New Forms of Consumption

New Forms of Consumption

Consumers, Culture, and Commodification

edited by Mark Gottdiener

ROWMAN & LITTLEFIELD PUBLISHERS, INC.
Lanham • Boulder • New York • Oxford

ROWMAN & LITTLEFIELD PUBLISHERS, INC.

Published in the United States of America
by Rowman & Littlefield Publishers, Inc.
4720 Boston Way, Lanham, Maryland 20706
http://www.rowmanlittlefield.com

12 Hid's Copse Road
Cumnor Hill, Oxford OX2 9JJ, England

British Library Cataloguing in Publication Information Available

Library of Congress Cataloging-in-Publication Data

New forms of consumption : consumers, culture, and commodification / edited by
    Mark Gottdiener.
      p.   cm.
    Includes bibliographical references and index.
    ISBN 0-8476-9569-7 (alk. paper)—ISBN 0-8476-9570-0 (pbk. : alk. paper)
      1. Consumption (Economics)—History.   2. Market segmentation—History.
    I. Gottdiener, Mark.

    HC79.C6 N49   2000
    658.8—dc21   00-032849

Printed in the United States of America

♾™ The paper used in this publication meets the minimum requirements of
American National Standard for Information Sciences—Permanence of
Paper for Printed Library Materials, ANSI/NISO Z39.48-1992.

Contents

List of Illustrations   vii

Introduction   ix
    M. Gottdiener

Part I: Theoretical Perspectives

1   Approaches to Consumption: Classical and
Contemporary Perspectives   3
M. Gottdiener

2   The Process of McDonaldization Is Not Uniform, nor Are Its Settings,
Consumers, or the Consumption of Its Goods and Services   33
George Ritzer and Seth Ovadia

3   Mass Tourism or the Re-Enchantment of the World?
Issues and Contradictions in the Study of Travel   51
Chris Rojek

4   Shopping and Postmodernism: Consumption, Production,
Identity, and the Internet   71
Minjoo Oh and Jorge Arditi

Part II: Case Studies

5   Brain-Suck   93
Eugene Halton

6   The Rise of "The Toddler" as Subject and as Merchandising
Category in the 1930s   111
Daniel Thomas Cook

7 The Body and the Country: A Political Ecology of Consumption   131
E. Melanie DuPuis

8 Packaging Violence: Media, Story Sequencing, and the Perception
of Right and Wrong   153
Karen A. Cerulo

9 The Commodification of Sports: The Example of Personal Seat
Licenses in Professional Football   177
Matthew D. Bramlett and Mark Sloan

10 The Commodification of Rebellion: Rock Culture and Consumer
Capitalism   203
Cotten Seiler

11 Fantasy Tours: Exploring the Global Consumption of Caribbean
Sex Tourisms   227
Beverley Mullings

12 Commodification and Theming of the Sacred: Changing Patterns
of Tourist Consumption in the "Holy Land"   251
Noam Shoval

13 The Consumption of Space and the Spaces of Consumption   265
M. Gottdiener

Index   287

About the Contributors   297

Illustrations

Table 8.1.	Sequences by Violence Type	160
Table 8.2.	Ratings of Violent Stories by Theme	166
Tables 8.3A and 8.3B.	Subjects' Violence Ratings by Sequence Type for High and Low Consensus Conditions	168
Table 9.1.	Work Stoppages in Major League Baseball since 1972	182
Table 9.2A.	1997 American League, Top and Bottom Four Teams by Salary	184
Table 9.2B.	1997 National League, Top and Bottom Four Teams by Salary	184
Table 9.2C.	1998 American League, Top and Bottom Four Teams by Salary	185
Table 9.2D.	1998 National League, Top and Bottom Four Teams by Salary	185
Table 9.3.	PSL Comparison	188
Table 9.4.	Comparison of Rams and Ravens PSL Statistics	191
Table 9.5.	Ravens PSL Zones	192
Table 11.1.	Ranking of Tourism's Contribution to Selected Regional Economics	236
Figure 11.1	The Caribbean Sex Trade	235

Introduction

M. Gottdiener

Our society is characterized by "changes in the interrelationship of different systems of production and consumption, or regimes of value, and the multiplication of relatively independent sites for the use of things." DuGay 1997:4

Cultural studies scholars have paid great interest over the last decade to the topic of consumption. Discussions have revisited well-trod ground, with Thorstein Veblen's writings experiencing renewed interest, for example, as well as explored new terrain, with analysis of shopping in cyberspace. Consumption is viewed as the central focal interest of people in advanced industrial societies and the cornerstone today for the construction of identity. Among postmodern cultural analysts, in particular, the new emphasis on consumerism heralds a qualitative change in society. Work is no longer the key existential experience behind lifestyle choices, and production is no longer the primary regulatory concern of advanced economies. Now self-realization through consuming modalities and the economics of credit, interest, comparison shopping, and new forms of buying via electronic means are the main ways people experience daily life. Postmodernists criticize Marxism for its "productionist" bias, echoing in diluted form Jean Baudrillard's critique of political economy in *The Mirror of Production* (1975). Proclaiming today's society as the Kingdom of the Consumer, attention is paid to McDonaldization, Disneyfication, and other rationalized means of distributing products to people rather than the work-a-day world of business or the factory.

Although there is little debate about the increasing relevance of consumerism to society, the picture drawn in favor of its primacy by postmodernists is overdone. After so many years of increasing theoretical sophistication by cultural analysts, it is remarkable that either/or choices are still being advocated for what are essentially dialectical issues. As with other topics that are equally fashionable, such as globalization, flexible accumulation, and postmodern geography, hypsters promote a radical break for social history by proclaiming a "new" kind of society, when in reality, there is none. If McDonaldization is viewed solely as an antidote to the "productionist" bias of the past (Ritzer 1999), that means other things are ignored, such as the destruction of the rainforest in Latin America by cattle breeders who supply the raw meat to the franchise. Persisting class biases that affect the ability to consume in different ways are also overlooked. In short, a different kind of partial truth emerges that creates the same single-minded blindness as did the putative predecessors who allegedly ignored consumption in favor of the work world of production.

Consumption and production are inexorably linked. As Paul DuGay observes, "The use or appropriation of an object is more often than not both a moment of consumption *and* production, of undoing *and* doing, of destruction *and* construction" (1997:1). Yet understanding this relation also requires paying more attention to how consumerism has changed ways of living. Although the broad outlines of capitalist society remain, fundamental shifts have occurred that require study. Not simply "trends," but basic daily life encounters have been altered most fundamentally from the recent past, in fact, from just a few decades ago. As the sites of consumption and the variety of its forms have multiplied, society is presented with a more complex world of consumption and consumerism. New analysis is required to reign in and understand the increasingly different modes of experience that characterize consuming and that help mold the self. The present collection addresses this issue. It embraces political economy while also transcending it through new modes of symbolic analysis. It deals with consumerism and commodification as they increasingly articulate with the mass media, new social spaces, new electronic forms, and new lifestyle modalities. Topics range from theories of consumerism and culture to case studies of commodification and the production of new forms of consumption.

Part I of the volume is dedicated to theoretical discussions about aspects of consumption. Chapter 1, written by the editor, presents an overview of the field. It discusses classical theories of consumption and commodification, paying particular attention to nineteenth- and early twentieth-century sociologists who were more concerned with the social bond and the operation of capitalism in general than with simple questions of buying and selling. This chapter spends some time on the ideas of Veblen because his work on consumption remains highly relevant to the present, that is, to social life one hundred years after the publication of *The Theory of the Leisure Class* (1899). His term "conspicuous consumption" has passed into everyday use, quite an accomplishment for a sociologist. Yet, the concepts behind this vocabulary remain complex and require thoughtful discussion.

Chapter 1 then deals with contemporary theories of consumption. Most especially, it addresses a series of issues that have emerged from cultural studies since writers have turned their attention to consumerism and its relationship to the historical development of capitalism. It discusses issues of political economy, history, and culture as they relate to the increasing role of consumption in society both as a social activity and as a dimension within which self-identity is forged and sustained. The chapter closes with a discussion of an integrated approach to the economic, symbolic, and personal aspects of the consumer experience.

Chapter 2, by George Ritzer and Seth Ovadia, explores the classic thesis of McDonaldization. Applying Max Weber's concept of rationality, Ritzer has shown in previous works how the bureaucratic approach to efficiency, control, calculability, and predictability has transformed the fast-food industry and has led to global franchising. McDonaldization, as a mode of business operation, however, has also been imported into the running of an increasing number of other sectors in American society, such as hospitals, schools, and theme parks.

Chapter 2 deals with four aspects of this thesis that have often been misrepresented in the literature. Ritzer and Ovadia contend that (1) McDonaldization is not a uniform process, it has several variants; (2) variation exists in the settings; (3) the attempt to mold consumer behavior is only variably successful; and (4) there is a great variety characterizing the kinds of consumers. In sum, this chapter introduces the much cited thesis of McDonaldization, explains it, and qualifies its relevance in the light of recent work in cultural studies.

Chris Rojek in chapter 3 supplies a general overview of the contemporary phenomenon of tourism. He locates the increasing interest in tourism as a symptom of dealing with the social changes associated with postmodernism. Tourism is a form of consumption that, by definition, is liberated from the world of work. It is flexible and mobile, like the postmodern forces sculpting the new contours of society. Yet for Rojek, this overly postmodern rendering of the tourist experience that characterizes contemporary cultural studies is an exaggeration. More often than not, tourism is simply a packaged, commodified form of consumption that is skillfully marketed as a respite from the economic content of the working life, but which in reality is merely an extension of late capitalism. On the one hand, Rojek demonstrates that so-called organized tourism is not new; rather it has its origins in the Middle Ages (see chapter 12 for a further elaboration). On the other hand, tourism today is characterized by its highly commodified nature. So ubiquitous is the tourist experience in modern society that it can be considered an aspect of everyday life. Entire cities, many of which have been deindustrialized, have given themselves over to travelers as tourist spaces developing those characteristics that attract outsiders.

Despite the increasing ubiquity of organized tourism, there exist limitations of the concept as a sign of the times, which Rojek addresses. Tourism still costs money. Hence, participation in this new consumer form remains tied to class and the ability of people who can afford it. Many Americans and Europeans now engage in ecotourism, visiting such places as the Amazonian rainforest. Few inhabitants of the rainforest, however, visit Western cities. Although some people have the luxury of exploring aspects of self-identity on holiday, many others remain too poor to experience what the postmodernists refer to as the "tourist gaze." In short, although tourism is increasingly more pronounced as a common mode of consumption, it is a form that is limited in very much the same way that other aspects of consumption are restricted, namely, by social differences based on class, race, and gender.

Chapter 4, written by Minjoo Oh and Jorge Arditi, brings Part I to a close. Their effort provides a discussion of the all-important issue of shopping. In most of the literature, shopping is cast either in a negative light as the passive, easily manipulated activity of consumption, or among recent postmodernists as a realm of liberation and self-expression. Placing themselves outside this either/or debate, the authors view shopping as a highly complex activity that is multifaceted and nevertheless critical to the survival of capitalism.

Oh and Arditi's chapter introduces three contemporary perspectives on shopping. First, they establish the important point that shopping is a gendered activity. In this sense, women have created a new subjectivity through participation in modernity and shopping. Second, the practice of shopping enables people to cement close ties with their intimates, especially family members. Third, shopping is linked tightly to our personal network of social relations. Although the authors explore in-depth the more contemporary approaches to shopping that view it in a positive light, they also discuss critical perspectives, especially the postmodern critique of Jean Baudrillard. For the latter, the freedom and exploration of self-expression allegedly afforded to shoppers is simply an illusion. Baudrillard discusses the ways shoppers remain manipulated by powerful capitalist interests and examines the specific techniques that are used in advertising, mass marketing, and stores to stimulate consumption.

The final section of this chapter explores a theory of shopping that synthesizes the different perspectives, both pro and con. The authors also revisit the concept of shopping as a multifaceted activity and develop it in useful ways. In the end, they strive for a greater understanding of the practice of shopping than that which currently exists in the literature.

Chapter 5 inaugurates Part II of the book, which contains case studies. Eugene Halton deals with the emerging culture of late modernism within which consumption plays such a central role. He is less concerned about the particulars of consumption culture per se than the removal of everyone from direct experience of the environment by the "techno-colonization of daily life." Halton examines the way mass media pull people into a virtual world that distances them from reality. This alienation is based on a person's own choices regarding the use of time, especially leisure time. For Halton, human qualities have been diminished in the wake of Internet ascendancy and the pervasive saturation of mass cultural images in daily life.

Chapter 6, by Daniel Thomas Cook, is an empirical study of commodification and the social production of a new form of subjectivity called "the Toddler." Clothing manufacturers marketed a particular style to young children, but in the course of this profit-making extension, they had to create a separate persona for children within the age limits of the new clothing style. As Cook maintains, "The case of the toddler speaks to some of the ways that agency can reproduce and be reproduced in commercial relationships." In his empirically meticulous case study, Cook shows how new markets for goods are created, in part by the invention of a new discourse that provides consumers with a matching subjectivity. This commercially induced persona reached its culmination in the global stardom achieved by the child actress Shirley Temple. In effect, Temple and Hollywood cemented the fabricated social distinction of toddlerhood through her fame. She also was the all-important mass image that became the referent for literally thousands of toddler-style commodities, effecting the intersection of fashion, Hollywood films, and toddler persona in daily life.

Chapter 7, by E. Melanie DuPuis, continues the empirical investigation into the creation of commodities and new forms of consuming. In this case, DuPuis explores the transformation of the dairy industry that created a mass market for cow's milk. Taking a different tack than Cook, DuPuis provides a more general account of how the body itself is usurped by capitalist processes of commodification. In the case of milk, not only were mothers transformed but so was nature, because the cultivation of dairy cows became a mass industry with its own requirements of land and other natural resources. All of these changes were predicated on the ability of profit-makers to commodify a product, which was readily and naturally produced for free by women after childbirth, in a mass, price-driven market. As DuPuis shows, with a combination of authoritative pronouncements by "professionals" and scare tactics that were based on false "scientific" information, the drinking of cow's milk became the normative family beverage for all ages by the 1950s in America. This transformation was remarkable not only for the way it changed the relationship between mother and child but also for the way it created a new "mythology of milk" that substituted for the close bond people once had with nature.

Chapter 8, by Karen A. Cerulo, concerns the commodification of violence. Today the explicit violent content of most media products is a staple of the industry. A growing body of evidence suggests that exposure to media violence may be harmful. Cerulo approaches this issue by delving not into the effects of violent programming per se but into the way violence itself is portrayed. According to Cerulo, "the ways in which those who tell the story of violence" or "order the elements of an account" have specific effects of their own that are relatively independent of content. Thus she draws attention to the packaging and commodification of violence as a separate area of social concern.

Cerulo presents an interesting discussion of the growing extent to which violent acts remain a problem in society. She also traces the use of violence in the media back to the first violent film made in 1903. But none of the early media examples impress much compared with the wholesale commodification of violence in children's video and computer games. Recent and horrible killings at high schools around the country give evidence, not just to the propensity for violence but also to the incredible *accuracy* with which children can use guns to kill other children. Violent computer and video games are training grounds for an entire generation of assassins precisely because of the way the killing experience is packaged.

The heart of Cerulo's analysis is the exploration of story sequencing that explains these views on the structuration of content. It is not possible to understand the differential effects of violent media content without appreciating how different sequences affect the audience in unique ways. Cerulo provides understanding of specifically why the particular sequencing of violence in computer and video games has such a real and deadly effect.

Matthew D. Bramlett and Mark Sloan discuss the increasing commodification of professional sports in chapter 9. They consider the sports world an economy. Owners are the capitalists, players are the workers, and fans are the consumers. Initially owners exploited players until this led to conflict, unionization, and contract negotiations that renegotiated the division of surplus value (mainly gate receipts but also media profits) more to the players' benefit. Owners then turned to the direct exploitation of consumers by raising prices for tickets and aggressive merchandising. Recently, according to Bramlett and Sloan, owners have been boxed in regarding more concessions from players, so fans have increasingly become the targets of a hyperexploitation that takes a variety of forms. The authors present a case study of one instance: the selling of personal seat licenses (PSLs) in the National Football League. Essentially, PSLs allow fans to purchase the "right" to buy a season ticket for a designated price that is offered for sale prior to the purchasing of actual tickets. In their chapter, Bramlett and Sloan discuss the changing nature of sports as a consequence of its penetration by capitalist relations and commodification.

Cotten Seiler, in chapter 10, discusses the commodification of youth subcultures in rock music. Much like Bramlett and Sloan's observations on organized sports, Seiler shows how rock music is, above all else, a business. The chapter begins with a general and useful discussion of cultural studies as a separate field of inquiry. It then examines popular music's special place in that tradition, which was not always a welcome one. Seiler then describes the progressive stages of commodification for popular music by the industry, culminating in an investigation of the rock concert as a kind of "hypercommodification" and exploitation of consumers.

For Seiler, rock music commodifies adolescent sentiments of rebellion in a way that always supersedes the latter's search for an oppositional stance. As with the larger culture, the rock industry can expropriate and commodify all forms, even ones that try to stand outside it in opposition. This flexibility and mobility of merchandising that is practiced without any inner norms or values, save the pursuit of profit itself, is peculiarly postmodern. Seiler's chapter is useful because he discusses the history of rock music, its increasing commodification by corporations, and the extension of consumer exploitation by new forms of packaging and merchandising that culminates in the rock concert and the megaconcerts, such as the recent Woodstocks.

In a fascinating discussion, Beverley Mullings considers the commodification of sex as an element of consumerism. Chapter 11 deals with the general phenomenon of the sex trade and contains a specific case study of the Caribbean that illustrates what has become a world-wide phenomenon—sex tourism. As an industry, global sex tourism includes Asia, Africa, Latin America, and the Caribbean, much like the globalization of manufacturing and for many of the *same* reasons. The sex trade has been highly developed for centuries in the more modern countries of America and Europe, but recently, travelers from these areas have included sexual adventures in their trips to the less-developed countries that were once "off the map." Interestingly, Mullings locates the growing sex tourist industry within the general shift of consumption in late modern society to the commodification of nonmaterial forms. The latter includes the consumption of images, media products, and in the case at hand, fantasy and intimacy that are for sale. By definition, tourism represents the consumption of symbols and cultures. It is also comprised, as Henri Lefebvre (1994) has observed, of the circulation of people through space with the commodification of their needs in new environments. In this sense, the sex tourism industry not only provides tourists with the visual consumption of places but also the visual consumption of bodies and of fantasy environments.

Another aspect of Mullings's discussion involves the development of a sex industry as part of the more general development of third-world places as a tourist economy. The purchasing of sex is considered one aspect of the "total" tourist experience. In fact, the selling of sex accounts for a significant share of total revenues derived from visits by foreigners in many areas of the world. One estimate is that now the global sex industry represents at least $20 billion, with "a growing proportion of trade being organized via the Internet." In fact, recently there has been an explosion of Web sites devoted to information about obtaining sex on trips to other countries. In short, both material places and native bodies are exploited by world-wide tourism, just as these same places and people are exploited by global manufacturing.

This chapter also describes the human aspects of the trade. Both women and men that sell sex tend to be young whereas their customers tend to be middle-aged men and women from affluent countries, although Mullings points out that increasingly consumers are of all ages and types. In the Caribbean, another distinguishing phenomenon is at work. Different islands host different sex markets. Some cater to tourist women more than men, while others attract tourist males. Race and color play a role in this distinction, as Mullings points out. Market niches of this kind are not simply "locally derived." Instead, as she remarks, the separate markets are created "by the same global processes of consumption and production" formalized elsewhere around the world.

In Chapter 12, Noam Shoval discusses another new form of consumption, namely the commodification of the sacred. In part, this phenomenon is directly connected to the growth of tourism, specifically tourist visits to Israel, or as it is known by Catholics and Muslims, "the Holy Land." In fact, travel to this area of the world is one of the earliest forms of tourism. For more than a thousand years, these trips took the form of pilgrimages. According to Shoval, these visits were "stimulated by a combination of fantasy, prayers, and dreams." Each of the three monotheistic religions, Judaism, Christianity, and Islam, had its own "mythological and historical narrative" that valorized aspects of the pilgrimage and specific "sacred" locations. Shoval claims that more recently, especially since the founding of the State of Israel in 1948, an increasing number of tourists combine visits to "holy" sites with trips to more secular attractions. He calls these travelers "religious tourists," as distinguished from both pilgrims and secular tourists.

Shoval presents a case study of how Jewish, Christian, and Muslim sites in Israel are increasingly developed specifically for the religious tourist. In fact, this category of visitor has become the backbone of the tourist industry. Sacred aspects of the environment are more generally staged and augmented by virtual-reality displays, museums, and according to Shoval, the commodification of "spiritual merchandise." Among the effects of this shift is the increasing consumption of models and staged displays as a substitute for first-hand excursions to places. Shoval also observes that this commodification of the sacred enables the tourist infrastructure to cater to both secular and religious visitors. Hotels, restaurants, transport services, guides, and the like make no distinction among tourists regarding the reasons they have for visiting developed locations. The pilgrim infrastructure, which still exists in the form of hospices and places of worship, has been eclipsed by this more industrialized mode of tourism, which relies increasingly on simulations, theming, and franchising, much like tourist places elsewhere.

The final chapter, *Consumption of Space and the Spaces of Consumption*, is written by the editor. It draws on more extensive studies elsewhere into the material basis of new forms of consumption. In particular, shopping and consuming today most often take place in appropriately engineered environments, such as malls, themed restaurants, department stores, theme parks, gambling casinos, "big box" warehouse stores, and the like. These milieus tap into fantasies and media linkages to invoke attractive aspects of popular culture as a way of stimulating consumption. The new environments are called "spaces of consumption" and they harken back to the earliest forms of markets in the development of society. What is new and different today is the way these markets are embedded in material structures that use symbolism and mass media connections to invoke a consumerist milieu.

To avoid the kind of either/or reductionism that this entire volume seeks to transcend, the final chapter also deals with the "other side" of these new spatial configurations. In particular, there is also a consumption of space, in addition to the spaces of consumption. Tourism and visits to theme parks or restaurants represent, perhaps, the best examples. Today people do not just consume products that are for sale. They also consume milieus. As mentioned, these material environments are skillfully engineered for effect. When people eat lunch at the Rainforest Café, Planet Hollywood, or the Hard Rock Café, they pay for the structured ambiance as well as the food. Finally, this chapter also deals with the production of such spaces as a new economic activity in society. Investment in themed and actively designed milieus has become a big business. Thus, the chapter links the consumption of space to its production in spaces of consumption.

BIBLIOGRAPHY

Baudrillard, Jean (1975). *The Mirror of Production.* St. Louis: Telos Press.

DuGay, Paul, ed. (1997). *Production of Culture/Cultures of Production.* London: Sage.

Lefebvre, Henri (1994). *The Production of Space.* Oxford: Blackwell.

Ritzer, George (1999). *Enchanting a Disenchanted World.* Thousand Oaks, Calif.: Pine Forge.

Veblen, Thorstein (1899). *The Theory of the Leisure Class.* New York: New America Library.

Part I

Theoretical Perspectives

1

Approaches to Consumption:
Classical and Contemporary Perspectives

M. Gottdiener

CLASSICAL SOCIOLOGICAL APPROACHES TO CONSUMPTION

Karl Marx

Karl Marx is best known from his writings on capitalism, and the founding fathers of sociology, especially Max Weber and Emile Durkheim, were highly influenced by him. In *Capital* [1867] 1967, Marx begins his monumental three-volume analysis by focusing on commodities and consumption. Conditions of production under capitalism are different than under other economic systems. Production is for the purpose of realizing a profit and the product is owned completely by the capitalist or company. Workers who make things are simply salaried employees. With their wages, they must buy the things they need that they and others make. Products are purchased in a market in which money is exchanged for goods and services. These products that have been reduced to a specific price are called "commodities." As Henri Lefebvre observes,

> In the first hundred pages of *Capital* Marx shows how a thing, a product assumes, under certain conditions, the form of a commodity. The thing splits in two; without losing its material reality and use value it is transmuted into an exchange value. (1968:47)

All commodities are measured by money and have exchange value. In Marx's terms, money is the universal equivalent under capitalism. Through this medium, the use value of any material good or service is converted effortlessly into a particular exchange value, its market price. It is this reduction of potential value based on use to one of exchange that is at the essence of the commodity form. Under capitalism all things have a price and all desires can be satisfied, for a fee. Personal, subjective valuations of a commodity based on its possession by a single person have nothing to do with the market price, unless that person is also part of a mass. In this way, exchange value dominates use value under capitalism.

Marx's analysis of the commodity in the early pages of *Capital* discusses the social-psychological aspects of consumption and its problematic, alienation, before commencing an extended treatment of the process of production that is more relevant to the economic analysis of capitalism. Marx was intrigued by the problem of alienation and saw the process of consumption as a key way in which people were estranged from their own humanity. He called this process *the fetishization of commodities*. According to Lefebvre,

> To Marx, the commodity form possesses the peculiar capacity of concealing its own essence and origin from the human beings who live with it and by it. The form is fetishized. It appears to be a thing endowed with boundless powers. (1968:47)

Marx argued that under capitalist conditions of production and distribution, products of labor appear as abstract things detached from the labor process. They are offered for sale in markets separate from the place of production. All kinds of special attributes are imputed to these commodities. They are fetishized, desired for the putative powers that they are thought to provide.

Although there are other aspects to consumption that will be discussed shortly, Marx's contribution is as relevant today as it was more than one hundred years ago. If anything the pervasive power of advertising has heightened the extent to which commodities of all types are fetishized and made to symbolize attributes that are craved. Advertisers market everything from shoes to toothpaste and underarm deodorant to cars as providing the lucky purchaser with special powers that they would not otherwise have. Products are fetishized because they are bought in the belief that they can enhance the purchasers' abilities to attain their desires for sex, success, notoriety, uniqueness, identity or a sense of self, privileged social status, and personal power. Through the all-pervasive power of advertising in today's society, what Marx only glimpsed one hundred years ago is now an ordinary fact of daily life—people see themselves and others through the possession of commodities. Goods are the tools that signal to others who we want them to think we are and who we want to be.

Max Weber

Max Weber, one of the first great sociologists, qualified many aspects of Marx's ideas. He particularly sought to show how cultural or symbolic aspects of society complemented the economic considerations that Marx emphasized. The dimension of signification adds to the complexity of society. As Weber quite rightly knew, people behave according to symbolic as well as economic needs. One of Weber's key insights was to hypothesize the existence of a social ranking based on prestige, or status, in addition to one based on individual wealth. Clearly wealth and status are highly correlated, and Marx did not see much difference between the two. For Weber, however, status and wealth measured slightly different distinctions in modern society and the former, in particular, played an important role in personal lifestyle. This insight was to have a profound influence on a famous American sociologist, Thorstein Veblen, as discussed below. In the United States, status may be more important than class in defining who one is, even if class still remains the principal determinant of life chances, as both Marx and Weber believed.

Max Weber is credited with contributing another important set of ideas to the contemporary study of consumption. He was fascinated by the emergence of bureaucracy as a decisionmaking structure and studied that form in great detail. He viewed the development of society as an inexorable progression to ever more bureaucratized modes of daily living. Recently George Ritzer (1996) has applied Weber's ideas about bureaucraticization and rationality to the analysis of McDonald's and its unprecedented global success in franchising fast food. For Ritzer, Weber's concept of rationality has four components that every bureaucracy strives to embody: efficiency, calculability, predictability, and control. Ritzer sees the same four features epitomizing the revolution in the process of people and fast-food service behind what he calls "McDonaldization" or "the process by which the principles of the fast-food restaurant are coming to dominate more and more sectors of American society." Ritzer's application of Weber's ideas is discussed in chapter 2.

Emile Durkheim

Emile Durkheim differed from both Marx and Weber because he was fascinated by the power of the social bond between people in society. In this sense, he was a pure sociologist and for most of his academic career, he labored to show how social ties inspire, channel, and constrain individual behavior. Although Durkheim obviously believed that symbolic processes could not be reduced to economic concerns, he did not explicitly address this issue. Yet many of his studies are about culture or what he called "nonmaterial social facts," that is, the social institutions of, for example, law and religion. Durkheim did not conceive of culture as a system of signs, unlike later analysts of culture. Rather he was more concerned with the kinds of moral values or sentiments that people held in common and which, in turn, reflected the social bond. He called these shared ideas that were social referents "collective representations." One of his classic studies, *The Elementary Forms of Religious Life* (1965), examined primitive religion to isolate the way solidarity was manifested symbolically. In this work, Durkheim analyzed the phenomenon of totemism, which ascribes to images the power of organized clans in traditional society. Through another distinction, that of the *sacred versus profane* elements of daily life, he demonstrated how religious distinctions can lead to an entire way of life—a culture that defines a separate domain from the "profane" aspects of secular society.

Durkheim's sociology does not address the issue of consumption per se and is less useful than the work of Marx. Yet the concept of "collective representation" and the way he showed how social bonds are expressed symbolically explains much about contemporary culture. The media are literally saturated by images that people value in common. Although they function as signs, something about which Durkheim had little to say, these images also operate to create commonalities among the otherwise diverse population groups. Hence mass culture and mass consumption unify people in the same ways as other more tangible "elementary forms" of social solidarity, such as religion or the legal system.

Durkheim's son-in-law, the French sociologist Marcel Mauss, extended his ideas and isolated an important aspect of the social bond, namely, the process of symbolic exchange. Mauss studied a certain kind of exchange in his classic work, *The Gift.* For Mauss, in true Durkheimian fashion, gift giving is symbolic of social solidarity because it helps to externalize reciprocal obligations. A gift received must eventually be returned in kind. The height of this particular social process is the potlatch ceremonies of Northwest Native Americans (e.g., Jonaitis 1991), which Mauss studied in great detail. Potlatch ceremonies are examples of consumption done in mass quantities for ritualistic purposes, compared with the mass consumption of our society.

Gift giving, according to Mauss, represents a certain kind of exchange that differs from the exchange of money for commodities studied by Marx. Yet for Mauss and also for Durkheim, the force behind the action was social in content. A discussion follows below about the development of approaches to consumption that emphasize the independent operation of symbolic factors at progressively higher levels. Sociologist Jean Baudrillard, for example, observes that Mauss missed the key point, which was to isolate the presence of "symbolic exchange" in gift giving, a phenomenon independent of both the social bond emphasized by Durkheim and the economic exchange studied by Marx.

Thorstein Veblen

Like Marx, Weber, and Durkheim, Thorstein Veblen (1857–1929) was a student of modernization and the effect of industrial capitalism on social life. Later in his life, Veblen focused on the operation of the economy and addressed questions that today are classified as inquiries into the nature of human capital. Earlier in his career, however, he wrote a definitive treatment of the emerging consumer society in America, *The Theory of the Leisure Class* (1899). In short, more so than others, Veblen created the field of consumer cultural studies.

Veblen worked very much within the purview of the Marxian world, the world of nineteenth-century predatory capitalism, with its relentless exploitation of both human labor and natural resources. Veblen went over the same ground as Marx and used the concept of class as an organizing referent. The moral visions of the two were also similar. The excesses of a system that manufactured an extreme form of inequality appalled them both. Marx sublimated that emotion into his project of historical theory and the critique of political economy. Veblen, in contrast, remained closer to the facts, to everyday life, and translated his moral vision into a peculiarly American idiom that is, in the *Theory of the Leisure Class*, the first important cultural critique of our society. As C. Wright Mills (1953) observed, Veblen sought to grasp the essentials of our society and "delineate the characters of the typical men within it."

Conspicousness as an Analytical Concept

Superficial and rapid turnover of ideas among academic sociologists forces complex conceptions into simple catchwords. Veblen is known today by the concept of "conspicuous consumption." Yet in the first chapters of Veblen's *Theory of the Leisure Class*, three distinct and seminal ideas are introduced—"pecuniary emulation," "conspicuous leisure," and "conspicuous consumption." Although only the last has survived the homogenizing Cuisinart of academic sociology and become a common term, each idea has its special place in the cultural analysis of American society. Veblen begins his analysis with the origin of private property in a system that also creates a special class of leisured people who possess power over the laboring masses.

> The present inquiry, therefore, is not concerned with the beginning of indolence, nor with the appropriation of useful articles to individual consumption. The point in question is the origin and nature of a conventional leisure class on the one hand and the beginnings of individual ownership as a conventional right or equitable claim on the other hand. (1899:33)

Interestingly enough, Veblen commences this inquiry with a discussion of the ownership of women and sees the juridical relations surrounding the claim of men over women in marriage as a foundation for contemporary property relations.

Conspicuousness and Social Positioning

For Veblen, commodities and consumption define social positioning. All societies exhibit this feature, as the Kwakiutl potlatch shows, but capitalist society has taken it to a particular extreme. Although acknowledging, no doubt, the problematic of capitalist political economy and its ownership relations in an implicit sense, Veblen views consumption practices as the differentiating criterion for social classes. The laboring and the upper classes are based definitionally on economic distinctions; but their *social differentiation* rests on the visible evidence of consumption practices. Through "pecuniary emulation" a status hierarchy emerges in society based on differences in consumption practice. In all societies, Veblen observes, the possession of wealth confers honor. The desire to accumulate in capitalist society, therefore, is "an honorific relation." Veblen considered the comparative possession of wealth between the bourgeoisie and the working class the basis for society's status hierarchy and called this social difference an "invidious comparison" implying critique. As he remarks, "Those members of the community who fall short of this, somewhat indefinite, normal degree of prowess or of property suffer in the esteem of their fellow men" (1899:35). Emulation is the driving force that is behind the accumulation of wealth in a capitalist society. Absent the visible presence of an aristocratic, landed class, as was the case in the United States, Veblen rightly pointed out how honor or prestige was bestowed on those the society considered "wealthy." In the United States, therefore, the accumulation of money, property, and goods was the socially decent thing to do.

Mere acquisition of property, however, was not sufficient in nineteenth-century American society to bestow honor, as Veblen observed. Pecuniary emulation required a demonstration of wealth, not simply its accumulation. Because the United States had no aristocracy, there was no other way of showing who was privileged and who was not. In this sense, the "most imperative" of the social demands of honor and prestige was abstention from work. For Veblen then, the social positioning that produced the status hierarchy of the United States was the visible evidence of distance from the workaday world. Veblen called this cultural feature "conspicuous leisure."

> From the days of the Greek philosophers to the present, a degree of leisure and of exemption from the contact with such industrial processes as serve the immediate everyday purposes of human life has ever been recognized by thoughtful men as a prerequisite to a worthy or beautiful, or even blameless, human life. (1899:42)

In short, before introducing the concept of conspicuous consumption, for which he is best known, Veblen shows how the premise of social positioning and status differentiation in American society depended on visible evidence of separation from the world of work, or conspicuous leisure. Among the examples of this phenomenon are exclusive golf and country clubs, charity drives, political activities, "high society" social activities, and religious observance. Among conspicuous leisure pursuits, Veblen listed politics, war, sports, and "devout observances." Today, tourism, golfing, and shopping can be added. But a word of caution. Veblen's basic condition for the formation of the leisure class, defined as the process of pecuniary emulation, was the absence from connection to the world of work. All those in society who had to work yet engaged in forms of conspicuous leisure Veblen defined as "vicariously" emulating the dominant class's life style. Today, by Veblen's definition, most conspicuous leisure is really vicarious. Considerable evidence of one's position in the status hierarchy of society was required. For the wealthy, it was not enough to engage in conspicuous leisure as an indicator of not needing to work. The leisure class also had to consume in a conspicuous way by engaging in expenditures that were unnecessary for basic human existence. It is in this context that Veblen introduces his concept of "conspicuous consumption." Ordinarily, the dominant class must pursue both forms of conspicuous display, leisure and consumption activities. The two work in tandem for social positioning. Veblen observes, however, that as society becomes more complicated and differentiated, conspicuous consumption becomes the principal means of designating superior status. Conspicuous consumption is characterized by possession of wasteful commodities. Veblen did not use the term pejoratively. By waste he meant the excesses of consumption that were not necessary for the mere functionality of objects. Wasteful elaboration of commodities and their possession were meant as evidence of honor, wealth, and social status.

Fetishization and Conspicuousness

Despite criticisms, both Marx's and Veblen's concepts are enduring. Decades of advertising, for example, have only accentuated beyond imagining the fetishization of commodities. The world of material objects has been extended by commodification to the farthest reaches of the human condition. There is no want or need that does not already have its correlate in some object manufactured for profit. Consumer society is fetishization writ large. And Veblen's conspicuous consumption is so applicable to behavior today that it has passed into the ordinary lexicon and is now a phrase commonly used in both advertising and daily speech. Yet both conspicuous leisure and pecuniary emulation also should be remembered as part of Veblen's conceptual triad. In the terms of his argument, however, current conspicuous displays are forms of "vicarious" leisure and consumption because there is no longer a separate leisure class nor abstention from work. Nevertheless, Veblen pinpointed an anthropological truth that is as characteristic of Western society as it is of the Kwakiutl Indians in the Northwest. Status hierarchy is based on possessions. Wealth is honorific. Prestige comes from possessing excess.

Symbolic Exchange

What did Veblen see that Marx did not? The fetishization of commodities is based on the conversion of use value into exchange value by the equivalence relation of the money economy. For Marx, life under capitalism is alienated and dehumanized because all things can be made to exchange for money. But objects not only have use and exchange value, they also possess sign value (see below).

This is implicit in the concept of fetishization as a form of alienation. Veblen made this quality explicit. Creation of a status hierarchy is based on symbolic distinctions along with ownership of the means of production. Commodities are not only the object of human alienation but they are also sign vehicles in the conveyance of social meanings. Status consists of display because conspicuous consumption and leisure signify prestige and they mark people according to society's hierarchy. This display function of prestige signs seems to operate in all cultures, from the most primitive to the most advanced. Commodities or material artifacts *mean* something about status in addition to their intrinsically functional significance. In short, they are visible symbols of status and they connote meanings as sign vehicles about social positioning in a way that class relations cannot.

Veblen's conception also does something more. By focusing on the creation and reproduction of a status hierarchy based on conspicuous public display, Veblen implies that sign vehicles have their own equivalence relation as symbols. Without the normative valorization of these signs of status, social judgments about what constitutes Veblen's invidious comparison could not exist. That is, the social construction of the status "wealthy" depends for its conception on *symbolic* difference in consumption practice. As Baudrillard (1993) observed, Marx's conceptualization of capitalism remains limited because it is based solely on the equivalence relation of the commodity market, the transformation of use value into exchange value through commodity exchange for money. For Baudrillard, Marx ignored the *other* equivalence relation in society, that of the consumption code and its basis in sign value. In other words, Marx was so preoccupied with the power of money under capitalism that he missed the power of symbols. Both dimensions implicitly involve exchange relations that help structure society.

Veblen studied goods and social activities intended for evidence of pecuniary excess, that is, as a sign of wealth. The social hierarchy created and sustained by this kind of activity is not based on commodity exchange as in Marx, but on symbolic exchange. In this sense, Veblen's analysis of conspicuous display, which implies public scrutiny and difference according to the code of consumerism, or the "invidious comparison" with the working-class "other," constitutes a precursor to Baudrillard's more sophisticated, if not extreme cultural criticism, which will be examined in the next section.

CONTEMPORARY APPROACHES TO CONSUMPTION

Precapitalist Social Formations and the Rise of Consumerism

Many analysts of the contemporary scene see consumption as a central aspect of society. In some cases, writers have criticized social theorists, such as Karl Marx, for privileging the process of production (see Firat and Venkatesh 1995). In contrast, they argue that it is consumption activities that dominate society, whereas an emphasis on the economic aspects of work constitutes a "productionist" bias. According to Ritzer (1999:28), for example, "American society is now better characterized by consumption than production." Yet one of cultural studies' more recent contributions has been to show that an emphasis on consumption can be traced back to emerging tendencies of Western European society occurring over the last three centuries. Although it is commonly understood that a so-called consumer culture is a necessary feature of capitalism, many of the qualities of that culture—consumption as social positioning, consumption as a mode of self-expression—can be found in European society in periods that predate the rise of capitalism.

Fernand Braudel (1967), the noted French historian, calls attention to the fact that both "superfluity and bare necessity" have always been found existing side by side. The rulers of society, the ones most privileged, are expected to possess luxuries that the common people do not and cannot ever have. Over time, Braudel notes, what was considered a "luxury" changed and was always relative to particular societies. For example, "Chairs are still a luxury in many parts of Asia, so is fresh fruit in other countries" (1967:122). As society matured, areas of everyday life were taken over by *habits of distinction* in the battle for status. However, the emphasis on consumption as social positioning was not created all at once but instead emerged over time (see also Elias 1978). Thus, Braudel observed that European eating habits were unsophisticated and food quite ordinary until the fifteenth and sixteenth centuries, at which time the idea of cuisine as a "skillful and expressive art" began to emerge first in Venice, Italy. By contrast, gourmet cooking was practiced centuries earlier in China and Arabia.

It is this variability across cultures and in the particular goods used in social positioning across societies, rather than the existence of an emphasis on consumption per se, that is most interesting in history.

> Luxury, therefore, has many facets, according to the period, country or civilization in question. In contrast, the social drama, without beginning or end, with luxury as its theme, scarcely changes at all. . . . Luxury does not only represent rarity and vanity, but also social success, fascination, the dream that one day becomes reality for the poor . . . . The rich are thus doomed to prepare the future life of the poor. (Braudel 1967:122)

In a penetrating study, Chandra Mukerji (1983) observes that the increasing presence of a wide variety of goods brought to Europe by trade created the conditions for consumption as a mode of self-expression centuries before the rise of capitalism. Mukerji adopts the premise, which will be developed more fully below, that objects in all societies assume a "symbolic and communicative character" (1983:12), so that they are used as sign vehicles in social relations. Deployment in the social hierarchy of status positioning is only one of many such aspects. According to Grant McCracken (1990:10), "It is precisely as expressions, creators, and innovators of a range of cultural meaning that goods have contributed to the rise of the modern west."

Mukerji notes that the quality of consumption by the upper class, which Veblen called "conspicuous" and wasteful and which he correlated with the success of American industrial capitalism, was developed as a dominant mode of social interaction during Elizabethan times at the end of the sixteenth century. Queen Elizabeth I used royalty's unlimited access to wealth as a means of subjugating the nobility to the nation-state through a spectacle of wasteful and expensive consumption. Among such innovations at her court was the practice of the "anti-supper." Guests were ushered into an extravagantly set dining room complete with expensive dishes and costly prepared food. After the guests took their seats, the entire array was removed in a spectacular fashion, only to be replaced by the "real" dinner, another extravagant meal.

Under pressure to engage in these "conspicuous" practices at the queen's court, the nobility were forced into changing their consumption habits. Not only did they have to spend recklessly, if only to keep their social position, but they also bought items that were frivolous and were used up quickly, rather than holding to their earlier practice of purchasing high-status goods that could be kept by their family in perpetuity as an inheritance. It is the latter aspect that is most characteristic of the consumer society of today. As McCracken argues,

> In summary, we see in Elizabethan England a consumer explosion of extravagant proportions. This boom is due chiefly to the new consumption of two groups. Elizabeth, for her own political reasons, had learned to use consumption as a means of creating a vast theater devoted to the aggrandizement of her power as a monarch. She had also learned to use it as a device for the impoverishment of her potentially over-mighty subjects. Noblemen, on the other hand, found themselves spending reactively. Both Elizabeth and social competitors demanded that they do so. The escalation of this spending meant that they were very soon the slaves of competitive consumption. (1990:15)

Consumption and Capitalism

Writers such as Braudel and Mukerji make an important point, namely, that conspicuous or luxury consumption did not start with the emergence of capitalism. Yet even though the fundamental elements of a consumer culture—the use of goods for both social positioning and as a symbolic means of self-expression— were both in place by the nineteenth century, it is only with the rise of industrial capitalism that a full-blown consumerism appeared. After the eighteenth century, activities that were once restricted to the elite were now practiced by the masses as well. A flood of common industrial goods swept over the market that itself expanded through new opportunities for buying. Innovations such as the department store made shopping a regular and attractive activity (Miller 1981). Fashion became a social force and led to the cyclical abandonment and adoption of different styles whether goods were still useful or not (Simmel 1957; Konig 1973; Barthes 1967; Baudrillard 1968). Status or standing was marked by consumption differences extending to the veritable limits of social groupings in society. The appearance of mass advertising aimed at ordinary citizens through newspapers, radio, popular magazines, consumer catalogues, and later television stimulated purchasing and innovated an entire language of media-assisted consumption (Tedlow 1990; Marchand 1985; Schudson 1984).

To many scholars, the active role of these aspects in the new system of industrial capitalism during the 1800s gave rise to a "consumer society" because consumption involved the masses of people, not just the elite (see McKendrick et al. 1982). As summarized by McCracken,

> What men and woman had once hoped to inherit from their parents, they now expected to buy for themselves. What were once bought at the dictate of need, were now bought at the dictate of fashion. What were once bought for life, might now be bought several times over. What were once available only on high days and holidays through the agency of markets, fairs and itinerant peddlers were increasingly made available every day but Sunday through the additional agency of an ever-advancing network of shops and shopkeepers. (1990:17)

Is a Consumer Culture Necessary to Capitalism?

Contemporary studies have established that both an emphasis on consumption rather than production and the use of consumer goods as signs in the conflict over social positioning *predate* the advent of industrial capitalism by a considerable period, even though it is also recognized that a full-blown consumer culture characterizes society today. A more recent debate has focused on the question of whether a fully realized consumer culture is a functional requirement of capitalism. For a considerable time, scholars have assumed that industrial capitalism both produced and needed a high-consumption economy, but recent writers have questioned this association and they look with some skepticism at the belief that consuming dominates our culture.

Earlier writings on this subject equated the democratization and increased level of consumption in society with the success of industrial capitalism. A consumer culture was a visible sign of modernism and progress (see Fox 1967; Potter 1958; Galbraith 1960; Baudrillard [1968] 1998). On the one hand, capitalism was successful, so it was believed, in creating a society of "abundance" or "affluence" in which all sorts of consumption goods abounded within easy reach of most Americans. On the other hand, these writers argued that the way out of the Great Depression of the 1930s was by following Keynesian principles of economic expansion through the stimulation of increased consumer spending. Together these elements of the new post-Depression economy created a dominant "consumer culture" that was both accessible to most Americans and also necessary for the survival of capitalism. According to Kenneth Galbraith, "The individual serves the industrial system not by supplying it with savings and the resulting capital; he serves it by consuming its products." (1960:152)

In contrast, writers such as Colin Campbell (1987) pointed out that a distinctly modern form of excessive consumption predated the rise of industrial capitalism and keynesianism. Although the beginnings of both the modern era and capitalism are rooted in the emergence of a "protestant ethic," as conceived by Max Weber, Campbell argued that alongside the ascetism of the protestant sects focusing on acquisition there was also a second cultural tendency tied to the emergence of "romanticism." Campbell suggested that the yearning of the romanticist movement in the nineteenth century for the pleasures of daily life, exemplified by the poems of Keats and Wadsworth and the writings of Thoreau, solidified a "hedonistic" sensibility that was expressed in fantasy as well as in new consumption styles. This romantic ethic characterized by fantasy and desire stood alongside the protestant ethic characterized by asceticism and personal desire, giving the early culture of capitalism its contradictory dimensions. Consequently, if the keynesianism of post-Depression Western society after 1930 purposely stimulated high levels of consumption, the implicit hedonistic indulgence in goods that this culture reflects existed much earlier and was only exploited rather than being created whole by new economic policies or advertising.

Other writers have addressed this same issue by also challenging the universal subscription to the ideology of modernism that celebrates the abundance of a consumer society in the twentieth century. According to Jackson Lears (1994), for example, "Protestant values of personal authenticity and plain speech formed an uneasy dialectic with promises of transformation offered by commercial culture" (*Kirkus Reviews*, Oct. 1, 1994). Abundance and the advent of a consumer "paradise" were largely myths propagated by modernist ideology. Whereas earlier writers argued that the elements of protestant asceticism in culture were eradicated by a new hedonism based on a desiring subject that craved constant spending on commodities, Lears agreed with Campbell that the antagonistic elements of the dichotomy between asceticism and hedonism remain an important cultural dynamic. He took care, however, to show how the mass advertising industry in particular is responsible for the myth of the "abundant society." Images of plenty and easy accessibility to the world of commodities constitute an ideology sustained by mass advertising.

George Ritzer makes a counterargument (1999). He believes that our society is dominated by consumption. This is manifested less as a simple aspect of abundance and plenty, as modernist ideology claims, than as a more complex process in which people have been so stimulated by the contemporary environment to engage in excessive consumption that they are saddled with considerable debt. According to Ritzer, most of us now live well beyond our means and this new consumer society has been produced in part by the expansion and easy availability of credit.

> Within a few decades, the U.S. has gone from a society that emphasized personal savings to one that focuses on debt. Banks have, to a large degree, shifted from the business of inducing people to save to luring them into debt. In 1997 Americans received 3.1 billion pieces of mail imploring them to sign up for a credit card. The profits from servicing debt, especially credit card debt, are much higher than those derived from savings. (1999:37)

Although Ritzer's analysis helps isolate the difference between society now and pre-Depression America in terms of increasing ease of credit and mounting debt, he goes too far by stating that present conditions are functional for capitalism and this explains why consumerism dominates our society. As he says, "people are kept in the workplace and on the job by the need to pay the monthly premiums on their credit card accounts and, more generally, to support their consumption habits" (1999:29).

On the positive side, Ritzer points out changes in society, such as ease of credit, casino gambling, and theme parks that have helped provide people with greater opportunities to consume. To his list, the growth of tourism (see chapter 3) and Internet shopping (chapter 4) should be added, although I maintain that the social significance of the new themed environments is more complex (see Gottdiener 1997). In addition, rather than viewing the current culture as contradictory to the vision of Karl Marx, many of the new ways people consume are directly attributable to the kind of commodity fetishism Marx wrote about (see above). Chapters 9, 10, and 12 provide examples of commodification that extend the world of consumerism to new objects previously untouched by the logic of consumption. Expansion of this kind to new markets by producers that make new products and convince us all that they are now needed is a key way in which capitalism itself survives.

Are Consumers Manipulated by Capitalism?

Another common assumption of earlier writers was that consumers are easily manipulated by advertising and the conformist pressures of a consumer culture. The thesis of manipulation has been challenged by more recent writing. Most characteristic of work done in the 1950s during a time when mass advertising and "Madison Avenue" influences were first recognized as powerful cultural forces, writers once extolled the ability of companies to create demand for their products through ad campaigns. Books such as Vance Packard's *The Hidden Persuaders* (1957) argued that people were swayed by mass advertising to spend more than they might on products that they did not think they needed. Most recently, this line of reasoning has been offered to explain how advertising creates a fantasy world that people increasingly depend on to acquire material means for personal self-expression (see Ewen and Ewen 1982; Ewen 1988).

Some contemporary writers have challenged this conception of the power of advertising. Michael Schudson (1984) showed that in many cases the ability of advertising to increase demand is highly overrated. Robert Goldman and Stephen Papson (1996) argued against the common notion that effective ads manipulate consumers. More often than not, people simply become cynical about product claims. At the same time, it is widely acknowledged, in agreement with writers such as Stuart Ewen, that consumption remains a major way people seek to realize aspects of self-identity. This is especially true for fashion or appearance. Designer clothes and logos are powerful tools in the realization of personal self-expression. They are also effective markers in the constant war for social position. In this sense, advertising does make a difference, and substantially so.

In sum, the social conflict over position has been a constant force in society for some time, and beginning with the success of industrial capitalism, this war was extended to the masses. Expressing aspects of the self or marking social status are social needs that have been features of organized societies for millennia. What is new and different is the way advertising and image production in our society creates the means of realizing these old needs in novel ways. As Goldman and Papson (1996) point out, advertising doesn't manipulate people by creating demand, as was once thought, but it is an effective force in the capturing of market share (see also Gottdiener 1997). Fights for market share, such as the war of the sneakers between Nike and Reebok or of new luxury cars between Lexus and Infiniti, are won by effective advertising campaigns. Successful ads tap into a wellspring of latent demand, rather than creating new demand. Precisely because ads can mobilize desire, they remain a powerful force in society and as Ewen (1988) asserts, they also provide a vocabulary that aids the realization of self-expression in the war for social position, whether that is a worthwhile fight or not.

A Consumption Culture or a Culture of Consumption?

Contemporary writers offer a convincing argument that society cannot be characterized as a consumer culture. Clearly work, careers, and the making of money remain the most powerful domains of social activity. Yet to the extent that people presently seek the realization of self and the exercise of identity through lifestyles grounded in consumption practices, there is a culture of consumption in the United States or, more accurately, *cultures of consumption* that characterize social groupings. The act of consumption itself is no longer viewed as a passive mode of behavior and the ability of producers to manipulate people's desires and purchasing habits via advertising has been greatly exaggerated. Now culture is fragmented and diversified into many market segments. Although these may not aggregate into a society in which consumerism dominates other activities, they do define many cultures of consumption through which people interact with society and find particular meaning for their lives.

Increasingly issues of work, production, and corporate daily life are not the building blocks that bind people together in friendship networks in modern society, if they ever did. Instead social ties are centered more around mutual concerns regarding lifestyle, leisure, family life, home ownership, and the spectacular aspects of consumption such as cars, vacations, and fashion that dominate everyday discourse. These activities are not simply aspects of consumer culture with concerns that eclipse other elements of society. They form commodified minimilieus based on the production of material goods within which the various social groupings in society that differ by lifestyle, location, race, gender, age, and class carry out daily life. Inside these everyday domains advertising, status goods, and the drive for self-expression through consumption remain powerful forces. Fantasy and desire continue to play themselves out through the purchase and use of material goods and through the active presence of people in spaces of consumption that increasingly encroach on public space. To paraphrase Braudel above, although the particular goods and symbols of social status vary from group to group, the drive for status in general remains a constant and important social force in society (see also Bourdieu 1984).

THE IMPORTANCE OF SIGNS: POSTMODERNISM AND BEYOND

The single most troubling aspect of the cultural studies approach to consumption is the way almost all analysts seek to establish a one-sided view. This quest for reductionism helps those that advance "straw-man" arguments but does not help explain the phenomenon of consumption in contemporary late capitalist society, because consumption is multileveled. For example, recent writers now criticize Marxists for holding a "productionist bias" that neglects the process of consumption at the expense of a focus on industry. Although many Marxists do analyze production, because it is the basis of all wealth, this criticism is quite odd. Karl Marx provided two seminal ideas that remain pertinent to consumer studies, commodity fetishism and the socially contextualized concept of alienation (see above).

Other analysts claim that critics of consumption, such as the Frankfurt School, go too far in picturing this domain as being functional for control by the dominant class in society. Yet they then go too far in the other direction by arguing that consumption defines a liberatory domain of society that can free people from the confines of capitalism and alienation. Fuat Firat and Alladi Venkatesh, for example, claim that consumption activities possess "emancipatory potential" and "there is no natural distinction between consumption and production: They are

one and the same, occurring simultaneously" (1995:254). One can rightly won-
der whether these two professors of marketing have ever visited a factory. Yet
their argument is echoed elsewhere in some of the new writing about consumption that seeks to counter the reductionist view of 1950s authors such as Packard
or Galbraith who argued that people form a mindless mass easily manipulated
by advertising. As elsewhere, recent critics of this position take a reductionist
stance of their own. John Fiske (1989) for example, saw resistance and pleasure
in consumption practices where others found only domination and alienation.
Although such observations do place the act of consumption in a new light, helping to show the complexity and creativity of consumer behavior, they also go too
far in the opposite direction. Douglas Kellner points out the troubling nature of
such arguments.

> There has been a fetishism of resistance in some versions of cultural studies. . . .
> There is a tendency in cultural studies to celebrate resistance per se without distin-
> guishing between types and forms of resistance (a similar problem resides with in-
> discriminate celebration of audience pleasure in certain reception studies). . . .
> Indeed, the resistance that Fiske valorizes . . . is not resistance at all but a very con-
> ventional replication of pleasure in violence that eliminates those who one positions
> as "bad." . . . Political struggle is thus displaced into "struggle" for meanings and
> pleasure, while "resistance" is equated with the evasion of social responsibility, as
> in Fiske's examples of youth in video arcades, hanging out at the beach, surfing or
> loitering in malls. Modes of domination are occluded, and resistance and struggle
> are depoliticized and rendered harmless, thus providing an ideology of "popular cul-
> ture" perfectly congruent with the interests of the powers that be. (1995:38–39)

The ultimate reductionist vision of culture comes, however, from French phi-
losopher Jean Baudrillard and those that follow his version of postmodernism.
Baudrillard's ideas have been assessed by a significant literature (see Gane 1991;
Gottdiener 1995; Kellner 1989, 1995). He is a complex thinker whose ideas are
often simplified by contemporary writers. Although he criticized Marx for fail-
ing to recognize the importance of consumption (1975), Baudrillard would not
subscribe to the simplistic view discussed above that Marx had a "productionist
bias." Instead he reversed the Marxian dialectic by positioning consumption as
the critical element in the capitalist system while retaining the tie between production and consumption that remains the core relation in the analysis of capitalism. Baudrillard's main contribution to cultural theory comes from his
periodization of society's developmental stages in a way that is different from
historical materialism. His particular approach is postmodernist because, unlike
Marx who defined the developmental stages of society according to their modes
of production, Baudrillard periodizes change according to society's dominant
modes of representation. Whereas Marx focuses on the materialist realm as the

central arena of social action, Baudrillard privileges the symbolic realm as the key structural element of social action. This way of posing the issue of periodization is semiotic and deconstructionist rather than economistic.

For Baudrillard, all earlier periods of social development, except the current one, used reality as a referent for representations. The period of social development prior to this present stage, for example, was an age of ideology. Nationalism, world wars, and the global imperialist conflict turned the representation of reality into propaganda during most of the twentieth century. Baudrillard terms this period the stage of *dissimulation*. Based on reality, dissimulation implies the masking of truth. Culture conceals a lie, like the ideology of Russian communism, National Socialism, or the American Dream. Now the present period constitutes a radical break with all other stages. For Baudrillard, culture today is characterized by *simulation*. As he states,

> To dissimulate is to feign not to have what one has. To simulate is to feign to have what one hasn't. One implies a presence, the other an absence. Dissimulation can be checked by reality but simulation destroys that link because it bridges the gap of absence. (1983:5)

Baudrillard's concept of *simulation* is difficult to grasp and is, at its core, an extreme, reductionist vision of culture. In all previous stages, the real existed as a counter to the process of representation. The real was the referent for truth. Critical theory was possible in this universe, and indeed all of philosophy and truth seeking became a domain that checked the world of ideology and the practices of power. In all previous stages, "speaking truth to power" still made sense. Contemporary society, however, has evolved into one whose mode of representation no longer takes the real as a referent. Simulation requires no link to reality. It is based on the "hyperreal." In this world, culture is produced and reproduced through the media and electronics. At the core of culture is mimesis. In advertising, for example, assumptions are made about the necessities of life that have no bearing on reality. People respond by organizing their consumption styles accordingly, regardless of need, regardless of practical concerns, and regardless of reality. Truth claims in today's society are based more on image than reality tests. Politics, consumerism, even current ideas of personal beauty and individual worth are now a function of representation and advertising.

In the postmodern world of culture, image becomes central. Material goods are not connected directly to the demands of daily life. Instead, they are converted to signs. People respond to these goods as images and symbols. Beyond social positioning, the consumption of goods as images constitutes a process of *representational positioning*. We are who we *appear to be*, who we emulate from mass culture (Ewen 1988), and culture itself is now about image (Kellner 1995). Consumption today consists of appropriating signs. When we consume, we use commodities in the context of lifestyle construction and we validate a specific image. Producers of goods compete with each other through *sign wars* (Goldman and Papson 1996) for market share. "In today's consumer goods markets, products require signs that add value to them. Product standardization makes it imperative that products attach themselves to signs that carry an additional element of value" (Goldman and Papson 1996:3).

The Image-Driven Culture

Although Baudrillard's approach is extreme and leads to a one-dimensional casting of society, his argument establishes the importance of the sign or image in everyday culture. Furthermore, in his critique of Marx, he establishes the fact that signs have value. This concept, *sign value*, is critical to the analysis of contemporary society and the understanding of consumption. For Marx every object has both "use value" and "exchange value." The system of capitalism superimposes a universal exchange criterion—that is, money—on the transfer of commodities, and a capitalist society measures everything in these terms. For Baudrillard, the exchange at the base of society is about symbols, not money (see the discussion of Durkheim and Mauss, above). His universal criterion is the code of culture. It is the sign value of goods that determines what is wanted and how they are used.

From a postmodern perspective, Baudrillard's ideas mean that people are now more engaged in consumption issues than production issues (Appadurai 1996) and that everyday life has become "aestheticized" (Featherstone 1991). As Michael Featherstone remarks about Baudrillard,

> For Baudrillard art ceases to be a separate enclaved reality; it enters into production and reproduction so that everything "even if it be the everyday and banal reality, falls by this token under the sign of art, and becomes aesthetic". . . . And so art is everywhere, since artifice is at the very heart of reality. (Baudrillard 1983:151 Featherstone 1991:271)

Others following this reductionist perspective see consumer culture dominating society, thereby producing a "re-enchantment" of daily life (Firat and Venkatesh 1995; Ritzer 1999). Contrasting this thesis with Weber's of the "disenchantment" of the world because rational thought drives out the symbolic, the sacred, and the superstitious, current writers argue that the infusion of symbols and simulation in society "re-enchants" daily life.

Ritzer (1999) in particular points to the importance of the "new means of consumption," such as malls, casinos, cruise ships, themed restaurants, theme parks, and the like, in re-enchantment because they have become "cathedrals of consumption"; these venues have taken on a "quasi-religious" nature. As he states,

"They have become locales to which we make 'pilgrimages' in order to practice our consumer religion" (1999:x).

In these and similar statements, writers go much too far, although, as pointed out above, characterizing American society as a "consumer culture" and one dominated by consumption are reductionist ideas that can be criticized. Ritzer goes even farther to argue that consumption is the new "religion." Today's society is better described as one in which both production and consumption are important, and although there is no dominant consumer culture, there are many cultures of consumption that differentiate the population. Most often these cultures of consumption work as lifestyle orientations that combine various consumer choices into a complex of daily living.

CONSUMPTION, IDENTITY, AND CONSUMER CULTURES

The formation and sustenance of individual identity through consumption activities is a good issue to illustrate the above discussion. There exists a proliferation of consumer cultures because of the increasing differentiation of consuming activities in late capitalism. The following list of social changes are most important to this recent development.

1. For just about every conceivable need, there is a product that is sold claiming to satisfy it. New needs and new products are introduced almost every day.
2. Producers engage in a continual differentiation of products. Greater differentiation develops along with ever-increasing market segmentation.
3. People experience an increasing pervasiveness of the force of fashion determining the appearance and desirability of more and more commodities. Fashion and its socially governed cycles have even been extended to consumer durables, such as cars and electronic equipment.
4. In settlement spaces there is a greater mobility of shoppers and an exponential increase in alternative ways to buy, including through both physical and virtual means. People can travel extensively by car to various malls, outlets, big-box warehouses, and shopping centers. They can also order through thousands of direct mail catalogues and, increasingly, directly through the Internet, in both cases never leaving their homes.
5. There is a growing emphasis in society on lifestyles and personal interests as a marker of who one is and as a means to connect with others. Now people increasingly relate to each other through commonly held consumption practices such as their preferences in sports, vacations, music, films, restaurants, and not the least, modes of shopping itself.

Given this fundamental background dynamic to daily life that emphasizes consumption activities, people more and more define themselves according to their style of living. Consumption practices have increasingly become the domain within which people explore and define their own identities, or at least, a kind of identity that exists in a somewhat separate state from the one constructed through careers and at the place of work. Some studies indicate that involvement in consumption penetrates one's own psychological experience of life (Lunt and Livingstone 1992). As Celia Lury (1996:233) observes, cognitively oriented studies of consuming reveal that people have definite strategies for engaging in consumption. Most importantly, these individualized approaches possess a "strong rhetorical component" as people verbalize their hopes, fears, goals, and aspects of self through discussing their strategies of shopping. It is precisely through these examples that social scientists can attest to the increasing role consuming plays in the formation and sustenance of identity. According to Anthony Giddens (1991, 1992), for example, society today is characterized by the dominance of an identity politics involving the quest for self-realization. The pursuit of distinctive lifestyles through consumption represents a means of developing a sense of self and of actualizing this identity politics.

Most commentators on the relationship between consumption and identity formation argue for a multitiered notion of consumer culture. According to Featherstone (1991), for example, because of changes in the economy of contemporary society, there are more people who are able to engage in a high level of consumption. Fueled by easy credit and the presence of a large disposable income, these people, many of whom are professionals with high salaries, constitute for Featherstone the "new middle classes"; note that he conceives of these consumption-oriented groups in the plural. The principal characteristic of these new classes, according to Featherstone, is the fickle way they attach themselves to particular styles of life only to abandon them later. Consumption is merely a playground of subjectivity rather than the determinant of individual identity. People play with their involvement in and their distancing from particular lifestyles. They can change their consumption modes as often as fashion and their own purses allow.

The notion of multiple consumer cultures is also imbedded in another idea in contemporary cultural studies, the concept of *neotribalism* (see Maffesoli 1996; Bauman 1992; Warde 1994). By neotribalism, Maffesoli refers to a resurgence of group belonging as the contemporary influence of overarching modern social institutions begins to wane. Tribes were tightly knit communities based on cultural and kinship commonalities that most characteristically claimed the allegiance of individuals for life. Neotribes arise from the individuals' acts of self-definition in a search for identity. Allegiances are formed to particular styles of life in a world of belonging that exists at a lower social level than the formal institutions of society, such as religion, work, and politics, or even the generic categories of race, gender, and class. The lifestyles that mark the neotribes are formed by a postmodern culture that mixes many influences—the media, fashion, local customs, loosely articulated political ideologies, styles of consumption, and friendship networks.

According to Bauman (1992:136) neotribalism is a phenomenon composed of such loose and flexible attachments that it confirms the view that today's society consists of shifting cultures of consumption. As he states,

> The tribes, as we know them from ethnographic reports and ancient accounts, were tightly structured bodies with controlled membership. . . . The neotribes—the tribes of [sic] contemporary world, are on the contrary formed—as concepts rather than integrated social bodies—by the multitude of individual acts of *self-identification*. Such agencies as might from time to time emerge to hold the faithful together have limited executive power and little control over co-option or banishment. More often than not, "tribes" are oblivious of their following, and the following itself is cryptic and fickle. It dissipates as fast as it appears. . . . *Neotribes "exist" solely by individual decisions to sport the symbolic tags of tribal allegiance* [my emphasis]. They vanish once the decisions are revoked or the zeal and determination of "members" fades out. (1992:136–37)

There is little doubt that consumption plays an increasingly important role in identity formation and actualization. Many of the new approaches to consumerism push this fact as a means of validating the importance of studying consumption as separate from production in society. In fact, too many of these scholars now suggest that the focus should be solely on the activity of consumption because, they claim, it now "dominates" society. I disagree with this perspective. Reductionism of this kind would be a big mistake. None of the approaches to the formation of identity bother to discuss the world of work and how work-related cultures are implicated in that same process. The culture of the workplace and the subcultures of specific professions, such as law, medicine, and banking, also play a formidable role in the formation and actualization of identity. Subcultures of the workplace are, in fact, an important topic in the management of industry (see DuGay 1997). Often these work- or career-related styles of life are also expressed in consumption practices. People who play golf because it is a requirement of their corporate culture also must purchase golf clubs, golf shoes, golf clothing, and golf club memberships. They may even obsess about and fetishize certain brands, designs, or fashions. Yet the role of these activities in the formation of identity cannot be separated from the role of the work culture itself, despite the fact that many advocates of the new cultural studies approach to consumption seem to suggest just that.

The concept of "belonging" has also become increasingly complex in society. People develop their identities through belonging—to family, friend, religion, racial, gender, cohort, and class groups, but also to the kind of belonging characteristic of the neotribes, or the *lifestyles* of contemporary society. In today's world, people belong to many subcultures, many lifestyles, because their social roles are increasingly complex. People work and have families, friends, leisure activities, and the like. Each of these areas defines arenas within which they cultivate and realize a sense of self. Both worlds—that of work and of shopping— are important to this cultural activity.

Self-identity formation through consumption relies on all of the complex aspects of social interaction described above. In addition to avoiding a reductionist view of the process, there is another aspect that is often neglected or ignored by those writers that emphasize consumption alone. Consuming takes place in specific venues (see Jacobs 1984; Kroker and Cook 1986; Shields 1992). Recently, the spaces of consumption have become increasingly important to contemporary culture (Gottdiener 1997; see chapter 13 below). The spaces of consumption are the articulation points of individual psychology, social pressures, the media, fashion, personal desire, the compulsion to buy, forms and structures of material culture, and the realization of group belonging.

The spaces of consumption, the material realm that is a conjuncture of many cultural influences, are heavily implicated in the actualization of identity. The shopping mall is, perhaps, the most familiar venue for the kind of consumption referred to here. More and more, however, society is characterized by a proliferation of consumer spaces selling all kinds of commodities that utilize some overarching symbolic theme (see Gottdiener 1997). Sneaker stores are themed, as in Chicago's Nike Town; so are restaurant franchises such as the Hard Rock Café and Planet Hollywood; gambling casinos such as the ones in Las Vegas have for decades explored theming, often to the point of neon and simulated extremes. All of these new spaces of consumption constitute the conjuncture of Hollywood, television, advertising, celebrity, magazines, and other popular culture influences. Consider the mall as a representative space of this kind:

> The mall experience is partly this finding of a self which is the self as conditioned consumer in the ludic, amusement sphere of commodity capitalism. This consumer self is only primed by TV and the advertising media. It becomes actualized within the consumption and quasi-public ludic space of the mall. This sphere is a commodified utopia where the vagaries of daily life and the inhumanity of the production process exist as but faint echoes of the economy. The mall presents a material, built environment that is an amusement space, a carnival center. The self, which is actualized as a consumer self, transports to the mall, encounters the disorienting design features of its architecture, and searches out the region of clear light past the parking stalls, the gangways, escalators, stairs, entrance doors, and into the grand avenues of consumption and consumerist communion. (Gottdiener 1995:96)

Yet the spaces of consumption do not exhaust the material realms within which this actualization of the self occurs. Increasingly too the consumerist self and the neotribalized self become forged in the crucible of the Internet. This process leads to a true *virtual* self, because one manifests only a computer identity. Today people define their tastes, their desires, by the touch of a button, or more accurately, the touch of a mouse. They spend hours picking and choosing images and activities that are brought into their homes or offices from the multiple universes of the virtual Web. Often their activities are held secret. For some people, their connection with the Internet may mean the biggest secrets of their lives. In any case, social interaction today plays out increasingly, not in any material realm staging social communion, but in a virtual space through a computer connection to other virtual selves.

Interestingly enough, the formation of this "virtual self" that is now so much a part of people's identities was already prefigured when consumerism began to dominate the nonwork time consciousness. Controlled as it is by simulation, in the Baudrillard sense, the influences of TV, cinema, fashion, and advertising already helped to create a virtual self even before the heavy use of the Internet connection. As Kroker and Cook observe about the mall,

> Shopping malls are the real postmodern sites of happy consciousness. Not in the old Hegelian sense of a reconciled dialectic of reason, but happy consciousness, now in the sense of the virtual self . . . the self now is a virtual object to such a degree of intensity and accumulation that the fascination of the shopping mall is in the way of homecoming to a self that has been lost, but now happily discovered. (1986:208–9)

In sum, consumerism plays a significant role in the formation and realization of the self. But that self is actually a multiply manifested existential construct. In today's society everyone has the option of being many things. The concepts of lifestyle, subculture, and neotribalism all capture the varied way in which people weave consumption activities into their daily lives, lives that also involve the more mundane world of work. Consumerism is less an obsession of a fetishized quest, as Marx thought, than an essential activity relating a conception of "action" for postmodern people within spaces that articulate with the most powerful cultural influences in society—TV, advertising, movies, fashion— coupled with that powerful social force emanating from the status hierarchy of society that works through material symbols of prestige.

THE THREEFOLD DIALECTIC AMONG SIGN VALUE, EXCHANGE VALUE, AND USE VALUE

As has been argued above, culture is not dominated by consumption. People still have to work for a living, and their career interests, the making and management of money, and the culture of the workplace are all important aspects of daily life. The famous comic strip *Dilbert* is popular precisely because so much of the everyday is devoted to jobs, even if the circumstances of employment have changed greatly in recent years. Consuming also plays an important part in daily life, but it is more accurate to speak of cultures of consumption and lifestyle, as discussed above, than the one-sided argument that sees consumerism dominating society, as advanced by many recent writers influenced by Baudrillard and other postmodernists.

To avoid reductionism, recall that material goods can possess three statuses that have importance in organizing behavior (this discussion is based on Gottdiener 1995, chapter 8). Commodities possess *use value* because they are deployed to remedy a certain lack, whether it is physical or psychological. Commodities are used as tools in everyday life because they are a means by which to satisfy desires, whether these are functional or symbolic. In addition, goods possess *exchange value* because they are purchased in the market with money. Money remains a universal criterion of measurement for the many status items that are part of the process of social positioning still prevalent in society. Although it is true that markets or shopping (see chapter 4) have become major institutions in society, it is wrong to believe with Firat and Venkatesh (1995) or Appadurai (1996) and Baudrillard (1983) that the market has supplanted other institutions of importance, such as the family, religion, politics, state governance, or education.

Goods also possess *sign value*. This has been so useful an idea that it is easy to excuse the exuberance of writers such as Ritzer who argue that signs or images now serve as the dominating referents in society. Sign value is clearly important, but not to the extent of Baudrillard's view that the system of signs dominates culture so that the real no longer is a referent (see Kellner 1989; Gottdiener 1995). Although some analysts have reduced all of culture to the play of images (Ewen 1988), others quite rightly position the importance of sign value within the political economy of late capitalism. As mentioned elsewhere (Gottdiener 1995, chapter 8), signs are tools in the process of social interaction, rather than compelling forces in their own right. Although goods have sign value, that value is used as a vehicle for the core activities of consumption; signs are used as modes of self-expression and in the battle for social position. Often it is the highly valorized signs, such as designer clothing or high-status cars, that also possess the most exchange value, that are the most expensive goods of their kind. In this way, both wealth and status interact, as Veblen and Marx suggested.

Social life is best analyzed as a constant interplay of different value statuses— use, exchange, and sign. Although today's media culture is "image driven" (Kellner 1995), advertising doesn't always work; alternative media abound; and the standard processes of political economy, such as the accumulation of wealth through capitalist profit making, remain forces alongside the more postmodern aspects of simulation and the infusion of symbols in daily life (Gottdiener 1995, chapter 8). For example, fashion is an important driving force of culture in society. There is a tyranny of fashion, caused by changes in style. This is so regardless of gender, because even men must conform to new fashions when they affect businesswear such as suits and ties. Men must wear suits with narrow lapels or three buttons when these things are in style to "fit in." Women who wear skirts with short hemlines when the "fashion" is long hemlines commit a public faux pas and risk sanction. Being out of fashion is a social judgment that few can bear in contemporary society, whether one is attending high school or involved in a professional career.

Despite the symbolic nature of this fashion pressure and the equally powerful significance of clothing as a sign of status in the battle for social position, clothes also possess use value. They must protect from the weather. They must help in physical activities, such as work or recreation. The same material objects also possess exchange value. Clothing can be expensive, even if it is purchased purely for its utility. Blue jeans or denim pants were first designed for their use value by Levi Strauss during the nineteenth century's California gold rush. Miners wore them because they were strong and durable. Later ranch workers in the western United States wore denim pants and vests or jackets for the same reason. In post–World War II America, however, wearing denim came to symbolize rebellion and nonconformity. As the latter dimension took hold, those qualities of use that endeared consumers to that product were overshadowed by the sign value of denim among a new American subculture. By the 1960s, denim pants were de rigueur fashion for college students and the counterculture. They also became high-status items for the young adult generation in foreign countries such as France and Russia. There the symbolic connotation of rebellion and nonconformity remained intact, making the wearing of Levi's a cultural universal of youth. Later in the 1970s and 1980s, Levi's were worked over by commodification again, subjecting them to the cycles of fashion through alterations in appearance and eventually becoming a sign of status. They were manufactured in different colors and in the newly fashionable style of wide bell bottoms. In the 1970s, they became symbolic icons of rock musicians such as Elvis Presley, just as in the 1950s and 1960s they were associated with Hollywood rebel icons such as James Dean and Marlon Brando. By the 1980s, through the articulation with urban street culture, denim pants became available in several contrasting styles—loose fitting, classic, boot cut, and the like. Status wars erupted through the use of "designer jeans" and more "up-scale" brands—Calvin Klein, Guess—whose exchange and sign values were produced in part by vigorous advertising campaigns.

Now denim jeans are ubiquitous in society. In more than a century, their "value" has been modulated by mass commodification, by fashion, by status demands, by their association with influential cultural domains in society such as the rock music industry, and by status wars among alternative lifestyles and youth subcultures. This hundred-year dynamic comprises the complex interplay among use, exchange, and sign values. No single perspective can capture the phenomenon of Levi's. To this day, they remain, simultaneously, useful practical pants that almost everyone possesses for this reason; social symbols expressive of important lifestyle differences; and at times, quite expensive signs of status.

Although the best way to avoid reductionism in cultural analysis is to appreciate the threefold dialectic of value in society, it is also clear that the contemporary environment is increasingly characterized by the visible display of signs and the exploitation of sign value. Some encounters with aspects of society, such as a visit to Las Vegas or Disneyland, may even seem to prove that Baudrillard is right—simulation and sign value supersede all other aspects of culture. It's easy to forget that these phenomena are simply capitalism's ways of extending profit making into new, formerly unexplored domains of daily life—that, in short, spectacular signing and simulation remain part of the political economy of capitalism. This is clearly demonstrated by the appearance of theming and new consumption spaces in society.

Although themed experiences are common, it is wrong to view them as dominating society or even "re-enchanting" daily life to the exclusion of instrumental, rational money making. As in the case of advertising, people tend to be simultaneously drawn to novel ways of theming and also resistant enough to these new practices to avoid making a consumer choice based on symbols alone (see Goldman and Papson 1996; Kellner 1989; Bauman 1992). To avoid a reductionist approach to theming, it is necessary to view the phenomenon in the same way as the changing nature of Levi's pants, through the threefold dialectic of use, exchange, and sign value. Themes act *in concert* with other aspects of political economy, especially production, in the ongoing effort of capital to accumulate wealth, on the one hand, and with cognitive and emotional elements, on the other, in a quest for identity and self-expression.

Simulation and theming are but singular aspects of an expanding media-driven environment that includes virtual reality wherein people increasingly consume. Within this multidimensional universe, overlaps occur in the valorized images constructed in the worlds of fashion, show business, professional sports, advertising, magazines, Hollywood films, and television. The themes that are used most in society are limited because they derive from the quest by owners and profit makers for exchange value, and these moneyed interests require that the symbols and themes they use for their products appeal to the widest possible audience or market. Most often the themes of restaurants overlap with the major entertainment industries such as rock music, fashion, or the cinema (as in the Hard Rock Café, the Harley Davidson or Fashion Café, or Planet Hollywood). Las Vegas casinos, although seemingly unencumbered by the amount of money that can be spent on the construction of new resorts, stick to a limited number of fantasies that echo hackneyed clichés of Hollywood films—ancient Egypt, Rome, the circus, the "wild" West, pirates, or tropical paradise. They also promise spectacular renditions of the best-known urban milieus, such as New York, Paris, or Northern Italy, again reproduced as simulations according to the engineering of Hollywood film sets (Gottdiener 1997; Gottdiener et al. 1999). It is in the very nature of these themes that they must be easily recognized by potential customers for the casino environments to be effective. The same can be said for other venues of consumption.

In sum, *sign value* combines with the political economic aspects of *exchange value* and the everyday life reality of *use value* in the satisfaction of needs to structure a complex environment for consumption that also remains related to the work-a-day world of production and that is intended for the realization of profit. If these sign worlds also entertain and give pleasure, that is simply Late Capitalism's way of making money.

BIBLIOGRAPHY

Appadurai, Arjun (1996). *Modernity at Large*. Minneapolis: University of Minnesota Press.

Barthes, Roland (1967). *Système de la mode*. Paris: Seuil.

Baudrillard, Jean (1968). *Les Système des objets*. Paris: Denoil-Gunthier.

——— (1975). *The Mirror of Production*. Thousand Oaks, Calif.: Sage.

——— (1983). *Simulations*. New York: Semiotext(e).

——— (1993). *Symbolic Exchange and Death*. Thousand Oaks, Calif.: Sage.

——— (1998). *The Consumer Society*. Thousand Oaks, Calif.: Sage.

Bauman, Z. (1992). *Intimations of Postmodernity*. New York: Routledge.

Bourdieu, Pierre (1984). *Distinction: A Social Critique of the Judgment of Taste*. Cambridge, Mass.: Harvard University Press.

Braudel, Fernand (1967). *Capitalism and Material Life, 1400–1800*. New York: HarperTorchbooks.

Campbell, Colin (1987). *The Romantic Ethic and the Spirit of Modern Consumerism*. Oxford: Blackwell.

DuGay, Paul, ed. (1997). *Production of Culture/Cultures of Production*. London: Sage.

Durkheim, Emile (1965). *The Elementary Forms of Religious Life*. Translated by J. Swain. New York: The Free Press.

Elias, Norbert (1978). *The Civilizing Process (Volume I)*. New York: Pantheon Books.

Ewen, Stuart (1988). *All Consuming Images*. New York: Basic Books.

Ewen, Stuart, and E. Ewen (1982). *Channels of Desire*. New York: McGraw-Hill.

Featherstone, Michael (1991). *Consumer Culture and Postmodernism*. London: Sage.

Firat, A. Fuat, and Alladi Venkatesh (1995). "Liberatory Postmodernism and the Re-enchantment of Consumption." *Journal of Consumer Research*, Vol. 22, Dec.: 239–67.

Fiske, John (1989). *Understanding Popular Culture*. Boston: Unwin Hyman.

Fox, Daniel M. (1967). *The Discovery of Abundance*. Ithaca, N.Y.: Cornell University Press.

Galbraith, Kenneth (1960). *The Affluent Society*. Boston: Houghton Mifflin.

Gane, Mike (1991). *Baudrillard: Critical and Fatal Theory.* London: Routledge.

Giddens, A. (1991). *Modernity and Self Identity.* Oxford: Politz Press.

—— (1992). *The Transformation of Intimacy.* Oxford: Politz Press.

Goldman, Robert, and Stephen Papson (1996). *Sign Wars.* New York: Guilford.

Gottdiener, M. (1995). *Postmodern Semiotics: Material Culture and the Forms of Postmodern Life.* Oxford: Blackwell.

—— (1997). *The Theming of America: Dreams, Visions and Commercial Spaces.* Boulder, Colo.: Westview.

Gottdiener, M., et al. (1999). *Las Vegas: The Social Production of an All American City.* Oxford: Blackwell.

Jacobs, J. (1984). *The Mall.* Prospect Heights, Ill.: Waveland Press.

Jonaitis, A. (1991). *Chiefly Feasts: The Enduring Kwakiutl Potlatch.* Seattle: University of Washington Press.

Kellner, Doug (1989). *From Marxism to Postmodernism and Beyond: Critical Studies of Jean Baudrillard.* Cambridge: Polity Press.

—— (1995). *Media Culture.* New York: Routledge.

Kirkus Reviews. October 1, 1994. *Review of: Jackson Lears, Fables of Abundance.*

Konig, Rene (1973). *A la Mode: On the Social Psychology of Fashion.* New York: Seabury.

Kroker, A., and D. Cook (1986). *The Postmodern Scene.* New York: St. Martins.

Lears, Jackson (1995). *Fables of Abundance: A Cultural History of Advertising in America.* New York: Basic Books.

Lefebvre, Henri ([1968] 1982). *The Sociology of Marx.* New York: Columbia University Press.

—— (1994). *The Production of Space.* Oxford: Blackwell.

Lunt, P., and S. Livingstone (1992). *Mass Consumption and Personal Identity.* Bristol: Open University.

Lury, Celia (1996). *Consumer Culture.* New Brunswick, N.J.: Rutgers University Press.

Maffesoli, M. (1996). *The Time of the Tribes.* London: Sage.

Marchand, Roland (1985). *Advertising and the American Dream.* Berkeley: University of California Press.

Mauss, Marcel (1967). *The Gift.* New York: Norton.

McCracken, Grant (1990). *Culture and Consumption.* Bloomington: Indiana University Press.

McKendrick, Neil, et al. (1982). *The Birth of Consumer Society: The Commercialization of Eighteenth Century England.* Bloomington: Indiana University Press.

Miller, Michael (1981). *The Bon Marche: Bourgeois Culture and the Department Store: 1869–1920.* Princeton, N.J.: Princeton University Press.

Mills, C. Wright (1953). "Introduction to the Mentor Edition." Thorstein Veblen, *The Theory of the Leisure Class* [1899]. New York: New America Library.

Mukerji, Chandra (1983). *From Graven Images: Patterns of Modern Materialism.* New York: Columbia University Press.

Packard, Vance (1957). *The Hidden Persuaders.* New York: David McKay.

Potter, David M. (1958). *People of Plenty.* Chicago: University of Chicago Press.

Ritzer, George (1996). *McDonaldization.* Thousand Oaks, Calif.: Pine Forge Press.

—— (1998). *The McDonaldization Experience: Explorations and Extensions.* London: Sage.

———— (1999). *Enchanting a Disenchanted World.* Thousand Oaks, Calif.: Pine Forge Press.

Schudson, Michael (1984). *Advertising: The Uneasy Persuasion.* New York: Basic Books.

Shields, R. (1992). *Lifestyle Shopping.* New York: Routledge.

Simmel, Georg (1957). "On Fashion." *American Journal of Sociology* 62:54–58.

Tedlow, Richard S. (1990). *New and Improved: The Story of Mass Marketing in America.* New York: Basic Books.

Veblen, Thorstein (1899). *The Theory of the Leisure Class.* New York: New America Library.

2

The Process of McDonaldization Is Not Uniform, nor Are Its Settings, Consumers, or the Consumption of Its Goods and Services

George Ritzer and Seth Ovadia

McDonaldization is "the process by which the principles of the fast-food restaurant are coming to dominate more and more sectors of the American society as well as the rest of the world" (Ritzer 1996:1). It is found not only in fast-food restaurants but also has become a significant part of daily life in the United States and as well as in much of the rest of the world. As of this writing, McDonald's is found in 115 nations, and numerous clones exist in the fast-food industry and many other sectors of society. Seeking to utilize the principles that have made McDonald's one of the most successful enterprises in modern capitalism, a broad range of organizations, both profit and nonprofit, have emulated the McDonald's model to varying degrees.

The model's principles are *efficiency, calculability, predictability, and control,* particularly through the *substitution of nonhuman for human technology.* The basic concept, as well as its fundamental dimensions, is derived from Max Weber's ([1921] 1968) work on formal rationality. Weber demonstrated that the modern Western world was characterized by an increasing tendency toward the predominance of formally rational systems. Thus, the process of McDonaldization obviously predates McDonald's as an institution. However, that franchise is the exemplar (as was the bureaucracy in Weber's model) of the contemporary development of rationalization.

Recent studies have supported the idea that "the McDonaldization thesis" (Ritzer 1998) applies well beyond the fast-food restaurant and even everyday consumption to such areas as higher education ("McUniversity") (Hartley 1995; Parker and Jary 1995), vegetarianism (Tester 1999), theme parks (Bryman 1995,

33

1999a; Ritzer and Liska 1998—Bryman 1999b has even recently proposed a process of "Disneyization" as a complement to McDonaldization), Southern folk art (Fine 1999), politics (Turner 1999; Beilharz 1999), and "three-strikes-and-you're-out" criminal laws (Shichor 1997). McDonaldization is a broad social development; even birth and death have undergone the process (Ritzer 1998). Of course, not all systems are equally McDonaldized; McDonaldization is a matter of degree with some settings more McDonaldized than others (this issue will be addressed below). However, few settings have been able to escape the influence of McDonaldization altogether.

Efficiency is characterized by the effort to get from one point (or condition) to another with a minimum of effort. This is measured in terms of both economic cost and overall systemic effort. McDonald's systems of producing food and serving customers with minimal amounts of physical and temporal waste have become increasingly streamlined throughout the history of the franchise. Other businesses, ranging from competing fast-food chains to automobile repair shops and health care systems, have sought to reproduce McDonald's level of efficiency by adopting similar principles and organizational structures. Systems seek to maximize their efficiency by streamlining various processes (e.g., the drive-through window), simplifying products (e.g., "finger food" such as Chicken McNuggets), and putting customers to work (e.g., by bussing their own debris after the meal is finished).

Calculability is an emphasis on things that can be quantified. In McDonaldized systems, quantity takes priority over quality. In many cases, large quantities of things come to be equated with quality. This increasing dependence on numbers as a proxy for quality is found in all aspects of life. For example, the health of a company is often not measured by the quality of its products but by the value of its stock. The price of the stock, in turn, is largely determined by regular reports of sales and profits. A company might post a loss for a quarter in which a major investment is made in some qualitative aspect of the company, say a human resources initiative. Even if the company's operations are substantially improved as a result of the investment, until reports of profits resume, the company might be considered a poor investment. In addition to emphasizing quantity rather than quality (in the fast-food restaurant business, this is represented by the Big Mac and signs bragging about the number of billions sold), two other aspects of calculability are (1) giving the illusion of (usually large) quantity (the shape of the french fry scoop and the striped boxes that make it seem like there are more fries than there actually are) and (2) reducing processes of production (e.g., how long it takes to assemble a Whopper) and services (e.g., how long it takes to deliver a Domino's pizza) to numbers.

Predictability is another key dimension in McDonaldized systems. Like the other areas, it both facilitates and is made possible by the other aspects of rationalization. Efforts are undertaken to make the behavior of employees more predictable so that the production of goods and services can be anticipated from minute to minute and day to day. Such predictability also serves to make the system more efficient and amenable to calculability. McDonaldized systems also seek to make the behavior of consumers more predictable by, for example, providing uncomfortable seats and bright clashing colors that make them want to leave quickly. Various aspects of predictability are treated under this heading, including creating predictable settings (the physical setup of a fast-food restaurant is pretty uniform throughout the world); scripting predictable interactions with customers ("will you have dessert with your meal?"); ensuring predictable employee behavior (uniform techniques for cooking hamburgers); providing predictable products (the Big Mac is pretty much the same wherever you go) and processes (the ordering and provision of food at the drive-through window); and minimizing the danger and unpleasantness (fast-food restaurants and other McDonaldized systems seek to keep "undesirables" out).

Control through the replacement of human by nonhuman technologies is a major means by which predictability, efficiency, and calculability can be ensured both in production and in interactions with consumers. The increasing use of technology to control, and more extremely, take the place of, humans in production has been of great concern to social analysts (Marx [1867] 1967; Braverman 1974). As systems become more rationalized, employees come to be increasingly controlled by technologies. Once humans are reduced to robotlike actions, it is possible to replace them with automated systems. Such systems can not only produce products, but situations also are arising in which interaction between employees providing services and consumers is being replaced by consumers dealing directly and exclusively with machines (e.g., the automated pumps at most gas stations, ATMs). The increasing use of such technologies is a sure sign of progress toward the goal of an ever-more rational system of production. This serves other objectives as well, such as a smoother-running organization, decreased labor costs, and in the case of for-profit organizations, greater profitability.

With techniques ranging from installing the maze of ropes that consumers must negotiate in banks and government offices to providing the conscripted menu in fast-food restaurants, organizations also seek to control their customers by limiting their range of options. The organization becomes more efficient by not having to deviate from its routines. Were a person free to request financial advice from a bank teller, the efficiency of the bank would be hampered significantly. With the replacement of the bank teller by the ATM, this possibility of uncontrolled behavior by the consumer is virtually eliminated.

In a McDonaldizing society, beyond gaining greater control over people as employees and consumers, there is also interest in increasing control over products and processes. For example, a more uniform (predictable) product is created when it is produced by nonhuman technologies or when such technologies tightly control what employees do. Similarly, various processes associated with production and service are more efficient and predictable when nonhuman replaces human technology.

As Weber noted, a paradox of rationalized systems is that in the pursuit of "perfect" rationalization, irrationalities develop. For employees, consumers, and the whole of society, rationalization is irrational in various ways, especially the fact that it dehumanizes the fundamentally social acts of production and consumption through the means described above.

Although it is dehumanizing, among many other irrationalities, McDonaldization offers a variety of benefits. It offers owners greater profitability and managers of McDonaldized organizations greater control over employees and customers. Consumers can get various goods and services more quickly and easily; indeed, they may come to seek out systems that offer greater efficiency, calculability, predictability, and control through nonhuman technology. In this way, McDonaldization should not only be seen as something that is forced upon consumers; they have come to value the process and are often well served by it.

For example, compare banking in the 1950s and today. In the 1950s, people had few options for accessing their money. Credit cards were not common (the "universal card" had just been invented at the beginning of the decade [Ritzer 1995]). Cash was available from banks, but they were only open the traditional "bankers' hours" of approximately six hours a day, five days a week. Checks were perhaps the only form of around-the-clock access to money, but the recipient of the check could not cash it outside of the bank's schedule either.

Today, cash is available in most places in the United States and the Western world twenty-four hours a day, seven days a week. Even in the absence of cash, credit cards have become almost universally accepted in the modernized world. Bank transactions can also be performed by telephone and computer, facilitating a broad range of acts of consumption from the customer's home at any time of the day or night. Ultimately, it can be argued, this liberation of consumption from the restrictions of the bank's clock may serve the producers of goods more than the consumers, but the increased service to the consumer made possible by the McDonaldization of the banking industry is undeniable.

However, the consumer's agenda is not the primary concern in the development of rationality in most systems. It is usually not consumers who persuade systems to become more rational, although exceptions to this generalization are certainly present in modern society. Most often, though, managers and owners are the engineers behind McDonaldization as they seek to increase their profits (and/or reduce their costs) through increased use of efficient, calculable, predictable, and controlled systems.

The objective in the remainder of this chapter is to deal with four aspects of the McDonaldization thesis that have often been misrepresented. First, to make it clear that McDonaldization is *not* a uniform process; it has a variety of "trajectories." Second, and relatedly, as a result of varying trajectories, there is great variation in the degree to which settings are McDonaldized; even in the fast-food industry, not all settings are highly and equally McDonaldized. Third, although McDonaldized systems seek to mold consumers so that they behave in a uniform manner, they are never totally successful in doing so; there are various types of consumers. And fourth, there is variation in the relationship between consumers and McDonaldized settings; consumers do not always simply act in accord with the demands of McDonaldized systems. Although McDonaldization is a powerful force with quite general effects, overall, it involves several variations and complexities. This chapter will not only clarify certain aspects of the McDonaldization thesis but also offer more of the nuances associated with it.

MCDONALDIZATION AS PROCESS: VARIATIONS IN TRAJECTORIES

Systems do not undergo the process of McDonaldization in the same manner and to the same degree. Sectors of society are amenable to rationalization in varying degrees and even within the same sector, organizations are transformed in different ways, to different degrees, and in varying time frames. It could be argued that every system has a unique "trajectory of McDonaldization"; operations become increasingly rationalized over time in a pattern that is a function of the conditions specific to that system. (It is even possible for systems to move in the other direction; to undergo de-McDonaldization [Ritzer 1998].)

For example, franchised businesses are typically highly McDonaldized operations. Specifically in the fast-food industry, all of the major companies have developed advanced systems of efficiency, calculability, predictability, and control, often seeking to keep up with, or even surpass, McDonald's itself. At the same time, McDonald's continues to rationalize further its operations in search of increasing profits and the retention of a competitive edge over other franchises. However, in response to each of McDonald's innovations, other franchises quickly adopt similar practices and strategies. Of course, McDonald's is no longer the sole or even the leading innovator among franchises. Thus, McDonald's must remain sensitive to its competitors and adopt the best and most relevant of their innovations. In general then, not only are fast-food chains and franchises all highly rationalized but they also have a tendency to be somewhat indistinguishable from one another. Nonfranchised restaurants are likely to be less McDonaldized than the franchises, but although some remain quite nonrationalized, most experience pressure to rationalize their operations to remain competitive.

The health care industry is an example of a sector in which it is more difficult to McDonaldize many operations and, as a result, it has been slower to incorporate the principles of rationalization. Although it might appear that medical care is inherently antagonistic toward the process of McDonaldization, the rise of McDoctors, the HMO as the predominant form of health care provision, the increased emphasis on hospitals as businesses, and increased government control over medicine all reflect the fact that McDonaldization has exerted an influence in this area. All elements of the health care process are amenable to rationalization in varying degrees, but some elements of the medical field (McDoctors) are becoming McDonaldized more extremely and more quickly than others (complicated surgical procedures).

Several factors are influential in determining whether a sector is more or less amenable to McDonaldization. One that appears to play an important role is the degree to which suppliers of goods and services must adapt to the needs of individual customers. There is a strong need and considerable pressure on physicians to adapt their "service"—medical care—to the specific needs of each patient. Although the McDonaldization of medicine has led to doctors being forced to practice a more uniform and structured form of diagnosis and treatment, health care is still more resistant to the mechanical "if–then" mentality that one finds in settings such as the fast-food restaurant where there is little need to adapt to the desires of specific customers.

Complexity of tasks is another factor. Simple tasks such as the cooking and serving of hamburgers is more amenable to McDonaldization than highly complex tasks such as preparing a gourmet meal. Within medicine, simpler tasks (taking vital signs) are more likely to be McDonaldized than complex tasks such as open heart surgery, although even the latter is not without its McDonaldized elements.

It is possible to further distinguish among degrees of McDonaldization in a given sector. In health care, for example, certain institutional characteristics influence the speed and extent of McDonaldization. For instance, a large hospital in a major city and a general practice doctor's office in a rural area provide similar forms of health care services (in comparison with a drugstore or research laboratory). However, the hospital is likely to be much more McDonaldized, and to become so much more quickly, than the doctor's office.

Another variable that affects the process of McDonaldization is the degree of competition in a sector. The fast-food industry is saturated with intense competitors, and customers have many options to any single restaurant or chain. As a result, the pressure to draw upon the benefits of rationalization is great.[1] In contrast, organizations that provide unique products or enjoy virtual monopolies in their field are likely to be under less pressure to rationalize their systems. Because customers do not have many alternative options for the product, streamlining production and capturing customers through efficiency and control are not as important.

A key factor is organizational size. Because the people in charge of large organizations are unable to exercise direct control at all levels, they develop rational systems of accountability and control. These rationalized structures allow administrators to ensure the efficient functioning of the organization without having to be knowledgeable about the activities of all subordinates at all times.

For example, most major business firms—IBM, General Motors, and so on—are significantly McDonaldized. The sheer size of these companies, with thousands of employees, requires extensive systems of rationalization to maximize the likelihood of meeting their institutional goals. The same can be said for large non-business entities, such as federal and state governments. A small local print shop is likely to exhibit little in the way of McDonaldization, however.

Then there is the overall degree of McDonaldization in the environment. As a general rule, restaurants in smaller cities and suburbs will tend to be McDonaldized to a greater degree than those in urban settings. McDonald's began as a smaller city and suburban phenomenon and its strength continues to be in those locales (although in recent years it has made substantial inroads into the city). Competitors to McDonald's in such settings are likely to follow the McDonald's model and become highly rationalized. Seeing the positive effect of McDonaldization on one's institutional neighbors, even in different sectors, will lead administrators to attempt to adapt what makes their neighbors successful to their own organization. However, there are a variety of successful models in a city such as New York, many of them with well-established roots and a loyal clientele. Thus, although McDonaldized fast-food restaurants have established a successful presence, other models are likely to survive and continue to prosper. The restaurant business, among others, in New York City is less McDonaldized than in Huntsville, Alabama, or the suburbs of Washington, D.C.

The case of New York City suggests another important factor—the amount of cultural and ethnic diversity in an area. Areas that are fairly homogeneous and dominated by members of the majority group (white, middle-class Americans) are likely to be highly McDonaldized, whereas those that are highly diverse culturally and ethnically are apt to be less so. A complicating factor is income and wealth. Areas where well-to-do members of the majority group predominate are likely to be able to sustain a variety of less McDonaldized settings. Areas where ethnic minorities predominate are likely to support many non-McDonaldized settings even though income may be low. Therefore, areas dominated by poor and middle-class members of the majority group are most likely to be highly McDonaldized.

Specific relationships and hypotheses aside, the key point is that there is great variety in the degree of McDonaldization in various economic and social settings. Although there is a general trend toward the McDonaldization of such settings, it is not manifest uniformly across various domains or even within a specific domain. McDonaldization is *not* a monolithic process.

THE VARIETY OF SETTINGS FOR CONSUMPTION

As a result of the varying trajectories, there is great differentiation in consumption settings. Pierre Bourdieu's concept of "field" can be used to consider these diverse settings. The field is a network of relations among the objective positions within it (Bourdieu and Wacquant 1992:97). Positions may be occupied by either agents or institutions and they are constrained by the structure of the field. There are many semiautonomous fields within the social world. Each has an objective structure that can be mapped.

Fields can be envisioned at the macro-social level as well as at several sublevels. Thus, for example, each of the following can be conceived as fields—retail establishments; traditional, non-McDonaldized restaurants; fast-food restaurants; the McDonald's chain; and so on. In deciding where to dine, the consumers' practice is determined, in part, by the overall structure of these fields as well as the more specific field that they are led, or forced, to choose. Of course, that choice is also affected by characteristics of the consumer, especially, in Bourdieu's terms, the consumer's habitus and capital (see below).

Thus, a wide range of fields can be discussed under the heading of McDonaldization. If American restaurants define the field, then there is a variety of positions, ranging from highly McDonaldized chains to almost totally non-McDonaldized gourmet restaurants. If American health care is the field, then the range might be from McDoctors to surgical theaters. Both of these could be refined further; for example, if McDonaldized chains of restaurants is the field, different positions in the field can be identified—McDonald's, Burger King, Olive Garden, Morton's, and so on. The important point here is that there is a wide range of fields and subfields and this serves to underscore the point that there is great variety in consumption settings, and many other settings as well.

THE VARIETY OF CONSUMERS

Throughout the development of the sociology of consumption, there has been very little consensus on consumers and their characteristics. Some of the earliest authors on consumption, such as Thorstein Veblen ([1899] 1934) and Georg Simmel ([1904] 1971), tended to view consumers as conscious, empowered agents who use the symbolic system of consumption as a way of establishing class differences and distinct personal identities. Later theorists of consumption have been divided between the visions of consumers as empowered or as victims. However, between these two extremes lies a broad range of types of consumers, some of which overlap and others of which differ substantially from one another.

In *The Unmanageable Consumer* (1995), Yiannis Gabriel and Tim Lang attempt to organize these conceptualizations into a typology of the modern consumer. They argue that "different traditions or discourses have invented different representations of the consumer each with its own specificity and coherence, but willfully oblivious to those of others" (1995:2). Their catalog of consumer types is not a comprehensive list, but it does illustrate the range of consumers. They are the consumer as chooser, communicator, explorer, identity-seeker, hedonist or artist, victim, rebel, activist, and citizen. By themselves, none of these is sufficient to describe fully any single consumer (in this sense, Gabriel and Lang are outlining types of consumption acts of which all consumers are capable at one time or another). Most consumers can be seen as fitting into different types at different times, and often, multiple types within a single act of consumption. Certain combinations of these consumer roles overlap quite often, as in the case of the communicator and identity-seeker roles. Other combinations are somewhat exclusive of one another, such as the victim and the rebel.

Gabriel and Lang argue that the emergence of these multiple consumer types is a characteristic of later capitalism and an indication that the idea of the consumer as a singular figure is losing its coherence. "Precariousness, unevenness, and fragmentation are likely to become more pronounced for ever-increasing sections of Western populations," and as the consumer becomes more of a mercurial character, attempts by marketers, producers, and social scientists to define the consumer will become untenable (Gabriel and Lang 1995:190). They foresee a future in which consumption is an opportunistic act, and the providers of market goods are increasingly unable to target their products to consumers in rational and systematic ways.

This conclusion is opposed to the view of the consumer implicit in both the McDonaldization thesis and Weberian theory in general. McDonaldized organizations seek to control the consumer, irrespective of the consumer's desires or needs. For example, fast-food restaurants and many other highly rationalized systems have strict codes and practices that constrain the options of the consumer. Even less McDonaldized systems seek to limit the options available to consumers. In either case, the interpretation of the consumer as "unmanageable" does not fit with the idea of increasing McDonaldization. Rationalized organizations are too dependent on control to meet their own needs for efficiency and profit to allow the consumers to escape from the boxes in which the system places them.

However, Gabriel and Lang are correct in recognizing that in spite of increasing McDonaldization and the best efforts of McDonaldized systems, the consumer is not likely to be reduced to a singular, highly predictable figure. Consumers will continue to be agents and the various roles that individuals can take on must be considered part of developing a full understanding of the relationship between McDonaldized systems and the consumers of their goods and services.

To illustrate the diversity of consumers, examine the way in which each of Gabriel and Lang's types of consumers might relate to highly McDonaldized settings in the fast-food industry. This is obviously a highly simplified analysis, not only because the ideal is relied upon—typical rather than fully complex human consumers—but also because only one type of setting is focused upon. Yet this allows for more complete consideration about consumers in a McDonaldized society.

Choosers are likely to be led by rational factors into opting to eat in McDonaldized fast-food restaurants. For example, low price, convenience, and the lack of available alternatives (an increasing likelihood in an increasingly McDonaldized society) would lead such a consumer to a franchised restaurant. The fast-food restaurant is a "rational choice" in a society where speed and efficiency are valued, consumers want to be sure that they are getting what they expect, and cost is an important consideration. Other choosers are likely, for other equally rational reasons, to opt out of eating in such restaurants, at least to the degree that they can find viable alternatives. Such reasons might be the adverse effect of the nature of the food served on consumers' health, the dehumanizing character of "dining" in fast-food restaurants, and the negative impact such restaurants have on the environment.

Communicators would be led in the direction of a wide variety of restaurants depending on what it is they want to communicate. In eating in a chain of fast-food restaurants, they might be communicating that they are frugal and sensible and that they belong to the group of people that frequents such restaurants in general and the specific chain in particular. In terms of the latter, those who frequent Burger King may be communicating that they are somehow different from McDonald's consumers. Those who prefer higher-priced McDonaldized chains, such as the Olive Garden, may be seeking to communicate the fact that they are different from those who choose lower-end chains. Those who eat in chains of any type may be seeking to communicate that they are more "down to earth" than the "swells" who dine at expensive, chic restaurants.

Explorers would be drawn to the chains as one of many different types of restaurants that they wish to experience. Similarly, they may be drawn to a wide variety of them because of their desire to experience the full range of restaurant chains rather than committing to one or another. One would also expect explorers to sample any new chain as soon as it opens. Of course the explorer, assuming there are no major economic limitations, will not be restricted to franchises and will seek to experience a range of restaurants, including expensive, less McDonaldized settings.

Identity seekers may, paradoxically, establish their identity based on one of the highly McDonaldized chains. They may revel in thinking of themselves as "Burger King kind of people" or as members of an informal "breakfast club" that meets at the chain every morning. The paradox involves finding a distinctive identity in a system that offers uniformity, the same identity to all. This is explained by Stephen Miles (1998) as the problem of trying to purchase an identity "off the peg." In other words, it is the question of whether purchasing an identity created and mass-produced by McDonaldized systems constitutes a "true" identity.

Hedonists go to McDonaldized chains because they derive pleasure from being there and consuming the food and perhaps even from the "ambiance" of such a place. The hedonist would also be drawn by the emphasis on large portions and the idea that there is going to be plenty of food to devour. The *artists*, a type that Gabriel and Lang closely link to hedonists, would be drawn to the franchises by the desire to be creative and the need to express themselves. This again gives rise to a paradox, as one wonders how artists can express themselves in a creative fashion in such a structured environment. Possibilities include making special requests ("hold the catsup"), mixing several types of drinks at the self-service counters, or making creative salads or other innovative concoctions at the salad bar. Of course, both hedonists and artists, assuming cost was not an insurmountable barrier, would probably be drawn more to the high-end, non-McDonaldized restaurants where there are far more possibilities for creative ordering of dishes and where the dishes are more likely to please the eyes of the artist and the taste buds of the hedonist. In fact, the recent emphasis on elegant designs for the presentation of food on the plate is designed with the artist in mind. However, it is worth noting that in at least one sense, the artist has more leeway for creativity in the chains than in the elite restaurants. The self-service available in fast-food restaurants offers the artist more opportunities for self-expression than in the elite restaurants, where everything is done for the diner.

Consumers can be seen as *victims* in all types of restaurants, although the nature of the victimization differs from one type to another. In the fast-food restaurant, consumers are victimized by the structure (the limited menu, the drive-through window, the uncomfortable seats) and by being forced to do things that they might prefer not to do. They are also victimized by the food that, given the large number of calories and the high fat, cholesterol, salt, and sugar content of much of it, is likely to have an adverse effect on their health in the long run. Consumers can also be seen as victimized by the efforts of the fast-food restaurants to lure their children into being lifelong devotees of fast food (and its poor nutritional value). However, these forms of victimization are not exclusive to the fast-food end of the spectrum. Consumers at expensive restaurants can also be seen as victims of often unhealthy food (say a large slab of prime rib or a dish with very rich sauce) and, distinctively, of extraordinarily high prices.

It is possible to be a *rebel* in a fast-food restaurant, but its rigid structure makes it difficult to do so. Rebels could demand such things as table service at a fast-food restaurant, but the nature of the setting makes it virtually impossible that they will get it. More extremely, consumers could cover the walls with graffiti as an expression of rebellion against the system. Interestingly, fast-food restaurants in general, and especially McDonald's, are often the site of violence. In the past decade, there have been several well-publicized murders at fast-food restaurants. Overseas, people unhappy with the United States in general, or with the invasion of fast-food restaurants in particular, often take out their anger by attacking McDonald's outlets or those of other chains based in the United States.

For example, during the 1999 NATO bombing of Yugoslavia, one response of the Serbians was the smashing of windows at two McDonald's restaurants in Belgrade. One is far less likely to see acts of rebellion of this, or any other type, mounted against elite non-McDonaldized restaurants. They simply do not have the same semiotic significance as McDonald's or other well-known American chains.

Also as a result of their powerful symbolic importance, there is also likely to be much more *activism* mounted against McDonaldized chains than against an elite restaurant. This is well reflected in the worldwide community that has emerged as a result of the so-called McLibel trial in Great Britain (Vidal 1997). A site was created on the World Wide Web <http://www.mcspotlight.org/> and it reports an average of 1.75 million "hits" a month—a total of 65 million hits by March 1999. It has become the heart of a worldwide movement in opposition to McDonald's, as well as other aspects of the McDonaldized world (Penman 1997). It serves as the repository for information on actions taken against local McDonald's throughout the world.

The consumer as *citizen* is, to a large degree in society, contrasted to the consumer being depicted in most of this discussion. Except for the rebels and the activists, the types of consumers are virtually all self-interested in one way or another. In contrast, the consumer as citizen is interested in the good of the collectivity. In today's society, which emphasizes self-interested consumption, it is very difficult to be a citizen in the world of consumption. Buying "green" products might be an example of good citizenship in the realm of consumption, but perhaps the best thing that the citizen can do is to abstain from consumption as much as possible. The difficulty of being a citizen has been exacerbated in recent years by the government policies, epitomized by the war cry "no new taxes," which have tended to deemphasize the collective good and have focused instead on individual self-maximization. As a general rule, the consumer as citizen would have problems with both McDonaldized and non-McDonaldized restaurants, but the nature of the problem might be different. A citizen might object to the exclusive character and high cost of "elite" restaurants, but the opposition to McDonald's would deal more with things such as health concerns and environmental damage.

Thus, there are different types of consumers and each would relate differently to McDonaldized restaurants, to say nothing of the full range of restaurants. In addition, this overview should be considered as relating to acts of consumption and not just consumers. Any one person may engage in each of these types of consumer behavior at one time or another. The point is that means of consumption are confronted with a wide array of consumers and acts of consumption. They may seek to impose great uniformity on consumers and consumption, and although they are often largely successful, those actions are always going to be limited by the great diversity among consumers and in acts of consumption.

CONSUMERS AND MCDONALDIZATION

A McDonaldizing society is characterized by neither singular consumers nor singular settings; there is considerable variation in both. One type of consumer will relate differently to highly McDonaldized settings than another type. Furthermore, from one act of consumption to another, the same person is capable of taking on a variety of different roles and role combinations. Similarly, the settings of consumption vary in their degree of McDonaldization (and many other things as well). This issue then is: What is this complex relationship between a wide range of consumer types (and acts of consumption) and a similarly wide range of settings in terms of their degree of McDonaldization?

Such a specific issue moves into the realm of social theory associated in the United States with micro–macro relationships and in Europe with the agency–structure linkage. Individual consumers can be thought of as micro-level phenomena and the settings in which they consume, varying in terms of degree of McDonaldization, as macro-level phenomena. Alternatively, most consumers have agency, at least some of the time. And the settings in which they consume can be seen as structures. There is a dialectical relationship between the agency of the consumer and the nature of the structures. The form and outcome of that relationship depends upon the characteristics of both within a particular setting. Agency–structure theories tend to be richer than micro–macro theories and one that suggests itself, especially in relation to the concept of field, is Pierre Bourdieu's theory of practice. Without delving deeply into this theory, it does offer a useful general orientation to the relationship between various consumers and the range of McDonaldized settings for consumption.

In *Distinction* (1984:101), Bourdieu offers a formula for social action that takes into account both the agency of individuals and the structures in which they are situated: [(habitus) (capital)] + field = practice. Although the "mathematics" of the formula are not expounded upon, and the nature of the details are not of significance here, the important point is that Bourdieu is arguing that individual practice is the result of individual agency, the product of an individual's habitus[2] and the capital (cultural, social, etc.) of that individual, and the structure as expressed by the field in which the agents find themselves. Differences in agency and/or field will lead to different practices. Further, there is recognition here that there are important variations in both agency and field.

Consumer behavior is generated in part by the habitus of the individual consumer. A person's habitus is "a structured and structuring structure," from which, among other things, practice, classificatory schemes, and taste arise. The individual's habitus facilitates the performance of certain consumer roles and discourages the adoption of others. In addition, the relevant stocks of capital that the individual possesses play a role in determining consumer practices. Capital, in its various forms (social, educational, economic), interacts with the habitus of the consumer to create "stances" vis-à-vis the field of consumer settings. For example, consumers who lack economic capital are unlikely to be very discriminating (to be "choosers") when it comes to the settings of consumption; they will use what they can afford. The consumer as citizen requires social capital to be an effective presence in the face of the power of McDonaldized systems. Capital, like habitus, leads to specific practices and tends to discourage others in certain circumstances.

As has been seen, Bourdieu uses the concept of the field to designate the array of settings, and it is there that people engage in practices that express their habitus and employ their various stocks of capital. The practice of the individual is the result of the interaction of the habitus and capital(s) and the nature and structure of the field. The structure of the field affects the range of practices that are available to the individual; the individual chooses among the practices available within the field. The result is the practice which, in this discussion, is an act of consumption.

Bourdieu's concepts of habitus, capital, and field suggest a way to consider the relationship between the consumer and the means of consumption (one of which is the fast-food restaurant [Ritzer 1999]) so that both influence the form and outcome of the interaction. By understanding the act of consumption (practice) as the product of the consumer as agent (habitus and capital) and the specific means of consumption (field), there is a dynamic rather than a static vision of consumption. The consumer and the means of consumption interact in a dialectical relationship, as each influences the form of the other, and the overall interaction is one that is dynamic in both the specific interaction and over time.

Using Bourdieu as inspiration, it is possible now to begin to think about ways in which the consumer and the means of consumption encounter one another and the range of possible results that emerge from that interaction.[3] In a highly McDonaldized society, especially one that has been so for quite some time, the habitus of most people can be expected to be endowed with a strong propensity to prefer McDonaldized settings. This is especially likely to be so for young people, with older people less inclined to McDonaldized settings if for no other reason than the fact that it is likely they were born into a less McDonaldized society. As time passes and the older generations die off, there will likely be a more uniform propensity toward McDonaldized settings across generations.

In terms of social class, a propensity toward McDonaldization would be expected across all social classes, but there would be differences among classes. The lower and middle classes would be most strongly inclined in that direction, and the upper class would have a propensity that would lead to somewhat less of a draw toward McDonaldized settings.

The social class differences, to the extent that they exist, are related to capital. The possession of economic capital by the families of upper-class children would permit them to expose their children to non-McDonaldized settings from a young age. Similarly, their cultural capital (e.g., appreciation of fine cuisine) would lead them to want to take their children to good restaurants and, in the process, develop their cultural capital in this realm (and many others). At the other extreme, the lower classes, lacking in economic and cultural capital, would be led not only to expose their children to McDonaldized settings but also to extol the virtues of those settings. The middle class would have the economic capital to expose their children to McDonaldized settings much more frequently than the lower class. However, they would, on occasion, have the resources to expose them to non-McDonaldized settings. Similarly, the moderate cultural capital of the middle classes would lead them to stress the virtues of McDonaldized settings, although there would also be an appreciation of non-McDonaldized settings. Thus, there is greater likelihood for ambivalence in the middle classes than at the two poles of the class system.

When one turns to the field in a highly McDonaldized society, one obviously finds it dominated by McDonaldized settings. The greater the predominance of such settings, the less the likelihood that anyone has any choice, whatever the relationship between their habitus and capital. In a fully McDonaldized field, there would be no choice. This is what Weber meant by the "iron cage." Of course, no field will ever be totally McDonaldized, but it is likely that many will achieve a high degree of McDonaldization. In such a field, even those whose combination of habitus and capital inclines them to seek out non-McDonaldized settings will have a hard time finding them. In many cases, they will be forced into a McDonaldized setting even though they are inclined to, for example, eat in some other kind of setting.

The preceding is but a brief illustration of the direction Bourdieu's theory can take a person in thinking about the relationship between agency and structure in a McDonaldized society. As with the discussion in the previous sections on process, settings, and consumers, the critical point is that there is no simple conclusion to be drawn about, and there is great complexity in, that relationship.

CONCLUSION

This effort to add nuance and specificity to the McDonaldization thesis has only scratched the surface of a complex set of issues. There is much more to be said about trajectories of McDonaldization, differentiation within McDonaldized settings and between those that are highly McDonaldized and those that are less so, diversity among types of consumers and acts of consumption, and most importantly the relationships between consumers and the range of McDonaldized settings. A fuller analysis of acts of consumption needs to allow the levels of McDonaldization to range across the full spectrum. The types of consumers require further specification; Gabriel and Lang's nine types are a useful starting point, but there may be other types of consumers that have been overlooked. Much more needs to be done with translating Gabriel and Lang's types of consumers into types of consumer practices. In addition, far more can be done with the analysis of the consumer within the range of McDonaldized settings based on nature of habitus, amount and types of capital, and so on.

Most importantly, perhaps, much more can be said about the dialectical relationship between the consumer and the means of consumption. One way in which the dialectical process might be analyzed is in a study of the patterns of association between specific consumer types or types of consumer practices and settings at various points on the trajectory of McDonaldization. Studying the reasons why people consume where they do and how the settings attract certain types of customers rather than others begins to get at the dialectical association between consumers and means of consumption. Another way to explore this process is through a study of the "negotiations" that take place once a consumer begins interacting with a specific setting. How the consumer and means of consumption mutually determine the role that the consumer will play in the act of consumption is a dialectical process that often goes unnoticed by consumers, organizations, and those who study both. Consumption, like McDonaldization, is devilishly complex.

NOTES

1. Of course, this does not explain why the fast-food industry (although it had precursors) pioneered McDonaldization. Ray Kroc was not faced with a saturated market for such restaurants.

2. While we will not go into it here, there are problems involved in thinking about agency from the point of view of such a structuralist notion as habitus. Given his structuralist bias, Bourdieu does not have as strong a theory of agency as, say, Anthony Giddens.

3. However, a consideration of the system of consumption in its full complexity is well beyond the scope of this essay.

BIBLIOGRAPHY

Beilharz, Peter (1999). "McFascism? Reading Ritzer, Bauman and the Holocaust," in *Resisting McDonaldization*, ed. Barry Smart. London: Sage: 222–33.

Bourdieu, Pierre (1984). *Distinction: A Social Critique of the Judgment of Taste*. Cambridge, Mass.: Harvard University Press.

Bourdieu, Pierre, and Loic Wacquant (1992). "The Purpose of Reflexive Sociology (The Chicago Workshop)," in *An Invitation to Reflexive Sociology*, ed. Pierre Bourdieu and L. J. D. Wacquant. Chicago: University of Chicago Press: 61–215.

Braverman, Harry (1974). *Labor and Monopoly Capital: The Degradation of Work in the Twentieth Century*. New York: Monthly Review.

Bryman, Alan (1995). *Disney and His Worlds*. London: Routledge.

——— (1999a). "The Disneyization of Society," *Sociological Review* 47:25–47.

———(1999b). "Theme Parks and McDonaldization," in *Resisting McDonaldization*, ed. Barry Smart. London: Sage: 101–15.

Fine, Gary Alan (1999). "Art Centres: Southern Folk Art and the Splintering of a Hegemonic Market," in *Resisting McDonaldization*, ed. Barry Smart. London: Sage: 148–62.

Hartley, David (1995). "The 'McDonaldization' of Higher Education: Food for Thought?" *Oxford Review of Education* 21(4):409–23.

Gabriel, Yiannis, and Tim Lang (1995). *The Unmanageable Consumer: Contemporary Consumption and Its Fragmentation*. London: Sage.

Marx, Karl ([1867] 1967). *Capital: A Critique of Political Economy*, Vol. 1. New York: International Publishers.

Miles, Stephen (1998). *Consumerism as a Way of Life*. London: Sage.

Parker, Martin, and David Jary (1995). "The McUniversity: Organization, Management and Academic Subjectivity," *Organization* 2:1–20.

Penman, Danny (1997). "Judgment Day for McDonald's," *Independent* (London), June 19:20ff.

Ritzer, George (1995). *Expressing America: A Critique of the Global Credit Card Society*. Thousand Oaks, Calif.: Pine Forge Press.

———(1996). *The McDonaldization of Society*, revised ed. Thousand Oaks, Calif.: Pine Forge Press.

———(1998). *The McDonaldization Thesis*. London: Sage.

———(1999). *Enchanting a Disenchanted World: Revolutionizing the Means of Consumption*. Thousand Oaks, Calif.: Pine Forge Press.

Ritzer, George, and Allan Liska (1998). "'McDisneyization' and 'Post-Tourism': Complementary Perspectives on Contemporary Tourism," in *Touring Cultures: Transformations in Travel and Theory*, ed. Chris Rojek and John Urry. London: Routledge: 96–109.

Shichor, David (1997). "Three Strikes as a Public Policy: The Convergence of the New Penology and the McDonaldization of Punishment," *Crime and Delinquency* 43(4):470–92.

Simmel, Georg (1904/1971). "Fashion," in *On Individuality and Social Forms*, ed. Donald Levine. Chicago: University of Chicago Press: 294–323.

Tester, Keith (1999). "The Moral Malaise of McDonaldization: The Values of Vegetarianism," in *Resisting McDonaldization*, ed. Barry Smart. London: Sage: 207–21.

Turner, Bryan (1999). "McCitizens: Risk, Coolness and Irony in Contemporary Politics," in *Resisting McDonaldization*, ed. Barry Smart. London: Sage: 83–100.

Veblen, Thorstein ([1899] 1934). *The Theory of the Leisure Class: An Economic Study of Institutions*. New York: Modern Library.

Vidal, John (1997). *McLibel: Burger Culture on Trial*. New York: New Press.

Weber, Max ([1921] 1968). *Economy and Society*, 3 vols. Totowa, N.J.: Bedminster Press.

3

Mass Tourism or the Re-Enchantment of the World? Issues and Contradictions in the Study of Travel

Chris Rojek

Before the 1980s, people interested in the study of society and culture accepted the concept of modernity. Modernity rested upon three cornerstones. First, the proposition that work is the central life interest and the auxiliary thesis that production is the key to social progress. Second, the declaration that the nation-state is the impregnable foundation of politics and culture. And third, the belief in science as the primary mechanism of social control and the verification of objective reality.

In the 1980s, these scholars were presented with a new thesis. The condition of modernity, it was argued, is being replaced with the condition of postmodernity.[1] The cornerstones of modernity were attacked as being unable to support the immense moral and analytical weight placed upon them. More particularly, postmodern critics maintained that the ground had shifted. Society and culture were moving in the direction of "post-work," in which consumption, not production, was the focal point in the organization of lifestyle. The boundaries of the nation-state were now breached externally by the rise of new systems of mass communications and the move toward cheaper international transport; and internally, nation-states were revealing their hybrid multicultural roots. Science was criticized as being unable to produce a tenable picture of objective reality. Out of this turmoil, the tourist emerged as a new emblem of the postmodern condition (Bauman 1997). Mobile, flexible, and consumption-oriented, the tourist was presented in some circles as prefiguring a new kind of "cosmopolitan citizenship" in which the narrowness and authoritarianism of science and the modern nation-state were superseded (Linklater 1998).

The counterargument to the thesis of postmodernism was simple. Postmodernists exaggerated the technological and cultural changes that were occurring around them. Rumors of the end of production, the nation-state, and science were much exaggerated. The ethnic wars in the 1990s in the former Yugoslavia and Rwanda seemed to support this counterargument. The violence and weaponry gave little comfort to those who believed that nationalism was withering away or that science was ceasing to be an effective mechanism of social control. Not everyone could be a tourist, and the concept of cosmopolitan citizenship ignored the plight of the socially excluded, for whom the prospect of world travel was remote indeed. Even those who traveled regularly were said to be subject to the same processes of calculation, standardization, and predictability that characterized the rationalization process. George Ritzer's (1996; Ritzer and Liska 1997) work invoked the concept of the McTourist presented with packaged commodified travel experience as a more accurate statement of modern travel experience than postmodern evocations of the tourist gaze (Urry 1990). Modernity was not over yet.

The twinning of the subject of tourism with the debate on postmodernity is unfortunate. Organized tourism reaches back to at least the Middle Ages. Medieval pilgrims to the holy sights of Western Europe traveled in groups led by a tour guide. Merchants along the routes sold a highly developed range of accommodation, food and drink, and souvenirs to the tourists (Jusserand 1888; Rowling 1971). The embodied habitus of the eighteenth-century aristocratic young man about town counted for nothing unless it included the experience of the Grand Tour. Young aristocratic men and women toured the principal capitals of Western Europe to cultivate knowledge, character, and contacts (Black and Stroud 1992). After 1776, increasing numbers of Americans trod the same routes with the same goals in mind. By the beginning of the twentieth century, expatriate American salon cultures had emerged in London and Paris and were important patrons in the emergence of modernism in the arts (Crunden 1993). In short, there is nothing new about tourist flows. A major weakness of postmodernism is that it reduces a historical perspective by emphasizing the allegedly radical character of current changes in lifestyle and practice. The importance of cultivating a historical perspective in the sociology of tourism will be addressed at the end of the chapter.

What is unquestionably new in travel experience since the 1960s is the volume and density of tourist flows. The expansion of air routes, the relative decline in the cost of travel, and the long-term growth in real incomes have combined to make international travel an ordinary feature of everyday life. It is estimated that between four hundred million and five hundred million registered tourists travel every year (Woolacott 1993; Theobald 1994). This has produced a huge global infrastructure catering to the needs of tourists. More than 250 million people are directly employed in the tourist industry. The expansion of global tourist flows has changed the face of cities, many of which are now surrounded by a periphery of airport facilities with major link roads connecting the center to the periphery. Visitors centers, hotels, and motels have sprung up to offer hospitality. Tourist buses, meeting places, and tourist groups have become established features of city life, especially in the holiday season. The presence of strangers is now so visible and continuous that city cultures of community and belonging have been forced to adapt.

A culture of tourism has emerged that is a highly significant component of most metropolitan and national economies. Prima facie, the McTourist is the logical corollary of the rationalization processes involved in organizing and marketing tourist experience. The rationalization and commodification of travel have intensified in direct proportion to the growth in value of the travel business. But before deciding whether to endorse such logic, it is important to be clear about the contrasting positions on tourism and travel in the field of academic study.

TOURISM AND SOCIOLOGY

The academic literature on tourism and the rise of tourist cultures has focused on questions of tourist motivation and the regulation of tourist behavior. Broadly speaking, three positions have emerged in the literature. First, *voluntarism,* which presents tourists as free agents engaged in a quest for authenticity. Second, *structuralism,* which treats tourism as basically controlled behavior and stresses the exploitation and artificiality of tourist experience. And third, *postmodernism,* which sees tourist experience as fragmented, plural, and without a dominant, overarching belief in absolute value (e.g., absolute authenticity or absolute inauthenticity).

Voluntarism

Voluntarism is associated with the writings of Joost Krippendorf (1984) and the early and seminal contribution to the sociology of tourism made by Dean MacCannell (1976). This position emphasizes subjective elements and individual choice. Tourists are presented as knowledgeable social actors with the capacity to produce change in the tourist environments they encounter. Voluntarism is connected with pluralism. The diversity and variety of tourist experience and tourist conditions are emphasized. Pluralism is often associated with conservative and liberal political orientations because it assumes that the market form is the freest type of social structure and that the alternatives to market organization are inferior. This does not mean that voluntarism inevitably analyzes tourism as a passive activity that reinforces market conditions. On the contrary, the recognition that tourists are consumers who can choose between competing tourist services carries with it the proviso that tourists may oppose market outputs and seek to change them. Instead of capitulating to the processes of standardization and calculability suggested by the figure of the McTourist, voluntarist accounts suggest that tourism enlarges reflexivity about the processes of global commodification and promotes resistance.

Within voluntarism, ecotourism is arguably the leading critical approach to analyzing tourist behavior. Ecotourism regards the environment as fragile and the exploitation of tourist sights as precarious (Var et al. 1994; Gilbert et al. 1991). It develops its criticism of tourist behavior along two fronts. First, it submits that the commercial development of tourist sights is hazardous to the aesthetic integrity of the location. The development of car parks, bus lots, hotels, motels, gift shops, restaurants, and tourist bars and pubs are held to contribute to the aesthetic degradation of the location. In this sense, the accessories of McTourism are condemned. Second, it holds that mass tourism may make some locations unsustainable. This is particularly evident in locations where the tourist attraction is a sight of nature. For example, Gilbert and colleagues (1991) maintain that the overdevelopment of safari tourism in East Africa has disturbed the breeding cycles of animals. In the long run, this will lead to a serious depletion in animal stocks. For ecotourists, the remedy to McTourism is to restore the ecological balance by controlling the economic development of sights and to regulate the flow of tourists.

Voluntarism is an attractive position because it insists that tourists have the capacity to change the circumstances that they encounter in tourist cultures. It assumes that tourist experience produces strong feelings of authenticity so that the tourist gets in touch with the underlying reality of the location.

The main weakness of voluntarism is that it is based on a naïve view of subjective freedom. It produces an inadequate analysis of the structural factors that shape tourist experience. An auxiliary criticism is that voluntarism is too idealistic in assuming a universal condition between sights and tourist experience. Tourist interactions are coded in different ways according to cultural backgrounds, race, gender, and ethnicity. By universalizing tourist experience, voluntarism oversimplifies the varieties of tourist experience and the diversities of tourist cultures.

Structuralism

Structuralism is associated with the writings of Ritzer (1996; Ritzer and Liska 1997); Henri Lefebvre (1976, 1991); the later writings of E. Cohen (1987, 1995); and feminist contributions from C. Enloe (1989), M. Swain (1995), and V. Kinnaird and D. Hall (1994). It presents subjective choice and values as an aspect of structural forces. Most contributors stop short of proposing that tourist behavior is a simple reflection of structural forces. They allow some measure for human reflexivity and creativity. By the same token, structural forces are theorized as being crucial in generating tourist predispositions and the pattern of tourist culture. The authenticity of tourist responses to sights is thus permanently destabilized. In presenting tourist interactions and tourist cultures as profoundly shaped by structural forces, structuralism includes manipulation and exploitation as preconditions of tourist encounters. The main structural forces analyzed in the academic literature on tourism are rationalization, class, and gender.

Ritzer's (1996) work on the McDonaldization process overhauls Max Weber's rationalization thesis and demonstrates its acute relevance in contemporary culture. Ritzer argues that McDonaldization is based on increasing predictability, standardization, calculability, and the application of nonhuman technology to control human behavior. Ritzer and Alan Liska (1997) apply the McDonaldization thesis to tourism. Here, McTourism is used for the phenomenon they describe. Ritzer and Liska (1997:97) characterize Disney World as the paradigmatic example of the fully rationalized theme park and they use this to illustrate the principal characteristics of McTourism. They note that it is based in calculated organization. Tourists are required to pay set prices for a daily or weekly pass; tourist routes are regulated by an elaborate system of sign posting; fixed opening and closing times determine access to the site; and Disney on-site staff ensure that visitors keep to the prescribed tourist paths. It is highly predictable. For example, the live attractions are well advertised and timed to the pattern described in the Disney guide books and travel brochures; the mechanized attractions perform the same functions for different batches of tourists throughout the day; maintenance staff cosmetize the park, constantly cleaning up litter and ensuring that the flow of tourists is as smooth and continuous as possible. It applies the extensive use of nonhuman technology to control human choice and behavior. This is evident in the range of mechanical and computerized attractions available and the mechanical systems of organization that control the behavior of Disney employees.

Like Weber, Ritzer and Liska emphasize the negative, dystopian consequences of rationalization. For them, McTourism is part of the disenchantment of the world because it removes novelty and excitement from travel experience. Instead, travel becomes a continuation of the bureaucratic processes that shape wider social life. McTourism is associated with what Weber called "the disenchantment of the world." It closes down options for variety, diversity, and difference. Paradoxically this does not necessarily mean that tourists cease to find satisfaction in McTourist activity. On the contrary, Ritzer and Liska (1997) acknowledge that McTourism brings satisfaction to travelers, but only on the terms set by the general pattern of McDonaldization in society. McTourists want predictable, efficient forms of entertainment that come with low levels of risk. "Raised in McDonaldized systems," elaborate Ritzer and Liska (1997:100), "accustomed to a daily life in those systems, most people not only accept, but embrace, those systems. Thus, instead of being put off by McDonaldized vacations, many will gravitate towards them." Ritzer and Liska's account identifies rationalization as one of the major characteristics of modern society. However, it also shows these critics to be sympathetic to many aspects of postmodernism. In particular, they argue against voluntarism that tourism is not part of a quest for authenticity. Ritzer and Liska agree with postmodern authors who maintain that contemporary life is saturated with simulations and artificial spaces. They portray McTourism as a quest for inauthenticity, that is, a method of leaving the simulated settings of modern-day life behind by entering super-simulated settings such as theme parks and theme restaurants. Virtual reality is seen as offering new opportunities for super-simulated tourist experience.

The strength of the McDonaldization thesis is that it encapsulates the leveling processes involved in mass tourism. The density and velocity of tourist flows mean that a certain amount of standardization is inevitable. Novelty and variety are undoubtedly curtailed. In some respects, the thesis parallels Walter Benjamin's (1995) proposition that mechanical reproduction diminishes the aura of cultural objects.

Preindustrial cultural tourist sights have a high degree of magic for tourists partly because it is so difficult to reach them. For example, in the eighteenth and nineteenth centuries, it took days and in some cases weeks for most Western Europeans to reach the ancient sights of Greece, Rome, and the Holy Land.[2] The mass communications revolution has vastly increased the unified access to the sights. The result is that the magic of the sight has dimmed. Benjamin's point is that aura is further diminished by reproductions of cultural objects through photography, posters, and the development of markers such as commemorative mugs, key rings, tea towels, and similar forms of merchandise.

Ritzer's McDonaldization thesis is compatible with this proposition. It therefore helps to clarify the sense of anticlimax and disappointment that many tourists now express in tourist experience.

The weakness of the McDonaldization thesis, and the auxiliary McTourist thesis, is that it tends to present rationalization as a monolithic process. It therefore underestimates levels of reflexivity and resistance. For example, John Urry (1990) argues that part of the pleasure in posttourism is seeing through the depredations of rationalization. Posttourists take an ironic view of McDonaldized tourist infrastructures and the bureaucratic paraphernalia involved in airline travel. They treat it as part of the travel experience. McTourism also underestimates the diversity of travel experience. The payload of the McDonaldization thesis is that experience everywhere is becoming standardized. But the reaction against ecologically damaging tourism and sex tourism (explained below) suggests new forms of variety are emerging that are significant enough to change some of the marketing and organizational patterns in the travel industry.

The class perspective emphasizes the commodification of tourist experience. It argues that the "naturalness" of tourist sights is neutralized by commercial overdevelopment. Transforming the tourist experience into a conveyor belt for making money renders the experience unsatisfying and ultimately dehumanizing. A parallel argument here centers on social exclusion. The class perspective argues that tourist experience is rationed according to disposable income. Class membership still ultimately determines choices to travel and influences access in tourist cultures. Tourist cultures are presented as stratified so that travel flows reproduce the class relations. Priority in determining class membership is typically assigned to the ownership or nonownership of capital. Production is therefore reaffirmed as the seat of personality and social interaction. Tourism is primarily theorized as a branch of consumption activity and consumption activity is presented as the mirror of property ties. The class perspective highlights the role of inequality and exploitation in tourist experience and tourist cultures.

The gender perspective carries similar points of emphasis but it is distinct in fastening upon gender relations rather than class relations as the decisive structural force. Tourism is presented as privileging action, power, mobility, and ownership. These are theorized as archetypal masculine values. It follows that tourism is categorized as a sphere in which women are, a priori, subordinate actors. The gender perspective argues that women have less freedom to travel than men. Even when women do travel, they encounter spaces in which masculinist values are paramount.

Sex tourism is the most extreme example of the masculine bias in tourism. Tourist cultures have emerged that prioritize the female as willing and available. Enloe (1989:36) argues that in the tourist capitals of developing countries such as Bangkok, Manila, Kingston, and Lagos, Asian, African, and Caribbean women are presented to Western tourists as more adventurous and uninhibited than Western women. Colonialism laid the foundation of these stereotypes. However, the development of postcolonial capitalism has strengthened them. For example, M. Hall (1994:150–51) argues that sex tourism in Southeast Asia has passed through four distinct stages: indigenous prostitution, in which women took local men as clients; colonialization and militarization, such as the period of the Vietnam War in which thousands of American servicemen were stationed in Vietnam and visited Thailand and South Korea on leave; international tourism, in which international male travelers emerged as the main part of client supply; and institutionalized sex tourism, which is the present condition where a staple industry relatively insulated from police and government interference operates as a semi-official part of the tourist trail. Chris Ryan (1991:161) estimates that there are half a million prostitutes in Bangkok, one million in South Korea, and one hundred thousand in Manila.

Thus sexism is twinned with racism to explain how women in developing countries are driven into "hospitality work" as an alternative to poverty. Structuralism recognizes a huge gap between the representations of tourism in the tourist industry and the realities of tourist experience. Tourist cultures tend to present sun, sea, sand, and sex as the classless, unstratified condition of tourist experience. In reality tourist space is heavily stratified by class inequality and saturated with sexual oppression. The package tour, in which tourist experience is intensive, segmented, and subject to high levels of social control by the tour operator, is often used as an example of inauthenticity in travel experience. MacCannell's (1992) later work on tourism elaborated the theme of inauthenticity by showing how entire communities were transformed into display sights for tourists. For example, the town of Locke in California was purchased by a developer who marketed the town as a "living example" of the original Chinese settlements that had done so much to bring prosperity to the West by working in agriculture and laying the railway lines. Mark Gottdiener's (1997) account of themed attractions plays on the same irony of presenting artificial sights as authentic slices of historical reality. Tourism does not permit an alternative to the unequal relations that prevail elsewhere in society. On the contrary, it is based in the continuation of these exploitative and demeaning relations.

The chief criticisms made of class and gender versions of structuralism mirror the charge of monolithic theory already laid at the door of the McDonaldization thesis. In general, structuralism tends to underestimate human capacities for reflexivity and resistance and to exaggerate the process of social control. An overreductive view of tourist experience is presented. At a human level, it raises the pertinent question that if tourism is really so exploitative, rationalized, and dehumanizing, why do so many millions want to engage in it? In the most extreme cases, structuralism is guilty of attributing false consciousness to tourists. Thus, the pleasure that tourists take in the authenticity of tourist experience is analyzed as a delusion orchestrated by the travel industry. In addition, structuralism is unable to produce a convincing alternative to market forms of tourist experience. The restrictions on the movement and access of foreign travelers in China, Burma, Iraq, and other "centralized" economies is hardly an appealing antidote to what currently applies in Western travel experience. Pluralism cannot be denied simply by asserting the centrality of structures of class and gender in the organization of everyday life. Within these structures there is a wide variety of differences in power relations. For example, U. Wagner's (1977) study of sex tourism in Gambia found that many of the "hospitality workers" were young men who catered to the sexual desires of Western women. Moreover, men who were carried back to the West as "trophy partners" were often abused and discarded. In general, structuralism fails to reflect the ambiguities inherent in actual tourist experience and tourist cultures. The analysis associated with it tends to be too monolithic and inflexible.

Postmodernism

Postmodernism is associated with the work of Umberto Eco (1986), Urry (1990), A. Lingis (1994), and Jean Baudrillard (1983). It exhibits a potent spirit of exhaustion with what it sees as the naiveté of voluntaristic readings of freedom and the inflexibility of structuralist accounts of control. The debate between authenticity and inauthenticity is portrayed as a category error. For postmodernists, it is pointless to debate the original or fixed meaning in tourist sights. Rather, the material element and the representational element constitute an inviolable whole. Authenticity can no longer be interpreted as a function of visiting a sight or possessing a tourist object, for the elan vital of the sight is present just as much in representations of the sight that circulate in myriad systems of communication throughout the world. For postmodernists, a postage stamp showing the Statue of Liberty is no less an authentic part of the sight than the French statue that stands at the entry to Manhattan harbor.

Postmodernism is sensitive to the modes of visual and representational culture in everyday life. It holds that these modes permeate ordinary cultural experience and now function, along with face-to-face interaction, as the essential channels through which culture is made. The omnipresence and plurality of these forms do not admit the possibility of privileged readings. In place of the singular or dominant meanings attributed to tourism by voluntarism and structuralism, postmodernism insists that tourism contains a multiplicity of meanings. The task of postmodernist analysis is to deconstruct meanings without positing an end point to deconstructivism. Postmodernism therefore takes the micropolitics of social behavior seriously. Instead of glossing over difference and diversity by invoking grand master concepts such as class domination or patriarchy, postmodern methods seek to reveal the anomalous and ambiguous characteristics of social interaction. Richard Rorty (1989) sums up matters well when he submits that the postmodernist is someone who profoundly questions the authority of any final vocabulary about reality.

In Urry's (1990) work, postmodern sensitivity to visual culture is invested in the concept of the tourist gaze. The postmodern tourist gaze greets the landscape of tourism as a limitless horizon in which objects and experiences lack fixed or overarching meanings. Instead the meaning of tourist experience is always conditional and plural and hence associated with diversity and variation. Because the tourist gaze recognizes no privileged reading of tourist sights, it follows that concomitant cultures of tourism are more playful and ironic. The tourist gaze turns to tourist experience to provide contrast rather than truth and momentary engagement instead of everlasting meaning. The tourist gaze acknowledges the processual, relatively open-ended, contingent character of tourist experience and tourist cultures. It is hostile to readings that seek to close tourism by invoking immanent structural forces. Artificiality is taken as a source of pleasure, as when Eco (1986) delights in the fantasy landscapes designed by Disney's imagineers in Disneyland or the kitsch reproductions of classical objects in his travels in "hyper-reality."

This approach also lends itself to reading distinctions based on national boundaries as spurious. Given the ineradicable character of visual modes of communication, the ideas of hermetic nation-states and neat borders are dismissed as outdated. Postmodernism looks to new global forms of transparency and belonging that derive from the collapse of master-narratives. The antagonism to privileged readings and grand narrative are characteristic features of postmodernism. They coalesce in the proposition that the humanist project of the Enlightenment has decomposed. In particular, humanism is held to deny difference and diversity by invoking universalism and rationalism. Postmodernism identifies a rationalist bias in voluntarism and structuralist accounts of tourism. This bias is expressed in the presupposition that tourist experience involves imposing the Western tourist presence upon cultures. In this sense, Western tourism is associated with the quest for mastery.

Postmodernist accounts of tourism are therefore often coupled with criticisms of colonialism. Indeed postcolonialism can be usefully considered as an adjunct of postmodernism.[3] Both emphasize the ambivalence and micropolitics of experience and tourist cultures. For example, Lingis (1994) presents tourism as an inherently liminal condition in which tourists move in and out of their embodied habitus and the mores of the cultures that they visit. His reading assigns pronounced significance to the senses in tourist experience. He maintains that travel disrupts the habits of rationalized predictability and calculability that dominate commodified culture. It presents the opportunity of exploring the repressed parts of oneself by opening one up to what he calls the "strangeness" of other cultures and, by extension, the arbitrariness of one's own embodied habitus.

The chief criticism directed against postmodernism is that it ignores the patterned social and historical character of tourist experience and tourist cultures. Sights, such as the killing fields in Cambodia or the Gettysburg battle site in Pennsylvania, do not have moral equivalence with the Universal film studios in Hollywood or the Las Vegas strip. The Disney Corporation found this to its cost when its plans to open a Civil War theme park outside of Washington, D.C., ran aground against protests that the amusement park would trivialize the moral significance of the Civil War in American history. By treating all tourist sites with an ironic, playful, deconstructive attitude, postmodernism is unable to generate the necessary moral distinctions between tourist cultures. For this reason, it is impossible to extract a tenable set of policies for tourism from postmodern principles.

How does one decide what item of heritage is worth preserving if the representational code is inviolable from the material object and each are invested with the same quotient of authenticity? A lack of seriousness is assigned to postmodern readings of culture so that the readings themselves are attacked for carrying a decorative rather than an analytic significance. One aspect of this is that postmodernism is regarded to exaggerate the apocalyptic nature of contemporary life. Historical continuities tend to be neglected or ignored and local differences are neutralized by the presumption of global uniformity. The predilection for prioritizing the senses over rationalism exacerbate this tendency by suggesting that emotional responses to sights are universal.

THE BODY AND SPACE IN TOURISM

Turning now to the subject of research issues in the sociology of tourism, it is evident that the body is emerging as a focal concern. Questions of what the body is, how it relates to culture and society, and what happens to it when it moves through space are fundamental to all three positions in the sociology of tourism. A correlative set of questions derive from the nature of tourist space. In what ways is it distinct from surrounding culture? Why is it necessary? How is it developing?

Not surprisingly, the three positions in the field differ greatly in their approaches to these two sets of questions. Voluntarism and structuralism tend to prioritize ontology over epistemology. They are generally more interested in tourist experience and tourist cultures as states of being rather than criteria of knowledge.

Of course to some extent, ontology and epistemology are inseparable. Every theory of being mobilizes a framework that establishes categories of knowledge that delineate being. It is a question of balance. In voluntarism and structuralism, the balance is very much on the side of ontology. For example, voluntarism approaches tourist experience and tourist cultures from the standpoint of the actor's sense of authenticity. The responses of individual tourists to tourist locations is at the heart of theory and research. If the immediate context of tourist experience is unsatisfactory, the voluntarist solution is to change the context by creating conditions that allow for higher levels of personal satisfaction.

In structuralism, the character of the context in which social actors are situated is the crux of the matter. McTourism is standardized, predictable, and dominated by nonhuman technology because the rationalization of the world extends these conditions throughout human life. Under McDonaldization, capitalism, and gender inequality, individual tourist responses to tourist locations may express high levels of authenticity and satisfaction. However, from a structuralist standpoint, because they are expressed in the general context of exploitation and oppression, they do not constitute reliable evidence. Structuralism regards the prevailing conditions of life governing tourist actions as flawed in the sense that it impoverishes and degrades human capacities. As the foregoing discussion indicated, rationalization, commodification, and gender domination are posited as the main structural sources of impoverishment and degradation. The remedy is to change the context in which behavior is situated by collective action so that repressed human capacities can be freely and more fully expressed. Postmodernism presents theories of ontology as the real problem of modernist social science. It argues that theories of ontology always produce a privileged theory of being that aspires to become the master narrative in the field.

The postmodernist emphasis on multiplicity, diversity, and contingency is partly designed to act as an antidote to privileged readings and the urge to articulate master-narratives. Practically speaking, this means that postmodernist accounts

of tourism are more attuned to the variations between states of being than determining the essence of a given state of being. Thus Lingis (1989:117) approaches
the appeal of travel not as arriving in a concrete place but as moving through
multiple feeling states and emotions. For him the physical tourist location is only
one link in the metonomyic chain of meaning. Rationalist approaches to tourism
automatically place boundaries between the self and the other. Postmodernism
seeks to conceptualize the self and other as boundless. This is why Lingis (1994)
dwells on the sense of touch in his account of visiting places. It is also why
postmodernism in general assigns prominence to visual culture. The "strangeness"
that Lingis finds in "otherness" and the "arbitrariness" he finds in the cultural
mores that he embodies is only accomplished by discarding the boundaries of
Western rationalism and freeing the senses.

P. Virilio's (1986, 1991) work on velocity offers another postmodern route into
the strangeness and boundlessness of otherness. He argues that the transport and
communications revolutions are contributing to a sense of life speeding up and
the constraints of the body being left behind. Technology has changed the conception of distance and bodily limits. So in Europe, the United States is no longer
thought of as thousands of miles away but as being seven hours coast to coast,
and vice versa. Virilio's work implies that as the movement between cultures
accelerates, the velocity of changing contrasts is pleasurable per se. Here the attraction of tourism is presented as the movement of the body between states of
epistemic rupture: the clash between core and periphery cultures—East and West,
Christianity and Islam, the city and the country, mountains and desert—is what
compels the tourist to keep traveling.

The preeminence assigned to velocity and boundlessness fits well with the
postcolonialist, postrationalist orientation of postmodernism. But as the opening
paragraphs of this chapter showed, many critics see the apocalyptic tone struck
by postmodernists as inappropriate for understanding today's social and cultural
conditions. It is one thing for Lingis (1989, 1994) to celebrate the otherness and
strangeness of tourist experience, but it does not nullify the part that rationalism
and rational organization play in contemporary travel experience. As Ritzer and
Liska (1997) show, contemporary travel fundamentally involves inscribing and
reinforcing rational boundaries between the tourist and others. Ticketing arrangements, insurance protection, passport rights, airline controls, and passenger rights
are just some of the common ways in which rational boundaries are remade
through the act of travel.

TOURISM AND THE CRISIS IN SOCIOLOGICAL THEORY

The sociology of tourism has emerged relatively late in the day as a distinct area
of academic study. For most of its history, sociology has treated work as the central life interest and privileged production over consumption. As a component of

the sphere of consumption, tourism has, until recently, received secondary attention. It is part of the challenge of understanding tourism today that it has emerged
as a subject for academic study at a moment when theoretical approaches in sociology are in a condition of some turmoil. The debate on postmodernism and
reflexivity (Beck et al. 1994) highlights the limitations of sociological approaches
and questions the idea of foundational principles in social theory. Moreover, the
various competing paradigms of social explanation offer incompatible readings
of social life. For example, a feminist reading of society contains different points
of emphasis and works in different assumptions about social life than semiotic,
Marxist, or ethnomethodological readings. Although similarities may be acknowledged between them, the first thing likely to strike the impartial reader is the lack
of fit. Although this does not require the student to follow the postmodern turn,
it privileges the notion of pluralism in sociological approaches to social issues.
The figure of the tourist embodies the mobility, flexibility, and difference that
sociological approaches are now urged to embrace by critics of "monolithic"
social theory.

But there are dangers in allowing a first-world reading of identity and practice to become, as it were, the imperial standard for analyzing tourism. The expansion of the tourist industry is associated with new forms of social inequality
and oppression. Given the prominence assigned to the body, space, and kitsch-
themed environment in recent accounts of tourism, it is appropriate to consider
these forms in terms of these subjects.

With respect to issues relating to the body, the connection between sex tourism and prostitution was discussed above. In 1996, the World Congress against
Commercial Sexual Exploitation of Children drew attention to another tragic layer
of this question by pointing to the relationship between sex tourism and child
prostitution. In Thailand, it is estimated that 800,000 children are in prostitution;
in India, the number is between 400,000 and 500,000; in Sri Lanka, 20,000; in
the Dominican Republic, 25,000; in Brazil, 200,000; and in Peru, 500,000. The
problem is not confined to the developing countries. It is estimated that in Paris,
five hundred boys and three hundred girls are in prostitution, and in the United
States and Canada, the figure is thought to be between one hundred thousand and
three hundred thousand for both genders (Castells 1998:155). The World Congress
highlighted the inhumane and brutal conditions of life for these sex workers and
indicated how sex tourism intensifies poverty. More generally, low pay and low
unionization are widespread features of the tourist industry. The seasonal character of tourism and the relatively low levels of occupational professionalization
weaken the market position of tourist workers. The economic decline in Southeast Asia since the mid-1990s has worsened the situation. Unemployed industrial workers are adding to the seasonal workforce, which results in wages being
driven down farther. The possibility of cosmopolitan citizenship may be in the
grasp of the cash-rich in the advanced industrial countries. But in a world in which
most people do not have a telephone, let alone the surplus income to buy a long-

distance airline ticket, tourism remains an unrealistic goal for the majority (Thomas 1995).

In the debate around the local and the global level of the poverty gap, it is well to retain a sober view of the real level of the poverty gap. A recent United Nations report (1996) stated that the wealth of the top 358 billionaires in the world is equivalent to the capital shared by 2.3 billion people, or 45 percent of the world's adult population. This kind of statistic does not encourage a sanguine attitude on the issue of broadening travel opportunities for all.

The increasing significance of the tourist trade to the gross domestic product of nations increases the value of the tourist as a target for attack. The mobile body is a vulnerable entity without the defenses of domestic property. Holiday makers tend to carry around surplus money and to be relatively relaxed in their attitude to others. The combination of surplus income and lower levels of vigilance means that tourist towns such as Las Vegas, New Orleans, and Miami are associated with delinquent cultures that prey on tourists. Random attacks on tourists in Florida in the early 1990s seriously damaged the tourist trade and provoked calls at state and federal levels for a crackdown on muggings and shootings. In addition, tourists have emerged as a prime target for terrorists. For example, disrupting the tourist trade in the United Kingdom was a major objective of the Irish Republican Army's mainland bombing campaign in the 1980s and 1990s. They launched attacks at Heathrow airport, mainline railway stations in London and the provinces, Harrod's department store, and other popular tourist shopping areas.

In addition to deterring tourists from traveling to countries where the risk of attack is high, terrorist outbursts are designed to gain publicity for their cause. For example, the Palestine Liberation movement launched airline hijacks in the 1970s and executed tourists. Similarly, in Manila, a terrorist group hostile to the Marcos regime bombed the meeting of the American Society of Travel Agents in 1980. Since 1993, the Kurdistan Workers' Party has waged a campaign of terror against tourists in Turkey. In 1997, fifty-eight foreign tourists and four Egyptians were massacred in Luxor near the ancient Valley of the Kings. The attackers were members of the Gama'a al-Islamiya (Islamic Group) movement who did the killing to gain international recognition for their cause. At a time when Western social scientists are seriously discussing the disintegration of the nation-state and the rise of "network society" (Castells 1996, 1997, 1998), terrorist groups are identifying tourists as symbols of colonial power. Highly visible and usually undefended and unprepared for attack, the tourist is a soft target in terrorist politics. This emphasis on the vulnerability of the tourist body is a useful counterpoint to critical approaches that focus on the colonialist, imperial aspects for Western tourism.

Moving now to the subject of space, a continuing critical issue in the growth of tourism is what Lefebvre (1976) calls the "pulverization" of tourist space. The rationalization and commodification of tourist space threatens the sense of contrast and escape that are traditionally associated with tourist locations. Lefebvre's sociology points to the urban-industrial colonization of tourist space. The same point is made by Claude Lévi-Strauss (1955:43), who deplores the rise of mass tourism on the grounds that it "contaminates" the "magic caskets" of countries and locations untainted by urban-industrial values. The fear that these writers articulate is of a homogenized world in which technological innovation overtakes nature as the only source of variation and contrast. It prefigures the McDonaldized view of the world developed so potently by Ritzer (1996).

CONCLUSION: RE-ENCHANTMENT TENDENCIES?

In concentrating on the disenchanting aspects of mass tourism, there is a danger of losing sight of the genuine opportunities for re-enchantment that tourism brings. Seeing other cultures, meeting people who display different embodied habitus, and experiencing different landscapes and climates are intrinsically pleasurable. McTourism may revolve around standardized travel experience and homogenize the physical setting of tourist cultures. But Sydney is not the same as Tokyo, and London is not the same as San Francisco; Niagara Falls and the Swiss Alps each still have a unique beauty. Tourism is still fundamentally an encounter with difference.

At its best, tourism really can broaden the mind. The growth in the density of tourist flows is part of the globalization process. The deregulation of air routes and the consequent relative decline in ticket prices means that increasing numbers of people will travel regularly throughout the world. The kind of world they encounter is already very different from the world of their parents. J. Clifford (1992) makes the point that it is not only tourists who travel—cultures travel too. The development of multiculturalism throughout the West is the product of migration, the globalization of mass communications, and the increase in the velocity and density of tourist flows. The growth in Anglo-American cities of ethnic regions such as Chinatown, Japan Town, Little Russia, or Caribbean, Hindu, and Sikh quarters transform the character of lived experience. Everyday life with others acquires a more varied and diverse hue. To some extent, this supports the McTourist proposition that the fate of the world is increasing homogenization and rationalization. But looking at it another way, methodologically, Clifford's (1992) observation problematizes the location as a homogeneous, bounded site for study.

The established dichotomy between tourist and host community breaks down in important respects. In particular, the tourist loses the characteristics of strangeness and difference that defined relations with the host community in the nineteenth century and for most of the twentieth century. The "strangeness" that Lingis (1994) refers to diminishes and the sense of the arbitrariness of cultural codes intensifies. Celia Lury (1997) argues that this loosening of boundaries is already undoing the hierarchical models of culture that have traditionally dominated the study of cultural practice. Culture is no longer tied to a place or a body of people. Instead, it is becoming superterritorial and superorganic. So tourist sights such as the Taj Mahal, Disneyland, the Eiffel Tower, and the London Houses of Parliament are simultaneously and symbolically displaced from their physical locations and reinserted in a new type of transnational culture that is more accessible and permeable than anything that has gone before.

The interest in the rise of themed environments as places of leisure and entertainment sheds further light on the deterritorialization of culture. Gottdiener (1997) describes the rise of themed environments in America. His account underlines the fusing of symbolic elements from other times and different cultural traditions as a central motif of new tourist sights. For example, the Luxor Casino and Hotel in Las Vegas is shaped like an Egyptian pyramid, complete with a reconstruction of the sphinx in the front; the Hotel Tropicana in Las Vegas includes a reproduction of a Kon Tiki village; the Excalibur Hotel in the same city is built in the style of a medieval Arthurian fantasy. Elsewhere, the Busch Gardens complex in Williamsburg, Virginia, offers visitors "imagined" reconstructions of typical villages in England, France, Italy, and Germany; in Torrance, California, a full-scale Bavarian village has been reconstructed, complete with inhabitants dressed in native costume; the town of Helen in Georgia plays on a similar theme with the reconstruction of a Swiss chalet-type settlement and a "native" host population. In the United Kingdom, the Chessington World of Adventures boasts reconstructions of the sights and sounds of the "Mystic East," notably Japanese gardens and the Golden Palace of Bangkok; and the "Great American Theme Park" in the English Midlands offers simulations of Niagara Falls, Mississippi paddleboat life, the Santa Fe Railroad, and Silver City—a "real" Wild West town. All of these sights play openly and self-consciously with kitsch culture. They mix symbols of ancient culture with the modern realities of urban-industrial space; they integrate references from uncivilized nature with the rationalized, controlled logic of modern civil society; they play on the distinction between reality and fantasy. To many commentators, they appear to support the proposition that society has moved into a condition of postmodernity.

But it is important to remember two things. First, the artificial mixture of ancient and modern styles and the use of fantasy-scapes for the purposes of entertainment have a much longer history in industrial society (Lowenthal [1961] 1985). J. E. Kasson (1978) in his study of fin de siècle amusements in the United States, notes that Luna Park in Coney Island boasted a reconstruction of an Irish village, Indian palaces, and a Venetian city complete with gondoliers. It also presented staged spectacles simulating the eruption of Mount Vesuvius, the explosion of Martinique, and Pennsylvania's Johnstown flood. Steeplechase Park offered a fantasy ride to the moon. Similarly, R. Bogdan's (1988) history of the freak show in America demonstrates a deep-rooted interest in abnormal bodies. Instead of positing a postmodern turn, a more interesting task facing students of tourism is to restore a historical perspective on the monstrous rise of modernity: the buckling of time-worn habits, the melting down of the distinction between town and country, the viral infection of transport and communication links across the face of the world created an accompanying interest in distortion, excess, and difference in cultural life. As entrepreneurs implored workers to develop the lean and fit musculature necessary for the industrial labor process, popular culture cultivated a fascination with transgression, aberration, and anomaly. Bodies and spaces that were manifestly out of control and flagrantly contrary to the urban-industrial norms became part of the daydreams of ordinary life.

The second thing to remember is that tourists are well aware of the kitsch character of these new themed sights. They do not regard them as a faithful representation of reality but an artificial reproduction. Herein lies much of their appeal. Out of the bleak *noir* settings of the cosmopolis created by industrialization emerged an urge to travel away from the confined existence of the rat race into a more gorgeous, anomalous world in which cultural simulations defied geographical space and historical time evaporated. Artificiality and supersimulation are key attributes of this expanded world. The themed landscapes that draw the day-tripper to Dollywood, the Luxor Casino and Hotel in Las Vegas, Universal Film Studios, and other popular themed attractions of the present day are not rejections of artificiality but revised versions of the artificial industrial-urban landscape that are more glittering and literally more incredible. These attractions obviously give pleasure. That is why the tourist flows to them are so dense.

The industrialization of tourism has certainly produced the rationalization and commodification of tourist experience. It may be impossible to replicate the relation that eighteenth- and nineteenth-century tourists had with sights. But in a sense, so what? It is in the nature of human development to change the relationship between subjects and objects in a dialectical process. The industrialization of tourism has displaced one form of enchanted relationship in tourist experience based upon a quest for authenticity. However, at the same time, in producing new types of urban-industrial superartificiality and in drastically increasing the velocity of movement, it has re-enchanted many aspects of urban-industrial life. The movement between disenchantment and re-enchantment is a continuous one, and tourism will remain caught up in twin tendencies for the foreseeable future.

NOTES

1. A vast literature has emerged dedicated to the inexorable task of explaining these terms. This literature is like the myth of Sisyphus revisited! Students have some reason to complain that it remains hard to pin down what exactly is meant by modernity and postmodernity. My (1995) own preference is to conceptualize modernity as a twin-headed process. *Modernity 1* refers to the attempt to impose a rational, bureaucratic, scientific

structure upon the human and physical world. *Modernity 2* refers to the critical consciousness of the boundaries imposed by Modernity 1. Prominent themes here are that the rationality of Modernity 1 has irrational consequences. These themes are taken up by critical theory, especially Marxism and feminism, and also by romantic movements in the arts. Modernity 2 seeks to transform the limitations of Modernity 1 by either raising popular consciousness or developing imaginative consciousness or socialist-feminist revolution. Postmodernism rejects the boundaries of Modernity 1 and the transcendent impulse of Modernity 2. It perpetuates the idea of living without boundaries. Deconstructivism is adopted as the primary method of combating the authoritarianism of Modernities 1 and 2. To some extent, postmodernism reflects the revival of idealism in social science and it is therefore associated with pluralism and the micropolitics of power.

2. The chief global tourist attractions of the eighteenth and nineteenth centuries were in fact Greece, Rome, and the Holy Land. Tourists believed they could short-circuit historical time and reenter the classical landscapes that had provided such a rich fund of images for Western civilization (Pemble 1987).

3. Both adopt a critical attitude to the notion of an overarching authority. Postcolonialism consists of two elements. First, it represents the historical tradition of acts of resistance against European colonialism. Second, it consists of the set of discursive practices generated against colonial ideologies.

BIBLIOGRAPHY

Baudrillard, J. (1983). *Simulations*. New York: Semiotext.
——— (1998). *The Consumer Society: Myths and Structures*. London: Sage.
Bauman, Z. (1997). *Postmodernity and Its Discontents*. Cambridge: Polity Press.
Beck, U., A. Giddens, and S. Lash (1994). *Reflexive Modernization*. Cambridge: Polity Press.
Benjamin, W. (1995). *Illuminations*. London: Jonathan Cape.
Black, J., and Alan Stroud (1992). *The British Abroad: The Grand Tour in the Nineteenth Century*. Sutton.
Bogdan, R. (1988). *Freakshow: Presenting Human Oddities for Amusement*. Chicago: University of Chicago Press.
Castells, M. (1996). *The Rise of the Network Society*. Oxford: Blackwell.
——— (1997). *The Power of Identity*. Oxford: Blackwell.
——— (1998). *The End of the Millennium*. Oxford: Blackwell.
Clifford, J. (1992). "Travelling Cultures," in *Cultural Studies*, ed. L. Grossberg, C. Nelson, and P. A. Treichler. London: Routledge.
Cohen, E. (1987). "Authenticity and Commoditisation in Tourism." *Annals of Tourism Research* 15:371–86.
——— (1995). "Contemporary Tourism—Trends and Challenges: Sustainable Authenticity or Contrived Post-Modernity?" in *Change in Tourism: People, Places, Processes*, ed. R. Butler and D. Pearce. London: Routledge.
Crunden, R. (1993). *American Salons*. Oxford: Oxford University Press.
Eco, Umberto (1986). *Travels in Hyper-Reality*. London: Picador.
Enloe, C. (1989). *Bananas, Beaches and Bases: Making Feminist Sense of International Relations*. London: Pandora.

Gilbert, D., J. Penda, and M. Friel (1991). "Issues in Sustainability and the National Parks in Kenya and Cameroon," in *Progress in Tourism, Recreation and Hospitality Management*, ed. C. P. Cooper and A. Lockwood. Chichester: Wiley.

Gottdiener, M. (1997). *The Theming of America.* Boulder, Colo.: Westview.

Hall, M. (1994). "Gender and Economic Interests in Tourism Prostitution: The Nature, Development and Implications of Sex Tourism in South-East Asia," in *Tourism: A Gender Analysis*, ed. V. Kinnaird and D. Hall. Chichester: Wiley.

Jusserand, J. (1888). *English Wayfaring Life in the Middle Ages.* London: Fisher-Unwin.

Kasson, J. E. (1978). *Amusing the Millions.* New York: Hill & Wang.

Kinnaird, V., and D. Hall, eds. (1994). *Tourism: A Gender Analysis.* Chichester: Wiley.

Krippendorf, J. (1984). *The Holidaymakers.* London: Heinemann.

Lefebvre, Henri (1976). *The Survival of Capitalism.* London: Allen & Unwin.

——— (1991). *Critique of Everyday Life.* Oxford: Blackwell.

Lévi-Strauss, C. (1955). *Tristes Tropiques.* Harmondsworth: Penguin.

Lingis, A. (1989). *Deathbound Subjectivity.* Bloomington: Indiana University Press.

——— (1994). *Foreign Bodies.* London: Routledge.

Linklater, A. (1998). "Cosmopolitan Citizenship." *Citizenship Studies* 2:1, 23–42.

Lowenthal, Leo ([1961] 1985). *Literature, Popular Culture, and Society.* Palo Alto, Calif.: Pacific Books.

Lury, Celia (1997). "The Culture of Tourism," in *Touring Cultures: Transformations in Travel and Theory*, ed. C. Rojek and J. Urry. London: Routledge: 113–36.

MacCannell, D. (1976). *The Tourist.* New York: Schocken.

——— (1992). *Empty Meeting Grounds.* London: Routledge.

Pemble, J. (1987). *The Mediterranean Passion.* Oxford: Oxford University Press.

Ritzer, G. (1996). *The McDonaldization of Society.* 2d. ed. Thousand Oaks, Calif.: Pine Forge.

Ritzer, G., and A. Liska (1997). "'McDisneyization' and 'Post Tourism': Complementary Perspectives on Contemporary Tourism," in *Touring Cultures*, ed. C. Rojek and J. Urry. London: Routledge: 96–112.

Rorty, R. (1989). *Contingency, Irony, and Solidarity.* Cambridge: Cambridge University Press.

Rowling, M. (1971). *Everyday Life of Medieval Traveller.* New York: Dorset.

Ryan, C. (1991). *Recreational Tourism.* London: Routledge.

Swain, M. (1995). "Gender in Tourism," *Annals of Tourism Research* 22:247–66.

Theobald, W., ed. (1994). *Global Tourism: The Next Decade.* Oxford: Butterworth-Heinemann.

Thomas, R. (1995). "Access and Inequality," in *Information Technology and Society*, ed. N. Heap, et al. London. Sage.

United Nations (1996). *Development Report.* New York: United Nations.

Urry, J. (1990). *The Tourist Gaze.* London: Sage.

Var, T., J. Ap, and C. Doren (1994). "Tourism and World Peace," in *Global Tourism: The Next Decade*, ed. W. Theobald. Oxford: Butterworth-Heinemann.

Virilio, P. (1986). *Speed and Politics.* New York: Semiotext.

——— (1991). *The Aesthetic of Disappearance.* New York: Semiotext.

Wagner, U. (1977). "Out of Time and Place: Mass Tourism and Cheap Charter Trips," *Ethnos* 42:38–52.

Woolacott, M. (1993). "When the Death of a Tourist Meets the Death of a Dream," *The Guardian* 14, 4, Manchester, U.K.

4

Shopping and Postmodernism: Consumption, Production, Identity, and the Internet

Minjoo Oh and Jorge Arditi

A growing number of commentators (Miller et al. 1998; Falk and Campbell 1997; Gabriel and Lang 1995; Radner 1995; Nava 1992; Shields 1992) consider shopping to be critical to an understanding of postmodern societies. Claims about the importance of shopping in contemporary societies abound. It has been seen as the dominant mode of contemporary public life or as the central form of organizing people's daily routines. In light of popular conceptions of shopping, the claims seem largely incongruous. Indeed, popular conceptions of shopping, as well as early theories of consumption, portray shoppers as gullible, superficial, loose, hedonistic, emotionally overstimulated, hyperactive, intellectually inferior, and banal. Shopping is seen as an undisciplined, unsupervised practice virtually out of control. It is, so the stereotype goes, an *irrational* activity.

Much of the sociological literature on shopping that has developed during the last fifteen to twenty years evolved, in part, as a reaction to this negative perception of shopping and, by extension, of shoppers as well. Writing about shopping became an integral part of the more contemporary trend in cultural studies that shifted the focus from the production to the consumption aspects of economic practice (Edgell 1997; Lury 1996; Lee 1993; Featherstone 1991).

The new trend in the literature on consumption focuses on "active" shoppers and on the processes by which people shape their everyday lives with materials provided to them by the dominant economic, social, and cultural forces (Featherstone 1991; Shields 1992; Ritzer 1999). Although the claims about the centrality of shopping to postmodern society may be overstated, there is growing consent that it is still a very significant aspect of public life within contemporary

71

environments and a virtually inescapable component of the everyday. Moreover, and more importantly, it is seen as an aspect through which self-expression has become increasingly possible (Miller et al. 1998; Friedman 1994; Lunt and Livingstone 1992).

This discussion takes a middle road between the negative view of the earlier scholarship and the overpositive one of the new literature, a view that, it will be argued, often verges on a glorification of shopping at the cost of obscuring the production-led impact of the circulation of commodities on the practice in general. The orientation can be formulated with the help of the widely held idea, already found in Karl Marx's argument on the fetishism of the commodity, that in the capitalistic mode of production, commodities, or goods, have been "emptied" of meaning (Lury 1996). The question that this raises, then, is what or who invests the commodities back with meaning? Production-led approaches, as well as most of the traditional literature on shopping, point the finger at the marketing aspects of goods, including advertising. Consumption-led approaches, as do much of the new literature on shopping in general, suggest that it is above all the shopper who invests goods with meaning. That is, contemporary subjectivities pursue their own desires, although these may be the product of varied influences.

This discussion suggests that instead of looking at the question as largely an either/or matter, shopping should be viewed as being invested by a multiplicity of frames of meaning, some coming from production and marketing processes, some from the shoppers' multiple frames of action (see also chapter 1). Shopping, in this sense, becomes a "fuzzy" practice, an immensely complex, multidimensional, often fluid activity that points at the complicated, multilayered, malleable nature of everyday life itself.

First examined are four works that exemplify the orientation of the new literature on shopping and introduce an understanding of frames of meaning originating with shoppers. Next, as a counterpoint to these studies, the perspective on consumerism developed by Jean Baudrillard in *The Consumer Society* (1998) is briefly pondered. The chapter ends with an important discussion of the explosion of on-line shopping and how the perspectives analyzed here shed some light on the new realities emerging in an Internet society with a consumer economy mediated by electronic means.

SHOPPER-CENTERED STUDIES

Gender-Based Shopping

Mica Nava's article, "Modernity's Disavowal" (1997), provides a good example of the new literature on shopping. Nava analyzes the construction of the discourse on shopping at the turn of the century and how this operated to forge a popular image of the shopper. Her claim is simple and persuasive. Neither the discourse nor the image, she argues, was gender neutral, and it is this gendered perception of shopping that underlies its negative associations. According to Nava, the turn of the century was indeed a critical period for the development of shopping. The financial power of the bourgeoisie accruing to consumers represented a force with vast implications for the unfolding of modernity, yet it also represented a threat to the established social order of the times.

The realm of shopping was, and to a considerable extent continues to be, considered a sphere of practice dominated by women. Male workers were largely confined to their places of employment while women, by necessity or by force, were increasingly moved to participate in the activity of consumption. Male workers' confinement, Nava argues, provoked their fear and anxiety toward shopping. The idea that women's unsupervised excursions to the department stores might offer them freedoms and pleasures and the expanding liberty and skills that the practices of shopping provided them did not fail to disturb the accepted conceptions of gender.

It is on these grounds that Nava explains the development of the popular discourses on shopping and the exclusion of the experiential aspects of consumerism from the historical perspective. The gendered nature of the practice was, at least in part, responsible for the discursive marginalization of shopping as a serious field of study. Because of its challenge to established patterns of gender practices, the discourse on shopping turned the activity into something based on a sexualized "other," which reinforced existing gender ideology. Women, as shoppers, were identified as surfaces and illusions, just like the commodities themselves. Like commodities, this gendered social practice of buying covered up the reality of natural decay, and like commodities, it encouraged the fetishistic fragmentation of the living body. In short, this gendered discourse, Nava suggests, still resonates strongly with today's popular conception of shopping and shoppers.

Nava not only exposes the gendered perceptions of shopping but also makes a strong claim about the role of shoppers, and by extension of women, as a modernizing force in society. Rather than being confined to the domestic sphere, women, she claims, modernized the public sphere and were modernized by it, because without question, the emerging public space of society helped to usher in Modernity. First, women's work as shoppers required, and still requires, substantial levels of skill and expertise in social interaction with strangers. Shopping, as a mode of agency, remains a core and indispensable constituent of the modern production–retailing cycle (see Harvey 1989; Gottdiener 1997). Yet shopping has also been far more profoundly marked by the materiality of the practice than the classic discourses suggest. Second, shopping is work. Despite this absolute centrality of shopping to modern Western economic life, this conception of the activity as labor has been remarkably neglected by commentators that privilege consumption practices as a kind of effortless world dominated by fantasy and enchantment (see Firat and Venkatesh 1995; Ritzer 1999).

Third, shopping is gendered because of its material basis. Thus, it is charac-teristically women's work and the sphere of women's self-actualization. Finally, shopping is quintessentially modern because it transpires in the public sphere. Increasingly consumption now takes place in new public spaces, such as depart-ment stores and malls (see chapter 13). Interaction within these spaces predomi-nantly involves women, young people, and children—a reality that in effect chal-lenges the popular image of the suburban-home-secluded woman largely removed from the public sphere. According to Nava, traveling to large cities to shop was always an adventure for women that also signified a middle-class status. Depart-ment stores were established for ease and convenience and were decorated with beautiful colors and scenery, juxtaposed by racks of clothing. Shopping became such an event that women considered it entertainment while still doing the family's work. This luxurious experience of dressing well, mingling, traveling, socializing, and spending money allowed participation in an activity originally reserved exclusively for wealthy women.

In sum, the gendered shopping experience that emerged along with other as-pects of modernity in the nineteenth century subverted the complex of qualities— inwardness, passivity, and purity—imputed traditionally to female subjectivity. Shopping allowed women to participate freely in the public sphere, even if it was initially confined only to the sphere of consumption prior to the twentieth cen-tury. That is, working in tandem, both shopping and modernity·helped create a new female subjectivity.

Conceptualizing shopping as an ambiguous activity that is neither clearly work nor clearly leisure challenges the traditional notion of work itself. Yet Nava is not concerned with conceptual issues nor with evaluating whether shopping has indeed played the crucial transformative role that she attributes to it. Her con-cern is to show how women have stepped outside of male-defined and male-con-trolled discourses, something that has entailed varying degrees of female exclu-sivity in regard to public space, activity, social perspective, and the definition of femininity.

It is in this sense that the question of the transformative role of shopping is, nevertheless, critical. For if shopping undeniably can be seen as a rupture with traditional gender roles and some forms of patriarchal domination, this break does not necessarily imply an emancipation, or liberation, or even an empowerment of women, as Nava suggests. More in line with Foucaultian arguments of a new form of enslavement, the new women's work of shopping could well be consid-ered a change in the power that, nevertheless, still dominates women. Nava's argument is grounded on the idea that emancipation and empowerment both fol-low directly the liberation of women from the traditional form of patriarchy. After this break, Nava suggests that women entered a new social world of freedom and self-expression with an unleashing of creative powers. Yet it could also be argued that women, and men too, have simply moved in the modernist transformation of society from one form of subjection to another. This contrasting view is, indeed, parallel to Michel Foucault's argument in *Discipline and Punish* (1979) and *The History of Sexuality* (1985) and will be discussed more fully below when the work of Jean Baudrillard is considered below.

Shopping and Polysemy

Another perspective that argues for the importance of shopping as a gendered sphere is provided by Mary Douglas, who takes a more analytical turn in an eloquently entitled article, "In Defense of Shopping" (1997). Douglas, like Nava, takes issue with the assumptions and implications of the "swing theory" (1997:15) of consumer behavior in market research, a theory that views shoppers, and particularly female shoppers, as irrational and purely reactive consumers mobilized by the waves of fashion. Douglas wants to show that, instead, shoppers are coherent and consistently rational beings. Rejecting the market-research framework, which is based on individualist psychology, Douglas argues for a culturally grounded framework, one that helps see consumption within distinctive "household cultures" (1997:26) as continuously and pervasively inspired by what she calls cultural "hostility" (1997:18). Fashion, or style, is not an external surface swaying people at whim; people are not blindly navigating over its waves. To Douglas, style is a way of constructing and maintaining a cultural form, not only by choosing one style but also by rejecting others. It involves simultaneously a positive dimension of self-construction, of allowing a person to define herself as part of a culture or group, and a negative dimension of exclusion, of establishing differences from others through "hostility." Acts of shopping are not haphazard responses to particular needs. They are conscientious and conscious activities, even rational activities, that help build one's cultural form and operate through the deployment of likes and dislikes.

Like Nava, Douglas does not consider the possibility of a power, or in her case, the larger consumer culture, setting the parameters within which the sort of cultural dynamics associated with shopping operate. She ascribes considerable freedom to this activity. Specifically, she defines four subjectivities or "lifestyles," allegedly universal, to which each person or family belongs: individualist, hierarchicalist, enclavist, and isolationist (1997:19). People buy some items and not others to affirm their individualist or their enclavist lifestyles and to reject the lifestyles of others. The shoppers' choices involve a constant assessment and calculation of an item's meaning in terms of this dynamic of hostility.

What is missing in Douglas's argument is the historical, sociological kind of transformations of social conditions and social reality underlying arguments such as those that Baudrillard (1998) discusses (see below). And yet Douglas's approach illuminates an aspect of shopping that is *absent* from Baudrillard—the idea that shopping can be framed by more than one cultural dimension and therefore can be invested with meanings by a multiplicity of frames of practice. In sum, Douglas introduces the idea of diversity in the experience of both men and women regarding the social meaning of shopping. Her approach is semiotic. Meanings generated by individual participation in the consumption sphere are polysemic and linked to differences in lifestyle.

Provisioning

Marjorie DeVault's notion of "provisioning" (1991) introduces another, perhaps more sociologically relevant, sphere of practice framing shopping. DeVault's provisioning (1991:58) takes into account a shopper's activities both before and after the actual shopping experience to articulate invisible "care work" (1991:19). To DeVault, shopping (provisioning) is more than the mere buying of things. Shopping involves the construction of a family as a socially organized material setting, which like any social setting, requires particular kinds of coordinative and maintenance activities. "The ideals have changed—hardly any contemporary wives or mothers even aim for 'perfect order,'" DeVault writes, "but housework is still a project of 'making meaningful patterns'" (1991:78). In a sense, DeVault locates shopping in the context of women's position in the family. Her argument indeed "is fundamentally about women's 'place' in family life rather than about identity, an argument that aims to show how women are continually recruited into participation in social relations that produce their subordination" (1991:13).

The frame brought into the activity of shopping here has nothing to do with the cultural sense of the family but, quite literally, with the *work* of making the family. DeVault puts it clearly: "Shopping for food can be seen as a complex, artful activity that supports the production of meaningful patterns of household life by negotiating connections between household and market" (1991:59).

Provisioning (shopping) is accomplished through a set of techniques and strategies that women have developed. These strategies and the process of provisioning in general have been trivialized as women's "natural" disposition. DeVault, however, deconstructs this alleged "naturalness" (1991:16) of shopping and brings to light the complexity of the activity. She points out that shopping requires a complex set of tasks such as planning, screening, sorting, and evaluating, as well as adapting, improvising, and revising—tasks that are performed under the name of "love" and "care" (1991:18) for the family. Indeed, for many women, shopping is defined as service to others. Women learn to care for others. Then the fact that so many women frame shopping as "choice" (1991:161) means that they are less likely to make choices in their own behalf when the interests of family members conflict. In that sense, DeVault suggests, the activity of men when they shop involves a different frame. Men have no terms through which they can think of shopping as service to a woman nor a cultural script suggesting that husbands should care for wives through domestic work.

As the quotation concerning how women produce their own subordination reveals, DeVault definitely recognizes the limits of providing a theory of family work as also providing a theory of empowerment. DeVault does not minimize the centrality of the market and in a way, just as Douglas does, she recognizes the polysemic, multiplicity of frames instructing shopping. To her, for example, shopping blurs the boundaries between the public and the private. DeVault theorizes shopping within the context of the unacknowledged yet critical role that women play in both the public and the private sphere. DeVault would agree with Douglas that shoppers do not merely respond to market fluctuations. She recognizes that shoppers respond to market forces, yet, she argues, they find ways to get the things that fulfill their household needs. When shoppers do not find products that are compatible with their daily needs, they become frustrated and anxious. In this sense, the market is but a context for the realization of women's family work. Shoppers engage and struggle with the market as context and with their family budgets as a material constraint. Consumers are located at the intersection of their own personal lives and the more impersonal social institutions of the economy. They are always drawn in two directions, negotiating the demands of both family members and market forces while contending with both personal desires and impersonal budgets.

Shopping and the Mediation of Personal Relationships

Daniel Miller (1998) also sees shopping as an activity whose primary meaning derives from the family relationships that it helps to produce and reproduce. Indeed, for Miller, like DeVault, shopping is not about the superficial world of consumption but about primary social relationships. The purpose of shopping is not so much to buy the things people want but to strive to be in a relationship with subjects that want these things. What shoppers desire above all is for others to want and to appreciate what they buy. For Miller, shopping involves a dynamic yielding a specific form of social relationship best understood as "love" (1998: 18). It involves being responsible and, above all, caring for others and for oneself. In return, this activity locates the shopper in an intimate relationship with others.

To Miller, commodities in themselves have no meaning other than the one shoppers give them. The experience of shopping in itself seems to have no unique effect. People do not develop a special subjectivity or attitude to things because of the experience, as the earlier critiques of the consumer society or the work of Baudrillard suggests. Consumerism, in the pejorative sense, is *not* an issue for Miller. Unlike the current craze among postmodern sociologists that focuses solely on the structural domination of consumption by society, Miller seeks an understanding through a study of basic social relationships for *why* shopping, and consumerism in general, have become dominant forms of practice in contemporary society. Nor does shopping, according to Miller, constitute the intersection between capitalism and consumerism, as DeVault argues. "Capitalism has its own independent logic of expansion, for which it matters little that goods are consumed within this or that context just as long as they sell." And, he asserts, "the consumer is not merely expressing some spirit of capitalism" (1998:153).

To Miller, the important question is how men, and especially women, interpret their own activities as shoppers and how as a consequence they invest commodities with meaning. In his view, shopping becomes, literally, a devotional rite that helps constitute a social order based on "love." In a sense, shopping is a site in which the kind of desiring subjects and the sort of practices that reproduce such a social order come into being. The meaning of shopping for shoppers is contained in this devotional practice, and the meaning of commodities is imbued with the significance that objects acquire as a function of this practice.

According to Miller, shopping is the modern expression of the universal ritual of sacrifice—one of the rituals by which concern for others takes shape in culture. As she shops for others, for example, a woman, as a member of a family, engages in a constant practice of "sacrifice" (1998:112), always having in mind a sincere concern for what others want and postponing the satisfaction of her own desires. In the process, a network of relationships with significant others develops. The meaning of shopping and the meaning of the thing bought derive only from this concern and this practice. In this sense, each thing acquires almost a particularized meaning that makes sense only in the context of the particular social relationship.

The Importance of Shopping

For Nava, Douglas, DeVault, and Miller, shopping is not a superficial, inconsequential activity, as is often claimed by cultural critics of consumerism—it is significant, deep, creative, laden with responsibilities, and richly polysemic with diverse meanings. These four writers encourage consideration of new ways of thinking about the apparently mundane, everyday act of shopping. They urge a reappraisal of the familiar experiences of selecting, preparing, and sharing food, often taken for granted, to see in greater depth the habits and choices, preferences and aversions demonstrated by consumers. Each argument points at different ways in which the practice of shopping is framed by shoppers through the influence of both institutional structure and personal agency. At the same time, these perspectives that value shopping also show how different dimensions of meaning associated with both shopping and commodities are invoked in this social activity that, like other aspects of modernity, is tied to the contemporary public sphere, and yet is still so much a part of the cherished intimate, personal relationships.

POSTMODERN PERSPECTIVES

Writers who are more interested in postmodern culture and consumerism than issues of gender serve as a counterpoint to the previous studies. Baudrillard (1998), for example, views contemporary production and marketing processes as transforming the nature of commodities in a society of abundance (see also Appadurai 1986). From the postmodern perspective, it is the structural aspect of shopping that provides meaning for commodities, rather than the subjective agency and gendered specificity observed above. Echoing a theme developed earlier in this century by the critical theorists, Baudrillard views the sense of freedom in the public sphere argued for by Nava, Douglas, DeVault, and Miller as simply illusory.

Shopping as an Imaginary Relation: Baudrillard

Baudrillard (1998) indeed, makes a strong argument regarding the shoppers' illusory sense of empowerment. This, he suggests, is more a consequence of the techniques of presentation by retailers and advertisers than a real property of shoppers. The profusion of commodities presented to shoppers and the specific strategies by which this profusion is displayed—"piling high" hundreds of clothes of different sizes and colors in department stores; hundreds if not thousands of cereal packs and canned foods and all kinds of foodstuffs in supermarkets; tens of thousands of books, records, and goods of all kinds in the superstores—create the *illusion of abundance* and plenty. In turn, Baudrillard argues, commodities appear as miraculous "gifts," in the Maussian sense, and their display appears as a spectacular "feast" (1998:26), not unlike the potlatch ritual of the Northwest Native Americans. Shoppers enjoy the freedom of the "feast" and happily take all the magical "gifts" up to their credit card limits. The feast allows a shopper to develop the very same feeling of being alive, which Nava makes so much of, but this time it is derived from simulated sources. For Baudrillard, this profusion of the "gift" in contemporary society creates the illusion of choice. And yet, Baudrillard insists, presenting commodities as gifts and as a feast are marketing and retailing techniques that establish constraints on shoppers by directing their freedom of choice and channeling their desires to the retailers' interests (see Ewen and Ewen 1982).

Shoppers have only an illusion that they are the ones who choose things. In reality, shoppers merely follow through directive "pathways" structured by basic stimulus and response mechanisms (Baudrillard 1998:27), which are arranged as a way to gain maximum economic profit. The whole network of commodities is arranged to captivate the purchasing impulse of shoppers. The profusion of commodities and their display have a subtle yet tremendous effect in orchestrating shopping behavior. Shoppers, Baudrillard explains, "will move *logically* from

one object to another. [They] will be caught up in a *calculus* of objects, and this
is something quite different from the frenzy of buying and acquisitiveness to
which the simple profusion of commodities gives rise" (1998:27, emphases in
the original).

Under contemporary, postmodern conditions, when the code of consumption
dominates social life, the alleged freedom of shoppers quickly turns into the most
rigid constraint. Buy more and need more becomes compulsory and mandatory.
The more shoppers buy, the more shoppers will desire to buy. In this affluent
society, Baudrillard contends, consumers are poorer than ever before. Their need
for more commodities and new experiences seems insatiable and thus never satisfied. Through the play of differentiation, one commodity induces another as
"ensemble" or "packaging" (1998:28). It is not a mere sequence of objects but
"a chain of signifiers" (1998:27) that impose a coherent and collective vision of
things. People are surrounded by the image of objects. An infinite play of signs
is thus the order of society. In this sense, shoppers are very passive and entrapped
in the "fantasmagoria" of the world of consumption (1998:147). People as consumers "live at the pace of objects, live to the rhythm of their ceaseless succes-
sion" (1998:25), not at the pace of their own daily life. Indeed, the human species
is buried under the images of objects. "We are here at the heart of consumption
as total organization of everyday life," Baudrillard declares (1998:29).

Not only is freedom illusory, then. To Baudrillard, the meaning of commodities has little if nothing to do with shopping. Commodities do not derive their
meanings from signifiers originating with shoppers but from the self-referential,
semiotic logic linking commodities together into "ensembles," into more complex "super-objects" that draw consumers into ever stronger complex "motivations" (1998:27). These ensembles are connected by the logic of fashion or visual fit alone; they are structured by the chain of signification or difference. A
commodity signifies only in the context of, and in reference to, the other commodities with which it is assembled. Objects are always placed in a context and
people literally buy into the environment or ambiance as a form of simulated
participation. In this consumer milieu, the meaning of objects is a function of
the multiple practices of assemblage—piling high, packaging, the placing of
commodities in a shop, the brand name, techniques of advertising, and so on—
to which is added, for example, the dispersed practices of commodity assemblage
developing in the Internet.

Near the beginning of his book *The Consumer Society* Baudrillard gives an
example.

> Few objects today are offered *alone* without a context of objects which "speaks"
> them. And this changes the consumer's relation to the object: [the consumer] no
> longer relates to a particular object in its specific utility, but to a set of objects in
> its total signification. Washing machine, refrigerator and dishwasher taken together

have a different meaning from the one each has individually as an appliance. The shop-window, the advertisement, the manufacturer and the *brand name*, which here plays a crucial role, impose a coherent, collective vision, as though they were almost an indissociable totality, a series (emphases in the original). (1998:27)

A THEORY OF SHOPPING

Baudrillard's argument is persuasive, though only to the extent that shoppers limit their activities to the most immediate experience of consumption. The semiotics of commodities that Baudrillard brings to the forefront of his analysis unquestionably sets the parameters within which all shopping occurs. Yet as the previous authors also persuasively argue, shoppers bring other frames of practice to the series set by the multiple assemblages that serve as pathways to the consumption experience. In this sense, shopping is a multiply framed, or a multilayered, practice unfolding from the primary layer formed by the play of signifiers of commodities toward greater personal and idiosyncratic modes of desire and meaning.

On another level, Baudrillard's argument that consumption practices have reshaped the very nature of everyday life seems on the mark. The natural seasons of the year, for example, that once structured traditional societies disappeared a long time ago in today's culture. Today, through e-commerce, the distinction between day and night seems to have collapsed altogether. Commodities are remaking seasons and days through a series of holidays—Halloween, Thanksgiving, Christmas, Mardi Gras, Easter, and the like—each with its own logic, celebrated through buying and consumption. Commodities reconfigure geography, neighborhood, family, and one's subjectivity itself. Yet as DeVault and Miller show, the network of one's social relations, mediated as they might be by the realities of consumerism itself, shapes the microscopic practices of which shopping is ultimately constituted. Commodities are not just pathways, they are vehicles by which "love," to use Miller's word, and the social or interactive order that ensues from it unfolds.

NEW DIMENSIONS: E-COMMERCE AND ON-LINE SHOPPING

The strength and limitations of each orientation briefly introduced above come graphically into view when the new realities of shopping emerging via the Internet are examined. With the easing of security fears, on-line shopping has developed into a multibillion-dollar industry and is expected to grow rapidly over the next few years, if not eventually defining the future of shopping itself. In December 1999, yahoo.com announced that business in its shopping site the day after Thanksgiving increased 400 percent from a year earlier. Market share of niche

Internet music sites that specialize in jazz or classical music, for example, out-perform their "real-life" counterparts—actual stores, even franchised outlets. Web-based "superstores" such as amazon.com have changed the face of shopping, forcing traditional companies such as Barnes & Noble, Borders, and Tower Records to open their own on-line stores. A November article in the *New York Times* celebrated Barnes & Noble's move to the Internet, describing it, without a trace of irony, as an act of survival for the traditional company.

In the fast-growing, ever-changing, cutting-edge realm of electronic market-ing, consumers find that they can now order even their groceries on-line. A site, americanfoods.com, which delivers items such as frozen gourmet steaks, chops, poultry, fish, vegetables, and desserts, advocates in an advertisement its advan-tage of convenience over traditional retail stores.

> Are you frustrated by supermarket shopping? Think about your last supermarket experience: the uncooperative shopping cart, the seemingly endless search for your desired items, the "friendly" sales help, the long check-out lines, the lugging of grocery bags to your car, and again into your home. Wouldn't you like to avoid the supermarket hassle?" (<http://www.americanfoods.com>)

No traffic jams. No parking hassles. No jostling crowds. No inattentive, har-ried sales clerks. The cyberstore stimulates people to shop on the Internet with alleged advantages emphasizing convenience, that is, the saving of time and money. This is one vision of shopping on the Internet as advocated by the mov-ers of e-commerce themselves; but that does not mean it is altogether inaccurate.

For shoppers, in effect, e-commerce does offer convenience, ease, and a flex-ibility that is absent from conventional stores. According to a Visa survey taken in November 1998, 46 percent of people polled planned to buy at least some of their holiday gifts on-line; 60 percent of e-shoppers reported doing so in their pajamas. Whether or not the last number is accurate is not the issue, for even if it is inflated by the answerers themselves, it points to a well-known and amply discussed aspect of on-line shopping. Internet stores are open twenty-four hours a day, seven days a week, even under the most extreme weather conditions. The cyberstores are accessible at a click of the mouse, and shoppers can enter and leave at will, starting to shop in the morning; leaving their shopping in a "bas-ket"; and coming back hours, days, or even weeks later to complete or just con-tinue their shopping. Try doing that at a "real" supermarket.

In addition, people can visit multiple shops and almost simultaneously check and compare, get the best prices, and more—from the ease and comfort of their own home. Whether shoppers also become smarter or actually save money, along with experiencing greater convenience, as e-retailers try to convince them they are, is a questionable conclusion, however.

In a sense, on-line shopping does little to change the situation described by Baudrillard regarding consumerism in general. It might actually magnify some of its most salient characteristics, and through this process of magnification, perhaps transform them in unexpected ways. Take the first point that Baudrillard raises in *The Consumer Society* (1998), the profusion of goods. With the Internet, this profusion attains a new dimension: it denotes not just abundance but limitless possibility. The Internet gives the impression that everything is attainable—the most obscure or rare item seems to be on sale, available to all. The Internet combines the supermarket, the department store, the specialty shop, the convenience store, the mall, and the flea market, all at once. It makes the abundance of things a profusion not just of quantity but of quality; not just of a limited number of items piled high but of a limitless number of qualitatively different things dispersed throughout cyberspace.

The magical effect of this hyperabundance takes on a new dimension in which any need can be invented and immediately satisfied. New needs and new "pathways" (Baudrillard 1998:27) for their satisfaction come and go at the ceaseless "24/7" rhythm of e-commerce. Rather than being liberated, shoppers are taken even deeper by their very own desires into the labyrinth of consumerism and the play of significations that create endless meanings through difference alone.

As a consequence too, the seduction of the play of commodities on shoppers works differently in the spaces of e-commerce, compared with the practices of seduction in force in the brick-and-mortar stores. In "real" venues, not only the presentation of the commodity but the entire environment of the shop itself is geared toward sparking the desire of shoppers to consume. From very early on in the history of department stores, managers mobilized shoppers' imaginations by attempting to recreate a sense of community and excitement (Williams 1982). Geared especially to middle-class women, department stores created a market *and* a public space. They furnished the stores with reading rooms, writing tables, free refreshments, art galleries, and of course, an architecture of the retailing space and a presentation of merchandise heightening the sensual relation of the shopper with the commodity—the touch of silk, the seduction of colors, the softness or coolness of the floor, and so on. Subsequently, department stores and shopping malls have spent large amounts of money to create the image of accessible and convenient "dreamworlds" of pleasure (Williams 1982; Gottdiener 1997).

The spectacular is a form of narrative, and part of the innovative force of department stores and the newer consumer phenomenon, shopping malls, is to create an imagery of the spectacle through which consumer behavior can thrive (Gottdiener 1997; Ritzer1999). Indeed, in contrast to these "dreamworlds," engineered to be fantastic and exciting, daily activities are experienced as flat and dull. Pleasure and excitement thus become associated with the act of shopping in these enchanted environments of fantasy and spectacle that stimulate the senses while shopping. No one is a rational shopper in what Guy Debord (1970) has called this veritable "society of the spectacle."

Cyberstores have a distinctive mode of mobilizing shoppers that contrasts with this fantasmagoria of real brick-and-mortar stores. In the computer-accessed world of e-commerce, the regime of needs and desires is, as is well known, literally disembodied. The direct engagement of the body is absent in cyberspace and, in a way, both pleasure and terror are absent from this "cool" world. Cyberstores do not create an experience such as the smell of perfume or the feeling of silky fabrics that are at hand in malls and department stores. Most Internet shopping sites promote their advantages strictly in terms of convenience and price, not in terms of a call to the senses. E-commerce does not need to take an instructive position nor "seduce" e-shoppers with "spectacle." In the cyberstores, there is no "place to be seen," no "spectacular commodity signs."

And yet, with the very spread of e-commerce and the proliferation of shopping sites, and with the need to constantly increase business, next-generation cyberstores are engineering their sites to encourage shoppers' irrational desires. The emergence and popularity of auction sites is a function both of price and of the gamblinglike quality of the practice itself. Auction sites on the Web do not appeal to the senses nor simply to the rationality of shoppers, as they often claim they do. They are like huge, interactive bingo parlors or betting places, in which the seduction of gambling adds to the economic incentive of buying Internet merchandise. The growing offering of chat rooms and user home pages within shopping sites, or the implementations of electronic "wine-tasting parties" or virtual "dressing rooms" with personalized 3-D mannequins are attempts to recreate the community-driven experience of the mall's department store in cyberspace (Cos 1999). Although by definition a disembodied experience, retailers in the cyberworld of e-commerce are using their Web sites to *simulate* a public space in the same sense that department stores once structured these environments of social communion adjacent to merchandise.

Seduction through the image of "personalization" is another example. Cyberstores talk about the death of the age of mass communication and their triumphant one-on-one relationship with customers through the Internet. They claim that the link between buyer and seller through the computer can be a personal one. The mail-order clothing company Lands' End now has a Web site that advertises access to a shopper's own "digital tailor." For example, shoppers are asked for their dress size, color, and style preferences; then they can sort through a massive selection of "virtual" dresses that match their tastes *without* the occasional embarrassment that often comes from telling others their measurements. Cybershopping, unlike interaction with real people, is also relatively stress free. It is much easier for customers to say no to a "virtual" sales person than to a live one.

Yet along with the different nature of the experience, e-commerce also exhibits some of the negative features first critiqued by Baudrillard (1998). New techniques of assemblage, for example, have also emerged, producing new patterns of associations between commodities and generating new plays of signifiers. These changes are produced in part as a consequence of the very move to produce new mechanisms of seduction, or new feelings of participation or community that fit the cyberspace world. The most interesting among them, and one that can hardly be replicated outside cyberstores, is the practice now common in on-line stores such as amazon.com, barnesandnoble.com, or CDnow.com of listing items that other customers have also bought when buying something. The copy usually says: "Customers who bought this book also bought . . . etc." or "Auctions and zShops sellers and our other stores recommend. . . ."

This last technique represents, in fact, an entirely new mode of aggregating merchandise not previously used in all of marketing. The assemblage of books from an on-line superstore that others have also read follows *none* of the traditional forms of organizing books: by subject, by author, by alphabet, and so on. Here, the association follows the rather random buying patterns at the e-store, one that reflects the idiosyncrasies or the momentary needs of a few people or perhaps the trace of shopping excursions meant for a variety of people and activities—self, family members, friends, school, work. These choices are then all lumped together by cyberstores with their instantaneous recall of computerized, stored information. The program does this automatically.

Still, for e-shoppers, these assemblages bespeak of "affinities" all the more attractive for their randomness and their foundations in the actual practices of people who, like the on-line shoppers, are attracted to what putative "others" are also buying. In this way, the individual buyer is linked to a "virtual" community of the like-minded by an electronic mechanism that works without human mediation.

A "calculus of objects" (Baudrillard 1998:27) of a different order thus takes shape—one that provides new pathways for shoppers to move "logically," or perhaps in this case, "naturally," from one object to another that is still for sale by businesses interested primarily in making a profit. It is a calculus that mobilizes, literally, a logic of affinities, commodities drawing their meaning from the allegedly "natural" likeness of tastes or interests among all shoppers. This new cybertechnique of assemblage remains a means to stimulate e-shoppers' desires and to facilitate the act of buying. It simulates the sort of frame that escapes the abilities of producers and retailers as discussed in the works of Nava, Douglas, DeVault, and Miller. Although this assemblage of the like-minded generated by a computer gives the impression of belonging to a community, there is nothing in this link anywhere close to the type of intimate, "thick" social relations that DeVault's "provisioning" or Miller's "love" implies.

And yet, as seen above, assemblages are not just electronic "pathways." In a manner that resonates with Anthony Giddens's concept of "double structuration" (1986) or Pierre Bourdieu's "habitus" (1977), they are also "vehicles" with which shoppers manifest motives originating in other frames of practice. This is as true for on-line shopping as it is for shopping in a brick-and-mortar supermarket or department store. Indeed, although it is clear that on-line shopping magnifies many of the points raised by Baudrillard and develops others in new directions, making the grip of consumerism even stronger, none of it affects the type of provisioning that DeVault talks about, or the unfolding of social relations as Miller discusses it, or the affirmation of identity that Douglas identifies, or other practices and meanings foreign to consumerism per se that e-shoppers *weave together* with the pathways generated by the play of commodities. Hence shopping, because of its social complexity, transcends each of these perspectives yet contains them all. This quality is exemplified by the framing mechanisms deployed by all types of shoppers.

GENERAL ASPECTS OF SHOPPING: TYPES OF FRAMING PRACTICES

There are three major types of framing practices originating in shoppers on-line and off-line alike. First, shoppers are using their purchases to sustain a particular sense of identity and as a framing device that brings the need to explore and develop their own sense of self or subjectivity. To paraphrase Bourdieu (1984), shoppers engage in self-construction by a process of acquiring commodities of distinction and difference. Although Douglas does not speak in terms of identity, this is the type of framing she exemplifies. Her argument about the affirmation of "household cultures" through the mobilization of "hostility," that is, active likes and dislikes, involves precisely a constant strategy of identification. Shoppers' definition of self, their sense of self as a relation to others, shapes what they buy and refuse to buy, makes them choose certain pathways and not others, or determines if they will be seduced by some commodities and not by others. In short, shoppers invest commodities with personal or deeply held cultural meanings deriving from their social situation.

Second, shoppers are seen as investing commodities with meanings of a more affectual nature, of which DeVault's "provisioning" and Miller's "love" are perfect examples. Shoppers incorporate values in the calculus of their purchases that are different than the sign value of the commodity and that sometimes have little to do with it. Affectual criteria related primarily to family concerns or the care of family members but are not limited to them permeate shoppers' practices and, simultaneously, sustain the social relations at their origin. Commodities become vehicles for caring, while caring is channeled, and sustained, by consumption. That does not make Western society less of a society of consumption, but it does make consumption something more than a purely production-led phenomenon.

And third, shoppers can be seen as recontextualizing the commodities and the play of commodities—their actions becoming, as Nava suggests, unintentionally subversive. The question of whether or not sign value dominates the use value of commodities, as Baudrillard argues, is not a real issue (but see Gottdiener 1997, and chapter 1 of this volume). As long as shoppers have a reflexive power to recontexualize, reterritorialize, and redesign sign value, they have constitutive power over the meaning of commodities and their own social interactions. This reflexive power does not always come from shoppers' intentionality or consciousness. To use Michel de Certeau's (1984) terms as he addresses the creative power of people in everyday practice, the shoppers' reflexive power consists of "tactics" rather than "strategies."

In this sense, meaning is not something related to what shoppers say or do. It is something accomplished through their engagement with and their practice of everyday life, especially the constraints of family budgets, and through a perspective that they develop as they manipulate space. In their everyday doings, shoppers manipulate established forms of material culture from their own perspectives. The embodiment of social life in established places, de Certeau argues, must be counterposed to the creative organization of experienced space. As Nava observes about the gendered nature of shopping, the practice of consumption highlights the liberating dimensions of shopping, its potential for reinvention and reconstitution, even though, as Baudrillard claims, it also becomes simultaneously a part of the new forms of domination.

Nava, Douglas, DeVault, and Miller all acknowledge the feminine side of shopping that mobilizes concerns and emerges from and helps to constitute the everyday experience of women. Moreover, consumption embodies the concerns and motivations that pertain to spheres of action conventionally identified with women: family, care, primary social relations, stylization. In male discourses, which Miller claims should not be identified as the discourse of all men, these particular considerations stay largely unrecognized and misrecognized. The view of shoppers as passive, then, has been formulated as a consequence of the invisibility of the discourses and spheres of action activated by women, which are a result of women's work.

Indeed, contemporary moves toward a more active view of shoppers, although limited in their own way, ultimately produce a more honest and gender-sensitive view. Yet at the same time, it is also a fuzzier view of the practice itself. As Douglas suggests (see also chapter 1), shopping is polysemic—a multidimensional and multilayered practice that parallels the multidimensional and multilayered nature of everyday life itself.

BIBLIOGRAPHY

Appadurai, Arjun (1986). "Introduction: Commodities and the Politics of Value," in *The Social Life of Things: Commodities in Cultural Perspective*, ed. A. Appadurai. Cambridge: Cambridge University Press.

Baudrillard, Jean (1998). *The Consumer Society: Myths and Structures*. London: Sage.

Bourdieu, Pierre (1977). *An Outline of a Theory of Practice*. Cambridge: Cambridge University Press.

———— (1984). *Distinction: A Social Critique of the Judgment of Taste.* Trans. R. Nice. London: Routledge & Kegan Paul.

Certeau, Michel de (1984). *The Practice of Everyday Life.* Berkeley: University of California Press.

Cos, Ana Marie (1999). "Just Browsing," *Time Magazine,* November, 1 (special issue: Your Guide to 250 Shopping Sites):25–28.

Debord, Guy (1970). *The Society of the Spectacle.* Detroit: Black and Red.

DeVault, Marjorie (1991). *Feeding the Family: The Social Organization of Caring as Gendered Work.* Chicago: University of Chicago Press.

Douglas, Mary (1997). "In Defense of Shopping," in *The Shopping Experience,* edited by P. Falk and C. Campbell. London: Sage.

Douglas, Mary, and Baron Iserwood (1996). *The World of Goods.* London: Routledge.

Edgell, Stephen, Kevin Hetherington, and Alan Warde, eds. (1996). *Consumption Matters.* Oxford: Blackwell.

Ewen, S., and E. Ewen (1982). *Channels of Desire.* New York: McGraw-Hill.

Falk, Pasi, and Colin Campbell, eds. (1997). *The Shopping Experience.* London: Sage.

Featherstone, Mike (1991). *Consumer Culture and Postmodernism.* London: Sage.

Foucault, Michel (1979). *Discipline and Punish: The Birth of the Prison.* Trans. by Alan Sheridan. New York: Vintage Books.

———— (1985). *The History of Sexuality: Volume I, An Introduction.* Trans. by Robert Hurley. New York: Pantheon.

Friedman, Jonathan (1994). *Consumption and Identity.* Switzerland: Harwood Academic Publishers.

Gabriel, Yiannis, and Tim Lang (1995). *The Unmanageable Consumer: Contemporary Consumption and Its Fragmentation.* London: Sage.

Giddens, Anthony (1986). *The Constitution of Society: Outline of the Theory of Structuration.* Berkeley: University of California Press.

Gottdiener, M. (1997). *The Theming of America: Dreams, Visions, and Commercial Spaces.* Boulder, Colo.: Westview.

Lee, Martyn J. (1993). *Consumer Culture Reborn: The Cultural Politics of Consumption.* London: Routledge.

Lunt, Peter, and Sonia Livingstone (1992). *Mass Consumption and Personal Identity: Everyday Economic Experience.* Buckingham, England: Open University Press.

Lupton, Deborah (1996). *Food, the Body, and the Self.* London: Sage.

Lury, Celia (1996). *Consumer Culture.* New Brunswick, N.J.: Rutgers University Press.

Miller, Daniel (1998). *A Theory of Shopping.* Ithaca, N.Y.: Cornell University Press.

Miller, Daniel, et al. (1998). *Shopping, Place, and Identity.* New York: Routledge.

Nava, Mica (1992). *Changing Cultures: Feminism, Youth, and Consumerism.* London: Sage.

———— (1997). "Modernity's Disavowal: Women, the City, and the Department Sore," in *Modern Times: Reflections on a Century of English Modernity,* ed. Mica Nava and Alan O'Shea. London: Routledge.

Radner, Hilary (1995). *Shopping Around: Feminine Culture and the Pursuit of Pleasure.* New York: Routledge.

Ritzer, George (1999). *Consumption and the Re-Enchantment of Everyday Life.* Thousand Oaks, Calif.: Pine Forge Press.

Shields, Rob, ed. (1992). *Lifestyle Shopping: The Subject of Consumption.* London: Routledge.

Williams, Rosalind H. (1982). *Dream Worlds: Mass Consumption in Late Nineteenth-Century France.* Berkeley: University of California Press.

Part II

Case Studies

Part II

Case Studies

5

Brain-Suck

Eugene Halton

The year 1990 ushered in the newest phase of postmodern decay: virtuality as virtue. That year is a convenient decade marker for the change, when superstores begin to blitz already mall-crazed America, when cheap imitation ethnic restaurants give way to high-quality virtual "local" ethnic restaurant franchises, when high-quality superbookstore and supercafé franchises colonize city and mall alike, when Americans finally and voluntarily surrender those chunks of time not already owned by television to their newly purchased smart typewriter contraptions. Could anyone imagine just twenty years ago the extent to which mass numbers of the leisure classes of the advanced industrial nations would spend significant leisure time "typing?"

The old modern vision of the human of the future was a spindly creature with an enormous brain. Now we know that vision was wrong, because we are making the human of the future right now; "it" is already well under way—that pathetic genderless creature, and we know in what remains of our Interneted souls that it will eventually be a pinheaded creature with huge, thick typing fingers. Evolution has selected carpal tunnel syndrome as the means of weeding out the mechanically weak stock and the Internet as the means of brain-sucking the populace or increasing its dependency on externally derived information that bypasses the need for actual thinking, feeling, and experiencing. We've already witnessed the brain-suck of check-out attendants, who formerly possessed the ability for common arithmetic, by calculating machines.

More and more information is pumped into the world every minute of every day, and yet America dumbs down: more and more information about the world and yet people know less and less about it; more and more sources of history available and yet less and less knowledge of history; more and more information about cultures of the world and yet less and less awareness.

Do people accumulate this information by day and have it removed, like night soil, by dark? There is a vast brain-suck occurring. But from where? How can you flood brains with information and by doing so, precisely in the act of doing so, suck them dry?

How is it that we can look at and listen to so much information bombarding our eyes and ears, yet apparently see not and hear not? It is not simply a physiological problem but a cultural and moral one that involves all the fibers of our being, including the physical. It is the same problem, I suppose, that causes me misgivings when I see those people in health clubs reading on bicycle machines, abstracted from the pure being of their bodies. You know when you look at them that they cycle away more miles on those machines than the ones they passed while driving in their auto-machines to get to the health club. But these are physiologically measurable and paid-for miles.

My technical term for this neurometaphysical disorder is "brain-suck." It derives from a technoculture bent on replacing *self-originated experience* with rationally derived commodity forms and on colonizing the inner life with substitute emotions. The result is what might be called, only half-fancifully, "brainoid tissue," surrogate synapses all linked to and ultimately produced by the Great and Powerful Machine. I want to explore some of the varieties of this process with reference to the colonization of the human self by consumption culture—mostly in its American version—with some gear changes.

GEAR CHANGE

A Day in the Life of Techno-Colonized Person

In the American version, a techno-colonized person moves by machine, spending a daily average of eighty-one minutes for males and sixty-four minutes for females driving an automobile, according to a study by the U.S. Department of Transportation (1998). Techno-colonized person enjoys this time in the auto and perceives hurtling speedily down the road as his or her "time to think and enjoy being alone." This auto-meditative attitude is more pronounced among the young, declining with age, and also increases with wealth (Edmonson 1998).

Far from the view of modern culture as a purely rationalizing system, there is this other side to it, its need to make connection to the human soul. American consumer culture, for example, represents a fully technototemic system in place. Do you need to make up a personal name for your automobile when it's already a Mustang, a Stingray, a Cobra, a Jaguar? If you want to display your luxus, what better way than through a Lexus?

The American car system functions as a crucial part of this consumer technototemic system. It is a pure example of a technical system at work, and yet it needs to attach irrational symbols of desire, either predatory or sexual, to itself, to a machine. Driving becomes a technical form of hunting or eroticism or luxury or musical emotion or even meditation, and the auto experience is supposed to confer those qualities onto the owner or the driver.

The word automobile means self-moving and that is an important part of the symbolism of cars. One can not only move in a solitary place, seemingly away from the rat race even while driving in it, but one also obtains the freedom to move within the social system.

American culture today highlights the more general modern battle between autonomy and the automaton. The great dream of the modern era has been to provide for and enlarge the autonomy of humankind through technical invention and control over the necessities of life. As that dream has been realized, it has all too frequently revealed itself in diabolical reversal. The vast technical culture and wealth of America have not led the way toward the good life but instead toward the goods life, toward a reified culture centered in commodities rather than citizens, toward an ultimate goal of automatic things and away from human autonomy. This is not the necessary outcome of the development of technology but the consequence of the withering of human purpose in the face of the "magic" of technique. Not only did the 1980s signify the new phase of the electronics revolution under way but also something more sinister. It was as if the long-held human tension between fear of and fascination for the robotic finally dissolved, as if the fascination for the magic of the automation overwhelmed the understandable fears for its power to alienate the human and left only the ideal of fusion of humans with the powerful instruments of the automatic: humanoids, terminators, carbon-based units.

Perhaps the young child playing with "transformer" robots, the older child playing video games and mall cruising, the adult in a health club exercising on an electronic bicycle while watching a video display or a large-screen television picture of a route are all symbols of an emergent creature that willingly would prefer to live in "virtual reality" than the real thing. Yet who can deny the conveniences that the machines launched in the 1980s and 1990s afford? Still the question is whether they truly enhance autonomy or automatism, and clearly both outcomes are possible.

Probably you, dear reader, and surely I would defend the word-processing computer as providing greater autonomy. But talk to an office worker whose keystrokes are being monitored or who has suffered repetitive-motion damage. What books are left unread on the shelf by the video-game-expert child? What drain does each additional device put on time families spend together in the home? The fact that the family meal has been increasingly fragmented through individualized microwaved meals, through the intrusion of television, through increased dependence on fast-food restaurants ought to be taken as a sign of how increasingly difficult it is to do simple activities together, relatively unintruded upon by high-tech.

The presumed purpose of the high-tech household is to transfer everyday necessities—heating, cooking, cleaning, and so forth—to machines to enlarge "leisure time." Yet leisure is itself largely a machine activity in America. Consider that the average American spent 3,000 hours consuming media in 1988, of which 1,550 hours were devoted to television and 1,160 to radio. It is alleged that the average American household has a television on for eleven hours per day, watched or not. These numbing numbers suggest that Americans devote an enormous amount of time to the daily habit of listening and watching. Americans seemed to enter the 1980s as "joggers" and to exit as quasi-stationary couch potatoes, going on to computer jockey status in the 1990s. Perhaps the great tendency to sit—in autos and in front of televisions—was perhaps offset somewhat by a reported rise in the "standing breakfast" eaten next to a kitchen counter, or by stand-up eating in fast-food restaurants. But these standing and sitting patterns only testify to overly mechanized life.

As part of the larger dynamics of the modern era, American culture has transformed technique from a means to the good life to a virtual goal unto itself, with the result that Americans have increasingly seemed to be willing to sacrifice the art and practice and struggles of concrete life to the conveniences of abstract technique: to give up the active cultivation of home life to the passive consumption of TV, TV dinners, take-out and fast road food; to multipurpose centers for civic life and local commerce; to self-enclosed, privatized, behavior-monitoring shopping malls; to surrender the pursuit of autonomy to the accumulation of dollars and the identity-confirming rituals of consumption.

In real life, as the expression goes, shit happens. Virtual automatic consumption culture is designed, in stark contrast, to habituate us to an ideal technokitsch realm immunized from the necessary baggage of human life. To the extent that it does, it sucks from us the anchors of everyday life, those problematic face-to-face relations with family, friends, neighbors, and coworkers that are anything but ideal and that, precisely in their limitations, force us to find our way in a common world. And for people living on the edges of sanity, those social anchors may be all that is keeping them from plunging, lemminglike, into the abyss.

GEAR CHANGE

The Triumph of Potterville

In the 1946 Hollywood Christmas film, *It's a Wonderful Life,* actor Jimmy Stewart's character, George, depressed and suicidal, experiences a vision of what it would be like if he had never been born. His small town becomes a glittery sin-city, Potterville, named after the heartless town millionaire. George sees that his job as town banker has been crucial in keeping the community spirit alive and not just ensuring the economic welfare of his neighbors and fellow citizens. He returns from his hopelessness, renewed as the solid-guy-who-holds-the-town-together, and succeeds in the end in staving off Potterville. Decency overcomes unbounded capitalistic greed and human baseness.

Moving from this image of late Depression and wartime America to 1950s postwar-prosperity America, something far worse happens in the small-town myth. In the 1956 sci-fi classic *The Invasion of the Body Snatchers*, the doctor, played by Kevin McCarthy, cannot hold the center together, losing everything—his town, his patients, his neighbors and friends, and even the object of his love, Becky.

Worse, the town is not lost to the tyrant but to the postpersonality system of emotionless, conforming drones—just as Vaclav Havel depicted the ascendance of the *posttotalitarian system* in the West. By posttotalitarian he meant that totalitarianism, far from being over, had entered a new phase, shifting from the cult of personality characterizing the first generation of totalitarianism—with its Stalin, Hitler, Mussolini, Franco, and Atatürk—to a system running on virtual "automatic pilot." Similarly, by a postdemocratic system, I mean a society that has lost its grounded democratic processes—ranging from vital neighborhood institutions to national political culture—in favor of the automatic pilot of media, commercial, and celebrity system requirements.

Like its posttotalitarian counterpart, the postdemocratic system that was under assembly in the 1950s and that shifted into higher gear by the 1990s selects for an elite of cool-thinking functionaries, expanding their vegetative ways (Halton 1999). Perhaps "Microsoft Man" would be a good term for this being, though the suggestion of a gender—male or female—however diminished, still seems beyond the capacities of this neutered creature. If the 1950s had its "organization man," who pledged allegiance to his company, perhaps the 1990s has seen the emergence of the postorganization person, whose only allegiance is to the system in general, regardless of the particular company or country.

One could take the various *Star Trek* TV series and movies as personifying this rootless elite, alienated from family, friends, and neighborhood; living in a purely artificial convenience enclosure, militaristic, progress-oriented; and propelled by extreme bewildering mobility. These are precisely the elites Christopher Lasch spoke of in his book, *The Revolt of the Elites and the Betrayal of Democracy*:

> Those who covet membership in the new aristocracy of brains tend to congregate on the coasts, turning their back on the heartland and cultivating ties with the international market in fast-moving money, glamour, fashion, and popular culture. It is a question of whether they think of themselves as Americans at all. . . . The new elites are at home only in transit, en route to a high-level conference, to the grand opening of a new franchise, to an international film festival, or to an undiscovered resort. Theirs is essentially a tourist's view of the world—not a perspective likely to encourage a passionate devotion to democracy. (1996:6)

Though the elite pictured by *Star Trek* has grown more gender-equal and "multicultural" over the years, not much has changed regarding the characters' alienation from their home planet or their colonizing—while appearing not to interfere—"prime directive." What is their real prime directive? To extend the federation of machines.

GEAR CHANGE

From Metropolis to Dark City: The Triumph of Post-Potterville

The recent science-fiction film *Dark City* (1998) chillingly pictures a virtual bee-hive of drones, soullessly searching for the enigmatic human soul while "experimenting" with tortures through nightly identity changes. Unlike medieval or modern torture chambers and their consciously induced pain, this urbanoid zone practices its experiments painlessly, taking its victims' identities instead of their physical lives through a form of circadian colonization. It is a kind of photo negative of Albert Camus's absurdist novel, *The Stranger*, whose strange hero, Meurseult, inhabits a world in which, as he puts it, "nothing matters," not even his shooting a man to death at the beach. In *Dark City*, by contrast, nothing matters to anyone except to the one falsely accused of murder, John Murdoch. Instead of a public concerned more with the keeping of convention than justice, here it is the strange chorus, insectlike, for whom nothing seems to matter. Known as "the strangers," they are dressed in trench coats ominously resonant with the group of alienated students of Columbine High School in Littleton, Colorado, who called themselves the "trench coat mafia," two of whose members would explode in a murderous and suicidal rage a year after the release of the movie.

In seeing the film, I suddenly imagined the strangers in the movie as a kind of cloned colony of Meurseult, the antihero of *The Stranger*. They gather every midnight in this night world to "tune," to chatter shrill little sounds, the result of which is a continually altering memoryscape projected into the city and into the shifting postmodern identities of its inhabitants. Buildings expand or shrink, new features appear, all is an unconscious mobility of place and identity, like a time-lapse film of contemporary life, a postmodern, constantly shifting Potemkin village.

The hero, Murdoch, somehow shares their "special" ability to tune. He is the individual, pitted against the mass of drones and power elite. He has a character that transcends the roles into which he is nightly projected.

The landscape is utterly claustrophobic: an old-time Hollywood grade-B detective-movie feel, set in a New York around the 1930s. There is no nature throughout the movie, not even urban nature: no trees, no fountains, not even a lawn. When Murdoch finally uses his tuning abilities in the finale, he creates a sun and an ocean beach. But it too is an illusory reality, set on a flat plane with swirling clouds, but no glorious globe of Earth. Murdoch, who shares that alien power, remains unable to conceive a natural planet or to return home again from virtual land. He gets the girl in a sentimentalized virtual reality through the same powers that the aliens possessed. Mind power—but no real soul power.

As in the 1982 film *Blade Runner*, there is the sci-fi fantasy of lost memory, lost identity, everything the life of the "false self." And *Blade Runner*, continuing a theme from Karel Capek's 1921 play, *R.U.R. (Rossum's Universal Robots)*, shows the machines to be more human than the humans who lost themselves through mechanistic master–slave delusions.

In *Blade Runner*, four advanced androids return to earth, the home they are forbidden to see because they are too indistinguishable from humans, to find their maker and learn how to prolong their lives beyond their allotted four years. They have all been programmed with false memories of childhoods and with special abilities by their genius "father," the head of the android corporation. These creatures have no maternity and function as one might expect humans deprived of the early childhood narcissistic phase of mother attachment and separation anxiety that occurs between the ages of one-and-a-half and three. They search desperately for the empathic connection that never was, for the gaze of care and warmth, using "special gifts" they possess.

Their extraordinary abilities of strength, sexuality, and cunning were "installed" as survival mechanisms but function psychologically in the all-too-human androids as compensations for abandonment. For they have unexpectedly begun to experience real human emotions, real empathy for each other if not for humans, and the urgent need to find their real humanity becomes murderous narcissistic rage. This is most poignantly illustrated when the android played by Rutger Hauer penetrates the high-security high-rise corporate ziggurat of the android corporation and confronts his maker about his origins and life expectancy. He cradles his surrogate "father's" head in both of his hands, looks him lovingly in the eyes, kisses him, and then proceeds to crush his skull.

Capek's play similarly involves a riff on Nietzsche—showing the potential dark consequences of Übermenschen, as the following dialogue illustrates:

Harry Domin: "I wanted to turn the whole of mankind into an aristocracy of the world. An aristocracy nourished by millions of mechanical slaves. Unrestricted, free, and consumated in man. And maybe more than man."

Alquist: "Super-man?"

In 1921, Capek saw the false promise of the machine and "progress": the old Mephistophelean deal in shiny metallic clothing. Fritz Lang pictured it well too in his film *Metropolis* in 1926. The pure exercise of the will to power releases powers beyond the ability to limit them. Such powers become "agents" unto themselves: robot nuclear weapons dictate world politics; robot automobiles dictate automotive habits of life; robot computers, televisions, bank tellers, and sex machines liberate from direct experience in the name of convenience.

Machines are the latest episode of the old master–slave relationship, and the world today is like the Jewish story of the golem that was prominent in Kapek's Prague. A rabbi made a golem, which grew throughout the day and served him. At the end of the day, the rabbi would put ashes on the forehead of the golem and it would die. One day he forgot to eradicate the golem, which continued to grow through the night, monstrous, and when the rabbi awoke, he found his "will to power" willed to a superhuman level, which then annihilated him.

Dark City strikes me as an important movie, though flawed, that pictures the dire state of virtual lives people exhibit today and that also finds expression in the ideas of the leading lights of social thought and philosophy. The last android of *Blade Runner*, played by Rutger Hauer, found his humanity at the conclusion of the film in letting his hunter, the blade runner played by Harrison Ford, live. But John Murdoch, protagonist of *Dark City*, merely assumes the power of the inhuman strangers, using it to project his own narcissistic, sentimentalized fantasy.

The highly efficient, highly stratified economy of the hive was discovered sixty million years ago by bees and ants, and now humanity thinks its own technological version of it represents "progress," caring little for the simple fact that as we become antlike and beelike, we forfeit all those qualities of empathy, spontaneity, and freedom that helped make us human.

GEAR CHANGE

What is "normal" in the consumption system of today may not be "normal" for a rich home life, neighborhood life, and civic life, because these things require qualities such as love, friendship, trust, sharing, and forgiveness. These domestic qualities are not as easily bought and sold, yet they are crucial for truly being "normal" in a vital way. Even more basically, a home is a place where memories should be far richer than any computer could store, where the home-cooked meal should be a prized standard of cooking, where intimacy requires a self not completely encased in a commodity-driven identity, where things are means or testaments to the practice of life rather than emblems and trophies of some great baboon hierarchy.

GEAR CHANGE

Scientists have discovered many amazing things in the past century, but is it possible to be right in the details and fundamentally wrong in the big picture? The ancient Hindus described a cyclical picture of the universe whose decline, the "kali yuga," corresponds to our present scientific time. It is a time of childish rampant destruction.

How is it that these "unscientific" ancient philosophers, using subjective sensing of the human creature and its follies, say such things, while "wise" scientists proclaim progress throughout the twentieth century? Think of that worldview of the religion of modern science that flowered in midcentury with its hydrogen bombs and totalitarian scientifically planned societies, with its cult that society could be governed by scientific principles: by bomb makers; by replacing mother's milk with "formula"; by building more and more roads and cars, more and more technology; by transforming all "undeveloped" forests and lands into modern, scientifically planned agricultural centers; by exterminating bugs with DDT; by transforming universities into research grant junkies; by building ever more complex machines that would free us from our drudgery through our increased dependence upon them. Here is an example of the power of science for you, from a priest of one of its deadliest temples, the Atomic Energy Commission: "Large nuclear explosives give us, for the first time, the capability to remedy nature's oversights" (1971:188).

This is indeed a worldvision of infinite possibilities, where, as Dostoyevsky's Grand Inquisitor predicted, "Everything is permitted." Only we have discovered that everything is not permitted, that one cannot format natural finitude according to scientific megalomania.

For that is what the big picture of science and technology has shown itself to be time and time again in the twentieth century: a crypto-religion of arrogant cult scientism, led by emotional infants (albeit intelligent and skillful infants). I don't think that is the real essence of science, any more than I believe organized religions express the real nature of religious feeling, but that is how the culture of science, institutionally, has repeatedly revealed itself.

Where were the scientists during the first half of the century who saw the dark and dangerous possibilities of the powers science was releasing? Why did it take a "fool" such as Henry Adams, using logically incorrect methods on the rise of power over the last few centuries, to predict in 1905 that it would not take another half century for there to be "bombs of cosmic violence," and conditions in which morality would become police and disintegration overcome integration? Why did it take a fiction writer such as H. G. Wells to call attention in his 1913 novel, *The World Set Free*, to the dangers of what he called "atomic bombs," in a war he placed at midcentury?

Why did humans evolve under conditions of reverence and awe, conditions that have sustained humans until modern "scientific" times? Do you think hominids could have evolved into humans under the kinds of scientific, technical, bureaucratic, ideological, academic, and artistic thinking that have predominated in the twentieth century? The answer is no. This would have been a starvation diet to the fierce passionate creatures who created us.

GEAR CHANGE

Normal Man normally kills that which does not fit into Normality. Traditionally he kills the inspired wise man. The wise man's followers form a religion or school. Then that religion or school becomes normal and kills its own original impulses to ensure that no genuine inspirations will happen again.

Creativity seems to work like that. Normal people like to steal the creativity and kill the creative one so that they can possess the creativity. Their very possession and use of it renders it normal and no longer creative. But they often do appropriate the worldly success.

Take al-Hallaj, a tenth-century Muslim from Baghdad who allowed his religious passion to flow—so of course he had to be put to death. Why was al-Hallaj, with his wonderful sense of play and irony, not a founder of a religion as were Jesus and Mohammed, who both seem to me so earnest? Who knows whether Jesus was killed a second time—and for me this would be his real death—by his normalizing followers, who deleted his sense of play and other unacceptable qualities, and "earnesthetized" him?

This battle goes on in us, individually, too. And that is why the poet and painter William Blake proposed a marriage between heaven and hell. Without those corrosives and fiery inspirations, we would go inert. Maybe that's why the bumper sticker says, "I like heaven for the climate, hell for the company."

Consider the contemporary image-consumption culture in this light. It takes as its task the absorption of human emotion through its projection of virtual transcendence; of appearances of corrosives and fiery inspirations whose sources run deep in sex, war, and religion; of magic celebrities whose images and actions are so many stimuli producing emotionlike responses in the spectatorial lonely crowd. Consider a populace socialized into this world from early childhood, carefully trained to experience the extremes of human emotion in virtual scenarios of TV violence and commercial abundance. These bright images of contemporary consumption culture are beacons shining dark lights upon the human soul, the old Faust deal done under slow habituation. It is the dance of the bees, the simulated scents of simulated flowers, compelling the populace to the rules of the hive, making them feel as if they're alive!

GEAR CHANGE

Materialism and Normalcy: Why Be Normal?

I probably don't need to tell the reader that the word normal means norm or average. Norms that set healthy limits are necessary to any society. You can't live without some norms. Yet if one's ultimate goal is to become normal, that is giving up on one's own possibilities of development. To be a healthy person, you need to be immersed to a varying extent within family, household, work, city. Everybody has different levels and degrees by which they identify themselves.

We like to believe that—although it is a fantasy—we are rugged people as we drive our mechanical broncos and otherwise named totemic chariots. So we live these fantasies of rugged individualism, although in reality we reduce ourselves to a pathologically "normal" existence. We become the norm of a vast, mega-technic machine. We produce and are trained to consume mass quantities of *low-grade experience* as a key system requirement of postdemocratic society.

GEAR CHANGE

Mourning and Melodrama: Reflections from 1997 on Media Narcissism and Substitute Emotions

What is the proper place of heroes and celebrities in social life? Public figures are supposed to be people who do things that, for various reasons, place them in the public eye. But what happens when an excessive emphasis on commercially produced celebrity takes over the socialization process and defines who counts as public figures and heroes?

Take, for example, the way artificially manufactured celebrity replaces genuine achievement, as in the rise of so-called entertainment news, whose purpose is to promote celebrities and their nonnews, or the way normal news excessively panders to celebrity sensationalism. The normal process of having role models in the environment, with whom we can either identify or internalize in the dialogue of the self, gets replaced by the elevation of celebrities and the kind of virtual world that celebrities inhabit.

Instead of contributing to the cultivation of the self, the system infiltrates the self at the core of the identification process, that "glassy essence" of which Shakespeare wrote, binding its images to those processes the psychoanalysts call "object-relations" and the social psychologists call "role modeling." It taps the roots of human emotion with its image/sound/product scenarios of ecstatic sex, violence, death, and the longings for transcendence.

Cut to commercial.

Consider the following statement issued by CNN concerning the funeral for fashion designer Gianni Versace:

MILAN, Italy (CNN)—Naomi Campbell, one of Gianni Versace's favorite models, wept openly Tuesday as she, Princess Diana, Elton John, and scores of international celebrities came here to say goodbye to the murdered fashion designer at the first public memorial in his native land.

Some 2,000 people, including Versace's brother, Santo, his sister, Donatella, and his companion, Antonio D'Amico, packed Milan's gothic Roman Catholic cathedral for the service, one week after the Italian designer was gunned down outside his Miami Beach home. Authorities continued their hunt for the shooter, believed to be spree-killing suspect Andrew Cunanan.

Famous Faces in Mourning

Those from the fashion world in attendance included model Carla Bruni and designers Giorgio Armani, Karl Lagerfeld, Carla Fendi, and Tai Missoni. Also present were singer Sting; Carolyn Bessette, the wife of John Kennedy Jr.; and Italian ski star Alberto Tomba. Sting and Elton John were to sing a setting of Psalm 23, "The Lord is my shepherd." Italian opera star Luciano Pavarotti also was expected.

Campbell, wearing a black dress and jacket and dark glasses, had to be supported prior to the service as she walked to the Versace empire headquarters in Milan. She was doubled over and crying.

Princess Diana, who loved Versace's glamorous, sexy clothes, wore a black dress and white pearls. The designer had named a handbag after her—the Lady Di. The princess was seated next to John. The pop singer, a fan of Versace's flamboyant outfits, was dressed in a dark suit.

End commercial.

GEAR CHANGE, IN A DARK SUIT

Killing the Creator

Last year I received one of those phone calls from a journalist, one in which the reporter solicits your expert opinion on a subject not even remotely connected to your expertise. My call came from Christopher Mason, who was writing a biography of Gianni Versace (Mason unpublished manuscript). I told him I was no expert on celebrity, but if I had any insights on the subject, I would be happy to share them. In fact, the first part of our conversation was more me interviewing him. He told me how the supermodels who attended Versace's funeral had been feuding with Versace's company for the previous year. Nevertheless, their agencies flew them to Milan, and when they arrived at their lavish hotel suites, each found a black Versace dress in her size waiting for her—a kind of gift from the grave. Mason also told me of the friendship between Versace, Princess Di, and Elton John, and how they too had been feuding before Versace's death. As we spoke, I improvised a theory of Versace's murder: that Andrew Cunanan, his murderer, had a rage toward his father, who never recognized him. He transferred it to Versace, who Mason said apparently met Cunanan at the San Francisco Opera a few years earlier and recognized him from seeing him at some earlier time with an old friend.

I would like to take Cunanan as an example of the colonization of the self by consumer celebrity culture. He was someone who liked money and its luxuries, the "visibility" it makes possible, and who acquired them by being a "kept man," his expenses paid for by wealthy gay lovers, typically older men. He seems to be a textbook case of a narcissistic false-self disturbance, someone whose identity was largely based not only on the commodity forms it desired and acquired but also by himself becoming a commodity for his lovers: "someone's amusing trinket" as the *Miami Herald* put it in an editorial.

As forensic psychologist Reid Meloy stated in an interview, Cunanan's rage and wanton killing-spree exhibited "the horrible flowering and self-destruction of a high-velocity young psychopath. . . . No one would know the name Sirhan Sirhan unless he killed Robert Kennedy. No one would know Mark David Chapman unless he killed John Lennon. Destroying a figure of that stature links you to that figure in perpetuity" (Viglucci 1997).

If Cunanan illustrates a self extrinsically shaped by exhibitionistic markers of prestige, masking an underlying narcissistic rage and psychopathic manipulativeness, then the breakdown of that false self—and consequent release of the rage—might be expected to find its target in the self-images it could destroy: ex-lovers, older wealthy men, and finally by a celebrity who once paid him attention by recognizing him. One can see how a narcissistically disordered self whose real feelings had been replaced by those of the consumption and status and celebrity world could be led by his self-images and released rage to destroy a celebrity, his Creator, the creator of his false self. In destroying the celebrity self-image, he could simultaneously merge with it, as another well-known raging American, Captain Ahab, did with his grandiose self-image, the whale Moby Dick.

Cunanan's creator, personified by Versace, was, like himself, a poor kid from a Catholic country who made it big in America, made it big in the world, was in a close friendship triangle with the megacelebrities Princess Di and Elton John.

And a month after Versace's celebrity murder, his friend Princess Di topped his death with an even more perfect celebrity death, resulting from the infamous chasing of her auto by the Parisian paparazzi. Her death provided an international outpouring of emotions, a perfect synthesis of mourning and celebrity, tapping the traditional idealization of royalty and fusing it with a woman whose image bridged Mother Teresa's Eastern world of poverty and suffering with *la Dolce Vita* of the West—not to mention a genuine "playboy of the Western World" of Middle-Eastern extraction, Dodi Fayed. No soap opera could come close to this script: talk about "global village"! But let us return to the American melodrama, the killing of the Italian celebrity in Miami by the Filipino boy-toy.

When Mason told me that Versace's everyday friends sat in the back of the funeral services in Milan because of the celebrities filling the front rows, I asked, "He wouldn't have wanted that, would he?" Mason replied enthusiastically that, quite to the contrary, a celebrity funeral would be precisely what Versace would have wanted, that he basked in the celebrity spotlight, thoroughly enjoying surrounding himself with other celebrities.

Think about it. You can buy your identity by buying a fine set of clothes, by watching the celebrity images of fashion. This is the profane level of everyday consumption culture.

Or you can go to the sacred level by appropriating the Creator himself—instead of buying through the medium of money, killing through the medium of a gun. You attain immortality in this act of identification with the Creator. If "clothes make the man," merging in death with the Clothes Creator makes the man immortal.

Cunanan had an intermediary step: he killed a Chicago businessman "father" and stole some of his suits with the car—a Lexus—and money. He acquired clothing through the bullet method of down payment, which also helped point the way toward the Creator.

Jesus killed sex and aggression: no sex with the Holy Mary Oedipal Mother, no sex with the prostitute Mary "lover." No aggression toward the Heavenly Father who condemned him to death, no aggression toward the carpentry inflicted upon him on the cross, which cut close to his earthly and absent father's own profession.

Cunanan the "altar boy," as his father described him in denying his son's homosexuality, could not act against his earthly father, who had come to America, failed financially, and returned home. But when all mediating defenses were undone, he could go straight to the heavenly father, the former altar boy Versace, who had risen from poverty and made it big in America. Like the androids in *Blade Runner*, he could seek out Versace and merge with him and his immortal celebrity in a final act of murderous, suicidal aggression: He could merge as the anti-prodigal son with the Creator, the Father, the Godfather, and the extrinsic identity!

Ironically, in doing so, he provided his earthly father with a potential for windfall profit. The elder Cunanan responded to the media by making almost immediate plans to have a film made about his son.

America is not only the land of democratic virtual royalty, it is the home of celebrity virtual Olympus, of a virtual heaven that is nevertheless becoming increasingly globalized.

Perhaps in this strange media melodrama, Princess Di is the new celebrity female Jesus, Versace is the good thief, Elton John—though not yet dead—is the bad thief, Mother Teresa is Holy Mother, George Solti—who also died in 1997—conducts in the background, while Madonna dances in her autoerotic "truth or dare" virtual video world in the actual grave of her mother. Meanwhile real human dramas and tragedies go unnoticed, thousands die in auto accidents—like the friend of an acquaintance who died in an auto accident in Spain two weeks before Princess Di and whose body required weeks of waiting before it could be returned to England for the funeral—and millions and millions of quiet lives of desperation remain attuned to the Great Broadcast of the technomaniacal media cult.

GEAR CHANGE

Consider the irony in this large claim I am making: the mechanical system of nature that replaced the Aristotelian worldview by the seventeenth century did so by ejecting teleology from nature. Yet, I am claiming, it secretly retains that teleology in its mythic goal of dehumanization. But how is it possible for a nonteleological mechanical system to do this? It is possible, in my opinion, because that entire system, the very basis for modern science and civilization, is a grand social construction, a mythic projection of that automatic side of the human psyche onto the world. It is a mythic projection that must fundamentally deny that not only are the machines of humans themselves projections of the human mind, but that the machine image of the universe is a projection of a portion of the human mind, of its automatic aspects, which must necessarily exclude the autonomous aspects.

So much of human life is engaged in the tension between the automatic and the autonomous, the rote habitual and the spontaneous engagement of the moment. The course of modern civilization has also been the simultaneous development of the automatic and the autonomous; of the mechanical features of existence one sees in the developments of natural science and the subjective dimensions of existence one sees in the rise of the novel, of perspective in painting, of tonality in music.

In the twentieth century, it was as if the cultural corpus callosum joining these two sides of the modern mind broke, leaving parallel but relatively incommunicable courses for each. Modern art embodied this split in its tendencies, especially by midcentury, toward purely "objective" or purely "subjective" works.

What Schoenberg intended in his serial music was one thing, what it resulted in—institutionally—was a rationalization of music comparable to the rationalization of architecture in the "international style"; to the rationalization of philosophy on logical positivism and Anglo-American "language analysis"; to psychological behaviorism; to scientism; to hyperrationalized, bureaucratized corporate and communist culture. As all these tendencies were particularly dominant in the 1950s, a rationalizing tendency whose other split-brain opposite in the twentieth century was formlessness, for example, John Cage's aleatoric, or "chance," music. From the burst of energy at the beginning of the century came an unenviable legacy: lifeless forms, formless life, subjectless objects, objectless subjects, the "originality" of nothingness, the realization of the ghost in the machine, the unintended consequence of the "via moderna," the end of modernism.

Though several artists—some yet to emerge—did not capitulate to the "advanced" image of pure subjectivism or objectivism, the majority of "avant-garde" artists did, only to find themselves on a dead-end street. Even postmodernism, as a movement, again, with exceptions, could not provide an alternative: If modernism is ultimately a dead end, postmodernism is the "no exit" sign at the end of the dead-end street.

GEAR CHANGE

If we think of America since the second world war, it may be good to remember that freedom was something very much in the air from a variety of perspectives—cold warriors, civil rights seekers, nascent feminists, teens cruising, artists seeking it or celebrating it through their work. Because today the very idea of freedom seems to have been reduced to that of the "freedom" to consume, to a consumption culture that truly found its form in the very same automaniacal, franchising 1950s.

Take the brainwashing of children and their parents by television—by thousands upon thousands of acts of anxiety (an average of three thousand per day) relieved by the purchase of a commodity, which is the basic physiological stimulus–response formula of commercials, and by thousands of acts of unfelt violence, by endless images of overflowing magical luxury, by a world of disposable celebrities who provide the children who identify with them substitute emotions the same way that drugs promise substitute feelings. Buy me, eat me, drink me, drive me, and you can be spontaneous, says the new Moloch of Megatechnic America. This is the reality of early education in America—mind-altering electro-chemical indoctrination—and why students can tell you everything about *I Love Lucy* and *Friends* while remaining clueless about the whys and whens of real history, outside of the box of the celebrity-image machine.

Or take the ways preemptive behavior-monitoring tests and surveillance in schools and the workplace are on the rise or of surveillance in malls. I suppose the point is that if you indoctrinate schoolchildren into submission to the surveillance state early on, they will grow up to be more docile to such losses of freedom at work and in the consumption zones and sheeplike in the loss of their neighborhoods when powerful and distant corporations so decree. For even more important to the surveillance sector and its agents and "educators" is to make students docile to the dictates of the bureaucratic consumption state and its technical devices of sedation. A conforming, consuming, dependent populace is much safer than a free and independent citizenry.

The celebrity machine functions as a great fantasia, providing all the virtual requirements of life, while it quietly absorbs the self as its "soul food." There is nothing new in this, perhaps: the ancient Romans knew that bread and circuses kept the population subservient. But what is different in the new "pax electronica" is that the entire mechanical universe of modern civilization has as its hidden teleology the absorption and ultimate replacement of human life with its own humanoid image: brain-suck.

BIBLIOGRAPHY

Adams, Henry (1947). *Henry Adams and His Friends*, ed. Harold D. Carter. Boston: Houghton Mifflin.

U.S. Atomic Energy Commission (1971). In *Man and the Atom: Building a New World through Nuclear Technology*, ed. Glenn T. Seaborg and William Corliss. New York: Dutton.

Edmondson, Brad (1998). "In the Driver's Seat," *American Demographics,* March.

Halton, Eugene (1999). "The Truth about That Quiet Decade," *Notre Dame Magazine*, May:43–48.

Lasch, Christopher (1996). *The Revolt of the Elites and the Betrayal of Democracy*. New York: Norton.

Mason, Christopher (unpublished manuscript). *Undressed: The Life and Times of Gianni Versace*.

U.S. Dept. of Transportation (1998). *National Personal Transportation Survey*. Washington, D.C.: U.S. Government Printing Office.

Viglucci, Andres (1997). "Last Piece of the Puzzle Is Gone with a Gunshot," *Miami Herald*, Friday, July 25.

Wells, H. G. ([1913] 1988). *The World Set Free*. London: Hogarth.

6

The Rise of "The Toddler" as Subject and as Merchandising Category in the 1930s

Daniel Thomas Cook

The ongoing hegemony of capitalism depends upon the continual integration of person with commodity. Basic, everyday notions of what makes a self and what constitutes a person figure strongly in the reproduction of capitalist culture to the extent that they serve as mediums for the realization of, and the time–space travel for, both economic and symbolic exchange value (see Marx 1978; Baudrillard 1981; Kopytoff 1986). Capitalism (re)produces its own culture(s) when the equation between self/person and the commodity form articulates with other historically embedded meanings, values, social relations, and institutions (see Comaroff and Comaroff 1997; Slater 1997; Leach 1993a; Featherstone 1991a, 1991b; Lears 1983).

The equation of self/person with commodity, like the process of cultural reproduction, is never exhaustive. Ample space exists for resistance to structurally given meaning. Agency is often exercised on a variety of levels and in a variety of social and cultural contexts (Radway 1984; Gottdiener 1985; Press 1990). This chapter focuses on a historical moment when one aspect of value equivalence materialized in a category of person the agency of whose members is problematic. What follows offers a perspective on part of a historical process referred to as the "commodification of childhood" by interrogating some relevant contexts out of which the "toddler"—as a named phase of the life course, as subject, and as merchandising category—arose during the 1930s in the United States.

Examining the rise of the toddler not only gives insight into how consumer culture emerges historically (Ewen 1976; McKendrick, Brewer, and Plumb 1982; Marchand 1985; Leach 1993b; Slater 1997) but also gestures toward opening a space for examining how something akin to a "consumption ethic" (Campbell 1989) reproduces itself over time. Consumers are made, not born. The tie between self and commodity becomes an intimate one when it is passed along between peers and through generations, that is, when it becomes (echoing C. W. Mills) part of both biography and history. The twin processes of learning to be a consumer and of the commodification of social relations occur at different levels of abstraction and in different cadences of time; they nevertheless rely upon each other. Neither occurs without some form of agency yet neither is isomorphic with autonomy. The case of "the toddler" speaks to some of the ways that agency can reproduce, and be reproduced in, commercial relations.

ON COMMODITIES, CHILDHOOD, AND COMMERCIAL PERSONAE

This chapter centers on how childhood has developed into a site for commercial activity in the twentieth century. The larger work from which this chapter is derived examines the rise, growth, and segmentation of the children's clothing industry in the United States, focusing particularly on the 1917–67 period. During this time, children emerged as consumers in their own right and childhood became a primary social medium for the creation and exchange of commercial value.

The empirical core of this endeavor consists of the statements, images, and documents produced primarily by those in the children's wear industry's trade press, *Earnshaw's Review* (initially called the *Infants' Department*), beginning in 1917. These serve as entry points into the public perspectives of those who sought to create and maintain a mass market for children's clothing. This discussion investigates how these cultural brokers rhetorically, visually, and symbolically have depicted "the child" (Cook 1999, 2000) and "the mother" (Cook 1995) as personae amenable to a market for consumer goods. In so doing, the way in which these actors collectively crafted particular versions of childhood (and motherhood) as sites for commercial activity and expansion are demonstrated.

It is assumed that the "meaning" of a garment, image, or good, like a piece of art, is constitutive of the actions performed on it by various actors, individual and corporate (see Becker 1982). In this case, these actors execute agendas in a context that may be tangential to, even independent of, the realm of childhood and children proper—the context of a market economy. Examining the agendas of the producers and sellers of children's wear allows one to problemitize their portrayals of children and childhood and to see them as a form of commercially motivated depiction rather than arising spontaneously from some collective ethos.

The "commodities" in this case consist not only of physical materials— children's garments and related goods—but also of discursive materials forged by the producers, retailers, and press in and through time. It is these discursive materials that serve to create the context in which an item can become a commodity. Commodity production, at least since the modern industrial period, is never exhausted with the making and selling of its good. Rather, commodity production always implicates the existence of and, indeed, the creation of social statuses, identities, and images; in short, the creation of symbolic persons or personae. (See for instance Csikszentmihalyi and Rochberg-Halton 1981; Baudrillard 1981; Lears 1983; Featherstone 1991b.)

In this work, it is those personages arising in and from the children's wear trade press—"commercial personae"—that are at issue. Commercial personae are assemblages of characteristics—known or conjectured, real or imagined—constructed by and traded among interested parties in the service of their industry. They are the negotiable currency of a merchant-class ideology that seeks to comprehend its subject, "the consumer" in the abstract, with the goals of opening new markets and of maintaining/expanding old ones. To put it another way, to "give the customers what they want" implies that the merchant somewhere and somehow proffers a model of those customers. Here, the customer becomes an admixture of specified quantities and intensities of priorities, concerns, abilities, wants, needs, and motivations. A commercial persona consists of both statements and images that together give shape to these imputed characteristics.

The commodification of childhood (and motherhood) in this way addresses the creation of social persons in commercial space. It refers to a historical process whereby childhood, as a phase of the life cycle, acquires exchange values in and for the larger market sphere. In the process, the figure of "the child" becomes a prime carrier of meaning and thus of value.

ON THE SACRED AND PROFANE

The commodification of childhood is entangled with a fundamental tension endemic to modern, Western childhood—that between the sacred and the profane. According to Viviana Zelizer (1985), a profound change in the economic and sentimental value of children took place between the 1870s and 1930s. Examining debates about child labor and children's life insurance, she argues that children had been expelled from the "cash nexus" of the American economy for largely cultural reasons relating to a child's sacred or sentimental "worth." Over this time, a child's value was measured less and less in economic–monetary terms and became constituted increasingly in sentimental–emotional ones. Except in some limited cases, Zelizer claims, children essentially had become extra-commercium—economically and productively useless (1985:11).

Zelizer's argument about the moral pricelessness of the economically worthless child in the twentieth century offers a great deal of food for thought and opportunity for expansion. The expulsion of young children from nearly all wage-earning, productive activity during this time signaled not the end of their economic participation but a fundamental change in it. As working-class children were gradually liberated from direct production over the first third of this century, middle-class childhood increasingly became a site for morally mediated consumption.

In the first three decades of the twentieth century, Americans witnessed the rise and proliferation of mass-produced goods specifically designed, manufactured, and merchandised for children, such as clothing, toys, furniture, and nursery ware (Cook 1995; Kline 1993:143–73; Leach 1993a; Leach 1993b:85–90, 328–30; Forty 1986:67–72). Since that time, the market for children's goods has burgeoned into an industry worth tens of billions of dollars annually in the United States alone (McNeal 1992:39–41). Market researchers have found that children influence the purchase of items such as major appliances, cars, and homes as well as the products for their own use (McNeal 1992; Guber and Berry 1993). Images of children have been brought to the service of many industries throughout the twentieth century in the form of advertising personae (Cook 1999; 2000), and children regularly star in television commercials hawking a variety of goods, many of which are not intended for children's specific use (e.g., automobile tires). Dozens of magazines, television shows, weekly or daily sections in newspapers, networks, and Web sites presently vie for children's attention, including *Sports Illustrated for Kids* and *Totally Kids* (the latter published by the Fox Children's Network). Many of these publications and shows laud the child as an expert on consumption and provide their own product-judgment panels or news columns in which children critique the merits of the newest shows, goods, and media stars.

Something of an accommodation between the marketplace and childhood has taken place. Under the tutelage of capitalism in the twentieth century, childhood has not been leveled to or equalized with all other commodity values as Georg Simmel ([1900] 1978); Karl Marx (1978: especially 101–6 and 302–29), and to a different extent, Max Weber ([1904–05] 1958) would have it. The peculiar ability of the capitalist market to equate disparate values under the umbrella of abstract Value has been met with the equally peculiar ability of culture to create meaning in the most diverse ways (see Comaroff and Comaroff 1997; Zelizer 1985; Lamont 1992; Parry and Bloch 1989; Kopytoff 1986). In fact, it would seem that childhood has intensified in its sacred–sentimental value even as a children's consumer culture has grown, as evidenced by rising public concern with child abuse, school violence, abortion, and other issues (see Best 1990; Woolons 1993; Giroux 1998).

The question then arises: how has "sacred childhood" come to coexist more or less alongside, or integrated with, the "profane market"? The tension that Zelizer identifies does not disappear but transforms. It transforms with changing social and economic circumstances and, in the process, authorizes the construct of "the child" as person, and thus as consumer. The tension between "child" and "market" is taken as the engine driving the emergence and growth of a now ubiquitous children's consumer culture, rather than as a foil to it.

There are two fundamental ways to reconcile "the child" with "the market." One is to (re)define commodities as beneficial/functional for children. When goods become framed as "useful," they become means to ends rather than intended for mere consumption or display. The most common way to frame children's goods as "useful" is to situate them directly in the child's growth and development.

Child development—the process of moving through predictable, specifiable, and sequential stages of the early life course—remains the quintessential mode for the adjudication of what may be legitimized as "beneficial" to children. Parents, especially mothers, can avoid being labeled hedonistic or ostentatious by purchasing products and engaging in activities that assist (or at least do not impede) a process of growth that is thought to be sanctioned by the timeless authority of "nature." At the same time, "useful" goods and their merchants can elude the criticism of being exploitative of innocent children or well-meaning mothers (see Seiter 1993:64–67).

The second way is to (re)define children themselves as persons who have the wherewithal and the right to be desirous of goods. Once children become treated more or less as autonomous, volitional subjects, they lose part of the cloak of sacredness and are enfranchised as participants in and through the marketplace. The functionality of products, the felt imperatives of development, and the definition of children as active, volitional consumers have, from time to time, served as alibis or justifications for the production, promotion, and consumption of children's goods. They are not exclusive of one another but intertwine in such a way that each strand remains identifiable.

Toys and books are also implicated in child development and the commodification of childhood and thus figure in the moral dimensions of consumption but in different ways and to different extents than clothing. Clothing speaks daily and publicly to the presentation of self. Clothing and personal display are visible in a continuous manner, whereas toys and books are intermittent, less conspicuous markers of consumption and social status. Perhaps because clothing is tied intimately to the body and the social self, it becomes a moral concern as toys do not (see Cross 1998; Kline 1993; Seiter 1993; Leach 1993a). Historically, "the toddler"—as subject, commercial persona, and merchandising category—arose in the arena of personal display during the period when the pattern of framing children's goods in functional and developmental terms was being set.

THE RISE OF CHILDREN'S WEAR

Children's wear industry pioneer George Earnshaw made extensive use of the first tactic throughout the 1920s on the pages of the *Infants' Department*—the industry's first trade journal, which he began publishing in 1917.[1] As discussed elsewhere (Cook 1995), Earnshaw deployed the rhetorical construct of the "mother as consumer" to persuade clothing buyers and department store managers that separate infants' departments were necessary and profitable.[2] This white, middle-class mother was said to be in a position to purchase garments for her children for two different reasons: an agentive one—out of "instinctual love" for her child; and a structural one—due to her position as "purchasing agent" for the family (see Marchand 1985:167–71; Gottdiener 1997:58–62) .

In several ways, the "mother as consumer" provided manufacturers and merchants with moral cover to target with impunity both mothers and children (particularly infants) as markets throughout the 1917–29 period. Because this mother thought of her child's needs first and foremost, Earnshaw and his staff writers reasoned, a separate infants'/children's department would be the initial draw for the family's purchasing agent, who would naturally be inclined to make all her purchases in one department store. During a time of high infant mortality and of "baby saving" campaigns, Earnshaw drew upon the discourses of health and medical motherhood (see Apple 1987; Ehrenreich and English 1978) to suggest that the garments themselves needed to be "healthful" (the criteria of which often remained unspecified or vague). Many clothing manufacturers also made claims to that effect. Besides the garments and accessories on display, Earnshaw envisioned the infants'/children's department as a center for maternal information and education. Trained nurses and infant/maternal health publications provided by the Children's Bureau and the American Medical Association, among other things, would serve these ends (see also Klaus 1993:136–71).

It was a logical and consistent step for many merchants (and manufacturers) to expand into and specialize in older children's sizes and styles. By the mid-1930s, department stores such as Wanamaker's in Philadelphia as well as the new discount chain stores such as Woolworth's erected entire "children's floors" replete with clothing, toys, and books that catered to boys and girls from birth through the high school years (see *Earnshaw's Review* 1936:48). In the process, they took advantage of the existing consumption patterns of middle-class mothers who were becoming habituated to the organization of the children's wear retail environment.

The infants'/children's departments of the late 1920s were organized according to the presumed perspective and priorities of the consuming mother—from the variety of stock available and the presence of empathetic saleswomen to the design and physical location of the department itself. By the 1930s, however, these departments and subdepartments began to change their focus of organization from the mother as primary customer to the child. In a relatively short period of time, juvenile clothing departments divided and subdivided along gender lines and along an emerging age–stage paradigm of growth, maturation and personhood. In the process, several new size ranges came into use indicating newly identified distinctions within the phases of middle-class childhood.

This was a gradual process of change, of course. Around the turn of the century, when there may have been as few as a half-dozen manufacturers exclusively devoted to making children's garments, standardized size ranges in children's clothes were virtually nonexistent. A gross categorization of something similar to the following was operative in women's magazines such as *Ladies Home Journal, Harper's Bazaar,* and *Women's Home Companion*: birth to eighteen months, eighteen months to six years, and six years to fourteen years. There do not seem to have been proper names to these age ranges, except for the youngest range known as "infants" or "babies."

From the 1910s onward, but especially in the 1930s, the internal chronology of middle-class childhood would undergo a transformation into finely graded series in which stages of the life course were nuanced by changes in appearance and clothing. The "new" stages of this version of childhood, especially those expressed in children's garments and in size ranges, gained their impetus primarily through an effort to closely match size and appearance to girls' physical growth and social maturation. Only the younger boys' ranges were made as a close parallel construction to girls. After about age seven or eight, boys' size ranges followed men's sizing, perhaps as a gesture toward the belief in the earlier maturation of males rather than for biological conditions thought immanent to boyhood.

The category and the persona of the toddler provided a first opportunity to make distinctions within an essentially genderless construction of early childhood (Paoletti and Kreglogh 1989). In the process of naming a new stage of "development," a new social person with her/his own needs and desires stepped onto the stage of commercial capitalism.[3]

TODDLERS

The term "toddler" appears to have been in use only since the late eighteenth century, according to the *Oxford English Dictionary* (1992). It refers simply to "one who toddles, especially a child" (1992:3340). Currently, it is both a scheduled period of child rearing and a clothing size. It starts at about age one when children begin to walk unsteadily, or "toddle," and ends around age three when toilet training is assumed to be complete.

As a clothing size, it is indicated by the letter "T" after a numbered size on clothing tags to avoid confusion with similarly numbered sizes for the "children's" range. That is, a 3T is a size 3 in the toddler range rather than a size 3 in the children's range of 3 to 6. Toddlers' clothing currently comes in sizes ranging from 1T to 6T to accommodate the varying body sizes of this age (see Jaffe and Rosa 1990:4).

The difference between a toddler's garment and a child's garment of the same numbered size is its style and fit—how the child looks rather than the physical size of the garment. Toddlers still wear diapers, and garments must be made full enough to accommodate them. Also the stance of the toddler is different from older children or adults because toddlers sway back and walk flat-footed in an effort to balance—consequently, their stomach protrudes. Children's wear designers closely adhere to these developmental constraints (Jaffe and Rosa 1990:4).

Sometime around 1930, the term "toddler" began to be used with great frequency as a size range and as a merchandising category and soon after, as an age–stage designation. Prior to the 1930s, "toddler" seemed to refer only to the children themselves, especially those aged around two, three, and four years. For instance, an article entitled "Summer Vogue for Toddlers" in the 1924 consumer magazine, *Babyhood* (June), displays fashion sketches of models but does not give an age range.

The market potential for toddlers as a size–style range, however, was not addressed until the mid-1930s. An *Earnshaw's* writer in 1934, after touring a manufacturing house that specialized in toddler dresses, speculated about the promise for this range:

> And if it requires so many dresses to take care of these one-two-threes, what about all the other garments worn by these same ages? Then, too, there are the little boys, with all their needs to be supplied. These little boys and girls grow up into two-to-sixers, and on and on. (*Earnshaw's Review* 1934:49)

A size–style range, just barely visible in the 1930s, had already aroused speculation about merchandising and stock turnover as the children grew into the next size–style range. This writer offers the emergent formula for what was to become the hallmark of children's wear merchandising: as each size range becomes associated with a general style or look for that age, the next older range offers the possibility of new distinctions upon which new value may be added.

In 1936, the "toddler" as a commercial persona/construct began to take shape. A long-time industry observer explained some of the characteristics of toddlers in terms that resonate with merchants catering to a small but commercially viable middle class:

> Toddler dresses are made up in crisp batiste, in organdy and dimity, in swiss or shimmering broadcloth, in dainty pastels and adorable prints. For the Toddler boy, they are more tailored, naturally, yet keeping a touch of the baby, which satisfies both mother and father. . . . All these are designed and cut to fit the busy little folks who are just beginning to realize their importance in the scheme of things. Little boys, little girls each have their definite niche in the world of style and merchandise today. . . . Infants' or baby clothes won't do. Clothes for these Toddlers are made with the proper fit and feel which do so much for a child's appearance and poise of mind. Even a small child likes to feel properly dressed.
>
> Toddlers require their own particular type of undergarments also: Proper underclothing for these toddler styles is also quite necessary. Undies must follow the

curves of the body and allow freedom of movement. They must be designed for ease and convenience in training to sanitary habits. Yet they must not interfere with the style and lines of the outer garments. The sagging panties and bulgy bloomers of yesteryear are gone from sight. (*Earnshaw's Review* 1936:70)

The article concludes by urging retailers and buyers to "study this interesting episode" and to include and feature toddlers in their infants' department, apparently as a subdepartment of infants.

The harsh economic conditions of the mid-1930s severely constrained the amount and scope of a customer base that would have the financial wherewithal and cultural capital to regard their children in such decidedly ostentatious terms. A toddler dressed in this manner clearly signaled that the family was not being fed with government assistance. These conditions limited the external, retail sales growth of the industry but did not, however, inhibit as drastically the industry's internal expansion and its infrastructure and perhaps encouraged it.[4] The imputation of agency, desire, and self-consciousness onto the child both helped assuage the concerns of merchants and manufacturers and situated demand in something other than a bourgeois preoccupation with conspicuous display.

In this view, the toddler is an emerging person whose "likes" and feelings count as much as those of anyone. Boy toddlers and girl toddlers are different from each other, of course. The girls manifest femininity in "dainty pastels and adorable prints" and boys' garments are more "tailored," more mannish for their "poise of mind." The special designation, "the toddler," is important not only for the parents; the toddler her- or himself is now a person available for scrutiny by others, whose feelings, needs, poise of mind, and choice are being discovered and invoked as legitimate authority. These toddlers are concerned with how they look and are more than aware of the distinction between "proper" and "improper" dress.

To the extent that the discourse of this trade article represents a moment in the commercial construction of "toddlerhood," it also stands for the first step in the transformation of the sacred child of sentimental domesticity. Note how the toddler's complete worth is not confined to some value thought to be intrinsic to the child; toddlers are valued partially for appearance, for how they display style and line outwardly to some observer. This narrative must invoke the child's own perspective. To do otherwise would be to profane the sanctity of the priceless child who is beyond all imposed value. The rhetorical move of placing desire and a degree of autonomy within the child effectively embeds the concern with appearance in the realm of agency and volition. "The child" here is several steps removed from dependency at only a year or two beyond infancy.

A year and a half later, a trade writer called catering to toddlers the "third stepping stone" in building an infants' department. She explained to the trade audience that "[t]he child at this age is leaving babyhood and each day becoming more of a personality. His clothes, too, must begin to have personality. Each little figure and individual type must be considered" (*Earnshaw's Review* 1937:54).

Manufacturers, the trade audience was told, now make clothes for one- two-three-year-olds with more "charm appeal," an appeal that sells. Repeating the "charming frock-manly suit" description for toddler-wear, the author lists eighteen different items of dress requisite for this classification (*Earnshaw's Review* 1937:54–92). She calls for toddlers to be "housed and treated as a separate division and given in charge of a saleswoman who has the understanding and interest of this group at heart" (92). This type of saleswoman "becomes interested in the personalities of these small toddlers themselves, and plays up to them, as well as to their parents and relatives" (54). Again, direct appeals to profitability are made by imputing personhood to the child. As a "personality," the child requires an "individual" style. Not yet autonomous but nevertheless a person, the toddler can be exploited through his or her parents and relatives who now supposedly can feel free to turn the youngster into a (carefully mediated) clothes horse.

"Toddlers' " as a category is made possible by "the toddler" as a social person who arises from the crawling dependency of a basically asexual and sartorially colorless infancy of the 1920s into a persona and fixture in the size–style commercial pantheon of children's clothing of the 1930s and beyond.[5] The toddler gains its identity in contradistinction to the infant by its ability to stand and walk. This event demarcates a biological and psychical transition in the life cycle, denoting the first stage of a willful individual capable of movement, choice, and direction. The invention of toddlerhood arises out social-psychological knowledge and concerns, as opposed to the invention of infancy, which was originally a medical category (Armstrong 1987).

The "upright child" has occupied a particular ideological place in the history of Western childhood. According to Karin Calvert (1992), seventeenth- and eighteenth-century practices of swaddling and corseting infants, combined with the extensive use of narrow, stiff cradles and walking stools were evidence of an anxiety about the direction and growth of the "inchoate child" (1992:27). These devices helped assure concerned colonial Calvinists of an orderly progression from animal-like infancy to divine, humanlike adulthood by limiting the child's time spent crawling on all fours, a position that put them physically and symbolically closer to Satan: "Children, if they were to assume their rightful place in the divine order, had to do so on the feet, not on their hands and knees" (1992:33).

In the 1930s, the upright child unfolded as a boundary condition for a market designation. The toddler was now both morally ready and socially able to take her or his rightful place in the emergent commercial order of things. Differentiated from the complete dependency and hypermoral arena of infants, a toddler was also a vehicle more amenable than an infant for the expression of style and gender. These expressions are concomitantly taken as expressions of "personality," of personhood, and are graphically depicted as such in various advertisements utilizing the images of toddlers that have extended into the present (Cook 1999; see also Higonnet 1998; Alexander 1994).

Two basic developments ground the discovery of and belief in "toddlerhood" and in the attendant personality of the toddler. One is the rise of a new morality in middle-class parenting, beginning in the 1920s. The other is the emergent visibility of young, popular culture icons, such as Shirley Temple, in the 1930s.

THE "NEW PARENTING" AND SHIRLEY TEMPLE

The new parenting was formed selectively from academic psychology (and perhaps helped along by the popularity of Margaret Mead's work; see, for instance, her "South Sea Tips on Character Training," 1932). Beginning in the 1920s, parents—mothers especially—were bombarded with numerous, often contradictory, messages about children's needs on the pages of women's magazines and in the new *Parents* magazine (established in 1926). Advice from experts such as J. B. Watson often merged with advertising appeals advocating the purchase of particular products. Both made use of a similar language of development and both offered essentially the same solutions to parenting problems (Seiter 1993:24).

This "new" morality has been characterized by Martha Wolfenstein as "fun morality," whereby fun, once thought "suspect, if not taboo, has tended to become obligatory" (1955:168). For Wolfenstein, who examined the parenting advice literature of the Children's Bureau from 1914 to 1945, the basis of the new fun morality was a change in the valuation of the child's impulses. Briefly, the impulses—such as crying, thumb sucking, feeding, and masturbation—were negatively appraised in the literature of 1914 as things to be controlled or eliminated. By 1945, the impulses "appear as benevolent rather than dangerous" (1955:171). They become positively valued as indications of what is good and right for the individual child; nature is to be individuated and nurtured. The consequence, she notes, is that it has become a mother's duty to nurture the play impulse, thus making "fun" an imperative that can not always be achieved.

This positive valuation of the child's impulses combined with the medicalization of mothering to form the basis of the new middle-class parenting. As Ellen Seiter (1993) notes:

> Experts advised mothers to care not only for the body and its (baby's) health but for the mind and its rate of development. They increased the demand for nurturing behavior in constant supply. The new child psychology was a child-centered model. Implicitly in its proscriptions was a disavowal of maternal authority and an upgrading of *the child's own desires* as rational and goal directed. (1993:23, emphasis added)

From its inception, *Parents* magazine has been a leader in the promotion and dissemination of parenting advice based on modern psychological and medical models of child care. Directed to the educated classes, *Parents* was an important vehicle for these views, especially in its ability to advocate developmental child psychology to a national, albeit middle-class, audience. According to Seiter, the publication helped to "popularize the idea that childhood is divided into discrete observable stages" and encouraged mothers "to see weekly and monthly changes in their children's development" (1993:65).

In the 1930s, the gaze of the psychologist (Rose 1990) and of medicine (Armstrong 1987) collapsed into the commercial persona of the toddler not only as a merchandising category but also as an embodied, individuated, and natural "personality." The surveillance of childhood made possible by discrete measurements also made for market distinctions; the imputation of toddler personality gave that market a face. During a period when "the autonomous self . . . was being rendered unreal" by the growth of an interdependent market (Lears 1983:9), those same market relations helped signify and bring to the fore an autonomous self in the person of Shirley Temple.

Americans in the 1920s witnessed the rise of the juvenile actor on the silver screen. Douglas Fairbanks Jr. and Jackie Coogan led the way not only with numerous screen appearances but also with frequent appearances in advertisements for boys' clothes. With the advent of the "talkies" in the 1930s, child stars such as Jane Withers, Gloria Jean, Virginia Weidler, Judy Garland, and Mickey Rooney burst on the scene.[6] All of them had their own line(s) of clothing or endorsed clothing for children.[7]

A cultural and merchandising space was defined for these actors by the early success of Shirley Temple, both as an actress and as a product endorser. Temple gave "toddlerhood" a boost with her on-screen persona as a befrocked, precocious, curly-haired young girl who exuded definite personality. She also became a commercial persona as she hawked her own lines of clothing. From her licensing debut in 1934 until the early 1940s, the Shirley Temple name and image added materially to sales of dresses, socks, coats and snowsuits, hats, hair bands, and raincoats. A 1936 advertisement in *Earnshaw's* by Kramer Bros. urged the trade to "Cash in on Shirley's Tremendous Popularity" with their line of Shirley Temple socks, which meet "No Sales Resistance." Besides the expected paid advertisements, *Earnshaw's* also printed unpaid listings of "Shirley Temple Resources."

Ms. Temple made her feature film debut in 1934 at the age of five. Her stage dresses were designed with a toddler "look," and her retail line of dresses maintained a toddler line throughout the 1930s, even though she was not one herself. One children's fashion observer attributes the success of Shirley Temple frocks to their simplicity:

> They follow one pattern almost invariably: a skirt (about the size of a postage stamp) that falls in soft pleats from a round collar of a contrasting material or appliqué; no belt—Shirley wisely favors the pinafore fashion which shows off a small round tummy to best advantage; and, for trimming, a bow of baby ribbon or an appliquéd

nursery figure. Even her party frocks use no trimming except touches of hand embroidery and edgings of narrow lace. (Owen 1935:20)

Note how the "round belly," a physical attribute of the toddler age, is described as being shown off as the marker of status—as if this feature adds to the positive valuation and authenticity of the actress and her appearance.[8] Note also how the author discusses Ms. Temple's "look" as a consequence of her deliberation, rather than that of her handlers.

As commercial persona, it may be said that Temple "performed" toddlerhood well past the toddler age and was looked upon as one even as she moved through middle childhood. The production of trademarked Shirley Temple dresses for the toddler range by the Nannette Manufacturing Company of New York City included numerous styles and variations on the basic silhouette and continued into the early 1940s. Her birthday became an annual occasion for special promotions. In addition, the Roseneau Bros. Manufacturing Company of New York offered Shirley Temple designs in Big and Little Sister styles, sizes 3 to 6½ and 7 to 12 years).[9]

Aware of the potential impact of children's on-screen appearances, by the late 1930s each of the big Hollywood studios (Twentieth-Century Fox, MGM, Universal, and Paramount) hired big-name designers to create the wardrobes of the child actors. Vera West of Universal and Edith Head of Paramount were the most famous of these designers. They crafted clothing with an eye toward the apparel market in addition to the movie-going market, although direct tie-ins from film to manufacturer did not exist at this time (see *Earnshaw's Review*, 1940:31).

The accessibility of Shirley Temple and others as child/juvenile stars provided visibility for style in the developing fashion system for children. Social theorists from Georg Simmel ([1904] 1971) to Herbert Blumer (1969) to Fred Davis (1992) have stressed the necessity of conspicuous display for fashion to develop and a fashion system to thrive. In the midst of the Depression, children and parents alike found that they could emulate screen stars, at least sartorially.

Both the "new" parenting and the increased visibility of the child star, especially Shirley Temple, informed and gave impetus to the rise and elaboration of the toddler size–style range, particularly for girls. The new mode of parenting uniformly recognized the young child as possessing personal desires and healthy impulses. This view enables a construction of the toddler as a person, or a person-in-progress, which is therefore "less" sacred—less sacred than the crawling, hyperdependent infant. The toddler-as-person is that much more able, developmentally, morally, and subjectively, to desire material goods, make choices, and to "feel properly dressed."

Once trade members and parents alike accepted that the toddler was no longer an infant but not yet a "full" person, then the way was paved to identify and take seriously the particular commercial "needs" of the toddler. These could be met, some would say, only by special merchandise. If the toddler was gaining or mani-festing a "personality," then Shirley Temple, and other actors, stood as publicly shared models for how that personality could be expressed appropriately by white middle-class girls.

Note how observers discuss Ms. Temple, and toddlers generally, from an aes-thetic point of view, for example, in descriptions of the visual "line" of the cloth-ing and the charming dresses. The toddler girl, especially, becomes one who is seen, viewed by others, and no doubt evaluated by onlookers. She also is imputed to be separately aware of her appearance and, as such, she stands as a model of agency. "The child" becomes an object for display and scrutiny and, at the same time, a subject to be engaged—at once a type and an individual.

CONCLUDING REMARKS

In the introductory chapter to *Children and the Politics of Culture* (1995), the late anthropologist Sharon Stephens argued, "To make sense of the history of a once localized, now globally penetrating capitalist order, we need to explore the ways in which certain objects and processes come to be invested with natural boundaries, objective solidity, and material force" (1995:xx). Childhood serves this project well because it is so strongly and so often invested with a sense of "naturalness." The toddler embodies and personifies how desire for consumer goods can be represented as something naturally occurring and thus beyond the realm of choice.

The toddler, however, also represents a renaturalizing of the self or "personal-ity" during a historical period that scholars have characterized as being ill at ease with notions of the self. T. J. Jackson Lears (1983:9) describes how a therapeu-tic ethos of consumption in the 1920s and 1930s offered defenses against the "loss of selfhood" which "lay at the heart of the modern sense of unreality." Warren Susman (1979) argues that those who drove the ascendance of "personality" over "character" in the early part of the century stressed the ability to cultivate, to create, a self through superficial or external means rather than through self-discipline. "Personality," and not "character," was better suited to a consumer rather than a producer culture. Marchand (1985) makes similar observations in his analysis of advertising and the advertising industry.

It appears that at the same historical period, among roughly the same white, urban, middle-class people, two different postures toward the self were present: a tenuousness about the self among adults and an imputation of naturalness about the self in children. These need not be at odds with one another so long as the idea of sacred, sentimental childhood is kept in mind. Uncertainty about the moral place of consumption and desire seems to be a reasonable response for adults who were experiencing, many without realizing it, a profound transition from a producer to a consumer economy. The crisis in both production and consumption during the Depression would understandably call into question the foundations of identity of a class fraction that had arisen in tandem with these material and ideal conditions.

When David Reisman and colleagues began their work immediately after World War II on what was to become *The Lonely Crowd* (1950), they interviewed members of the same race–class constituency that had embraced the new parenting and who had produced the first "toddlers." For these adults, to see cultural images of young children performing as personalities, to become parents in a milieu of fun morality, and to have fewer and fewer alternatives to mass-produced goods must have made the acceptance of the toddler-as-natural-person not only a possible social identity but a viable one. The "other-directed" personality—one that seeks guidance and direction from contemporaries—has its clearest expression when self and commodity commingle.

Other-directedness took root during this time not just as a contrived manipulation by advertisers but as a way in which a particular version of the self came into existence. The performative self became the natural self—a notion that Erving Goffman (1959) not too long afterward would institutionalize as social theory and research perspective. What Goffman missed, as many have, is the place of commodities, commodity culture, and symbolic exchange value in the creation of "natural" selves and consumers. Children's market research, since its inception in the 1930s, has sought the locus of desire in children themselves. The task since that time has been to find developmentally cognitively appropriate ways young children could "express" these preexistent desires (see Cook 2000.).

It is becoming increasingly difficult to conceive of any form of social action that will not eventually be subsumed under some form of market structure or market idiom. It has also become increasingly difficult to deny a child's "right" to enjoyment in the world of goods. If children are presently enfranchised as persons, as they seem to be in many contexts, they have become so necessarily through the medium of the marketplace over the course of successive generations of youth/consumer culture. And if consumer capitalism reigns triumphant at the dawn of a new century, if alternatives to its hegemony are virtually incomprehensible, it is because the line dividing person and commodity is becoming academic.

NOTES

1. It continues today as *Earnshaw's Review*, the premiere publication of the trade, based in New York City.

2. Prior to 1917, there were few, if any, separate children's clothing departments in urban department stores. Clothing was stocked and displayed by item (i.e., hosiery, shirts) rather than by age (see Walker and Mendelson 1967).

3. Left out of this discussion is the concomitant rise, in the 1930s, of the "children's" size range (3 to 6 years) and the "girls'" size range, which subdivided the 6-to-14 range into 6-to-10 and 10-to-14. In the 1940s the "teen girl" (ages 12 to 16) became a size range as well as a social type, and in the 1950s, so did the "preteen" girl (10 to 12 years).

4. Between 1929 and 1939, according to the Census of Business for those years, retail sales for "infants' and children's stores" decreased more than 55 percent in receipts (just under $30 million in 1929 to $13.4 million in 1939) as measured at these two points. These figures pertain only to independent specialty stores and do not include department store or chain store data.

5. According to Paoletti and Kreglogh (1989), clear gender markers for infants, such as the girl-pink, boy-blue coding, became solidified only after World War II in the United States (1989:26–29).

6. Child actors and performers were widespread in the Vaudeville circuits from the late 1800s through the 1930s. However, the growth of the film industry effectively killed Vaudeville by creating a star system that featured only a handful of key performers and actors on screen, rather than the tens of thousands on stage.

7. Zelizer (1985) points out that one major exception to child labor laws, child actors, presented a paradox in that they had to work to portray the sentimental, priceless child on screen and stage (1985:92–96).

8. That toddlers became an object of social scrutiny and concern is suggested by a *Parents* article in 1937 (June), which assured apparently concerned mothers that their toddler's "pot belly" was "normal" and would go away as the child ages, advising against subjecting the child to stomach-flattening exercises (28–107).

9. Sidney Roseneau, of Roseneau Bros., was appointed Shirley Temple's guardian by Supreme Court Justice Edgar L. Lauer in 1935 to act for her in matters regarding litigation. She was suing Lenora Doll Company for producing dolls in her likeness and advertised as Shirley Temple Dolls (*Earnshaw's Review* 1935:76).

BIBLIOGRAPHY

Alexander, Victoria A. (1994). "The Image of Children in Magazine Advertisements from 1905–1990," *Communication Research* 21(6):742–65.

Apple, Rima D. (1987). *Mothers and Medicine*. Madison: University of Wisconsin Press.

Armstrong, David (1987). "The Invention of Infant Mortality," *Sociology of Health and Illness*. 211–32.

Baudrillard, Jean (1981). *For a Critique of the Political Economy of the Sign*. St. Louis: Telos.

Becker, Howard S. (1982). *Artworlds*. Berkeley: University of California Press.

Best, Joel (1990). *Threatened Children*. Chicago: University of Chicago Press.

Blumer, Herbert (1969). "Fashion: From Class Differentiation to Collective Selection," *Sociological Quarterly* 10:275–91.

Calvert, Karin (1992). *Children in the House: The Material Culture of Early Childhood, 1600–1900*. Boston: Northeastern University Press.

Campbell, Colin (1989). *The Romantic Ethic and the Spirit of Modern Consumerism*. Oxford: Blackwell.

Comaroff, John L., and Jean Comaroff (1997). *Of Revelation and Revolution, Volume Two*. Chicago: University of Chicago Press.

Cook, Daniel Thomas (1995). "The Mother as Consumer: Insights from the Children's Wear Industry, 1917–1929," *Sociological Quarterly*, 36:3, 505–22.

——— (1999). "The Visual Commoditization of Childhood: A Case History from a Children's Clothing Trade Journal, 1920s–1980s," *Journal of Social Sciences* 3(1–2) (Jan-Apr):21–40.

——— (2000). "The Other 'Child Study': Market Research and the Construction of Children as Persons, 1930s–1960s." *Sociological Quarterly* 41(3).

Cross, Gary (1998). *Kids' Stuff*. Cambridge, Mass.: Harvard University Press.

Csikszentmihalyi, Mihaly, and Eugene Rochberg-Halton (1981). *The Meaning of Things*. Cambridge: Cambridge University Press.

Davis, Fred (1992). *Fashion, Culture, and Identity*. Chicago: University of Chicago.

Earnshaw's Review (Jan. 1934). "What About Toddlers?" 18(1).

Earnshaw's Review (Feb. 1936). "Toddlers?" 20(2).

Earnshaw's Review (Nov. 1937). "The Fourth Stepping Stone," 21(11).

Earnshaw's Review (Nov. 1940). "Dressing the Juvenile Film Star," 24(11).

Ehrenreich, Barbara, and Deirdre English (1978). *For Her Own Good: 150 Years of the Experts' Advice to Women*. New York: Doubleday.

Ewen, Stuart (1976). *Captains of Consciousness*. New York: McGraw-Hill.

Featherstone, Mike (1991a). "The Body in Consumer Culture," in *The Body: Social Process and Cultural Theory*, ed. Mike Featherstone, Mike Hepworth, and Bryan S. Turner. London: Sage:170–96.

——— (1991b). *Postmodernism and Consumer Culture*. New York: Sage.

Forty, Adrian (1986). *Objects of Desire*. London: Thames and Hudson.

Giroux, Henry (1998). "Nymphet Fantasies: Child Beauty Pageants and the Politics of Innocence." *Social Text* 57,16:4(Winter), 31–53.

Goffman, Erving (1959). *The Presentation of Self in Everyday Life*. New York: Doubleday.

Gottdiener, Mark (1985). "Hegemony and Mass Culture: A Semiotic Approach," *American Journal of Sociology* 90(5):979–1001.

——— (1997). *The Theming of America: Dreams, Visions, and Commercial Spaces*. Boulder, Colo.: Westview Press.

Guber, Selina, and Jon Berry (1993). *Marketing to and through Kids*. New York: McGraw-Hill.

Higonnet, Anne (1998). *Pictures of Innocence*. New York: Thames and Hudson.

Jaffe, Hilde, and Rosa Rosa (1990). *Childrenswear Design*. New York: Fairchild Publications.

Klaus, Alisa (1993). *Every Child a Lion*. Ithaca, N.Y.: Cornell University Press.

Kline, Stephen (1993). *Out of the Garden: Toys and Children's Culture in the Age of TV Marketing*. London: Verso.

Kopytoff, Igor (1986). "The Cultural Biography of Things: Commoditization as Process," in *The Social Life of Things*, ed. Arjun Appadurai, Cambridge: Cambridge University Press:63–91.

Lamont, Michele (1992). *Money, Morals, and Markets*. Chicago: University of Chicago Press.

Leach, William (1993a). "Child-World in the Promised Land," in *The Mythmaking Frame of Mind*, ed. J. Gilbert et al., Belmont, Calif.: Wadsworth:209–38.

——— (1993b). *Land of Desire: Merchants, Power and the Rise of a New American Culture*. New York: Pantheon.

Lears, T. J. Jackson (1983). "From Salvation to Self-Realization," in *The Culture of Consumption*, ed. T. J. Jackson Lears and Richard Wrightman Fox. New York: Pantheon:3–38.

McKendrick, Neil, John Brewer, and John H. Plumb (1982). *The Birth of a Consumer Society*. Bloomington: Indiana University Press.

McNeal, James U. (1992). *Kids as Customers*. New York: Lexington.

Marchand, Roland (1985). *Advertising the American Dream*. Berkeley: University of California Press.

Marx, Karl (1978). "Commodities," in *The Marx-Engels Reader* (Second Edition), ed. Robert C. Tucker, New York: Norton:302–29.

Mead, Margaret (1932). "South Sea Tips on Character Training," *Parents* 7(3):13–16.

Owen, Hortense (1935). "Hollywood's in the Nursery Closet," *Pictorial Review* 37(6).

Paoletti, Jo B., and Carol L. Krelogh (1989). "The Children's Department," in *Men and Women, Dressing the Part*, ed. Claudia Kidwell and Valerie Steele. Washington, D.C.: Smithsonian Institution Press:22–41.

Parry, Jonathan, and Maurice Bloch, eds. (1989). *Money and the Morality of Exchange*. Cambridge: Cambridge University Press.

Press, Andrea (1990). *Women Watching Television*. Philadelphia: University of Pennsylvania Press.

Radway, Janice (1984). *Reading the Romance*. Chapel Hill: University of North Carolina Press.

Reisman, David, Nathan Glazer, and Reuel Denney (1950). *The Lonely Crowd*. New York: Doubleday.

Rose, Nicholas (1990). *Governing the Soul*. London: Routledge.

Seiter, Ellen (1993). *Sold Separately: Parents and Children in Consumer Culture*. New Brunswick, N.J.: Rutgers University Press.

Simmel, Georg (1971 [1904]). "Fashion," in *On Individuality and Social Forms*, ed. Donald N. Levine. Chicago: University of Chicago Press:294–323.

——— (1978 [1900]). *The Philosophy of Money*. Edited and transl. by David Frisby. Oxford: Blackwell.

Slater, Don (1997). *Consumer Culture and Modernity*. Cambridge: Polity Press.

Stephens, Sharon, ed. (1995). *Children and the Politics of Culture*. Princeton, N.J.: Princeton University Press.

Susman, Warren I. (1979). "'Personality' and the Making of Twentieth-Century Culture," in *New Directions in American Intellectual History*, ed. John Hingham and Paul Conklin, Baltimore: Johns Hopkins University Press:212–26.

Walker, Herbert, and Nathaniel Mendelson (1967). *The Children's Wear Merchandiser*. New York: National Retail Merchant's Association.

——— (1994). *The Social Meaning of Money*. New York: Basic.

Weber, Max (1958 [1904–05]). *The Protestant Ethic and the Spirit of Capitalism*. New York: Charles Scribner's Sons.

Wolfenstein, Martha (1955). "Fun Morality," in *Childhood in Contemporary Cultures*, ed. Margaret Mead and Martha Wolfenstein. Chicago: University of Chicago Press.

Woolons, Roberta, ed. (1993). *Children at Risk in America*. Albany: SUNY Press.

Zelizer, Viviana A. (1985). *Pricing the Priceless Child: The Changing Social Value of Children*. New York: Basic.

7

The Body and the Country:
A Political Ecology of Consumption

E. Melanie DuPuis

Food is the nexus between nature and the body. In 1980, Carolyn Merchant declared the "death of nature" in her analysis of changing representations of the countryside from feminine nurture to masculine artifice. A few years later, Emily Martin (1987) declared the "end of the body" in her analysis of cultural representations of the body and the increased masculine control of bodily existence. Their pronouncements of the demise of nature and the demise of the body were, in fact, calls for greater attention to how nature and the body were represented, particularly in Western society. Rather than declaring "the end of food" (which would leave everyone unhappy at mealtimes), this chapter will attempt to link cultural analyses of body and country to explain the rise of industrial food consumption, in this case, the rise of fluid milk drinking.

Analysis of the industrialization of food has given little attention to the burgeoning literature on the role of cultural representations of nature or the body in the formation of the industrial food system. Most of the work on this topic relies on the framework of political economy, particularly the analysis of the food commodity chain, which looks at the way the food system for a particular commodity is organized, from production to consumption. This analytical framework has been an extremely fruitful alternative to classical economic studies that explain food production according to universalistic ideas of production efficiency and comparative advantage. Commodity-chain analysis explains how, where, and why people produce food the way they do according to macro-economic trends, such as industrialization and globalization, as well as within local historical and political contexts.

Recently, however, several analysts critiqued commodity-chain analysis for not taking nature into account (Grossman 1998) and argued that the framework should be expanded to include ecological factors. Many of these authors referred to this expanded framework as "political ecology" (Blaikie and Brookfield 1987). Therefore, political economy has now incorporated one "side" of the body–nature nexus into an analysis of agricultural commodities, especially food commodities.

However, the other side of the nature–body food nexus has yet to be incorporated into a political ecology/commodity-chain analysis of food. As a result, explanations of the consumption end of the chain tend to be overly simplistic and especially economistic. In particular, the historical analysis of changes in food consumption tends to focus on changes in women's role in the family without painting a sufficiently complex picture of those changes. This is unfortunate in light of the significant amount of historical work that recently has been done on the changes in family relationships as the United States became more urban and industrial.

This chapter will draw on this new historical work on the family in the history of industrialization to extend the analysis of the food system to the other end of the nexus: the body and its centrality to family relationships. Diagrammed, the extension of the framework might look like this:

**Political ecology Political economy/Commodity chain
Consumption Studies/Embodiment**

Nature ← —— → People ← —— → People ← —— → Nature (Body)

The arrows in this case represent relationships that need to be considered in an analysis of the food system. Because the relationship between people and their own bodies is also a relationship with nature, one could argue that an inclusion of a sociology of the body is a "natural" extension of the political ecology framework.

Milk is an exemplary food to utilize in this extension of commodity-chain analysis (Apple 1987). Fluid milk as an industrial food originated primarily as an infant food. Fluid milk could be considered, historically, as a subsistence "crop" that was produced in the "countryside" of women's bodies specifically for children and others in need of "nursing."[1] Milk was then "commodified" by "outsourcing" the food, appropriating (Goodman, Sorj, and Wilkinson 1987) a function that once occurred within the family (infant feeding) and making it an industrial product (fluid milk, condensed milk, and infant formula). This is an uncomfortable way to talk about fluid milk as a commodity, because it is difficult to separate out women as members of society and women as "nature" in this explanation. However, what this explanation points to is a very complex relationship between women, children, and bodily nature that needs more sociological attention.

One way to give these consumption factors the attention they deserve is to look carefully at the way people, especially women and children, bodies, and nature were represented in certain food discourses. In particular, how did people think about these relationships during the time period (1850–1920) when the rise in industrialized, commodified fluid milk was happening? This chapter will look at two different "voices" in the discourse on fluid milk consumption during this period: reform tracts in the "fight for pure milk" in the mid-nineteenth century, and milk advertisements during this period.

The most common story told about milk consumption in the United States centers on the extraordinary rise of milk drinking in America over the past 150 years. These histories of milk consumption follow one particular story line: that milk was dangerous and impure before public intervention in the industry. As a result, city people did not drink much of it, and when they did, especially if they were children, they often died. After pasteurization, the story goes, milk was healthy and wholesome, and milk consumption, as a result, rose rapidly (Spencer and Blanford 1977). These triumphalist histories display charts showing the rapid rise of milk consumption after pasteurization (see, for example, Catherwood 1931:6).

Interestingly, even a contemporary children's book, *Milk: The Fight for Purity,* tells the tale of "the struggle to ensure a safe, reliable supply of milk for the world's children and adults" (Giblin 1986:3). The narrative in all these stories describes how industrial technology and state institutions come to the rescue of dying children by providing the safe, pure milk demanded by the public. This milk history story parallels the booster histories of many other industrial foods.

In fact, the rise of milk drinking at the turn of the century is not simply a rise in *average* consumption but an expansion in the proportion of the population (the number of bodies) consuming milk. One hundred years ago, the idea of milk as an everyday drink for anyone older than twelve years of age was not part of the public dietary landscape. Milk was a children's beverage. Although people did drink milk on the farm, they did so not because milk was essential to the diet but as a way to dispose of the by-products (buttermilk) of other dairy activities, such as the household production of butter and cheese. If milk was not available, which it often was not in the winter months, this was not a social problem. In fact, milk and other dairy by-products such as whey were often fed to livestock rather than consumed by the farm family.

Like most industrial food commodities, fluid milk as a food arose as a form of urban food provisioning. However, the first urban consumers of the urban milk supply were infants who were not breast-fed. This history of milk consumption is therefore a history of how a food produced in a mother becomes a food produced by cows and then how this food becomes a major source of nutrition for the majority of the American population.

It is difficult to estimate the average American's milk consumption before the 1900s. However, it is clear that, in the mid-1800s, the supply of milk going to

Northeastern cities went primarily to the feeding of infants and children. However, one hundred years later, most North Americans drank significant amounts of milk, nearly a pint a day. For example, between 1930 and 1940, per-capita milk consumption increased 1 to 2 percent a year. By the 1950s, milk had become a necessary food for most Americans. Nearly everyone—children, adults, older people—drank milk in large quantities.

The most common explanation for the rise in milk drinking links it to the rise in sanitary standards, consumer education, and dairy science early in the twentieth century. This is a triumphalist narrative commonly expressed by the organic intellectuals of the dairy industry. For example, dairy economist Leland Spencer and New York City and northern New Jersey Milk Market official Ida Parker noted the substantial rise in milk drinking after "a market improvement in the sanitary and keeping quality of milk" (Spencer and Parker 1961:54), particularly the institution of mandatory pasteurization in this urban area. The link between the rise of milk drinking and the rise of "pure" milk is made in a great deal of the institutional economics literature on the subject. The explanation in a 1960s-era food marketing textbook is typical:

> Since the early 1900s, fluid milk has been a staple in the American diet. The "perfect food" has maintained popularity, as information regarding its nutritional value has spread. Improvements in the breeding and feeding of dairy cattle, almost sterile cleanliness in every part of the milk-handling operation, and advances in processing such as homogenization have contributed to better quality and flavor of milk. (Hampe and Wittenberg 1964:186)

Yet this triumphalist narrative of science and government making food safe and flavorful for the public does not explain the earliest stage of the milk supply system and its infant feeding purpose. Although few people drank milk in cities in the mid-nineteenth century, the feeding of milk to infants began, and even expanded, despite the clear evidence that this food—as produced at the time—was dangerous, even deadly. Some even referred to it as "white poison" (Atkins 1992). Yet city people increasingly supplied this milk to their infants and children. In 1842, milk reformer Robert Hartley, with information based on the claims of local physicians, estimated that three-quarters of all infants and children in New York City were being raised on cow's milk. Although this claim was probably an exaggeration, it does indicate that substantial numbers of children were drinking milk in New York City long before sanitary protections were in place.

According to this "progress" history of milk, consumers began to purchase and consume industrial foods when science, government, and industry made the food safe and economical. Clearly recent studies of the industrialization of food have been more critical of the role of these institutions and the Durkheimian idea that modern institutions exist to preserve the order of society and the safety of the populace. Populist rants characterize industrial food as the downfall of modern society.

From this critical perspective, previous forms of food production that are simpler, more local, less industrial, and more craft-based are often romanticized as lost, ideal forms of producing food. For example, Jim Hightower's article, "Food Monopoly," in the Naderite *Big Business Reader* begins:

> Americans have come a long way since the first Thanksgiving meal was brought to some New England colonists by local Indians, in a spirit of sharing, 367 years ago. Maybe we've come too far. At least those Pilgrims knew where their meal came from—it was the bounty of nature, delivered by Indian people, and presumed to be the blessing of God.
>
> No longer is that the case. These days, nature has less and less to do with our meals, which are often not even put on the table by farmers, much less Indians; and if modern food is God-ordained, as Earl Butz once suggested, then the religious fundamentalists are right—we've ticked off the Lord something awful. His revenge is a Brave New Thanksgiving that, unbeknownst to most Americans, is the product of monopolized markets, conglomerate bookkeeping, genetic engineering, integrated factory systems, centralized procurement, national advertising, chemical artifice, standardized taste, and The Bottom Line. It's not especially good, or good for you, and it's very expensive, but you can be thankful for one thing: there's plenty of it. (Hightower 1973:3)

From this "downfall of food" perspective, the modern food system and state regulatory systems "captured" by modern big business interests have degraded the quality of our diet, making it less God-given.

Studies of food from the political economy perspective tell a less black-and-white story about the industrialization of food. Political economy, however, is also critical of the triumphalist narrative of food and progress and looks closely at the relationships of power within a capitalist system. These studies provide in-depth analyses of the institutions and relationships involved in the industrial food system, including such factors as contract farming and other forms of vertical coordination, as well as the social history of land use in various food-producing regions. More recently, political economists have turned to explaining the globalization of food, particularly the new global emphasis on "outsourcing," or playing different production regions off of each other in competition for being the source of supply for a multinational company. These studies have been synthesized to provide an overview of the rise of industrial food. Three book-length studies are Sidney Mintz's (1986) *Sweetness and Power,* David Goodman and Michael Redclift's (1991) *Refashioning Nature: Food, Ecology, and Culture,* and Richard Pillsbury's (1998) *No Foreign Food.*

Goodman and Redclift focus more on the farm side of the commodity chain, whereas Pillsbury, a geographer, focuses on the organization of retail sales.

However, both make similar statements about the changes in the family that prompt the acceptance of industrial foods. Both see a woman's role in the family in terms of her labor. Changes in women's labor availability is central to their explanations for the rise of the industrial food system. In their chapter, "Food into Freezers: Women into Factories," Goodman and Redclift state:

> Changes in the preparation of food, outside and inside the home, need to be related to shifts in the labour process, which have taken women into more wage employment and brought new domestic technology to bear on housework. More and more household tasks—the tasks of servants in nineteenth-century middle-class households—have been handed over to outside specialists. This process, which reached deep into the social fabric of British and other industrialized societies, mirrors the wider process through which industry has appropriated the domestic labour process. In being commoditized, domestic labour was converted into an arena for accumulation. (1991:43)

Pillsbury (1998), in his chapter "Too Busy to Cook: The Rise of Prepared Food," also portrays the "consumption side" of the industrialization of food as resulting from the changes arising as women found employment outside the home, a "transformation of the American household [that] demanded the creation of an entirely new set of foods" (1998:98).

The study that gives the most consideration to cultural aspects of consumption is that of Mintz (1986). He does pay a great deal of attention to English family relationships in his history of sugar. His explanation for the rise of sugar consumption in Britain is an extremely sophisticated analysis of the link between the relations of consumption and the relations of production. Even Mintz's approach, however, can be enhanced by greater attention to feminist views of the family as contradiction and to ideas of eating as embodied nature.

Women's employment, cited both by Goodman and Redclift and by Pillsbury as a major source of the rise in consumption of industrial foods, cannot fully explain the rise of milk as an industrial food in the United States. This reason is weak because it doesn't explain the vast incorporation of industrial foods into American eating long before the rate of women's outside employment rose in the late nineteenth century. Figures on women's actual participation in the labor force in the mid-1800s, when they began to replace breast milk with swill milk, are difficult to determine. The significant amount of informal work and industrial homework performed by working-class women and children during this period— none of which is recorded as employment in the census figures of the time—complicates the picture.

However, it is clear that the "artificial feeding" of infants with cow's milk was not directly correlated to employment status. A look at which women were feeding cow's milk to their children in 1850s New York illustrates the problem with the "labor process" explanation. Only one of these groups—indigent female heads of household—was employed outside the home and therefore unable to breast-feed. The other group feeding cow's milk to their children during this time period was upper- and middle-class women who were neither breast-feeding nor employed. It was widely understood during this time period that working-class women—even those with informal or home employment—were more likely to breast-feed than *either* upper-class women *or* indigent single mothers who were often forced by social service providers to work outside the home.

Taking a feminist cultural point of view, the consumption of cow's milk can best be explained by looking at milk as a social and political construction in which the eventual landscape of milk industry power was first forged in the arena of culture and power. The rise of milk drinking cannot be explained by simple "progress" perspectives of the march of science and technological progress, nor through populist perspectives about the selfishness of monopoly capitalism. Nor can the political economy's current "proletarianized mothers" explanation fully grasp the consumption side of the industrialization of milk.

To illustrate the fruitfulness of this broader focus, the next two sections of this chapter will look at two voices in the discourse on milk during the rise of the industrial milk system, from the mid-nineteenth century to the early twentieth century: consumer and industry voices. From these discourses, it will be shown that the rise of the modern industrial dairy system did involve (as Goodman and Redclift [1991] call it) a "re-fashioning" of food. However, this re-fashioning will be extended to include the re-visioning of body–nature relationships and how these re-visionings reflected much more complex changes in family relationships than simply a proletarianized mother. To this end, the way consumer and commercial discourses represented bodies (particularly women's and children's bodies) and nature will be examined, as well as the way these representations changed with the further industrialization of the milk system.

THE CONSUMER VOICE: "PURE MILK" REFORMERS IN THE MID-NINETEENTH CENTURY

The earliest consumer voice in the public discourse on milk is Robert Hartley's 1842 political tract, *An Essay on Milk*. He was an urban food reformer with a vision, a milk "booster" at a time (the mid-nineteenth century) and in a place (New York City) where people drank very little milk and what they did drink was basically adulterated, filthy, and germ ridden.[2] Hartley was interested in ridding the city of the poisonous substance called "swill milk," which was drunk primarily by infants and children. However, he was even more interested in ridding the city of liquor and beer. Swill milk accomplished both these purposes, because it was an adjunct of the brewery/distillery system. In this system, milk cows in stables next to distilleries/breweries were fed primarily on brewery waste grains, which in turn affected the milk these cows produced, causing them to create an unhealthy substance that came to be called swill milk. At the time of Hartley's writing, most of the milk provided to New York City, and most milk in other large cities, was swill milk.

Hartley's treatise was primarily an exposé of the unsanitary way in which this milk was produced. However, rather than warning people off of milk altogether, he wrote at length about the indispensability of milk, the complete nutrition it provides, and the universality of its consumption through time and throughout space.

One of the many surprises in this essay is the source Hartley used to establish the indispensability of milk: the Bible. He spent a full third of his 350-page essay describing the biblical evidence of milk's perfection as a food. Hartley's argument for the perfection of milk drinking rested on three main arguments: the universality of milk consumption through time and space, milk as the most complete source of nutrition available, and the role of large-scale industry in providing this "perfect food" to the public.

Hartley establishes the universality of milk consumption by linking it to God's intended "design," that is, God's plan as to how people would eat. His chapter, "The Primary Design of Milk," is a biblical exegesis based in Natural Theology that demonstrates that milk drinking was God's intention. Starting with Genesis, Hartley notes that the Bible mentions milk use soon after the fall from Eden, "certainly the result of [Divine] design, as was the creation of man" (1842:34). To Hartley, this early use substantiates his claim that milk

for thousands of years has constituted so important and valuable a part of human sustenance. Being ready prepared by nature for food, it could at once be appropriated by the rudest savage, as well as the more cultivated. This peculiarity indeed, in an unimproved state of society, before the arts were invented, and when culinary processes were unknown, was in itself sufficient to determine his choice in favor of this form of aliment before all other kinds, which required the intervention of cookery to fit them for use. (1977:34)

In a subsequent section, "The Importance of the Bovine Tribes," Hartley quotes early biblical commentaries that paint Abel's herding as a more noble profession than Cain's tilling:

Abel brought milk and the first fruits of his flocks as offerings to the Creator, who was more delighted and more honored with oblations which grew naturally of their own accord, than with the inventions of a covetous man whose offering were got by forcing the ground. (Josephus Book 1:9, quoted in Hartley 1977:37)

This biblical romance is continued with bucolic descriptions of the "wandering life" in which "every inhabitant and every family was free to pasture their flocks and herds and pitch their tents, wherever fancy might direct or Providence guide" (1842:37). In this way, Hartley painstakingly establishes the "naturalness" of milk drinking as intrinsic to human society and given to humans by God:

> By miraculous power certain species of animals are preserved from the abyss of waters in sevenfold greater numbers, than of others. Need we inquire wherefore this special interposition and indication of Divine favor? It certainly was not on account of the animals themselves, but evidently with prospective reference to the wants of the future families of man. "Doth God take care for oxen?" was the inquiry of the inspired Paul; and from his own response we learn, that this care was altogether for man's sake. (1842:39)

Hartley places milk drinking as a practice not only universally over the time of human subsistence but universally over space as well: "The ox and his kind have followed man in all his migrations. There is scarcely a country in which they are not either indigenous or naturalized" (1842:27). This is a surprising statement, given the fact that Hartley is speaking from a continent where a domestic bovine species had been introduced only a few hundred years before.

Ten years later, another milk reformer in New York City, John Mullaly, wrote a similar treatise on the problems of the city milk supply (1853). Although Mullaly was less prone to cite scripture and more prone to cite statistics, he, like Hartley, assumes the historical universality of milk, citing a French public health publication that states, "Milk is an object of great importance to man. . . . Is it not, therefore, wonderful, that in every age this liquid should have attracted considerable attention?" (Mullaly 1853:110).

The universality of milk consumption became an accepted fact in the mythology of milk, so much so that the average dairy management textbook often started with a phrase such as this one: "The milk of animals was used for human beings before the dawn of history" (Roadhouse and Henderson 1950:608).

The milk booster's second argument in favor of the milk-drinking habit was that milk represented, in words repeated by Roadhouse and Henderson, "the most nearly perfect food" (1950:608). This constantly repeated phrase echoes through the literature on the nutritive value of milk. This "special value" comes from the fact that milk's role is to "nourish the species before a mixed diet can be taken" and for this reason it "occupies a unique position." It is, therefore, "the one food that supplies most of the nutritional requirements in the proper form and balanced proportions" (Roadhouse and Henderson 1950:608).

Hartley, writing before the discovery of vitamins or the development of nutritional science, relies heavily on William Prout's *Bridgewater Treatises on the Power, Wisdom, and Goodness of God, as Manifested in the Creation: Treatise VII –Chemistry, Meteorology, and the Function of Digestion Considered with Reference to Natural Theology* (1834). This treatise combines scientific expertise of the time with a heavy use of William Paley's natural theology. Hartley quotes Prout as referring to milk as "the most perfect of all elementary aliments":

> Being a natural compound of albumen, oil and sugar, which constitute the three great
> staminal principles that are essential to the support of animal life, it is a model of
> what a nutritious substance ought to be, and the most perfect of all elementary ali-
> ments. Such being its characteristics, it possesses both animal and vegetable prop-
> erties, and naturally takes its place at the head of nutrient substances. (Prout, cited
> in Hartley 1842:3)

Hartley cites directly a passage in which Prout goes so far as to call milk the
prototype of all food.

> After all his cooking and his art, how much soever he may be disinclined to believe
> it, is the sole object of his labor; and the more nearly his results approach to this
> object [milk], the more nearly do they approach perfection. Even in the utmost re-
> finements of his luxury, and in his choices delicacies, the same great principle is
> attended to; and his sugar and flour, his eggs and butter, in all their various forms
> and combinations, are nothing more or less, than disguised imitation of the great
> alimentary prototype *milk*, as furnished to him by nature. (Prout, cited in
> Hartley1842:106)

John Mullaly, who took up the milk crusade in the 1850s, states the issue simply: "Good milk contains, as is well known, all the elements necessary not only
for the nutrition, but the growth of the body" (1853:116).

The science behind Hartley's and Mullaly's support for the idea of milk as a
perfect food is vastly different from that cited by Roadhouse and Henderson a
hundred years later. However, the basic argument is the same: milk is the first
food to sustain the human body, and it contains within itself the universe of nutritional needs. Therefore, milk is not only universally used over time and space
but contains within itself the universe of nutrition. These three universals—history, geography, and the commodity itself—make milk boosterism almost a spiritual quest for the unification of time, space, and the body. Although Hartley's
claims may seem more outlandish and less well informed, his final goal is not
so different from that of Roadhouse and Henderson. Hartley is attempting to reunite a city population with its milk-drinking history and God's Divine Will,
whereas Roadhouse and Henderson are instructing a milk distributor on how to
educate the public on "the importance of his product to the health of his community" (1950:608). In both cases, however, the goal is the same: to unite the
public with milk drinking, for its own good.

Hartley, a temperance reformer, was writing as much against alcohol as in favor of pure milk. In his vision of a pure milk supply, he had a clear alternative to
the distillery-based dairy system, which he laid out in a chapter titled "Appeal
to Farmers." He notes that, due to the increasing exposure of the problems of
distillery milk,

there is now a growing demand for pure milk produced from natural food. Such, briefly, being the attitude of this community in relation to the business, a fine opening is presented to men of enterprise who live in grass regions, within a convenient distance of the city. . . . Why should you not engage in this branch of business? Many of you are the proprietors of some of the finest grazing farms in the world, which are already stocked with cows. These you can turn to immediate and profitable account. The conversion of your milk into butter or cheese, with the loss of the labor of making it, will not pay more than two cents a quart, for which you may realize six cents in these cities. Is not this sufficient pecuniary inducement for you to engage in the business, aside from the human consideration that such an enterprise will probably be the means of saving the lives of thousands of innocent children, and of warding off numerous evils [the distilleries themselves] which now afflict and oppress the population? (Roadhouse and Henderson 1950:608).

Yet the building of railroads into New York City lagged behind many other cities at that time, making its overall food supply higher priced and of poorer quality than many other cities (Spann 1981:458). Spann describes the relationship between the development of the rail system into New York City and the consequent improvement in food supplies:

Before 1845, supply by land was limited to farm wagons, droves of cattle herded on the hoof, and New York's still feeble rail system. Railroad development after 1845 rapidly opened up new inland areas. By 1850, besides its connections with New England, New York was served by some 762 miles of railroad; by 1860 the figure was 1,110. The railroad may not have increased the area of the city's food supply by the 4,600 percent estimated by rail enthusiast Henry Varnum Poor, but the new system did effectively supplement, and increasingly supplant, the older water and land routes by providing faster and more flexible service. (1981:121)

Ten years after Hartley's treatise, one third of the city's milk supply was brought in by rail. This new type of dairy industry was heralded by John Mullaly and the next generation of milk reformers as the alternative that would achieve the goal that Hartley originally set out: to reunite the city public with its fresh milk-drinking destiny. This new system brought "country milk" over the newly constructed rail lines into the city.

At the turn of the century, New York City saw "rapid progress in milk supervision," beginning in 1904 when Dr. Thomas Darlington became the city's health commissioner. He began the system of dairy farm and plant inspection, which became the norm in most cities by World War I. By the time of Roadhouse and Henderson's writing in 1950, the industry had achieved "a high point in sanitary production, transportation, processing, and distribution" (1950:8). In addition, "consumption of milk per capita has markedly increased during recent years" (1950:8). More than one-third of all milk produced went into the fluid market milk system by this time, compared with only a small percentage of milk produced in Hartley's time. By 1950, the fluid milk industry had become "the most important branch of the dairy industry in value of products, investment in buildings and equipment, and the number of people required to do the work" (Roadhouse and Henderson 1950:8).

Looking to the future, Roadhouse and Henderson state that "the responsibility of market-milk producers is to maintain the present quality and to strive toward even higher standards." Maintaining this responsibility is necessary because "the public's confidence in and appreciation of the product will always influence the demand for it" (1950:8).

Why did the early milk reformers need to recommend milk, despite the deadly, disease-ridden state of most milk at that time? Why did they insist that milk was indispensable? Why was the "completeness" of milk so important? Why didn't they simply recommend that people stop drinking milk altogether and, like European health movements of that time, recommend a return to breast-feeding?

MILK, NOT MOTHER

Given the unhealthiness of the product in the mid-1800s, why did anyone drink cow's milk at all, much less vulnerable infants and children? Accounts that celebrate the perfection of "country" milk and the poisonous nature of swill milk tend to ignore another widely available and widely used source of pure milk at that time: the human mother. Hartley's hundreds of pages linking humanity to milk drinking and animal herding leaves out the basic historical fact that the milk drunk most commonly by humans across history and geography has been, in fact, breast milk. Mullaly's book on the milk trade extols the purity of country milk but never mentions this alternative and traditional source of milk for children. Hartley, extolling the benefits of cow's milk, describes it as "the natural food of the infant . . . when pure it is at once the most palatable, healthy, and nutritive aliment with which our nurseries and tables can be supplied" (1842:205). He does not mention that human women had been, until that time, supplying milk but instead moves to the idea that this natural—and divinely ordained—food must be "supplied."

Experience at foundling hospitals made the relationship between artificial feeding and infant mortality rates widely known even before the time of Hartley's writing (Baumslag and Michels 1995). Yet Hartley's description of mother's milk betrays multiple suspicions about the healthfulness of breast-feeding. His 350-page treatise mentions breast-feeding only twice. In the first section, titled "Popular Mistakes," he follows a lengthy discussion on the milk of diseased animals with a query about the health condition of breast-feeding mothers: "Who does not know, for illustration, that the health of the infant is affected by the condition of the sustenance it receives from its mother? . . . Is the mother diseased? The virus generated in the vitiated secretions, taints the nourishment, and is communicated to the child" (1842:203). One might attribute these statements to ignorance about the communication of antibodies and other immunities—as opposed to the potential but much less crucial transmission of disease—through breast milk. However, Hartley's statement is more striking, considering that breast milk was for centuries (up to the nineteenth century) considered a curative, almost sacred substance that women often used as a medicine in their role as healers (Salmon 1994).

But beyond the suspicion of diseased mothers—which was an exceptional circumstance—he expanded his suspicions of the quality of mothers' milk for a reason much more common and much more likely to resound with average middle-class urban women of that time: nerves. Although he listed diet and health as two factors that affect the quality of a woman's breast milk, he adds that these "irregularities" can be attributed "probably more frequently to the influence of mental emotions, which as they happen to be unfavorably affected, produce corresponding changes in the milk that seriously injure the health of the infant, and in some instances have proved fatal" (1842:96).

To prove this claim, Hartley offers an anecdote, quoted in 1836 by a doctor quoting in turn another doctor who was supposedly physician to the king of Saxony. In this story, a soldier billeted to the house of a carpenter began to argue with the man and drew his sword on him. The carpenter's wife came between the two men and wrestled the sword away from the soldier, with neighbors assisting in separating the two men.

> While in this state of strong excitement, the mother took up her child from the cradle, where it lay playing and in the most perfect health, never having had a moment's illness; she gave it the breast, and in so doing sealed its fate. In a few minutes the child left off, became restless, panted and *sank dead on its mother's bosom*." (1842:97)

Despite the frequent occurrence of such stories about "nerves" and the inability to breast-feed, most nineteenth-century child-rearing texts did not agree with Hartley's views. They encouraged mothers to breast-feed and admonished those who refused (Golden 1996; Fildes 1986). In addition, a "cult of domestic motherhood" arose with the growth and expansion of urban industrial society, separating men and women—who had worked together in rural contexts—into public and private spheres (Cott 1997; Mintz and Kellog 1988; Clement 1997). Domestic motherhood made women responsible for creating a private space outside of the competitive work world that raised children and revived men in an atmosphere of caring.

Domestic motherhood, however, was a contradictory ideal that put severe cross-pressures on middle-class wives. "The pattern of family life that began to appear in the late eighteenth century often proved in practice to be a source of conflict and personal unhappiness" (Mintz and Kellog 1988:63). Another historian of Victorian motherhood, Mary Lynn Stevens Heininger (1984), argues that the cult of domestic motherhood was a highly contradictory concept in practice. Victorians were subject to "conflicting cultural demands" (1984:19) that in fact separated them further from their children. For example, the social demands placed upon middle-class women—visiting, entertaining, and making consumption decisions, particularly in furnishing and running the home—required a great deal of time. Unlike women's earlier roles, these errands and obligations were not ones in which children could tag along. Visiting was one example of this type of social obligation:

> The sophisticated language of the calling card was beyond the vocabulary of a child, and the ritual of the social visit itself, with its peculiar and changing etiquette, did not welcome them. "Fortunately," wrote Miss Leslie in 1864, "it is no longer fashionable for mothers to take their children with them on morning visits." Four years earlier, Florence Hartley had proclaimed, "To have a child constantly touching the parlor ornaments, balancing itself on the back of a chair, leaning from a window, or performing any of the tricks in which children excel is an annoyance, both to yourself and to your hostess." (Heininger 1984:21)

For fathers: "Adult recreation, with the exception of such sports as baseball and ice skating, was likely to take place in smoke-filled clubs, hunting expeditions, or other social functions at which children were unwelcome" (1984:20). As a result, Heininger states, childhood became not only a separate time of life but increasingly occupying its own separate space in the middle-class home:

> children were increasingly relegated to—a special world apart. Cribs with guardrails and bars made bed a safer place than an unwatched cradle . . . varieties of toys and books enabled children to entertain themselves easily for substantial periods of time without active supervision. . . . [C]are that once had demanded physical presence could now be administered from a distance by means of substitutes for or extensions of personal contact. (Heininger 1984:19)

Heininger also notes a relationship between the growth of an industrial society in which women and children played increasingly marginal roles and the sentimentalization of these roles:

> The disparity between what was considered truly important in adult society and what children were in fact capable of doing begins to explain why adults began to widen the distance between themselves and their children at a time when cultural regard for childhood appeared to be at its highest level ever. At work was the process of sentimentalization, involving womanhood as well as childhood. Ann Douglas, in discussing the phenomenon of sentimentalism explains how this impulse "asserts that the values a society's activity denies are precisely the ones it cherishes." (1984:21)

Mintz and Kellog (1988) write of the increasing isolation of the middle-class mother from the outside world during this time period:

> By the early nineteenth century, the American family had been deprived of a range of traditional economic, social, and ideological supports. . . . The middle-class family existed in a society that rewarded independence and self-reliance and tended to isolate domestic ideals—deference, obedience, and loyalty—from broader economic and political values. (63)

This discussion of isolation tells only part of the story. As Cott (1997) described, middle-class women of the mid-nineteenth century were not isolated in every way: they created new networks around another romantic ideal—friendship. Friendship involved the formation of intimate bonds revolving around the expression of personal, heartfelt feelings. However, these new networks of friendship and feeling entailed different forms of obligation than the earlier economic networks women had formed with kin and neighbors. Although these women increasingly discovered networks of emotional self-expression, they were missing the earlier networks of "helping out" that were an integral part of an earlier "women's economy." Women visited, wrote, and unburdened their hearts, but they were also increasingly expected, as Mintz and Kellog described, to be independent and self-reliant in the functioning of their households.

It is exactly this contradiction between the independent family and women's role within that family that formed another source of conflict. As Alexis de Tocqueville noted, American women before marriage, many with jobs, education, and control over determining their marriage partners, were given greater freedoms and were more independent than European women. However, after marriage, American women appeared more isolated. Individual independence became the independence of the family unit, and the mother's role was taken to be self-sacrifice for the sake of her family. According to Mintz and Kellog (1988:63), "The latent contradiction between woman's preparation for self-fulfillment and her role as the family's key nurturing figure often resulted in enormous personal tension, sometimes manifested in the classic nineteenth-century neurosis of hysteria."

Ironically, the increased economic insecurity of working-class families in urban areas made them retain the "helping out" network. A male breadwinner's wages were not sufficient to feed and clothe a family. Therefore, other family members, including mothers and children, were forced to gain an income of some sort. Kin also depended on pooled resources to make ends meet. "For many immigrants the kinship network provided day-to-day assistance with housing, child care, and loans" (Mintz and Kellog 1988:88). In working-class neighborhoods, a form of helping out network often extended to neighbors as well. Therefore, although working-class women were increasingly uncertain about income, they existed in a larger support network that included a network of work.

For middle-class women, the helping out network must have seemed increasingly beneath their class status. According to Janet Golden (1996), the system of domestic work changed from one of mutual hiring systems to one in which certain people worked as "domestics" for hire by others whose labor was not available in return. In addition, many "hired hands" in the earlier system were relatives, such as children boarded with kin to help out, learn a trade, and receive further discipline. This system of boarding out children stemmed from the Puritan era, when parents felt they needed to send children to relatives for their education and discipline (Hareven 1989). For working-class children, their labor became increasingly used in unskilled factory jobs but without moving away from home. For middle-class children, apprentice work away from home was replaced with play and education in the home to develop their skills for the new professional world of work.

This new system, in which children remained at home with women while men spent most of the day away from home, made women responsible for the upbringing of children, not just ideologically but through their physical proximity. This occurred at a time when the upbringing of children—ensuring their readiness for the professional world—and not the property they were to inherit became the main source of their future status. This led to a certain "status anxiety" in the middle class. According to Priscilla Clement (1997:38), "Because the job market was so much in flux, and new job skills necessary in an industrial economy might render learning traditional crafts useless for advancement, middle-class parents agonized about how best to rear and prepare their children for the future." Therefore, mothers become increasingly important to the raising of children, particularly older children, who had commonly left the household in earlier times or had been expected to help with the younger children. In the new middle-class household, children of all ages required education and could not be depended on as helpers. As a result, "By the early 1800s middle-class parents were experiencing such an intensified sense of responsibility for the proper upbringing of their children that many described parental responsibilities as 'awful'" (Grant 1998:14).

In summary, the middle-class mother of the mid-nineteenth century was faced with the loss of husband, kin, friends, neighbors, and older children as physically available help in child rearing. In addition, the increased claims on her time for the education and discipline of older children as well as a growing number of demands from an adult world increasingly separate from children must have had a great deal of influence on her decision whether or not to breast-feed her infants. Contemporary studies of influences on breast-feeding note the importance of support networks for a mother to successfully perform this task (Visness and Kennedy 1997). The drop in rates of breast-feeding with the urbanization of the family throughout the developed and underdeveloped world is an indication that people in cities have a hard time building these networks. Breast-feeding as a practice may need to be seen as requiring a network of social capital that was less available to upper- and middle-class women beginning in the early nineteenth century.

The cultural declaration by religious reformers that milk was a "perfect food" and necessary for infants, even when milk was a very bad choice for infant feeding, melded with the contradictions of the middle-class urban family to create a new food habit. It is important to note that this discourse did not come from those who would financially benefit from increased sales of milk, but from religious "divines" and social reformers. As the industry developed a voice of its own, it took up the idea of milk's perfection and added its own embellishments to that story.

INDUSTRY'S VOICE

Given this strong ideological boosterism on behalf of cow's milk and against mother's milk, it is worth looking at whether the industry itself reflected these views. How did milk sellers represent their product at this time? Although there is little in the way of industry voice in the public discourse of the mid-nineteenth century, there are some handbills from the time. How the industry itself represented purity and nature in its advertising, from mid-nineteenth-century handbills up to early twentieth-century milk advertisements, shows an interesting progression. The product moved from regular cow's milk to specialized milk formulas. (Cow's milk moved from being an infant food to being consumed by older children and increasingly other members of the family.) In the mid- and late nineteenth century, the symbol for pure milk was the milkmaid. Many of the earliest food bills, posters advertising the product, link the idea of pure "country milk" with the associated images of a cow and a milkmaid. In art, the milkmaid represented the human embodiment of the pastoral ideal—she nurtured the cow and its product to protect health and purity.

Conversely, exposés of the poor quality of "city milk" played on the irony of male milkmaids, emphasizing the maleness of city milkers, seedy ones at that. Newspapers published vivid pictures to accompany reports of the city "swill milk" industry, in which cow stables were attached to breweries and cows ate strictly brewery waste. The men in these pictures were dirty, milking dying cows, and selling the poisoned milk for their own profit. The image of the milkmaid, however, was of a clean, healthy women, caring for her cows, and nourishing the cities with clean country milk.

The image of the milkmaid tending the cow and overseeing the purity of the milk for her customers reflects a connection between motherliness and the purity of the natural product. As an extension, this also reflects the nurturing, feminine countryside producing food to nourish the active, rational, and therefore masculine, city. This "pastoral" view, which made rural places feminine and cities masculine, had existed since ancient times. Yet according to Merchant (1980:20) "pastoral imagery could easily be incorporated into a mechanized industrialized world as an escape from the frustrations of the marketplace." The milkmaid, overseeing the purity of milk, therefore symbolized this nostalgia for the nurturing countryside.

With the development of the industrial economy, ideas concerning nature changed. Rather than the nurturing "mother earth," nature became "matter," a fuel used for the sustenance and growth of human machines, particularly children. Although, according to Merchant, this mechanical view entered scientific thought centuries earlier, the emphasis on the body as a human machine only entered food advertisements at the turn of the twentieth century. In milk advertisements, this resulted in a drastic change in the images portrayed to sell milk: they began to emphasize the product of milk input—the healthy, happy child.

This prize child, pictured in endless milk advertisements, represented the product of good mothering that was clearly linked to the new cult of domestic motherhood. The prize child catered to middle-class women's anxieties about their new role preparing children for the professional world. The chubby bodies, the obviously upper-class names, and the smiling faces no doubt prompted mothers to compare their own children with these products of lactated milk foods and condensed milks. Advertisements encouraged such comparisons with comments such as the number of pounds a child weighed at a certain age (one even boasting an astronomical twenty-eight pounds at eight months!), and the stories of how the child was saved from the door of death because it would eat "nothing else."

By the 1930s, this voice of authority had become dominant. Advertisements were encouraging mothers to make comparisons between the perfect "test children" in advertisements and their own. Although the ads always insisted that breast-feeding was best, the fact that breast-fed babies did not tend to be as chubby as the babies pictured in these advertisements must have prompted many mothers to turn to the bottle. In addition, although cows had disappeared from most milk advertisements, the symbol of milk purity that appeared in many government reports and some advertisements was the veterinarian inspecting the cow with a stethoscope. This picture of modern male science replaced the milkmaid as the major icon of milk purity.

The rise in science and rational control over nature, and the concurrent rise in urban control over the countryside, changed the symbolism of purity in food advertisements. The new "overseer" of purity was the expert, the veterinary doctor, who was always depicted as a man. Therefore, advertisements replaced the nurturing milkmaid in her generative partnership with nature with the expert male who made pure milk through scientific inspection of the subject, the cow. These advertisements inevitably show the veterinarian holding his stethoscope up to the animal's lungs, a scientific, not a motherly, gesture.

These changes in worldview also reflect changes in demography and the consequent political changes that went with them. By the 1920s, urban dwellers had gained a majority over the rural population and politicians and businessmen had to take into account these changes in their constituencies. The transformation of the countryside from mother to managed could not have taken place without these demographic changes.

The otherness of nature, through management, was therefore overcome. Not only was the cow domesticated but even the bacteria in her milk was now under control. Nature was perfectible through human intervention, with milk now leading the way as "the perfect food." Women, no longer in charge of nature, were instead grateful recipients of managed nature through pure food and were themselves managed through home economists' exhortations to be good shoppers. Ironically, the perfect shopper was embodied in that bovine image of the 1960s, Elsie the Cow, which combined the two worlds that men managed, women and nature, into a housewife cow who gave shopping advice.

These changes in the representation of milk in food advertisements reflected changes in the "political ecology" of consumption. In particular, these advertisements reflected the rise of industrial consumption from an earlier merchant era. Merchant-era advertisements—and particularly their milk wagons—represented the purity of their product by associating it with the countryside and the production source. As the industrial system developed, the images of nature and body changed from countryside, females, and cows to consumers, males, and birds.

Why birds? Answering this question once again uncovers the complex nature of relationships (of people to each other, particularly within the family) and embodiment (the relationship of people to their own natural bodies and—particularly for women—the bodies of their family) in the industrialization of food. Looking at the ways in which these issues were represented in food advertisements can provide some clue about how advertisers attempted to intervene in these relationships.

An overview of early twentieth-century food advertisements shows that the image of the "maker" of the food was often problematic. The actual production process involved in making the food was seldom portrayed (no factories are in evidence in these advertisements). Instead, a "replacement" maker or provider of food was often necessary. The Quaker in Quaker Oats was one of the first successful portrayals of a replacement maker that consumers identified with. In many cases, racial or childlike "others" represented the "maker" (someone who could not be confused with a consumer's actual local baker or grocer). For example, the replacement food provider was often a black man (as in the Cream of Wheat advertisements) or a child.

In milk formula advertisements, an obvious replacement for the maker would be the cow. Instead, the bird became the prominent symbol of milk formula. Borden advertised its "Eagle Brand" condensed milk through a fatherly bird-authority figure. Nestlé's earliest advertisements feature a bird feeding its children in a nest), an image that it eventually enhanced into the protective stork. Why did these companies feel the need to replace the cow with the bird?

To explain this phenomenon, it is necessary to look not at the food itself but at the ideal process that the advertiser wanted to encourage. A bird gathers food and brings it home to the family nest. A cow produces food within its own body. In other words, the cow too closely represented the process of embodied feeding, whereas the bird more accurately represented the mother participating in a process of commoditized consumption—shopping and bringing the infant's sustenance back home. The "replacement" nature icon in this case becomes part of a discourse about embodiment, nature, and family relationships around milk.

CONCLUSION

As this analysis shows, the relationship between consumer consciousness and the rise of industrial food is more complex than current narratives about the industrialization of food currently acknowledge. Changes in family relationships, with the rise in urbanization, changed the symbolism of food images. Nature was perfectible through human intervention, but the ideology of milk as "perfect" came not from food industrialists but reformer divines who linked milk's perfection to natural theology. Industrialists, economists, and dairy scientists later took up this claim using science and nutrition as their supportive evidence, but the message was basically the same. From religious authority to industrial and governmental authority, male authorities mediated the relationship between women, their families, and their bodies.

Yet the irony of this analysis is that the discourse separating female nature from milk did not originate with the industrial voice. The consumer voice, a part played in this discourse by the male urban reformer, had already reorganized the relationship between body, country, and food. In fact, it took the industry time to catch up with this ideology, abandoning the milkmaid as the representation of purity and replacing it with the child, the bird, and the veterinarian. The difference between milk as a substance and milk as a food is the relationship surrounding the provision and consumption of this substance. Understanding these relationships requires that analysis go beyond class as a factor and its simple focus on labor, particularly women's labor, as the major force influencing changes in consumption. To understand the rise of milk as a food requires bringing in the social history of family relationships and how these relationships relate to nature through the process of embodiment. Without these perspectives, commodity chain and other political economy approaches to consumption will always be missing a crucial link.

NOTES

1. The overlap in the meaning of this word is not accidental. Women traditionally breast-fed invalid and elderly members of the family as well.

2. While the suspicious populist side of me keeps looking for some economic relationship between Hartley and capitalists—primarily the train barons—that would benefit from his boosterism, so far I have found none.

BIBLIOGRAPHY

Apple, Rima D. (1987). *Mothers and Medicine: A Social History of Infant Feeding, 1890–1950*. Madison: University of Wisconsin Press.
Atkins, P. J. (1992). "White Poison? The Social Consequences of Milk Consumption, 1850–1930," *Social History of Medicine* 5(2):207–27.
Baumslag, Naomi, and Dia L. Michels (1995). *Milk, Money, and Madness: The Culture and Politics of Breast-Feeding*. Foreword by Richard Jolly. Westport, Conn.: Bergin & Garvey.
Blaikie, Piers M., and Harold Brookfield (1987). *Land Degradation and Society*. London: Methuen.
Catherwood, M. P. (1931). "A Statistical Study of Milk Production for the New York Market." Bulletin 518, Cornell University Agricultural Experimental Station.
Clement, Priscilla Ferguson (1997). *Growing Pains: Children in the Industrial Age, 1850–1890*. New York: Twayne.
Cott, Nancy F. (1997). *The Bonds of Womanhood: "Woman's Sphere" in New England, 1780–1835*. 2d ed. with a new preface. Edinburgh: Edinburgh University Press.
Giblin, James C. (1986). *Milk: The Fight for Purity*. New York: Crowell.
Golden, Janet Lynne (1996). *A Social History of Wet Nursing in America: From Breast to Bottle*. New York: Cambridge University Press.
Goodman, David, and Michael Redclift (1991). *Refashioning Nature: Food, Ecology, and Culture*. New York: Routledge.
Goodman, David, Bernardo Sorj, and John Wilkinson (1987). *From Farming to Biotechnology: A Theory of Agro-Industrial Development*. New York: Basil Blackwell.
Grant, Julia (1998). *Raising Baby by the Book: The Education of American Mothers*. New Haven, Conn.: Yale University Press.
Grossman, Lawrence (1998). *The Political Ecology of Bananas: Contract Farming, Peasants, and Agrarian Change in the Eastern Caribbean*. Chapel Hill: University of North Carolina Press.
Hampe, Edward C. Jr., and Merle Wittenberg (1964). *The Lifeline of America: Development of the Food Industry*. New York: McGraw-Hill.
Hareven, Tamara (1989). "Historical Changes in Children's Networks in the Family and Community," in *Children's Social Networks and Social Supports*, ed. Deborah Belle, 15–36. New York: Wiley.
Hartley, Robert Milham (1977 [1842]). *An Historical, Scientific, and Practical Essay on Milk as an Article of Human Sustenance*. New York: Arno Press.
Heininger, Mary Lynn Stevens (1984). *A Century of Childhood, 1820–1920*. Rochester, N.Y.: Margaret Woodbury Strong Museum.
Hightower, Jim (1973). *Hard Tomatoes, Hard Times; A Report of the Agribusiness Accountability Project on the Failure of America's Land Grant College Complex*. Research coordinated by Susan DeMarco. Foreword by James Abourezk. Cambridge, Mass.: Schenkman.

Martin, Emily (1987). *The Woman in the Body: A Cultural Analysis of Reproduction.* Boston: Beacon Press.

Merchant, Carolyn (1980). *The Death of Nature: Women, Ecology, and the Scientific Revolution.* 1st ed. San Francisco: Harper & Row.

Mintz, Sidney (1986). *Sweetness and Power: The Place of Sugar in Modern History.* New York: Penguin.

Mintz, Steven, and Susan Kellog (1988). *Domestic Revolutions: A Social History of American Family Life.* New York: Free Press; London: Collier Macmillan.

Mullaly, John (1853). *The Milk Trade of New York and Vicinity, Giving an Account of the Sale of Pure and Adulterated Milk.* With an introduction by R. T. Trall, M.D. New York: Fowlers and Wells.

Pillsbury, Richard (1998). *No Foreign Food: The American Diet in Time and Place.* Boulder, Colo.: Westview.

Prout, William (1834). *Bridgewater Treatises on the Power, Wisdom, and Goodness of God, as Manifested in the Creation: Treatise VIII–Chemistry, Meteorology, and the Function of Digestion Considered with Reference to Natural Theology.* London: Pickering.

Roadhouse, Chester Linwood, and James Lloyd Henderson (1950). *The Market-Milk Industry.* 2d ed. New York: McGraw-Hill.

Salmon, Marylynn (1994). "The Cultural Significance of Breastfeeding and Infant Care in Early Modern England and America," *Journal of Social History* 28(2):247–70.

Spann, Edward K. (1981). *The New Metropolis: New York City, 1840–1857.* New York: Columbia University Press.

Spencer, Leland, and Charles J. Blanford (1977). *An Economic History of Milk Marketing and Pricing, 1800–1933 Volume I (Amended Version).* Columbus, Ohio: Grid.

Spencer, Leland, and Ida A. Parker (1961). *Consumption of Milk and Cream in the New York City Market and Northern New Jersey.* Bulletin 965, Cornell University Agricultural Experimental Station (July).

Visness, Cynthia, and Kathy I. Kennedy (1997). "Maternal Employment and Breast-Feeding: Finding from the 1988 National Maternal and Infant Health Survey," *American Journal of Public Health* 87(6):945–50.

8

Packaging Violence: Media, Story Sequencing, and the Perception of Right and Wrong

Karen A. Cerulo

Violence is a staple of current media offerings, and usage statistics indicate that U.S. readers and viewers are "buying" it. But increasingly, research suggests that the media's commodification of violence may prove costly for American society. Specifically, many scholars contend that repeated contact with violent media content may be reshaping public views of normalcy and deviance and ultimately reshaping behaviors. A growing body of data supports this premise, documenting a significant link between long-term, heavy exposure to violent media stories and aggressive attitudes and behaviors. This chapter takes note of how the potential effects of media violence extend beyond issues of content. To determine fully the impact of violent media stories, one must carefully attend to the ways in which text and image are organized, or "packaged." Specifically, the research outlined in this chapter attends to the *sequencing* of violent media content—*the ways in which those who tell the story of violence unfold and order the elements of an account.* Packaging strategies such as sequencing demand the most serious attention, for the "putting together" of content commodifies violence in important ways. This chapter will demonstrate that the sequencing of a violent story's elements can significantly influence readers' and viewers' evaluations of violence as right, wrong, or something in between.

VIOLENT ACTS

On May 8, 1999, a New Jersey trial judge sentenced twenty-year-old Thomas Koskovich to death by lethal injection. That pronouncement ended a grisly, horrific saga that drew much attention in and around the state. The story began two years earlier on April 19, 1997. Pizzeria owner Georgio Gallaro and his employee Jeremy Giordano agreed to make one last delivery before "calling it a night." The delivery led Gallaro and Giordano to an abandoned home in Sussex County, New Jersey. When the men ventured out of their car, they were ambushed, shot eight times, and left to die in the road. Within thirty-six hours, police made arrests in the case. Teenagers Jason Vreeland, then seventeen, and Thomas Koskovich, then eighteen, were charged with two counts of first-degree murder— murders reportedly motivated not by theft or vendetta, but rather for the thrill of killing.[1]

The Gallaro and Giordano story is not the most famous of the decade; it is not the most unusual or the most brutal act of this time. Rather, these murders represent just one of many violent events that have become a routine feature of modern American life. Homicide now represents a leading cause of death for various demographic groups. It is the number-one killer of African American males between the ages of fifteen and forty-four. For all Americans between the ages of fifteen and twenty-four, homicide is eclipsed only by accidents.[2] Violent assaults at the hands of intimates are at an all time high. Every fifteen seconds in the United States, a woman is battered by her husband, boyfriend, or live-in partner. And in a recent survey, one out of every three teenagers reported knowing a victim of acquaintance rape.[3] Recent statistics also establish weapons of violence as a clear and present danger. Each day, approximately 370 people are shot and 93 people die of gunfire in the United States. Nearly 15 percent of gunshot fatalities claim this nation's children, a rate that is nearly sixteen times higher than the combined rate for children in twenty-five other industrial countries.[4]

Violence in the United States represents a complex problem. No single factor can satisfactorily account for its high levels of occurrence. Criminologists point to the growing availability of handguns and other weapons.[5] Philosophers suggest that a "moral poverty" has engulfed American society—especially its children and adolescents.[6] Many media scholars argue that current levels of violence may be linked to the graphic images now so central to newspapers, films, television, and video games.[7]

Among the many "probable causes" of violence, the role various media play has garnered consistent attention—and with good reason. Violence remains a regular feature of daily newspaper coverage.[8] The topic also dominates most audio-visual media. Sixty-one percent of television programs now contain some type of violence. During any weeknight, the average American viewer witnesses about three acts of violence per TV viewing hour. On Saturday mornings, a time period dominated by child viewers, the rate of violence increases to eighteen acts per hour.[9] Comparable figures can be cited with regard to motion pictures. Social activist Dock Rolfe reflects on the current state of film:

The first violent film that "moved" an audience was the *Great Train Robbery* in 1903. Ticket holders reportedly ran from the theaters in terror when the villain pointed his phony prop gun directly into the camera. In 1931, when James Cagney starred in *Public Enemy*, a *New York Times* film critic berated the picture as "sensational and incoherent ending in general slaughter." In fact, there were a total of eight deaths, each one taking place off screen. Compare that with the 1990 Bruce Willis film *Die Hard 2* with 264 brutal killings, all in front of the camera.[10]

Video and computer games, the newest addition to the media scene, promote explicit violence as well. And recent studies show that games involving fantasy violence represent the most popular genre for seventh and eighth graders—the primary users of such games.[11]

The first section of this chapter highlights the importance of sequencing in the attribution of meaning. The second section identifies four distinct sequences that drive the media's packaging of violence. (Examples of each format are supplied.) Noted are the circumstances under which storytellers are likely to apply one sequence type over another. Third, the impact of sequencing on audience interpretations of violent stories are reviewed. Recent focus-group data show that certain story sequences are systematically associated with negative assessments of violence, whereas other sequences typically elicit positive evaluations; still other sequences are associated with readers' and viewers' ambivalence. The conclusion speculates on the importance of these findings for those dedicated to fighting violence. If certain story sequences indeed reduce public tolerance for violence, then attention to sequencing as part of the media commodification process may ultimately prove an important tool in reducing the incidence of violent behaviors.

STORY SEQUENCING—WHY IS IT IMPORTANT?

Most social scientists approach media accounts as value-laden instruments of meaning, instruments with the power to confirm certain cultural beliefs and construct specific social realities.[12] This tradition locates the power of media stories primarily in their content; meaning is derived from *what* a story says or *what* an image depicts. The analysis explained here moves beyond the content of violent media accounts, emphasizing instead the *how* of violent accounts—the manner in which story content is deployed. Of particular importance is the temporal order by which information enters the foreground and then recedes to the background of readers' and viewers' attention, the *sequence* of a message. Sequencing is treated here as a "packaging strategy"—a method by which those who tell the stories of violence unfold and arrange the dimensions of a violent event.

Story sequencing is an important factor in the commodification of violence. This is because sequencing plays a vital role in readers' and viewers' attributions of meaning. In essence, a sequence operates as a silent narrator, one that initiates and meticulously guides the way in which an event is revealed. The directing voice of a sequence is first felt in the initiation of an account. By defining an event's beginning, a sequence creates what Merleau-Ponty[13] referred to as a perceptual "point-horizon." A story's entry point serves as a porthole from which people view the dimensions of the broader horizon. People come to inhabit the point, grasping all other elements of a story from this entry location.

By positioning people within an event, a sequence channels their experience. Sequences move them step by step through a finite series of facts and observations. Throughout the process, each move circumscribes the next, as every move limits the information options ahead. In so doing, a sequence ultimately assures a specific point of exit from the action; movement through the story is targeted toward a particular ending.

To be sure, other media scholars have explored sequencing and the role it plays in the acquisition of meaning. But in such studies, definitions of sequencing have traditionally been guided by elements tangential to temporal ordering—elements such as the inclusion and exclusion of material, the emphasis or deemphasis of content, and so on.[14] Such factors, and the knowledge of their workings, are undeniably important. But the information in this chapter promotes a more stringent inquiry. Ultimately, what is of interest here is the effects that may ensue when one changes the temporal ordering of *identical* story content. This research strives to discover if one can alter readers' and viewers' assessments of violence simply by repackaging the same materials. Probing this issue will allow the exploration of message structure as an independent source of meaning. In holding story content constant, it is possible to learn something new of the ways in which packaging strategies impact those who consume violent words and images.

THE FOUR SEQUENCES OF VIOLENCE

Before exploring the effects of sequencing, one must become familiar with the various sequence styles by which media storytellers package violence. Toward that end, I have reviewed literally hundreds of newspaper and television reports, motion-picture scenes, novels, short stories, paintings, photographs, and comic strips. (Note that I consider violence in its broadest sense, dealing not only with incidents of murder, assault, terrorism, and war, but with verbal attacks, corporal punishment, violent sports competition, and attacks of nature.) My review of these data reveals strong patterns guiding the packaging of media violence.[15] Specifically, *all* media storytellers use one of four informational sequences to unfold violent accounts. I refer to these four options as victim sequences, performer sequences, contextual sequences, and doublecasting sequences. Newspaper and television accounts help to illustrate the differences between these four packaging techniques.

Victim Sequences: Victim sequences present violence through the eyes of the injured. Information about the victim initiates the story and serves as the audience's point of reference. Details on violent perpetrators appear much later in the information chain, and contextual qualifications are reserved for the story's conclusion. A victim sequence guides this newspaper lead below;[16] the story reports a hit-and-run killing:

TEXT ELEMENT	SEQUENCE
A pregnant St. John's University student	Victim
was struck and killed	Act
by a hit-and- run driver	Performer
near the Queens campus.[17]	Context

Similarly, a victim sequence organizes this television news report of an aggravated assault:

AUDIO ELEMENT	VIDEO	SEQUENCE
A Continental Airlines agent, Angelo Sottile, is in critical condition tonight	Picture of the agent	Victim
following a brutal attack	Picture of the agent	Act
by passenger John C. Davis.	Picture of perpetrator in police custody	Performer
Sottile tried to stop the passenger when he did not show his boarding pass. Davis claims he was pursuing his straying toddler.[18]	*Picture of perpetrator in police custody*	*Context*

In each of these stories, victims and their fate provide the porthole to the action. The victim sequence prioritizes those whom violence strikes.

Performer Sequences: Performer sequences locate readers and viewers at the perpetrator's vantage point. Facts regarding the perpetrator's identity, intentions, and actions take precedence. Information on victims and context emerges later in the information stream. A performer sequence steers this description of a police shooting:

TEXT ELEMENT	SEQUENCE
Police yesterday	Performer
killed	Act
a man	Victim
who had shot to death two SWAT team members, ending a 16-hour standoff that began with a fight between neighbors.[19]	Context

Similarly, a performer sequence directs this description of nature's violent attack:

AUDIO ELEMENT	VIDEO	SEQUENCE
The surging Cedar river	Picture of surging river	Performer
split	Picture of surging river	Act
the town of Waverly Iowa	Picture of townspeople	Victim
in half and demolished property.		
Vice President Gore	Picture of townspeople	Context
announced federal disaster	and demolished property	
aid to the area.[20]		

In each of these stories, perpetrators introduce the violence. Readers and viewers "witness" the act from the performer's perspective.

Context Sequences: In contrast to the packaging styles heretofore reviewed, context sequences prioritize information on an act's setting or circumstance. Storytellers set the stage before "placing" victims or perpetrators. They locate readers and viewers in the "why" of violence before addressing the "who" or the "how."

In the following story, a context sequence reveals a suicide to readers:

TEXT ELEMENT	SEQUENCE
Apparently distressed about having	Context
to go to prison,	
a 29-year-old Jersey City man	Performer
hanged	Act
himself in the Union County jail.[21]	Victim
	(location)

Similarly, context introduces us to a controversial police shooting in Brooklyn, New York:

AUDIO ELEMENT	VIDEO	SEQUENCE
Was it self-defense? While	Picture of a residential	Context
investigating a car theft in	neighborhood	
Brooklyn yesterday morning,		
Police officers	Picture of several	Performers
	police officers	
shot and wounded	Pictures of teens on	Act
	an ambulance gurney	
two teen-age suspects.[22]	Picture of teens on	Victims
	an ambulance gurney	

In these story leads, circumstance takes center stage. Complexities and qualifications of the act precede the knowledge of the actors.

Doublecasting Sequences: Doublecasting sequences immediately impose a point/counterpoint perspective on an event. At their initiation, these formats simultaneously cast the central subject of a violent act as both victim and perpetrator.

This *New York Times* headline, announcing the murder of serial killer Jeffrey Dahmer, illustrates the doublecasting style. Dahmer's dual status—victim and performer—initiates the event:

JEFFREY DAHMER	MULTIPLE KILLER	IS BLUDGEONED TO DEATH IN PRISON
(Victim)	(Perpetrator)	(Act/Context)

Doublecasting drives the story lead as well:

TEXT ELEMENT	SEQUENCE
Jeffrey L. Dahmer,	Victim
whose gruesome exploits of murder, necrophilia, and dismemberment shocked the world in 1991,	Perpetrator
was attacked and killed today	Act
in a Wisconsin prison where he was serving 15 consecutive life terms.[23]	*Context*

The doublecasting formats displayed in these examples delay the connection of victim and act. Before allowing readers to sympathize fully with Dahmer's fate, the sequence presents readers with his sins. In this way, doublecasting disrupts the typical subject-predicate structure of media text. Instead, the sequence prioritizes Dahmer's dual status.

CHOOSING A STORYTELLING SEQUENCE

The four sequences of violence are not randomly applied. Rather, storytellers' sequence choices are very strongly tied to the type of violence they are recounting. In my analyses, three types of violence prove to be critical. The first, *deviant violence,* refers to acts generally classified as illegal. These include criminal assaults, criminal murders, forcible rapes, certain acts of terrorism, and so on. *Normal violence*, a second category, refers to acts typically judged to be legal, necessary, or in some cases, common and tolerable. Violence waged in self-defense, capital punishment, figurative verbal attacks, attacks of nature, sports violence, and so on typically exemplify this category. The final category, *ambiguous violence*, refers to acts that may exhibit necessity or justifiability. Yet such acts may also carry harsh negative sanctions. Suicide, the murder of a serial killer, and so on, provide examples of ambiguous violence.

My research shows that storytellers working in various media (i.e., newspapers, television, comic books, fiction, films, paintings, photos, and short stories) overwhelmingly prefer victim sequences for the display of deviant violence. Performer sequences are most often applied in presenting normal violence. And storytellers typically reserve context or doublecasting sequences for the telling of ambiguous violence.

The data contained in table 8.1, for example, summarize the sequence types used to build 130 different newspaper accounts of violence. (The table also provides information on my sampling strategy.) By looking down the columns of the table, one can easily see the patterns guiding storytellers' sequence choices. When journalists choose victim sequences, they are most likely using them to report instances of deviant violence. In contrast, when journalists select performer sequences, they are most likely packaging stories of normal violence. Journalists typically adopt context or doublecasting sequences for presentations of ambiguous violence.[24]

The patterns that characterize journalists' packaging of violence can be found in other media products as well. In motion pictures, for example, these same

Table 8.1   Sequences by Violence Type

	Sequence Types			
	Victim	*Performer*	*Doublecasting or Contextual*	*All*
Violence Type				
Deviant	71%	25%	4%	100%
Violence	(40)	(14)	(2)	(n=56)
Normal	0%	96%	4%	100%
Violence	(0)	(46)	(2)	(n=48)
Ambiguous	7%	7%	86%	100%
Violence	(1)	(1)	(24)	(n=26)
	(n=41)	(n=61)	(n=28)	(N=130)

Chi Square = 167.35; p<.001; d.f. = 4.

Note: These statistics derive from the analysis of newspaper stories on violence. The sample was drawn from twelve U.S. newspapers, newspapers selected with an eye toward both regional variation and variation in readerships: *The Atlanta Constitution, The Boston Globe, The Chicago Tribune, The Dallas Morning News, The Denver Post, The Los Angeles Times, The Miami Herald, The Philadelphia Inquirer, Reuter's News Service* (on-line news reports), *The St. Louis Dispatch, The Star Ledger,* and *USA Today.* During the period of December 1, 1995 to November 30, 1996, I randomly selected four issues of each newspaper for a total of forty-eight issues. Within each of the forty-eight issues, I coded all stories pertaining to violent action. This strategy resulted in a sample of 130 stories.

sequence choices distinguish deviant, normal, and ambiguous acts of violence. Several classic moments of motion picture violence help to illustrate filmmakers' sequence preferences. Consider first Francis Ford Coppola's saga, *The Godfather*. Frame-by-frame analysis suggests that Coppola's sequencing style changes with reference to the role of the violent actor—antagonist versus protagonist. For example, violence *against* the film's protagonists represents deviant action. Thus, when protagonists such as Vito Corleone or Sonny Corleone fall to enemy fire, viewers move through the scene with the victims. Victims introduce the scene, and during the violent act itself, viewers first witness the victim's surprise and suffering. Perpetrators typically occupy the final frames of the visual sequence.

In contrast, violence committed by *The Godfather's* protagonists constitutes normal violence. Such scenes are sequenced in ways that differ from deviant violence events. When the Corleones strike, viewers witness the acts from the perpetrators' perspectives. Viewers approach the shootings of Solozzo and McClosky, for example, from the viewpoint of protagonist Michael Corleone. Viewers witness the act through Michael's eyes; they flee the scene with Michael. Similarly, the bloody massacre that ends the movie is shot via the perpetrators' perspectives. Audience members prepare for the "job" with each "hit man"; they view the attack through each perpetrator's gun sight. By sequencing deviant and normal violence in different ways, Coppola provides viewers with contrasting views. Victim sequences place viewers with the injured, presumably encouraging sympathy for the characters' plight. Performer sequences put viewers "in the perpetrator's shoes," allowing for affinity with a violent strike.

The pictorial sequences used by Coppola to differentiate deviant and normal violence are common to a wide array of other motion pictures. Scenes from several Hollywood classics support this point. In Oliver Stone's *Midnight Express*, for example, viewers witness the sadistic warden Hamidou beating American prisoner William Hayes. In filming the action, audiences are positioned with the victim, viewing every blow from Hayes's perspective. In contrast, viewers watch the murder of Hamidou through perpetrator William Hayes's eyes. Hayes's justifiable attack, an act of self-preservation, is filmed from the perpetrator's spatial location.

Like Oliver Stone, Martin Scorsese uses visual sequences to distinguish types of violence in the *Taxi Driver*. Recall that Scorsese presents Travis Bickle's first violent act as heroic and normative. Bickle shoots a convenience-store intruder after the burglar attempts to murder the store owner. Scorsese films this normal violence from the violent actor's perspective. He places the camera over Bickle's shoulder, allowing audiences to experience the shooting with the performer. As *Taxi Driver* progresses, Scorsese makes it clear that Bickle is more disturbed than heroic. The famous vigilante spree near the film's conclusion is framed as brutal, alarming, and purely deviant. As Travis kills both Sporto the pimp and his partner,

Scorsese locates viewers with the victims. Each striking shot forces the audience to take the "hit" along with Bickle's prey.

Brian De Palma's *Scarface*, a film frequently cited for its violence, also contains visually distinct presentations of deviant and normal violence. The movie's famous "chain saw" scene, for example, depicts a heinous moment of violence. True to form, this deviant attack follows a classic victim sequence. The sequence begins with a quick camera series that takes viewers from victim to chain saw blade to the face of the threatening drug lord. As the actual assault occurs, viewers see the victim's eyes, they hear his screams. The scene concludes from the eyes of Scarface, the victim's friend. The onlooker is sickened by what he sees; he is splattered in the victim's blood. Contrast this presentation with the assassination of Scarface himself, an act portrayed as just punishment for a ruthless killer. DePalma unfolds Scarface's murder via a performer sequence. Viewers watch the assassin approach Scarface; the camera fixates the audience on the barrel of the assassin's gun. Through the gun's sights, viewers see a close-up of Scarface. As the scene concludes, viewers experience the shooting from the assassin's spatial location.

Director Scott Kalvert applies the same sequencing distinctions in his recent and controversial film, *The Basketball Diaries*. Kalvert uses the character Jim (based on artist Jim Carroll) to unfold carefully the destruction of drug addiction. As Jim's drug involvement deepens, the viewer watches him succumb to a violent, savage existence. Kalvert underscores the deviance of Jim's growing aggression (i.e., muggings, assaults, and eventually, murder) by presenting his violent acts via victim sequences. Each time Jim punches, shoves, or stabs another person, the viewer experience the violence from the victim's vantage point—the camera places the viewer at the shoulders of victims as they receive forceful punches; the camera locates the viewer flat on the sidewalk with victims being brutally kicked and beaten. Interestingly, the director abandons victim sequencing for only one of the film's violent scenes—a scene designed to help understand what is motivating Jim's violent rage. As this scene opens, Jim is narrating an entry from his diary. Groggy and drifting toward sleep, he shares with the audience his reasons, his pain, and his justifications for his actions. For these few moments, viewers leave Jim's victims behind; they are beckoned into the core of Jim's agony. Viewers then "fall asleep" with Jim and accompany him through a violent, painful dream. The dream finds Jim entering his high school classroom and slaughtering those who have tormented, attacked, and made him feel inferior. Throughout the scene, the camera places viewers in the role of shooter or cheering spectator—but never in the role of victim. By maintaining a performer perspective, Kalvert keeps viewers participating in the action. The director rivets viewers to the perpetrator and gives them a temporary space in which to experience the character's motivations (Woodruff 1995).[25]

Film portrayals of ambiguous violence conform to systematic patterns as well. As might be expected, prototypical film scenes of ambiguous violence unfold via contextual or doublecasting sequences. Consider, for example, the striking conclusion to Spike Lee's *Do the Right Thing*. Within the continuous stream of violent attacks that bring the film to a close, camera angles doublecast each of the characters as both victim and perpetrator. For example, when Sal, the pizzeria owner, angrily takes a bat to Radio's boombox, viewers watch the destruction from the victim's perspective. The camera places audiences over the shoulder of Radio as he fearfully watches Sal's angry attack. Radio's retaliatory assault of Sal also is filmed from the victim's vantage point. The camera positions the audience on the floor. Here, lying next to Sal, the audience experiences every blow of the brawl. Lee's juxtapositioning of these two scenes forces audiences to consider each character's dual role. Within moments, viewers live with both Sal and Radio, seeing them as both offenders and offended. The technique can leave audiences unsure regarding the appropriate target of blame.

In a similar way, director Tim Robbins uses doublecasting to capture the ambiguity surrounding the violence of capital punishment. Recall the execution scene in *Dead Man Walking*. As prison officials put victim Matthew Poncelet to death, Robbins interjects scenes of Poncelet as perpetrator. Thus, audiences view flashbacks of the murders for which Poncelet was convicted amidst the harrowing moments of Poncelet's execution ritual. The scene's conclusion presents Poncelet's corpse, framed by ghostlike silhouettes of his victims.[26]

ARE SEQUENCE CHOICES CONSCIOUS?

The sequencing of deviant, normal, and ambiguous violence exhibits strong and visible patterns. Where do these patterns originate? To explore the issue, I analyzed instructional texts written for journalists, broadcasters, and other artists.[27] I also conducted intensive interviews with reporters and other narrators.[28] Finally, I analyzed published interviews done with artists, filmmakers, and novelists.[29] Such analysis revealed *implicit formulae* that guide the sequencing of violence. These formulae are referred to as implicit because storytellers' application of these formulae is not directly recognized.

In pedagogical examples and in storytellers' accounts of "on-the-job training," certain sequence types were regularly coupled with particular kinds of violent stories. Storytellers "in training" were repeatedly exposed to specific ways of unfolding certain topics. This practice establishes "sequence conventions," and these conventions appear to guide media narrators as they temporally order a violent story's elements. Yet neither instructors nor storytellers fully perceive the role of professional socialization in establishing such conventions. Rather, instructors and storytellers link the sequence choices to what they call a "natural logic."

Among media storytellers and books that "teach" narration, the temporal ordering of a story's elements takes on an essential, or inherent, characteristic. This essentialist view is possible because storytellers assume that their readers and viewers hold a singular moral consensus. Instructional texts and interview data clearly show that *narrators attribute one uniform conception of right and wrong to their readers and viewers.*

Two textbook writers, Johnson and Harris (1942), powerfully capture the sentiment: "The descending order of importance by which one organizes facts will be referred to as *the logical order.* This term is useful in distinguishing between arrangements of events as they actually occur (chronological) and the rearrangement imposed on these events by the narrator. The term *logical order* implies also that the rearrangement of facts is not haphazard. Rather, *it happens in rational accordance with reader sentiment"* (1942:64).

This quote (and others like it) illustrates an important aspect of storytellers' professional socialization. The four sequences of violence are not explicitly itemized as alternate methods for reporting violence. Narrators are not expressly urged to learn specific sequence alternatives and apply them when faced with certain circumstances. Instead, the systematic application of the four sequences is downplayed and storytellers are urged to "develop a feel" for natural or logical hierarchies of facts—hierarchies believed to emerge from a universal moral code. In this way, the appropriate sequencing of a story's elements appears to *emerge* from the audience rather than being *imposed* on the audience via professional standards. Sequence choices appear to *reflect* a unified moral consensus rather than to *create* it.

Throughout my interviews, media storytellers deemphasized professional technique, opting instead to characterize their sequence choices as a response to public demand. For example, I posed the following question when interviewing journalists and reporters: "How would you typically order facts (i.e., the who, what, when, where, why, and how) surrounding a particularly heinous crime such as murder, rape, or a brutal assault?" Initially, my subjects could not provide a definitive response. Ninety-three percent of those questioned said that there was no specific formula to which they could refer in unfolding these stories. Rather the specific circumstances surrounding each event would dictate their story lead. Yet when I asked those same subjects to provide a sample lead for three deviant crimes—a "stranger homicide," a "husband-to-wife assault and battery" or a case of "child molesting," 90 percent of the respondents provided a victim sequence. I asked each subject why he/she had sequenced the story in this way. In response, the subjects spoke of their choices not as a "trick of the trade," or a professional convention but as *the only* appropriate—*the naturally logical voice*—for the stories in question.

One reporter explained: "With these kinds of stories, I lead with the victim. That's the most human approach. Most of these crimes are atrocious. Who could really sympathize with the murderer? But the victim, that's something else. The victim is someone the reader can relate to. He or she matters to the audience."

Another reporter said: "Few of my readers are likely to be perpetrators of a crime like this. But any one of them could be victims. So, that's the starting point . . . the victim, the act. That's the thing they will relate to. I start a story by putting them in that victim's shoes."

Appealing to a natural order is a practice waged by storytellers in other media as well. For example, in published interviews, filmmakers describe an "essential" moral perspective that helps them to unfold correctly a violent tale. Directors never discuss patterned storytelling formulae. They never describe their portrayals of violence as the product of filmmaking conventions. Rather they describe the trial and error involved in capturing the single most "appropriate" approach to certain violent scenes. Many filmmakers imply that success in this regard occurs almost mysteriously, as the camera lens reveals a shared understanding—a vision of the scene that directors immediately know will resonate with audience judgments.

Director Quentin Tarantino expounds on the process in discussing a particularly gruesome moment from *Reservoir Dogs*. In this now famous scene, a sadistic mobster named Blondie cuts off a policeman's ear and attempts to set the policeman on fire. The grizzly attack unfolds via a victim sequence. The audience watches Blondie approach the officer from the victim's vantage point. During the actual attack, viewers are spared the visual elements of the act. The camera picture fades, leaving viewers surrounded by the audio pleas and screams of the victim. Only when the violence is complete does a picture reemerge, a picture that now provides the perpetrator's perspective. Tarantino comments on this ordering:

> That was one of the only scenes in the movie that I actually shot two ways. I did a second version where the camera was directly behind Blondie as he straddles the cop and cuts off the ear. The camera is right there with him showing it. Then there was the version that made it into the film. I wanted to be sure about which way to go. . . . In the movie, we knew that the fade-away scene was "it" the minute we viewed it. . . . It's the one that really disturbs people and that's what I wanted. . . . I wanted it to be disturbing.[30]

Tarantino's position, like that of most media storytellers, paints the portrayal of violence as natural—void of professional technique. By subscribing to the theory of natural order, storytellers reject the notion of sequence conventions. Instead, storytellers link their sequence choices to the moral "pulse" of their audience.

SEQUENCING AND THE ASSESSMENT OF VIOLENCE

As has just been explained, media storytellers utilize one of four sequences when packaging stories of violence. These sequence choices are associated with the type of violence they are recounting: deviant, normal, or ambiguous. Although the art of sequence selection is part of storytellers' professional socialization, storytellers attribute their sequence choices to a natural or logical order. They describe their selections as choices motivated by a single moral consensus.

Are storytellers' sequence choices really reflecting shared public morals . . . or are these choices unfolding violent stories in ways that might sway public sentiments on violence? If the latter statement is true, do storytellers' sequence choices always lead readers and viewers to the conclusions that storytellers expect? Or do storytellers often commodify violence in unintended ways?

To explore these issues, I assembled twelve focus groups. In these sessions, I studied subjects' reactions to several newspaper and television depictions of violence. Data garnered from these groups allowed me to explore the role of story sequencing in the evaluation of violence. In particular, the twelve sessions allowed me to compare subjects' reactions to distinctly different methods of unfolding identical content. This was accomplished by matching focus groups along sociodemographic lines and then comparing group responses with differently sequenced versions of the same media report.[31]

The focus groups convened for this research ranged in size from six to twelve members, with a median group size of nine. Overall, a total of 109 people participated in the study.[32] In focus groups, subjects were exposed to ten violent accounts. Table 8.2 lists the story themes.

Table 8.2   Ratings of Violent Stories by Theme.

	EVALUATIONS OF VIOLENCE			
	Normal	*Ambiguous*	*Deviant*	*Total*
STORY THEME				
Police Violence	41%	30%	29%	100% (n=109)
Public Execution				
Foreign Culture	26%	31%	43%	100% (n=109)
Wartime Violence	16%	37%	46%	100% (n=109)
Parent-to-Child				
Spanking	34%	18%	48%	100% (n=109)
Bar Room Brawl	12%	30%	58%	100% (n=109)
Teacher-to-Student				
Spanking	18%	20%	62%	100% (n=109)
Violence Between				
Male Friends	14%	19%	67%	100% (n=109)
Drug Related Violence	3%	25%	72%	100% (n=109)
Female-to-Male				
Self-Defense	81%	4%	15%	100% (n=109)
Spousal Violence	9%	4%	87%	100% (n=109)

Chi-Square = 211.18; p<.001

Each subject privately rated these narratives as deviant violence, normal violence, or ambiguous violence.[33] Then in each group, I chose a portion of those stories and engaged subjects in a group discussion of their ratings. This discussion helped me to zero in on the reasoning behind subjects' ratings.

A review of table 8.2 demonstrates something important about subjects' evaluations of violence. (Note that the table summarizes subjects' reactions to violent scenarios across all sequence types.) In rating the rightness or wrongness of acts, recall that storytellers believe their audiences share a unified moral consensus. Yet the data do not support that position. Subjects' ratings for six of the ten themes (the first six) show substantial disagreement. In these cases, respondents' evaluations were sometimes evenly split across the three rating categories. Subjects' moral consensus proved high in only four of the ten themes examined (the last four categories).[34] Here, two-thirds or more of subjects agreed in their evaluation of the acts at hand.

Reviewing account themes with reference to moral consensus proves important to this study's goals. Tables 8.3A and B reveals that the impact of sequencing on subjects' evaluations of violence varies with reference to subjects' levels of moral consensus.

Tables 8.3A and B break down the focus group findings by levels of moral consensus, with table 8.3A devoted to themes that displayed low moral consensus and table 8.3B devoted to themes that displayed high moral consensus. Consider first the data addressing low moral consensus themes (table 8.3A lists the themes). The columns of the table show that different information sequences can alter subjects' ratings of violence. The figures in column 1 indicate that contextual sequences are most strongly associated with normal violence ratings. Column 2 shows that doublecasting formats are most often associated with ambiguous violence ratings. Column 3 shows that victim sequences are most strongly associated with deviant violence ratings.

When the violent themes that generated high moral consensus are examined, it is possible to note some substantial changes. Again, doublecasting formats are most strongly associated with ambiguous violence ratings (see column 2). However, the figures in column 1 of table 8.3B show that victim sequences are most strongly associated with normal violence ratings. Column 3 shows that both performer and contextual sequence are most strongly associated with deviant violence ratings.

Table 8.3 is important because it presents three critical pieces of information. First, *the data suggest that sequencing plays a crucial role in subjects' evaluation of violence.* When faced with identical material, different sequences can lead subjects to different conclusions as they decipher and react to violence. Second, *the data specify the precise nature of sequencing's impact.* By attending to the consensus that surrounds an act of violence, it is possible to predict the ways in which a particular sequence will steer subjects' "reading" of the event. Third, and

Tables 8.3A and 8.3B   Subjects' Violence Ratings by Sequence Type for High and Low Consensus Conditions.

3A: LOW CONSENSUS ACTS — *police shooting, public execution, wartime, parent spanking child, barroom brawl; teacher spanking student.*

| | VIOLENCE RATINGS | | | |
SEQUENCE TYPE	Normal	Ambiguous	Deviant	All
Victim Sequence	20%	20%	60%	100%
Performer Sequence	18%	34%	48%	100%
Contextual Sequence	39%	25%	36%	100%
Doublecasting	19%	41%	40%	100%[1]

8.3B: HIGH CONSENSUS ACTS — *violence between male friends, drug related, female to male self-defense, spousal.*

| | VIOLENCE RATINGS | | | |
SEQUENCE TYPE	Normal	Ambiguous	Deviant	All
Victim Sequence	37%	11%	52%	100%
Performer Sequence	19%	17%	64%	100%
Contextual Sequence	27%	10%	63%	100%
Doublecasting	7%	36%	57%	100%[2]

[1]$N = 654$ scenarios; Chi-Square = 25.57; p<.001
[2]$N = 436$ scenarios; Chi-Square = 14.92; p<.02

perhaps most importantly, *the data highlight a glaring discrepancy in the thinking of storytellers and their audiences.* Above, the distinct formulae that characterize the telling of violence were described. Recall that storytellers favor victim sequences in presenting deviant violence, they prefer contextual or doublecasting sequences for the telling of ambiguous violence, and they most often choose performer sequences in unfolding stories of normal violence. Also noted was the fact that narrators believe such formulae reflect a natural logic; they believe that they are ordering violent stories in ways that meet the moral expectations of their audiences. The data in tables 8.3A and B clearly challenge storytellers' assumptions on this score. The logical order of violent accounts as it exists in the minds of narrators often is quite different from the order that rests in the minds of readers and viewers. This discrepancy carries important implications. Indeed, those who continue to format their stories in concert with sequence conventions may fail to convey the message they intend. Storytellers must pay careful attention to the interaction of theme, moral consensus, and sequencing if they wish to maximize the chances of a story achieving its desired effect.

SEQUENCING AND THE DE-NORMALIZATION OF VIOLENCE

Violence is an established presence in the current media market. And for those involved in the "war on violence," the media's commodification of the issue represents a serious social problem. To date, researchers and activists working in this area have focused almost exclusively on media content. Yet this study suggests a new line of attack. Knowledge of story sequencing and its impact on audience evaluations may contribute another important piece to the puzzle of violent media effects.

This study suggests that the variable sequencing of identical violent content can generate different evaluations from those exposed to a violent story. In particular, certain packaging strategies appear more likely than others to normalize violent behaviors. Knowing this, media storytellers may wish to reconsider the ways in which they report or represent violent acts. Some may wish to adopt the sequence forms most likely to "de-normalize" violence. Systematically packaging violence in ways that link it to deviance may decrease readers' and viewers' tolerance for violence. By decreasing public tolerance, media storytellers may, in turn, contribute to more effective violence control.

To systematically de-normalize media violence, storytellers must familiarize themselves with the intricate "workings" of story sequencing. They must take careful note of the fact that the sequencing of a violent story has consequences— consequences that may differ significantly from storytellers' professional expectations. The focus group subjects aptly demonstrated this point: subjects' readings of violent stories often were at odds with the general intentions of media storytellers. For example, recall that storytellers typically favor performer sequences for the telling of normal violence. Yet in the focus group setting, performer sequences rarely elicited normal violence classifications.

Similarly, storytellers frequently choose contextual sequences in unfolding ambiguous violence accounts. Yet among focus group participants, this format was more strongly associated with normal violence evaluations (low moral consensus themes) or deviant violence evaluations (high moral consensus themes). Such discrepancies between senders' intentions and receivers' reactions indicate that storytellers may need to rethink the assumptions upon which their communication choices are based. Routine packaging conventions must be revisited. Indeed when it comes to violence, media storytellers must consider the very real possibility that sequence conventions can sometimes "sell" violence in unintended ways. Storytellers must attend to a more empirically based gauge of public morality if they hope to achieve a cognitive match between what is "said" and what is "heard."

"Traditional" media storytellers—journalists, television programmers, filmmakers, and so on—are not alone in their need to consider the potential effects of sequencing. Designers of video games, a growing media sector, stand to benefit from such reflections as well. At present, some researchers argue that a person's experience with "virtual violence" may contribute to her/his expression of "real world" violence. In this regard, the sequencing of virtual images may be key to video games' violent effects. For example, most home computer or video arcade games create a context of "necessary violence."[35] They place players in the role of a "righteous actor" and demand violence in the name of protection, progress, or honor. As a game ensues, players experience violent action from the perpetrator's point of view. They experience the excitement of attacking rather than the agony of being attacked. Perhaps most importantly, they experience violence in a context that redeems it as obligatory action.

Should video games be designed in ways that force players to experience victimization as well? Should players be required to endure both the exhilaration and the devastation of violence? Do players' porthole or game perspective influence their ultimate evaluations of violence? Lieutenant Colonel David Grossman believes that the answer to these questions is a resounding yes. (Grossman is a former professor of psychology at West Point. Currently, he teaches a course on the psychology of killing to both Green Berets in the military and to federal agents.) Grossman notes that the very same games being used in arcades and home computer systems (including the best-seller *Doom*) are also used to help police officers and soldiers increase their shooting accuracy. Thus according to Grossman, the average American child spends countless hundreds of hours perfecting her/his performance on what he calls "murder simulators" (*60 Minutes* 1999).

Grossman contends that the contextual and performer sequences upon which newer video games are built help players overcome the natural reluctance to kill. Because of the ways in which these games "position" players, the games give players a positive experience of violence. Players deliver rather than receive; they experience no costs in the execution of violence. Further, the positioning of players makes them "capable of extraordinary acts of accuracy with the weapon" (*60 Minutes* 1999).

Consider the case of Michael Carneal, the fourteen-year-old gunman in the Paducah, Kentucky, high school shooting. Carneal had never shot a real gun before he initiated the school siege. However, he was an avid video game player. In the Paducah attack, Carneal fired eight shots. Those bullets hit eight children— five of them in the head. According to Grossman, Carneal "never fired to the left, he never fired to the right, never far up, never far down. He just put one bullet in every thing that "popped up on his screen." His "success rate" was 100 percent" (*60 Minutes* 1999). Contrast this with a recent headline case in New York City: the Amadou Diallo shooting. Here, says Grossman, "four elite law enforcement officers at point-blank range fired forty-one shots and they hit with nineteen. The officers hit with less than 50 percent at point-blank range" (*60 Minutes* 1999). How did Carneal's accuracy surpass that of trained law enforcement professionals? Grossman believes that Carneal's virtual experience both trained him for the shooting and normalized the violence for him. (Interestingly, the parents of the

Paducah victims agree, and they have initiated a lawsuit against eighteen video game makers, saying that the games are partially responsible for turning Michael Carneal into a committed sharpshooter.)

The claims waged by Grossman and others demand further study. At present, knowledge of story sequencing and its effects are preliminary. Yet greater attention to the workings of sequencing could prove a sound investment. Further research on this issue could help to combat the commodification of violence in both traditional media and new, emerging formats.

CONCLUSION

This study brings up an old adage: It's not just *what* you say, it's *how* you say it. Sequencing represents one of many "hows" involved in media presentations of violence, and the practice represents a new avenue of inquiry for those concerned with the commodification of violence. My research suggests that reorienting those who package violence may help to reconfigure the ways in which media users ultimately think about and react to violence. Thus in many ways, this chapter provides a preliminary blueprint by which to commodify antiviolence agendas. But instituting the "correction factors" described in this chapter will prove a formidable task. Altering sequence conventions represents change of the most basic kind. More than twenty years ago, Herbert Gans[36] wrote of the rarity with which basic format changes ensue, noting that media communicators view such innovations as risky to standard operations.

Any organized attempt to direct systematically storytellers' presentational strategies also may be viewed as a threat to narrators' creative freedom. If new directives demand that stories be sequenced in ways that encourage specific audience evaluations, then journalists and reporters, as well as novelists, directors, screenplay and teleplay writers, video game designers, and others would be forced to unfold their products in highly similar and predictable ways. Thus, initiatives designed to synchronize story sequences with antiviolence goals introduce difficult moral terrain. Such initiatives may pit the community against the individual, as action is weighted for the common good against individual creativity and freedom of expression.

NOTES

*Some of the data presented in this article as well as certain limited lines of text appeared in Cerulo (1998). Thanks go to Mark Gottdeiner and Janet Ruane for helpful comments on earlier versions of this chapter.
    1. At this writing, Jason Vreeland is awaiting trial.
    2. U.S. National Center for Health Statistics (1998); U.S. Bureau of the Census (1998).

3. Statistics taken from "Domestic Violence: The Facts" <http://ci.longview.wa.us/services/police/flyers/DV6.html> [accessed August 1999].

4. Children's Defense Fund (1999); Cook and Ludwig (1997); Fingerhut (1993); Kistner (1997).

5. Kennedy, Piehl, and Braga (1996); Livingston (1996: 155–57); *Los Angeles Times* (1999).

6. Bennett, DiIulio, and Walters (1996).

7. Cerulo (1998); Comstock (1991a; 1991b); Comstock and Scharrer (1999); Jhally (1994); *National Television Violence Study* (1996–1998); Signorielli and Morgan (1990).

8. Cerulo (1998: Chapter 3).

9. Gerbner et al. (1994); *National Television Violence Study* (1996–1998); Reiman (1998); Signorielli, Gerbner, and Morgan (1995).

10. Rolfe (1997).

11. *Mediascope* (1997).

12. I refer here to scholars such as James Carey, David Eason, John Fiske, Michael Gurevitch, Elihu Katz, Michael Schudson, or Gaye Tuchman.

13. Merleau-Ponty (1962: 68).

14. See e.g. Gurevitch and Kavoori (1994); Rimmon-Kenan (1990); or Smith (1981).

15. In earlier work, I analyzed a representative sample of violent newspaper and television story leads. I also analyzed a selection of famous and highly visible examples of violent artwork, film scenes, short stories, and photographs. Cerulo (1998: chapter 3) provides a detailed discussion of these data.

16. *Leads* represent the opening sentences of a factual account, those designed to provide a concise, definitive statement of the action. Story leads occupied my primary analytic attention as such segments are typically identified as the guiding frames of factual narratives. Indeed most journalists argue that the lead "steers the rest of the narrative" (Harrington and Harrington 1929: 68).

17. Fenner, A. and J. Marzulli (1999). "Hit-run Kills Pregnant Student," *New York Daily News* (July 25, 1999):12.

18. Broadcast on WNBC New York 11PM news (July 25, 1999).

19. "Standoff Ends in Death." *Sunday Star Ledger* (July 25, 1999) Sect. 1: 14.

20. Broadcast on WABC New York 11PM news (July 24, 1999).

21. "Prisoner Hangs Self in County Jail Cell." *Star Ledger* (July 23, 1999) Sect. 1: 49.

22. Broadcast on WNBC New York 11PM news (March 20, 1999).

23. Terry, D. T. "Jeffrey Dahmer, Multiple Killer, Is Bludgeoned to Death." *New York Times* (November 29, 1994) A: 1.

24. To perform this analysis, I classified the theme of each story as deviant, normal, or ambiguous violence according to the criteria previously mentioned. Once classifying the type of violence, I analyzed and coded the sequence of each story's headline and lead.

25. In tune with this film's antiviolence, antidrug stance, most violent scenes follow a victim sequence. The classroom scene, the one exception to that rule, has been the subject of much controversy. Kalvert abandoned the victim sequence in the classroom scene reportedly for the sake of character development. He wished to convey to audiences that "the desire to kill and be killed—the vacillation of outward and inward blame—are at the heart of self-destructive behavior" (Woodruff 1995). Yet many feel that the failure

to bond viewers to the victims made the scene dangerously powerful. Indeed, families of the victims in the Paducah, Kentucky, school shooting are suing the makers of *The Basketball Diaries*, arguing that the classroom scene motivated Michael Carneal's murderous tirade. Similarly, many contend that Eric Harris and Dylan Klebold, perpetrators of the Columbine high school shootings, patterned their attack after this classroom scene.

26. For information on the sequencing of violence in cartoons, fiction, paintings, or photographs, see Cerulo (1998:chapters 3 and 4).

27. Forty instructional texts formed the sample for this analysis. For a full listing of the texts and the sampling strategy, see Cerulo (1998:155).

28. I targeted twelve reporters representing newspapers from distinct U.S. geographic regions: Atlanta, Boston, Chicago, Dallas, Denver, Elizabeth, Los Angeles, Miami, Milwaukee, Philadelphia, St. Louis, and Seattle. After each interview, I asked reporters for five referrals. I randomly ordered each reporter's referrals and contacted the number necessary to complete two interviews per list. This strategy resulted in a thirty-six member snowball sample.

29. Some of these interviews are quoted and referenced in this section. Data from additional interviews of this nature can be found in Cerulo (1998:79–99).

30. Taken from an interview filmed for a 1995 episode of *American Cinema* entitled "The Edge of Hollywood."

31. A story lead reporting a public execution in Pakistan was one of many materials used in my focus groups. I present the lead here to illustrate the differential sequencing of identical story content. The victim sequenced version of the story read, "PESHAWAR, Pakistan (AP) Two Pakistani men were executed today by the relatives of their murder victims. The two men were previously convicted for the murders. Crowds of thousands looked on, many shouting pleas for mercy. The executions were in accord with Islamic law." In contrast, the performer sequence read, "PESHAWAR, Pakistan (AP) Relatives of murder victims executed two Pakistani men today. These men were previously convicted for the murders. Crowds of thousands looked on, many shouting pleas for mercy. The executions were in accord with Islamic law." The context sequence version looked like this: "PESHAWAR, Pakistan (AP) Crowds of thousands looked on, many shouting pleas for mercy. Amidst this scene, two Pakistani men were executed today by the relatives of their murder victims. The two men were previously convicted for the murders, and the executions were in accord with Islamic law." Finally, the doublecasting version of the story read: "PESHAWAR, Pakistan (AP) Two Pakistani men, previously convicted of murder, were executed today by the relatives of their murder victims. Crowds of thousands looked on, many shouting pleas for mercy. The executions were in accord with Islamic law."

32. I recruited subjects by placing a display ad in two New Jersey daily newspapers. Thus all individuals are self-selected and the subjects constitute a nonprobability sample. Within this limitation, however, I attempted to maximize the heterogeneity of the sample by soliciting via newspapers that served highly varied populations. Thus the demographic profile of my subjects displays substantial demographic variation. Demographic breakdowns of the sample can be found in Cerulo (1998:114–15, 158–60).

33. Subjects used two different tools for this task. The first was a 5-point scale, in which 1 signaled justifiable violence, 5 indicated deviant violence, and moderate scores suggested ambiguity. The second tool allowed for a categorical rating of the violence:

"Unacceptable," "Justifiable," or "Can't Decide." These two measures were nearly perfectly correlated (Cramer's V = .96; Gamma = .99).

34. When 67 percent or more of the subjects agreed on the evaluation of a violent act, I classified the act as a "High Consensus" act.

35. *Mediascope* (1997).

36. Gans (1979: 164).

BIBLIOGRAPHY

Arredondo, S., T. Aultman-Bettridge, T. P. Johnson, K. R. Williams, L. Ninneman, and K. Topr (1999). *Preventing Youth Handgun Violence: A National Study with Trends and Patterns for the State of Colorado.* Boulder, Colo.: Center for the Study of the Prevention of Violence.

Baran, S. J., and D. K. Davis (2000). *Mass Communication Theory: Foundations, Ferment, and Future.* Australia: Wadsworth.

Bennett, W. J., J. J. DiIulio, and J. P. Walters (1996). *Body Count: Moral Poverty—and How to Win America's War against Crime and Drugs.* New York: Simon & Schuster.

Bureau of Justice Statistics—U.S. Department of Justice (1998). "Homicide Trends in the U.S.: Age Trends." <http://www.ojp.usdoj.gov/bjs/homicide/teems.htm> [accessed August 1999].

Cerulo, K. (1998). *Deciphering Violence: The Cognitive Structure of Right and Wrong.* New York: Routledge.

Children's Defense Fund (1999). "Children and Guns." <http://www.childrensdefense.org/youthviolence/childandguns.html> [accessed August 1999].

Comstock, G. A. (with H. Paik) (1991a). *Television and the American Child.* San Diego: Academic Press.

——— (1991b). *Television in America.* Newbury Park, Calif.: Sage.

Comstock, G. A., and E. Scharrer (1999). *Television: What's On, Who's Watching, and What It Means.* San Diego: Academic Press.

Cook, P. J., and J. Ludwig (1997). *Guns in America: Results of a National Comprehensive Survey on Firearms Ownership and Use*, Summary Report. Washington, D.C.: Police Foundation.

Fingerhut, L. A. (1993). *Firearm Mortality among Children, Youth, and Young Adults 1-34 Years of Age, Trends and Current Statistics, United States, 1985–1990.* Advance Data from Vital and Health Statistics, No. 231. Washington, D.C.: National Center for Health Statistics.

Gans, H. (1979). *Deciding What's News.* New York: Vintage.

Gerbner, G., M. Morgan, and N. Signorielli (1994). "Television Violence: Profile No. 16: The Turning Point from Research to Action," *Cultural Environment Movement.* Philadelphia: University of Pennsylvania City Science Center.

Glasgow, G. (1999). "Media the Message?" *Boulder News* (July 26, 1999), <http://www.bouldernews.com/shooting/27acult.html> [accessed August 1999].

Gurevitch, M., and A. P. Kavoori (1994). "Global Texts, Narrativity, and the Construction of Local and Global Meanings in Television News," *Journal of Narrative and Life History* 4:1, 2:2–24.

Harrington, H. F., and E. Harrington (1929). *Writing for Print*. Boston: D.C. Heath and Co.

Jhally, S. (1994). *The Killing Screens: Media and the Culture of Violence*. Northhampton, Mass.: The Media Education Foundation.

Johnson, S., and J. Harris (1942). *The Complete Reporter*. New York: Macmillan.

Joseph, J. (1997). "Fear of Crime Among Black Elderly," *Journal of Black Studies* 27: 5:698–717.

Kennedy, D. M.; A. M. Piehl; and A. A. Braga (1996). "Youth Violence in Boston: Gun Markets, Serious Youth Offenders, and a Use-Reduction Strategy," *Law and Contemporary Problems* 59: 1: 147–96.

Kistner, W. (1997). "Firearm Injuries: The Gun Battle Over Science." <http://www.pbs.org/wgbh/pages/frontline/shows/guns/procom/injurics.htm> [accessed August 1999].

Livingston, J. (1996). *Crime and Criminology* 2nd ed. Upper Saddle River, N.J.: Prentice Hall.

Los Angeles Times (1999). "Crime: The Stats' Story," Section B; page 5; column 1, (January 2).

Maguire, K., and A. L. Pastore (1994). *Sourcebook of Criminal Justice Statistics*. Washington, D.C.: U.S. Government Printing Office.

Mediascope. (1997). "Video Game Violence." <http://www.mediascope.org/fvidviol.htm> [accessed August 1999].

Merleau-Ponty, M. (1962). *Phenomenology of Perception*. Trans. Colin Smith. London: Routledge and Kegan Paul.

National Television Violence Study vols. 1–3. 1996–1998. Edited by the Center for Communication and Social Policy, University of California at Santa Barbara. Thousand Oaks, Calif.: Sage.

Reiman, J. (1998). *The Rich Get Richer and the Poor Get Prison*. 5th ed. Boston: Allyn and Bacon.

Rimmon-Kenan, S. (1990). *Narrative Fiction: Contemporary Poetics*. London: Routledge.

Rolfe, D. (1997). "Movie Violence Then and Now." <http://www.dove.org/dove/columns/1997/column9704.htm> [accessed August 1999].

Shoels, V., and M. Shoels (1999). "Simplistic Approach Will Not Work" *Denver Rocky Mountain News* (June 19, 1999), <http://www.insidedenver.com/shooting/0619shoe3.shtml> [accessed August 1999].

Signorielli, N., and Michael Morgan, eds. (1990). *Cultivation Analysis: New Directions in Media Effects Research*. Newbury Park, Calif.: Sage.

Signorielli, N., G. Gerbner, and M. Morgan (1995). "Violence on Television: The Cultural Indicators Project," *Journal of Broadcasting & Electronic Media* 39: 2: 278–83.

60 Minutes (1999). "Who's To Blame." CBS News, New York, N.Y. Broadcast on April 25.

Smith, B. H. (1981). "Narrative Versions, Narrative Theories," in *On Narrative*, ed. W. J. T. Mitchell. Chicago: University of Chicago Press: 209–32.

U.S. Bureau of the Census. 1998. *Statistical Abstract of the United States* 118th ed. "Table 142: Death Rates by Leading Causes and Age: 1980–1995." Washington, D.C.: U.S. Bureau of the Census.

———— (1997). *Sourcebook of Criminal Justice Statistics Online*. <http://www.albany.edu/sourcebook/> [accessed August 1999].

U.S. National Center for Health Statistics (1998). *National Vital Statistics Report, Vol 47: No. 4*. "Table 17: Deaths and Death Rates for the Ten Leading Causes of Death in Specified Age Groups, United States, Preliminary 1997." Hyattsville, Md.: National Center for Health Statistics.

Woodruff, Z. (1995). "New Film Reviews." *Tucson Weekly* <http://www.desert.net/tw/06-22-28/> [accessed August 1999].

9

The Commodification of Sports: The Example of Personal Seat Licenses in Professional Football

Matthew D. Bramlett and Mark Sloan

There is no question that modern sports have become commodified. Escalating player's salaries, the increased presence and intrusiveness of advertising in stadiums and on team uniforms, the sponsorship and creation of sporting events by commercial entities (the Virginia Slims tennis tournament, the Kemper Open in golf, and the Mobil Cotton Bowl in college football, just to name a few), and the selling of stadium-naming rights (e.g., USAir Arena, Qualcomm Stadium) indicate this. What follows is an explanation of how the roles of laborer, capitalist, and consumer are enacted in professional sports in America today. Within the context of professional sports, this chapter shows how the capitalist supplements profit from laborers' surplus-value with *surplus-profit* extracted from the consumer. Discussed is an extended empirical example of this process in action: personal seat licenses in the National Football League (NFL).

Throughout his discussion of the creation of commodities in the capitalist system, Karl Marx relies on an underlying, unspoken assumption. Simply put, Marx assumes that there are three main categories of people participating in the commodity creation process: capitalists, laborers, and consumers (Marx 1977). Consumers, despite their fundamental importance to the process, are largely left out of Marx's discussions of commodities, money, profit, and surplus-value extraction. The unspoken assumption is that consumers will consume what labor produces. Marx hangs his theory of capitalism on the idea that capitalists realize profit by extracting surplus value from labor. But what happens when capitalists have already maximized the surplus value from labor? Or when laborers become powerful enough to prevent capitalists from extracting that surplus value? In the case of modern American professional sports, owners have turned to the consumer as a new source of profit.

ON GAMES AND PLAYERS

One constant across the great variety of human cultures is that everyone plays games. The importance of games in human social and psychological development has been well documented (Mead 1934; Piaget 1965; Kohlberg 1969). Games can be defined as contests between two or more opposing teams or players who seek to achieve a specific goal or set of goals according to an agreed-upon set of formalized rules.[1] Furthermore, intellectual and strategic activities are of paramount importance in reaching those goals. In fact, in most nonsports games, intellectual and strategic activities are the only things that matter. Although a physical manifestation of the game almost invariably exists (i.e., a checkerboard, playing cards), they are mere representatives of the intersection between the strategic thought of the players and the formalized rules. The game occurs not on the playing surface but in the minds of the players.

Take the game of chess as an example. What does one really need to play a game of chess? All that is required is the set of agreed-upon formalized rules. If players do not have a board, they can draw one in the dirt. If players do not have pieces, they can use bottle caps or rocks. Players do not even need to be able to move their own pieces. Because it is the decision to move the piece that is important, not the movement of the piece itself, players can have someone else move their pieces, even their opponent. People living in different cities can play chess matches over the phone or by letter or electronic mail. Thus in games of pure strategy such as chess, the physical aspect of the game, although highly convenient, is not actually necessary for the play of the game.

Games that involve luck as well as skill (i.e., card and dice games) do require a greater element of physicality than games of pure skill such as chess. However, the importance of physicality in these games is still minimal. Here the physical manifestation of the game is necessary for the play of the game but is still a minor consideration in the play of the game itself. Quadriplegics could play a game of gin as long as there was someone, perhaps even their opponent, to draw and hold their cards for them.

In terms of Marx's system, when examined on their own, games only have one of the three roles represented: the laborer, who in this specialized case is called the player. In a general sense, sports combine two of the roles: laborer, or player, and consumer, or spectator. Professional sports add the third actor, the capitalist, or owner, completing the trio of roles necessary for the capitalist system to thrive and creating an arena for the exploitation of laborers and consumers.

ON SPORTS AND SPECTATORS

Although all sports are games, all games are not sports. Sports are games in which the physical component takes on additional meaning. It is the physical aspect of sports that sets them apart as special kinds of games. Unlike other games, the players must perform the physical aspects of the game themselves. Tennis players could not, for example, ask their opponents to serve for them. Nor can two teams play baseball over the phone or by mail.

The physical nature of sports is of fundamental importance when dealing with commodification because it is the physicality of sports that lends itself more to spectatorship than other kinds of games. It is simply more fun to watch people running after a ball, as in football or field hockey, or trying to outdo each other physically, as in boxing or gymnastics, than it is to watch two people staring at a chessboard or a handful of cards. An entire chess or bridge match can be re-counted in print and not lose much of its appeal. Not so with sports. The exciting thing about sports is watching them happen, watching the physicality.

At this point the consumer is a consumer in the pure sense, one who consumes the product or service but who does not pay for the right to consume the product/service. People who watch recreational sports in the park would fit this description.

PROFESSIONALIZATION

Historically, increasing numbers of spectators in various sports lead to the ability of people to play sports for a living, or at least for money (Ward and Burns 1994). In ancient Greece, the Olympians were supported much the same way artists were during the Renaissance by wealthy patrons so that they did not have to do anything other than be athletes (Mandell 1984). Their counterparts in the modern era are known as professional (or semiprofessional) athletes: people for whom sports is a primary (or the only) source of income.

Interest in professional sports leads to the inclusion of owners into the cast. If people want to see organized sports on a regular basis with the best players, then someone needs to organize matches, sell tickets, and distribute money to the players. In typical Marxist fashion, the owners of these professional sports teams and leagues try to extract as much surplus profit from their labor (the players) as possible. Here for the first time is the intersection of all three of the roles in Marx's scheme: laborer (player), consumer (spectator), and capitalist (owner).

In the early part of the twentieth century, this tendency to exploit the players' labor led to problems with gambling and the fixing of games. In 1919, in one of the most famous incidents of this kind, eight members of the Chicago White Sox baseball team were accused and later found guilty of intentionally losing the

World Series, Major League Baseball's (MLB) championship, in exchange for small monetary payments from known gamblers (Smith 1977; Voigt 1969). This incident, dubbed the Chicago Black Sox scandal, became so famous and so captured the imagination of the American public that several major motion pictures have since been made about it.[2] Interestingly, although the players involved in the scandal were thought of as the villains of this story, at the time very little was made of the fact that that year the owners had changed the World Series from a best four-out-of-seven series to a best five-out-of-nine series, without any concomitant increase in pay for the players (Ward and Burns 1994). Similar but less publicized problems were not uncommon in baseball and other professional and amateur sports of the time (Ward and Burns 1994; Nelli 1990).

In the latter part of the twentieth century, spectatorship of live sports in America rose dramatically. In major league baseball, for example, total attendance rose from 43,014,136 in 1980 to 70,601,148 in 1998, a 61 percent increase over the period (Thorn et al. 1999). Along with a rise in the number of consumers came increased revenues. Just between the years of 1995 and 1996, there was an increase of 30.9 percent in average revenue for MLB teams, from $50.4 million to $66 million (Lahman 1995, 1996).[3] Over the same two years, 1995 to 1996, players' salaries also increased but more slowly than revenue. In 1995 player costs averaged $31.2 million, and in 1996 player costs rose to $35.4 million, an increase of only 13.4 percent. Once again the owners failed to give the players increases in their wages that were in line with the increased revenues the games were generating; owners' profits were increasing faster than players' wages.

Over time, as the number of spectators increased, the players in American professional sports leagues have become more and more conscious of their impact on revenues and more and more conscious of the owners' drawing off the surplus value of their labor. There are several illustrative examples from the history of MLB that highlight the change in power relations over time between the owners and the players. Standard in all baseball contracts until 1973 was what was called the reserve clause, which stated that a team had the exclusive right to sign any of its players to a one-year contract. This clause essentially indentured players to their teams for as long as the teams wanted them. Or the team could trade away the rights to a player to another team without the player's consent. The player's only option was to play for the designated team or retire. In 1941 Joe DiMaggio, one of the greatest players in baseball history and arguably the best player of his era, asked for a salary increase from $15,000 to $40,000. The owner of the Yankees, Colonel J. Ruppert, offered DiMaggio $25,000, clearly less than he would have been able to receive on the open market. Ruppert is quoted as saying, "If he [DiMaggio] doesn't sign [the contract for $25,000] we'll win the pennant without him" (Ward and Burns 1994). DiMaggio signed for less than he wanted, and less than he was worth.

In 1966 Los Angeles Dodgers pitchers Sandy Koufax and Don Drysdale, two of the most talented and popular players in the league at that time, together refused to play unless each of them received new three-year contracts for approximately $165,000 a year. They further demanded that the team negotiate not with them but with their managing agent. Koufax and Drysdale felt that the Dodgers would do so poorly without them, both on the field and at the box office, that eventually the team would give in to their demands. After missing spring training, the two players returned to the team with significant raises in pay but without all of their demands met (Ward and Burns 1994). This episode was significant in that it was the first time players had some measure of success with collective bargaining.

In 1969, Curt Flood of the St. Louis Cardinals challenged the reserve clause and sued MLB. Flood was being traded from the Cardinals to the Philadelphia Phillies and refused to play for his new team. Instead Flood insisted that he had the right to become a "free agent," to allow teams to bid for his services. Flood's case went to the Supreme Court, where he eventually lost. But the high court warned MLB that the reserve clause would not stand up to future challenges. Flood's case signaled the beginning of the end of the reserve clause.

The major effect of ending the reserve clause was to usher in the era of collective bargaining and players' unions in professional sports. The level of conflict that exists between owners and players is illustrated by the fact that there have been work stoppages (strikes and/or lockouts) in all four major American sports in the last dozen years. Table 9.1 shows all of the work stoppages in MLB since 1972. The NFL Players' Association staged a prolonged players' strike in 1987; and in 1994 and 1998–99, respectively, the National Hockey League (NHL) and National Basketball Association (NBA) locked the players out, forcing the cancellation of several regular season games. Even minor sports in the United States have had strikes and lockouts threaten leagues in recent years, such as the Women's National Basketball Association in 1999. Nor have non-U.S. leagues been immune, as a threatened players' strike in the British Professional Footballers Association shows (*San Francisco Chronicle* 1996).

COMMODIFICATION

The profit motive has existed in modern sports since the first professional game was played. But it is the "undisguised primacy of the profit motive" (Sewart 1987) in sports that has arisen since the advent of free agency that has pushed professional sports over the line into the realm of commodification.

Commodification occurs when the outcomes of the games themselves become less important than the commercial interests associated with them for a majority of the parties concerned. Owners are always interested primarily in the commercial interests. It is when a second group, in this case the players, have become more interested in the commercial interests that it is possible to say that professional sports have truly become commodified. Symbolic content is traded for cash.

Table 9.1 Work Stoppages in Major League Baseball since 1972

Year	Work Stoppage	Games Missed	Length	Dates	Issue
1972	Strike	86	13 days	April 1–13	Pensions
1973	Lockout	0	17 days	February 8–25	Salary arbitration
1976	Lockout	0	17 days	March 1–17	Free agency
1980	Strike	0	8 days	April 1–8	Free-agent compensation
1981	Strike	712	50 days	June 12–July 31	Free-agent compensation
1985	Strike	0	2 days	August 6–7	Salary arbitration
1990	Lockout	0	32 days	February 15–March 18	Salary arbitration and salary cap
1994	Strike	920	232 days	August 12–March 31	Salary cap and revenue sharing

Source: Infoplease.com <http://www.infoplease.com/ipsa/A0764915.html>.

What follows is a *brief* series of examples demonstrating commodification in professional sports today, followed by an extended explanation of a new concept in revenue generation in professional sports: the personal seat license.

Top athletes, such as Michael Jordan, can now make more money from product endorsements than from playing their sport (*Seattle Times* 1997). *Forbes* magazine estimated that in 1997, Jordan made around $47 million from endorsements compared with his (relatively) low player's salary of $31.3 million (Spiegel 1997). *Forbes* also estimated that players in sports as diverse as golf, auto racing, and tennis earned more from endorsements than from actually playing their sport (Spiegel 1997).

Since the advent of free agency, a new trend has popped up: players leaving teams because salaries in the multimillions are "too low." In 1999 NHL player Brian Leetch threatened to leave the New York Rangers because of what he felt were low salary offers, in the $6 million–$6.5 million per season range. (Dellapina 1999). In the NBA, Rod Strickland was reported to be "insulted" by an $11 million per year salary offer from the Washington Wizards (Asher and Justice 1999).

It has become common practice for entire teams to threaten to relocate to different cities if local governments fail to fund new stadiums for them. The Yankees have threatened to leave New York (Finnegan 1998). Owners of hockey's Dallas Stars and basketball's Dallas Mavericks "persuaded the city council to contribute $125 million of taxpayers' money towards a new downtown stadium for their teams" (*London Financial Times* 1997). Seattle, Los Angeles, Buffalo, Milwaukee, Washington, D.C., Arlington (Texas), Cleveland, Denver, and Baltimore have all had public money contributed to building or renovating sports arenas in the 1990s (*London Financial Times* 1997; *USA Today* 1994).

Revenue and payroll disparities determine which teams are successful and which are not. In MLB, organizations such as the Montreal Expos are unable to put a competitive team on the field because of low salaries; teams with the highest player payrolls are the ones that make the playoffs (Chass 1999). As shown in tables 9.2A–D, spending more money does not guarantee success, but not spending does seem to ensure failure. In spring of 1999, MLB considered a proposal to sell advertising space on MLB uniforms (Newhan 1999).

Add to these incidents the increasing number, duration, and severity of work stoppages in professional sports and generally increasing fan interest in player salaries and salary negotiation, and commodification in professional sports is abundantly apparent.

Commodification has several deleterious effects on the sporting world. It causes a "divestiture of symbolic content" (Gottdiener 1997:34) and "blocks the realization of sport's emancipatory and liberative values" (Sewart 1987). Sports' emancipatory value lies in the spectators' ability to identify with and take a kind of emotional ownership of the symbolic conflict taking place before them. Teams are not just teams, they are symbolically "owned" by the spectators, and in this

Table 9.2A   1997 American League, Top and Bottom Four Teams by Salary

Team	Salary (millions) of dollars)	Salary Rank (out of 14)*	Winning Percentage	Participated in Playoffs
New York	73.8	1	.592	Yes
Baltimore	64.6	2	.604	Yes
Cleveland	58.9	3	.537	Yes
Toronto	48.9	4	.469	No
Minnesota	32.2	11	.416	No
Milwaukee	26.6	12	.484	No
Detroit	21.0	13	.487	No
Oakland	12.9	14	.401	No

Source: USA Today (1997) and MLB Player's Association

way spectators become members of the team. Success for the team means success for the spectator and the community in which the team resides. With sports becoming business first and sport second, the sport's ability to represent symbolically the fans through the action on the field is taken away. When, in the perception of the spectator, the priorities of players and owners shifts from winning the contest to increasing the profits, the ability of the spectator to feel like a member of the team is lost. The fans are no longer "members" of the team and as such are no longer important as people. The spectator is transformed from an individual to part of an interchangeable mass, in much the same way that workers become interchangeable in the capitalist system (Marx 1977). Players are defined as much by their salaries, and teams by their ticket prices, as they are by their ability to play the game. Salary figures become as important as box scores.

Table 9.2B   1997 National League, Top and Bottom Four Teams by Salary

Team	Salary (millions) of dollars)	Salary Rank (out of 14)*	Winning Percentage	Participated in Playoffs
Atlanta	53.1	1	.623	Yes
Florida	52.5	2	.567	Yes
St. Louis	50.2	3	.450	No
Los Angeles	46.4	4	.543	No
Philadelphia	31.1	11	.419	No
Chicago	30.8	12	.419	No
Montreal	18.0	13	.481	No
Pittsburgh	15.1	14	.487	No

*Arizona and Tampa Bay joined the National and American leagues respectively in 1998
Source: USA Today (1997) and MLB Player's Association

Table 9.2C 1998 American League, Top and Bottom Four Teams by Salary

Team	Salary (millions) of dollars)	Salary Rank (out of 15)	Winning Percentage	Participated in Playoffs
Baltimore	74.0	1	.488	No
New York	73.8	2	.704	Yes
Texas	62.2	3	.543	Yes
Boston	59.3	4	.568	Yes
Tampa Bay	27.6	12	.389	No
Detroit	23.3	13	.401	No
Minnesota	22.0	14	.432	No
Oakland	18.6	15	.457	No

Source: USA Today (1997) and MLB Player's Association

Commodification hurts sports by taking the focus away from the on-field product, the game itself, and elevating the importance of the business of sports.

Players become like their own owners (owners of their own labor power) and, as a group, use their control over the supply of labor to extract increasing amounts of profit from the team owners. This is possible because of the team owners' reliance on the noninterchangeable labor the players provide. If the best players refuse to play, then the quality of the product goes down, which means that revenues go down, which means that profits go down. Owners must not only find new ways to extract profit but must also find a new source of profit: the consumer.

Capitalists have developed new strategies for increasing revenues, and, contrary to Marx's original assertions, some of these strategies increase profits *without* further exploitation of the labor of wage workers. Instead of exploiting the labor power of the worker, capitalists develop alternate strategies that exploit the

Table 9.2D 1998 National League, Top and Bottom Four Teams by Salary

Team	Salary (millions) of dollars)	Rank (out of 15)*	Winning Percentage	Participated in Playoffs
Atlanta	61.7	1	.654	Yes
Los Angeles	60.7	2	.512	No
New York	58.7	3	.543	No
San Diego	53.0	4	.605	Yes
Cincinnati	20.7	12	.475	No
Florida	19.1	13	.333	No
Pittsburgh	13.7	14	.426	No
Montreal	8.3	15	.401	No

Source: *USA Today* and MLB Player's Association

buying power of the consumer. One alternate strategy for increasing profits is the extraction of profit *directly* from the consumer, such as the fees levied against bank customers who use automatic teller machines (ATMs) that are not owned by the customer's bank (fees that may be charged both by the customer's bank and the bank that owns the ATM) or the new fees introduced by some credit card companies that penalize customers who maintain a zero monthly balance. Another strategy for increasing profits without further exploitation of labor involves the mechanization of consumption, in which the consumer is the new production machine that releases the labor of wage workers, thus lowering costs. Examples of this include the practice of having consumers bus their tables at fast-food restaurants such as McDonald's or the practice of handing out trash bags to park visitors and asking them to clean up after themselves. A third alternative to surplus-value extraction as a strategy for increasing profits is the imposition of mandatory fees prior to a commodity or service purchase, such as the practice of requiring a donation of a set amount prior to allowing the purchase of a YMCA membership, and the example focused upon here: the new practice of requiring a personal seat license to purchase season tickets to certain professional sports teams.

PERSONAL SEAT LICENSES

Personal seat licenses (PSLs) have become mandatory for certain professional sporting teams that have recently relocated or are new league expansion teams. PSLs are a new strategy for increasing profits by raising revenues without increasing surplus-value extraction. Thus far, PSLs have mainly been instituted by specific teams to help finance the construction of a new stadium and other relocation costs.

The way PSLs work is to compel fans who want season tickets to pay a fee; for example, the fee is between $250 and $3,000 for the Baltimore Ravens and between $600 to $5,400 for the Carolina Panthers (Henry 1997:4; Morgan 1996b). This up-front payment grants the buyer the right to buy season tickets for a specified amount of time: thirty years for the Ravens, ten years for the Oakland Raiders (with annual maintenance fees of $50–$100, and after ten years, the fan must renew the personal seat license and pay again; Morgan 1996b). Please note: these fees *do not entitle the buyer to any product or service*. Rather, the buyer purchases the "right to buy" a product (i.e., a game ticket or series of tickets) at a later time. In essence, the consumer must pay for the right to pay.

Personal seat licenses, also called permanent seat licenses or premium seat licenses, were originally the brainchild of Carolina Panthers owner Jerry Richardson and "seat license guru" Max Muhleman. They developed the plan for the Carolina Panthers NFL expansion team in Charlotte, N.C., in 1993, and for the Rams' move to St. Louis in 1995 (Eisenberg 1995; Morgan 1994; Steadman

1995a). As of the summer of 1997, four NFL teams had PSL plans in place to finance relocation costs and/or new stadium construction costs: the St. Louis Rams, the Oakland Raiders, the Baltimore Ravens (all teams that relocated), and the Carolina Panthers (one of the recent NFL expansion teams). Nashville, Tenn., offered a PSL plan that has succeeded in attracting the Houston Oilers to relocate to the city (Preston 1995; *Baltimore Sun* 1995b). The Nashville PSL plan aimed to raise $71 million for a new stadium (*Baltimore Sun* 1996). The city of Cleveland was promised an NFL expansion team to replace the Browns (who moved to become the Baltimore Ravens), and the city has developed a PSL plan to finance stadium renovations (Morgan 1996b). Table 9.3 provides a summary of some characteristics of the various PSL plans around the NFL.

NFL franchise moves must be approved by at least three-quarters of NFL owners (twenty-three of thirty) (Murray 1995). Relocation costs include moving expenses, construction costs for a training facility, and relocation fees mandated by the NFL (Stellino 1995d). The NFL "charged the Cardinals $7.5 million to move to Phoenix in 1988" (Stellino 1995b). However, the NFL's relocation fees are not consistently levied: "The Raiders' move back to Oakland . . . was approved by league owners without a relocation fee. The NFL imposed a $29 million relocation fee and took a $17 million cut of seat license money when they approved the Rams' move from Anaheim" (*Baltimore Sun* 1995c; Associated Press 1995b). Some feel this inconsistency to be unfair: "If the Raiders don't have to pay a relocation fee to the NFL for moving to Oakland, the Rams shouldn't have to pay for moving to St. Louis" (Associated Press 1995b). League relocation fees levied against the St. Louis Rams and the Baltimore Ravens have been financed by the sale of PSLs. Construction costs on new stadiums associated with these relocations have been mainly covered by the state the team is moving into, and other moving expenses have been at least partially offset by the sale of PSLs.

The Carolina Panthers and the city of Charlotte started the original PSL plan in an attempt to raise $150 million for the construction of their new stadium and to attract the attention of the NFL to award the expansion team to that city (Morgan 1996a). As late as November 1995, the Carolina franchise still had "10,000 [out of 60,000 total] unsold premium seat licenses starting at $2,500 each . . . worth $30 million [total]" (Stellino 1994; Stellino 1995d; Eisenberg 1995). Vito Stellino (1995a) reported that, "[Carolina was] playing its first season in Clemson, S.C., a two-hour drive from Charlotte, where a new stadium was being built, and had sold only about 42,000 season tickets so far. Only 30,000 of the 50,000 premium seat license holders bought tickets." Fifty-four thousand of the sixty thousand Carolina PSLs had been sold as of May 1996 (Morgan 1996a).

The Oakland Football Marketing Association created its PSL plan to raise $197 million for renovations to the Oakland Coliseum and to finance the Raiders' return to Oakland (Reddy 1996; Stellino 1996c). Oakland's PSLs are good for ten years, after which they must be renewed (rebought) (Morgan 1996b). Oakland had sold only 35,000 PSLs (out of 45,000) as of December 1996, and the sta-

Table 9.3 PSL Comparison

	# Seats	# PSLs	Potential Revenues	PSL Price Range	Average PSL Price	# Single-Game Seats
Ericsson Stadium, Charlotte	72,685	53,960	$144.2 million	$600 to $5,400	$2,673	5,787
Transworld Dome, St. Louis	66,000	46,000	$67.25 million	$250 to $4,500	$1,462	11,930
Nashville Tenn.-New Stadium	65,000	57,600	$71.16 million	$250 to $4,500	$1,235	N/A
Baltimore Ravens-New Stadium	68,400	60,200	$68.4 million	$250 to $3,000	$1,136.2	6,000
Cleveland Browns-New Stadium	70,900	55,320	$41.5 million	$250 to $1,500	$750.27	15,580
Oakland-Alameda Stadium	61,309	56,309	$103.7 million	$250 to $4,000	$1814.6	5,000

Source: Morgan 1996b

Note: Figures for Oakland, Nashville, Cleveland, and Baltimore are estimates. Cleveland plans to offer discounts to season-ticket holders that will bring average PSL price to $574 and potential revenues to $29 million.

dium renovations were running $29 million over budget (Stellino 1995d, 1996c; Eisenberg 1995; Reddy 1996).

Whereas Carolina and Oakland have had some trouble selling all of their PSLs, St. Louis has had more luck. The civic group FANS, Inc., which designed the PSL plan to finance the Rams' move to St. Louis, announced in 1995 that with 74,000 applications for PSLs and only 46,000 seats available, 28,000 requests would be refused (*Baltimore Sun* 1995a). "Hardest hit were fans seeking the cheap seats. All 11,000 applicants for . . . the least-expensive category at $250 were bumped by applicants for higher-priced seats that listed [the cheap seats] as their second or third choice" (*Baltimore Sun* 1995a).

If the PSL holder does not buy season tickets in any one year, then the PSL becomes void (Morgan 1996b). The Ravens' PSL contract comes with several fine-print limitations, such as the requirement of purchasing tickets to every home game, including playoffs (or risk having the license revoked); restrictions on transferring the PSL (no transfers allowed until April 1999 except in the case of the death of the PSL holder, a $50 fee for transfer of a PSL, and only one PSL transfer per year); liability of the PSL holder for repair costs for seat damage; and an agreement not to sue the Ravens if the team should move again, or for "'spills of food or beverage and the unruly behavior of other patrons,' among other things" (Morgan 1997).

Some commentators have reacted with outrage to proposed seat license plans. These plans have been labeled "permanent seat larceny" and "a controversial scheme . . . that smacks of extortion" (Steadman 1995d); "a contaminated situation that smells worse than raw sewage" (Steadman 1995a); and a "broad-daylight mugging" (Steadman 1995b). Stellino (1995a) described the NFL as an illegal monopoly and stated, "The NFL is a cartel, and a cartel will use illegal means to maintain power." The owners "know that more cities are desperate to become major-league towns than there are major-league franchises, so they can demand anything they want and move if they don't get it" (Armacost 1995). Elise Armacost (1995) offers the image of states "prostrating themselves at the feet of the franchise owners."

The fans may not always take well to PSL schemes either. Dr. Robert Baade, an economics professor who testified at congressional hearings regarding NFL team relocation, was quoted as saying that team owners worry about fan resistance to PSL plans and "the league is courting disaster" (Steadman 1995d). Stellino reports that "seat licenses . . . have been a tough sell at times," citing the low sales of Oakland and Carolina PSLs (1995d).

The Baltimore Ravens' PSL Plan

The Baltimore Ravens were known as the Cleveland Browns until they moved to Baltimore in 1995. Team owner Art Modell and the Maryland Stadium Authority worked out a deal whereby the Browns (now the Ravens) pay no rent in the new stadium; keep all ticket, concession, parking, and advertising revenues; and only compensate the state for operating and maintenance costs (about $4 million a year). The state of Maryland gets a 10 percent tax on ticket sales and splits revenues from non-NFL events fifty-fifty with the team (Stellino 1995d; Morgan 1995; Armacost 1995). Maryland had pledged $200 million toward construction costs of the new 70,000-seat football stadium in Baltimore (*Baltimore Sun* 1995c; Stellino 1995d). The Ravens played at Baltimore's Memorial Stadium for the 1996 and 1997 seasons and moved into the new stadium for the 1998 season (Murray 1995).

In addition to all the concessions the state of Maryland had made to Modell, he also got PSL fees, about $68 million altogether, to offset moving expenses, construction costs for a new training facility, amounts owed to the city of Cleveland, and an NFL-mandated relocation fee of approximately $30 million (Steadman 1995d; Preston 1995). A paltry $5 million in PSL revenues went toward the cost of the new stadium (Associated Press 1996).

By comparison, the Rams pay $250,000 in rent per year to play in their new $260 million stadium in St. Louis (Stellino 1995d). The Rams' PSLs ranged in price from $250 to $4,500, averaging $800 for 50,000 season tickets (Associated Press 1995a; Stellino 1994a). In contrast to the Ravens, Rams PSLs were sold by the city, not the team (Stellino 1995b). The money raised by Rams PSLs ($68 million, identical to that of the Ravens) was used to cover the costs of a new training facility ($15 million), amounts owed to the city of Anaheim ($30 million), and an NFL relocation fee of $29 million (*Los Angeles Times* 1994; Steadman 1995a; Stellino 1995d). Thus, despite the difference in ownership of PSL money (St. Louis sold the Rams' PSLs, whereas the Ravens sold their own), it was used to offset identical costs associated with moving the team. Table 9.4 summarizes this comparison between the Rams and the Ravens. Differences exist in terms of which entity sold the PSLs; the stadium costs—the Rams' stadium will cost $60 million more; and rent payment—the Rams are paying rent, whereas the Ravens are not (although it would take 240 years before the rent would compensate for the $60 million additional stadium cost).

A PSL, according to the Baltimore Ravens, is "a permanent seat license which transfers control of the season ticket from the team to the fan, permanently. The cost of a PSL is a *one-time fee*, often not much more than the cost of one or two season tickets" (Henry 1997; emphasis in original).

Baltimore Ravens PSLs range in price from $250 to $3,000, according to the stadium zone. Table 9.5 summarizes the number of seats and prices of the Ravens' PSLs in each zone. The Ravens sold 57,000 season tickets for the 1996 season (51,000 in the first two weeks of availability) and received 14,000 orders for the 7,800 premium club seats at Memorial Stadium (Henry 1997:3). Full capacity at the new stadium will be 68,400.

Table 9.4 Comparison of Rams' and Ravens' PSL Statistics

	St. Louis Rams	Baltimore Ravens
Stadium construction costs	$260 million	$200 million
Stadium costs paid for by	State	State
Rent paid to state	$250,000/year	$0
PSL revenues	$68 million	$68 million
PSL revenues raised by	City	Team
NFL relocation fee	$29 million	$30 million
NFL fee paid for with	PSL revenues	PSL revenues
Other costs paid for with PSL revenues	New training facility other moving expenses $ owed to Anaheim	New training facility other moving expenses $ owed to Cleveland

Source: Steadman 1995a, 1995d; Stellino 1995b, 1995d; Preston 1995; *LA Times* 1994.

Table 9.5   Ravens PSL Zones

PSL Zone	Price	# of Seats	Revenues Potential
Club Seats (Clubs 1–4)	$1,000	7,900	$7,900,000
Zone A	$3,000	5,800	$17,400,000
Zone B	$1,500	9,000	$13,500,000
Zone C	$750	16,000	$12,000,000
Zone D	$2,000	2,500	$5,000,000
Zone E	$1,000	5,500	$5,500,000
Zone F	$750	7,900	$5,925,000
Zone G	$500	9,000	$4,500,000
Zone H	$250	2,100	$525,000
	Total:	65,700	$72,250,000

Source: Henry 1997:11.

Some criticize PSL plans as exploitative, but one can't fault a capitalist for trying to put a positive spin on profit extraction: Modell is quoted as clarifying how his PSL plan is less exploitative than others in the NFL:

> Mine is permanent seat licenses, not personal . . . personal in Oakland is in 10 years you've got to renew it and pay again. Mine runs for 30 years. Take 30 years, if a guy spends . . . for a 50-yard line and pays $3,000, that's $100 a year for 30 years. That's $10 a game and he can sell that, he can will it, he can do whatever he wants with it. It's like a condominium. He owns it. (Preston 1995)

Information provided by a marketing representative of the Baltimore Ravens in 1997 included a section labeled "PSL Highlights," which stressed "positives" associated with the Ravens' PSL plan. Included among these highlights were: (1) that season ticket prices have been set through the year 2000 season; (2) that 75 percent of Ravens PSLs are priced at or below $1,000; (3) that a new, lower PSL price ($250) has been added to make season tickets more affordable; (4) that almost half of club seats' season ticket prices are below those set by the Maryland Stadium Authority in 1993; (5) that the first set of Ravens PSL season ticket holders will have their names inscribed in a wall of honor at the new NFL stadium at Camden Yards; (6) that none of the PSL money goes to the Modell family—it all goes toward relocation costs (Henry 1997:2).

Of course, by offsetting relocation costs that otherwise would have come out of Modell's pocket, the effect of PSL revenue generation is the same as if it had all gone straight into Modell's pocket. Furthermore, *Baltimore Sun* sportswriter Ken Murray (1996) reports a great amount of discontent among PSL holders regarding their zone assignments: "The growl of discontent was loud enough to keep the teams' hot-line number (1-888-9RAVENS) tied up in a constant busy tone." Murray quotes Roy Sommerhof, director of Ravens ticket operations, as saying that 30 percent of calls to the hot-line number were in reference to discontent from zone assignment.

Commentators have also touched upon the exploitive relationship owners are building with consumers through the PSL schemes. John Steadman (1995b) reports: "how can the NFL be looked at as anything other than a business? It's . . . taking advantage of the fan to line its own pockets with millions in windfall income it isn't entitled to have. The game that's being played is to find new ways to extort money from the public."

In another article, Steadman (1995c) clarifies the exploitative nature of PSL sales: "Fans are now being asked to tax themselves to build the stadiums and provide them to team owners rent-free, pay the owner's moving expenses and then pay for their seats twice . . . it seems as if NFL owners and players no longer feel obligated to pretend they want to entertain us." Marx's theory of capitalist exploitation through surplus-value extraction cannot explain this exploitative nature of PSLs.

THE APPLICABILITY OF MARXIST THOUGHT TO PSLs

PSLs are commodities in the sense that they are sold in a commodity-exchange market, but there is no production process involved in the value of PSLs (other than the minimal cost of printing up a contract). The laborers in the industry that is called the National Football League (the players, coaching staff, stadium personnel, ticketing and team administration personnel) are not even involved in the production of commodities and hence can not possibly be involved in surplus-value production (they are thus unproductive workers, by Marx's definition of unproductive as not involved in the production of surplus-value; Marx 1977:644). Rather, the laborers in the NFL are involved in the provision of a service; specifically, entertainment in the form of professional sporting events. Extending the workday (making the players practice longer, for example) or intensifying the "labor process" (making the players practice harder) will have no effect on the value of the PSL. The PSL may thus be conceptualized as a "simulated commodity," in that it is sold in the commodity-exchange market and has a definite value attached to it, but there are no raw materials, production, or labor involved in the creation of the value of the PSL.

Despite the general inapplicability of Marx's theory of the labor process of production to these simulated commodities, some aspects of Marxist thought may still apply to the study of PSLs. The revenues generated through the sale of PSLs, revenues that are inexplicable in terms of surplus-value extraction, represent pure profit extraction. Marx did not have much to say about profit; his focus was on the exploitation of labor-power through surplus-value extraction. In fact, his discussion of profit revolves around surplus-value extraction as the source of all profit.

In *Capital*, Volume I, Marx defines the rate of profit only in contrast to the definition of the rate of surplus-value. Because the value of constant Capital is exactly transferred into the value of the commodity, it can be set to zero; total Capital advanced, the sum of constant and variable Capital ($c+v$) thus becomes only (v), and the value of the product (($c+v$)+s) becomes ($v+s$). The ratio of surplus-value to variable Capital (s/v) is the ratio by which variable Capital has valorized its value and is called the rate of surplus-value (the rate of exploitation), in contrast to the rate of profit, which Marx defines as $s/(c+v)$, the ratio of surplus-value to the total Capital advanced, constant plus variable (Marx 1977:324, 442; Marx 1959:42).

Marx deals with the rate of profit more extensively in Volume III of *Capital*; however, his assumption is still that profit derives from surplus-value alone. He presents a formula for the value of a commodity (C): $C = (c+v+s)$, where c is constant Capital consumed in the production of the commodity, v is variable Capital used to pay the wages for the labor-time invested in the production of the commodity, and s is the surplus-value extracted from the worker that is proportionally represented in the commodity. Marx modifies the formula such that $C = k+p$, where k represents the cost-price of the commodity (total Capital advanced in the production of the commodity, $c+v$) and p represents the profit associated with the commodity (surplus-value, s). The Capitalist realizes the profit (surplus-value) only when the commodity is sold. When a commodity is sold at its value, "profit is realized which is equal to the excess of its value over its cost-price, and therefore equal to the entire surplus-value incorporated in the value of the commodity" (Marx 1959:36–7). In this context, the rate of profit is given as p/k, the ratio of profit to cost-price, which is mathematically equivalent to $s/c+v$ (Marx 1959:42).

Nowhere in this discussion of the rate of profit does Marx allow for profit extraction that does not involve surplus-value extraction. Yet there are many examples of new techniques for profit extraction that Marx had not anticipated that do not involve surplus-value extraction, including bank ATM fees for using an ATM machine not owned by the customer's bank, credit card fees levied against customers who maintain a zero monthly balance, and "right-to-buy" fees, such as PSLs or required donations prior to the purchase of a YMCA membership.

A new term can be added to the formula for the rate of profit ($s/c+v$): let p represent the new concept *"surplus-profit,"* which shall denote profit accruing to the capitalist above and beyond the normal (expected) amount of profit realized by the exchange of commodities from which surplus-value was extracted during production. The rate of profit, including this surplus-profit, would then be given as $(p+s)/(c+v)$. This denotes the "true" rate of profit, taking into account sources of profit beyond surplus-value extraction (the ratio of total profit to total Capital advanced). Surplus-profit extraction occurs independently of the production process: it is extracted directly from the consumer.

Looking beyond Marx's focus on the exploitation of labor through surplus-value extraction leads to a new Marxist term with which PSLs, and other sources of profit that do not involve surplus-value extraction, can be analyzed: surplus-profit. There is another way in which Marxist thought can be applied to the PSL phenomenon: predicting the extent of PSL plan adoption in the future.

In his discussion of new production techniques that increase surplus-value extraction relatively (by increasing the productivity of labor), Marx indicates that successful techniques eventually become widespread throughout the industry. Increasing the productivity of labor, such that more commodities are produced in the same amount of time, results in a decrease in the value of each commodity (each commodity requires less labor-time to produce). However, the capitalist is able to reap higher profits for a period of time because the social value of the commodity continues to be based on the prior, less productive, method of production, until such time as other producers of the commodity react by upgrading their production techniques to tap the higher productivity of labor, which has the lagged effect of decreasing the social value of the commodity (Marx 1977: 434, 436). Once the social determination of the value of the commodity takes into account the more efficient production techniques, any producers of the commodity who do not upgrade production to meet that level of efficiency will be disadvantaged in the competition of different producers of the same commodity. As a result production techniques that are demonstrated to be successful in increasing surplus-value extraction eventually are adopted by all competitors (Marx 1977:436).

Even though this rapid adoption of production techniques is largely governed by competition in the market, this idea of other capitalists adopting techniques for increasing surplus-value extraction that have been demonstrated to be successful may be applied to PSLs. Following this train of thought leads to a prediction that PSLs, as a successful technique for raising surplus-profit, will eventually be adopted by all team owners in the future.

THE FUTURE OF PSLs

The Washington Redskins and late owner Jack Kent Cooke are an example of a team that moved to a new stadium without starting a PSL scheme. Cooke paid for the new stadium himself (Armacost 1995). "The Redskins plan to pay for their own stadium, but demanded and received assurances of $73 million in state aid for roads, sewers and other infrastructure" (Morgan 1995). Prior to his death, Cooke was vocal in his rejection of PSLs; he is quoted as saying, "I'm absolutely opposed to them [PSLs]. This, in my opinion, is a form of gouging, and I don't think it's fair to the fan that he should have to pay twice, as it were, for a seat" (Stellino 1996a).

Cooke is an example of an "altruistic capitalist," one who could, theoretically, justify earning an additional profit to cover new expenses, using a technique with precedent among his peers, but who chooses not to (and foregoes the risk of losing fan support or loyalty to an unpopular scheme). It will be interesting to see if new Redskins owner Daniel Snyder feels the same way as Cooke did, or if the Redskins ever do initiate a PSL plan to help finance the move to the new stadium or the stadium construction costs.

Unlike the Carolina Panthers, the Jacksonville Jaguars are an example of a new NFL expansion team that is not using a PSL plan to finance start-up costs. So far, the Jaguars stand alone among the three expansion teams in not using PSLs (Cleveland developed a PSL plan for its promised expansion team).

The Cincinnati Bengals is the first example of a team using a PSL plan without being able to justify it to the fans because of relocating or being a new expansion team. The plan aims to raise only $20 million, much lower than other PSL plans around the league that have been justified to the fans in terms of relocation or construction costs. The Bengals are calling its PSLs Charter Ownership Agreements (COAs), and rather than trying to justify the plan to fans, they are simply forcing season-ticket holders to comply or lose their seats by selling COAs to current season-ticket holders and non–season-ticket holders at the same time (Stellino 1996b).

A new development in PSL schemes may be an NFL plan to charge $10,000 for the right to buy Super Bowl tickets for four years. Stellino (1995c) reported that NFL owners presented a plan involving the sale of five thousand Super Bowl premium seat licenses at $10,000 apiece to "create a $50 million fund to help various teams with stadium improvements." The plan would raise $50 million every four years (Stellino 1995c). In other words, the price for Super Bowl tickets for the next four years would jump from $800 ($200 per ticket for four seasons) to $10,800. Such a price increase would put the Super Bowl out of reach of many fans who might otherwise be able to afford a ticket and would eventually result in Super Bowl attendance becoming a conspicuous indicator of the social status of members of the "leisure class" (Lury 1996:45–46).

The PSL trend seems to be growing and different takes on the PSL idea seem to be cropping up, but examples such as the Redskins and the Jaguars show that it is still too early to tell if PSLs will become widespread throughout the league. Marxist theory would tend to predict a growing proliferation of PSL plans in the future; however, team owners may choose to postpone PSL plan enactment until such time as the revenues generated by the PSL are sorely needed (because the revenues raised by PSL sales are largely restricted to one point in time). The future will tell whether the NFL will be able to initiate PSL plans throughout the league without incurring fan hostility, or whether team owners will utilize PSL schemes only when they can be justified or only when they are most needed to offset unusually high costs associated with factors such as relocation or stadium renovation.

The sale of personal seat licenses is an example of a new strategy for exploitation used by the capitalist class. There are two major ways in which these new strategies differ from those described by Marx. First, rather than creating profit through the extraction of surplus-value, they create what has been termed surplus-profit; profit accruing to the capitalist above and beyond the normal (expected) amount of profit realized by the exchange of commodities from which surplus-value was extracted during production. Second, and perhaps more significantly, the target of the exploitation changes from the laborer to the consumer, opening up new realms of profit, and therefore new realms of power, for the owners of capital.

In his description of the capitalist system and the creation of commodities, Marx was primarily concerned with the relationship between capitalist and laborer. In modern capitalism, the consumer has taken on a much more prominent and active role. The interaction of these various roles in the American professional sports industry has led to the commodification of the industry, which in turn has lead to the adoption of methods for the generation of surplus profit, most notably to date the creation of personal seat licenses in the National Football League.

At this point, it should be clarified that the commodification of sports is not as yet an all-consuming phenomenon. There are some indications of a trend against commodification. Fans seem to be turning away from the major mass-marketed sports toward sports that have to date smaller fan bases. The creation and popularity of ESPN2, an all-sports network showcasing sports such as snowboarding, billiards, motorboat racing, and soccer (which is still considered a minor or alternative sport by American audiences) is evidence of this trend. More proof can be found in the fact that television ratings for major sports have gone down in recent years, whereas ratings for minor sports have gone up. The ratings for the 1999 National Collegiate Athletic Association (NCAA) men's basketball tournament were the lowest since 1982 (Associated Press 1999), whereas the ratings for the NCAA women's basketball tournament were up 25 percent in one year (Smith and Orton 1999). These examples can be taken as anecdotal evidence of a trend against commodification in sports or perhaps the desire on the part of the consumer for a less commodified sporting world.

Owners and players also occasionally express the desire to exist in a less commodified realm. In an interesting recent development, prior to the eventual sale of the team to Daniel Snyder, the NFL owners effectively blocked the sale of the Washington Redskins to the highest bidder for a price nearly $300 million higher than paid for any American sports franchise up until that time (Shapiro 1999). The NFL owners seemed to prefer that the team be sold to John Kent Cook, the son of the late owner.[4] In a thoroughly commodified environment, the highest bidder would have been rapidly embraced.

There is also the occasional tale of a player such as Rex Chapman of the Phoenix Suns who in 1997 accepted the NBA league minimum salary to play in

Phoenix rather than move to a new team for a higher salary (*USA Today* 1997), or of a superstar such as the Denver Broncos' quarterback John Elway accepting a reduction in salary so that the team could sign another marquee player (Schefter 1998). But in the end, although some noncommodifying trends do exist in sports today, they are manifestly overwhelmed by the commodifying influence.

Although this focus has been on professional team sports in the United States, commodification of sports in the modern world goes beyond those limited boundaries. Further examinations of the issues of commodification are needed at the different levels of competitive expertise in sports: the Olympic games, collegiate athletics, Little League, and recreational sports. Likewise, the path that commodification took in individual sports such as golf, figure skating, and auto racing should be examined. And of course, the commodification of sports in the United States needs to be compared with similar processes in other nations.

The sports industry is also interesting in that a host of other actors are involved in the industry and in the commodification process in addition to owners (capitalists), players (laborers), and fans (consumers). On-the-field referees, coaches, and managers all have vested interests. In the executive offices, administrators, athletic directors, and general managers play an active role in the day-to-day operations of their sports. Finally, groups with increasing amounts of influence on the landscape of sports are those outside interests such as advertisers, media operators, politicians, and community leaders. Each of these groups has made a contribution to the commodified nature of the modern sporting world that should be examined.

NOTES

1. In this manner games are distinguished from play, which has no formalized set of agreed-upon rules.

2. Some of the more famous of these movies include *Eight Men Out* with John Cusack and Kevin Costner's *Field of Dreams*.

3. Total attendance in these years rose from 50,464,375 in 1995 to 60,100,715 in 1996.

4. Interestingly, many Washington Redskins fans objected to the fact that the NFL blocked the sale, because it meant dragging out the ownership question longer. Thus, in this case consumers objected not to the commodification of the sport, but to the lack of commodification.

BIBLIOGRAPHY

Armacost, Elise (1995). "Stadia Past the Point of Diminishing Returns," *Baltimore Sun*, December 10:4C.

Asher, Mark, and Richard Justice (1999). "Wizards, Douglas' Agent Hold Contract Discussions; Re-Signing Free Agent Strickland Is Uncertain," *Washington Post*, January 18:1D.

Associated Press (AP) 1995(a). "Rams Go for Gold in St. Louis," *Baltimore Sun*, January 18:5C.

——— (1995 b). "Rams Ask Why They, Not Raiders, Must Pay Fee," *Baltimore Sun*, July 23:14C.

——— (1996). "State Board OKs Funding for Stadiums; Public Works Panel to Vote April 10 on Issuance of Bonds," *Baltimore Sun*, March 28:14B.

——— (1999). "N.C.A.A. TOURNAMENT MEN'S CHAMPIONSHIP; UConn Wins, CBS Does Not," *New York Times*, March 31:4D.

Chass, Murray (1999). "1999 BASEBALL PREVIEW; The Haves Have It and the Nots Don't," *New York Times*, April 4: Section 8:2.

Dellapina, John (1999). "Leetch Top Ranger, Drama Negotiations Could Get Sticky," *Daily News* (New York), March 26:104.

Eisenberg, John (1995). "Take A Seat: It'll Be A Hot Ticket To Ride," *Baltimore Sun*, November 8:1D.

Finnegan, Michael (1998). "Rudy Biz Tax Plan is a Home Run, Hevesi Sez," *Daily News* (New York), April 22:3.

Gottdiener, M. (1997). *The Theming of America*. Boulder, Colo.: Westview.

Henry, Ginnie (1997). Facsimile Correspondence: Baltimore Ravens' PSL Information, Baltimore Ravens, Broadcasting Department, 11001 Owings Mills Boulevard, Baltimore, Maryland, 21117 Tel.(410)654-6296; Fax.(410)654-6212.

Kohlberg, Lawrence (1969). "Stage and Sequence: The Cognitive-Developmental Approach to Socialization," in *Handbook of Socialization: Theory in Research*, ed. D. A. Goslin. Boston: Houghton-Mifflin.

Lahman, Sean (1995, 1996). Sean Lahman's Baseball Archive, Baseball1.com <http://www.baseball1.com\bb-data\95-biz.html> and <http://www.baseball1.com\bb-data\96-biz.html > [accessed April 1999].

London Financial Times Staff (1997). "Corporate Welfare for the Super-Rich?: Multi-Millionaire Sports Team Owner Persuades Voters to Fund New," *Financial Times* (London) USA Edition, October 10:4.

Los Angeles Times (1994). "Rams, St. Louis Huddle Near Goal Line but TD Not Assured," *Baltimore Sun*, December 30:9C.

Lury, Celia (1996). *Consumer Culture*. New Brunswick: Rutgers University Press.

Mandell, Richard D. (1984). *Sport: A Cultural History*. New York: Columbia University Press.

Marx, Karl (1959). *Capital* Volume III. Moscow: Foreign Languages Publishing House.

——— (1977). *Capital* Volume I. New York: Vintage.

Mead, George Herbert (1934). *Mind, Self and Society*. Chicago: University of Chicago Press.

Morgan, John (1994). "Will Rams' Short List be Long on Frustration?" *Baltimore Sun*, October 2:1C.

——— (1995). "Browns, 'Skins Deals Draw Fire: Lean Times Warrant Renegotiation, Md. Lawmakers Say," *Baltimore Sun*, December 23:1A.

—— (1996a). "Ravens Set for First Test: Seat Licenses; Details of Team's Plan to Raise $60M–$70M to be Unveiled Today; Fans' Cost: $500 to $3,000; Memorial Season-Ticket Prices as Low as $170," *Baltimore Sun*, May 16:1D.

—— (1996 b). "Ravens Set Ticket Prices for New Park; '98 Seats to Range from $45 to $360 a Game, Including PSLs; To Be Below NFL Average," *Baltimore Sun*, October 12:1D.

—— (1997). "Ravens PSLs Not License to Sue; Many Restrictions in Six-page Document Sent to Potential Buyers," *Baltimore Sun*, February 22:1C.

Murray, Ken (1995). "Modell's Exit Ramp Eerily Close to Irsay's," *Baltimore Sun*, November 7:1D.

—— (1996). "Ravens Seats Not All Sights to Behold; Some Ticket Holders Ticked Off by Location," *Baltimore Sun*, July 11:1A.

Nelli, Humbert S. (1990). "Herman L. Donovan and the Emergence of 'Big-Time' Athletics at the University of Kentucky," *Register of the Kentucky Historical Society* 88(2):163–82.

Newhan, Ross (1999). "Ad Idea May Be a Little Patchy; Baseball Revenue Plan Would Have Players Wearing Small Advertisements on Sleeves," *Los Angeles Times*, April 1:1D.

Piaget, Jean (1965). *The Moral Judgment of the Child*. New York: Free Press.

Poulantzas, Nicos (1975). *Classes in Contemporary Capitalism*. London: New Left Books.

Preston, Mike (1995). "Extra Fees for Seats Is Possible; They're Baltimore's Browns; Ticket Depositors Could Face Surcharge on Required Licenses; Prices Still Up in the Air; Modell Reassures Fans on Seat Availability," *Baltimore Sun*, November 7:1D.

Reddy, Dave (1996). "Raiders Seek Lost Mystique; Oakland Apathetic to Troubled Club," *Baltimore Sun*, August 29:1D.

Resnick, Stephen, and Richard D. Wolff (1987). *Knowledge and Class: A Marxian Critique of Political Economy*. Chicago: University of Chicago Press:109–63.

San Francisco Chronicle Staff (1996). "Soccer Players Threaten to Strike," *San Francisco Chronicle*, August 13:5E.

Schefter, Adam (1998). "JOHNNY CASH; Elway Restructures Contract to Free Up Millions," *Denver Post*, August 11:1D.

Seattle Times (1997). "Usual Ringing Endorsements for Jordan," August 23:2B.

Sewart, John (1987). "The Commodification of Sport," *International Review for Sociology of Sport* 22(3):171–94.

Shapiro, Leonard (1999). "Tagliabue Hopes for Bid by late May," *Washington Post*, April 18:6D.

Smith, Dean (1977). "The Black Sox Scandal," *American History Illustrated* 11(9):16–24.

Smith, Michelle, and Kathy Orton (1999). "ESPN's Ratings Rise Through Tournament," *Washington Post*, March 27:8D.

Spiegel, Peter (1997). "Sports Top 40: His Airness Reigns Supreme," *Forbes Magazine*, December 15.

Staff and Wire Reports (1995). "St. Louis' Seat-Selling Campaign Is Too Good," *Baltimore Sun*, March 3:2C.

Steadman, John (1995 a). "St. Louis, Charlotte Seated in Low Places," *Baltimore Sun*, February 3:1C.

—————— (1995b). "NFL Shows What It Thinks of the Fans: Selling the Right to Buy Tickets Is an Outrage," *Baltimore Sun*, November 5:1F.

—————— (1995c). "Modell Must Reap Whirlwind He Didn't Know He Was Sowing," *Baltimore Sun*, November 9:2C.

—————— (1995d). "Seat-License Larceny Brings Disrepute: NFL Should Ban It," *Baltimore Sun*, December 10:2D.

Stellino, Vito (1994a). "Switzer Ready for NFL Debut," Baltimore Sun, September 29:4C.

—————— (1994b). "Montana or Young? 49ers Made Right Choice by Passing on Legend," *Baltimore Sun*, December 4:13D.

—————— (1995a). "Rams' Moving Saga Is a Matter of Money, Not Sense or Tradition," *Baltimore Sun*, March 12:15C.

—————— (1995b). "Rams Get Go-Ahead to Move," *Baltimore Sun*, April 13:1C.

—————— (1995c). "League Looks at Stadium Fund," *Baltimore Sun*, March 15:2C.

—————— (1995d). "Lease Deal for Browns Is 30 Years; Club Could Receive $75 Million from Sale of Seat Licenses; Funds to Cover Moving Cost; Owner Modell Signed Agreement 10 Days Ago," *Baltimore Sun*, November 6:1A.

—————— (1996a). "In Choosing Frerotte, Redskins Coach Admits Mistake," *Baltimore Sun*, August 25:5D.

—————— (1996b). "It's 49ers vs. Cowboys and Rice vs. Sanders," *Baltimore Sun*, November 10:11C.

—————— (1996c). "Free Agency Can Mean Reversal of Fortune" *Baltimore Sun*, December 1:7C.

Thorn, John, David Pietrusza, Michael Gershman, and Pete Palmer, eds. (1999). *Total Baseball, 3rd Edition*. Total Sports Publishing, March.

USA Today Staff (1997). "Chapman Chooses Suns Instead of Hefty Raise," *USA TODAY*, July 9:9C.

USA Today (1994). The Complete Four Sport Stadium Guide. New York: Fodor's Sports.

USA Today (1998). The Complete Four Sport Stadium Guide. New York: Fodor's Sports.

Voigt, David Quentin (1969). "The Chicago Black Sox and the Myth of Baseball's Single Sin," *Journal of the Illinois State Historical Society* 62(3):293–306.

Ward, Geoffrey C., and Ken Burns (1994). *Baseball: An Illustrated History*. New York: A. Knopf.

Baltimore Sun (1995a). "Road Is Clear for Oilers to Make Move to Nashville: Mayor, Team Owner Expected to Sign Today," November 16:1D.

—————— (1995b). "Modell Tours Oriole Park, Insists Move Will Happen; Says Finale in Cleveland a 'Draining' Experience," December 19:3D.

—————— (1996). "Cowboys' Holmes Sues NFL, Alleges Improper Drug Test; NFL Notes," January 8:5C.

10

The Commodification of Rebellion: Rock Culture and Consumer Capitalism

Cotten Seiler

POPULAR MUSIC AND CULTURAL STUDIES

As Frank Zappa observed, "the single most important development in modern music is making a business out of it" (Volpacchio 1991:125). In the Marxian sense, the "value" of music is an ambiguous concept at best, problematized by the technical inability to contain music within the manufactured commodity form for the great majority of human history. Sound recordings developed as commodities only in the twentieth century, during the early years of consumer culture. Their success as products "was dependent on the corresponding creation of a new social use value for popular music in its record form" (Buxton 1990:429). This new social use lay in the symbolic meanings that could be invested in the musical commodity, its ability to *signify* the status, interests, affinities— indeed, the very identity—of its purchaser. Of course, this system of symbolic investment in commodities presupposed the existence of a radical new view of the self in late modernity, one asserting the constitution and anchoring of identity through association with objects (see Bauman 1988; D. Miller 1995).

Academic analyses of popular music have their roots in the early twentieth-century Marxist turn to culture and the problem of "false consciousness" among the working class. In theories of hegemony as elaborated by the Frankfurt School theorists in the 1920s and 1930s, Theodor Adorno, Max Horkheimer, and Herbert Marcuse, the mass-marketed products of the "culture industry" function exclusively to normalize hegemonic ideologies and to provide an escapist realm of leisure in which workers psychically renew their capacity for work. Adorno in particular vehemently opposed popular music—"the dregs of musical history" (1976:29)—as a product created to gull and pacify the masses, as well as the ultimate debasement, enacted in the name of capital, of the sublime beauty and power one found in "serious" music. Popular music speaks to its listeners "in a language they think is their own" (Adorno 1990a:311), through repetitive narratives of idealized social relations and material conditions. This identification with prefabricated utopian dreams forecloses the possibility that one's desires might deviate from the utopias currently for sale. The effect is to naturalize the present system of political economy and to "reconcile (listeners) . . . to their social dependence" (Adorno 1990a:314). Similarly, the work of Jean Baudrillard, though not specifically concerned with popular music, addresses the ways in which hegemonic forces produce and circumscribe the parameters of consumer desire (see especially 1981).

A central difference between the Frankfurt School and Baudrillard, however, is the latter's insistence on consumption as a social practice based primarily on the exchange of signs. In this view, products are less important for what they *do* than for what they communicate about the consumer. However, as in the totalizing regime theorized by the Frankfurt School, Baudrillardian "sign value" is a function of domination, representing "the final triumph of capitalism in its attempt to impose a cultural order compatible with the demands of large-scale commodity production" (M. Lee 1993:23). Although continuing to influence the study of popular music, the Marxist model has been challenged by more recent scholarship for its excessive determinism, aesthetic elitism, and derogatory characterization of consumers as spoon-fed automatons.

Contemporary critics have tended to "*use* their involvement with popular culture as a site of contestation in itself" and to "appeal to the liberatory body, the creativity of consumption" (Ross 1989:11). These studies have suggested ways out of the "closed system" of domination theorized by the Frankfurt School, insisting instead on the unpredictable nature of popular culture commodities, their openness to symbolic revision, and reappropriation by a diverse range of consumers for equally diverse purposes (see, for example, Certeau 1984; Fiske 1987; Hebdige 1979; Lipsitz 1994). The most incisive of these studies indicate ruptures in the ideological order, moments and spaces in which the culture industry cannot control the social meanings and political uses consumers attach to its products. Others, however, tend to valorize popular culture consumption as an emancipatory practice *in itself*, with each purchasing choice made by the consumer indicating resistance, subversion, and empowerment. Hence Greil Marcus's observation that "a lot of the people in cultural studies these days remind me of the FBI in the fifties: they find subversion everywhere" (Kleinhans 1994:1). These opposed positions on popular music—one stressing domination, the other emancipation—may well be analogous to the aesthetic dictates of music itself, as the medium "represents at once the immediate manifestation of impulse and the locus of its taming" (Adorno 1990b:26), pleasure as well as pleasure's regulation and subordination to formal and hierarchical control.

In terms of commodification, the change in popular music has been quantitative rather than qualitative: when Thomas Edison recorded himself reciting "Mary Had a Little Lamb" onto a tin-foil cylinder (Sanjek and Sanjek 1996:vii), it was the commodification of sound he had in mind. In the 1990s, with annual music sales reaching more than $10 billion (1996:670), innovations in communications technologies, flexible production and distribution techniques, and new marketing strategies have expanded opportunities for commodification. As with most other consumer goods, the market for rock music has fragmented since the 1960s, when producers began to respond to new forms of demand that "followed from a global shift towards the pluralism of 'roots' . . . and . . . 'identity politics'" (D. Miller 1995:7). The music industry, part of an increasingly global and oligopolistic mass media (see Bagdikian 1997), has correspondingly diversified its product to sell to a wider range of specific markets, which were often structured around markers of identity such as race, nationality, gender, class, religion, and age.

Most recent work on popular music has focused on the "the dominant industrialized commercial medium of popular music": the recording (Shank 1994:172). To a degree, this is rightly so, as it was the sound recording that enabled music to become "popular," in terms of large-scale and efficient dissemination to disparate groups of people all over the world. Most cultural studies scholars focus on the profound effects of recorded music as a medium of value, ideology, and resistance and tend to derogate the subject of live performance to cultural historians, who, in turn, tend to privilege live performance in its heyday before the advent of the recorded text (see, for example, Erenberg 1981; Southern 1971).

The aim here, however, is to investigate the practice of live performance in postwar popular music. Though the recorded commodity has superseded live performance as the essential medium of artistic communication and as "chief symbol of musical mercantilism" (Gould quoted in Chanan 1995:132), the concert stage remains a site of authentication at which an artist's music is gauged by audiences as legitimate, pleasurable, and therefore worth buying in record form. Live performance also functions to affirm the audience's commitment to musical artists and what they and their music represent. As such, attendance at a rock concert demonstrates one's membership in an "affective alliance" (Grossberg 1992), a coalition of shared affection for a particular music and, potentially, shared social and political sensibilities. Standing amid some seventy thousand other fans at a Bruce Springsteen concert in Detroit, one writer affirmed rock's ability to provide "materials around which to construct social relationships and self-images" (Pratt 1990:178).

Of course, affective alliances are often also predictably cohesive groups of consumers. This chapter will point to some of the ways in which the culture industry has amplified its exploitation of consumer affect—the pleasure and distinction of "being there"—through merchandising and increased ticket prices and by delivering audiences to advertisers in the concert setting itself. And the tensions between rock music's historical status as a popular form espousing resistant or countercultural values and the unprecedented "incorporation" of rock and its values since the 1960s will be examined.

ROCK CULTURE, WOODSTOCK, AND THE RISE OF THE CONCERT INDUSTRY

One reaction to the commodification of popular music was the post–World War II folk movement, which asserted the authenticity of American regional and rural musics (forms that, for a variety of reasons, resisted commodification) over mass-produced, mainstream sounds. Folk continues to be figured as "noncommercial musics," consumed by "people who aren't willing to be spoon-fed something that the music biz has concocted as a commodity" (Redhead, quoted in Best 1997:27). However dubious the claims of folk exceptionalism, the movement deeply influenced the animating myth of the rock culture that emerged in the 1960s—that "rock is, or should be, art, and that commerce is inimical to art" (Weinstein 1999:57–58).

Rock culture's adoption of the art/commerce dichotomy did not coincide with the origin of rock music; instead, it responded to the cultural and economic power rock attained in the 1960s, the time when popular music became a billion-dollar industry (see Sanjek and Sanjek 1996) as well as a primary communicative tool of youth culture. As several scholars have noted, the genre "rock and roll" as it was isolated in the 1950s did not necessarily distinguish aesthetic consistencies; rather, it named the marketing category for popular music aimed at young white consumers (see, for example, Chapple and Garofalo 1977; George 1988; J. Miller 1999). Unlike their descendants, the earliest rock and roll artists had little concern for keeping their music pure, unsullied by market forces or with making any explicit political statement; rather, they wanted their records to *sell*. Little Richard, Elvis Presley, Jerry Lee Lewis, and other rock and roll progenitors cared little about artistic integrity or the quest for authenticity and social significance, "so long as their little black 45's hit number one and made them rich and famous" (Marcus 1990:4).

Popular music assumed a catalyzing role in the political and social upheaval of the 1960s, especially in terms of communicating the mission of social and political progressives (see Gitlin 1987; Grossberg 1992; Marcus 1990). It was in this decade that rock emerged as a generic form distinct from blues, folk, country, rhythm & blues, soul, and funk. Produced and consumed (like rock and roll) mainly by young whites, rock cohered around an ethical stance of rebellion, expressive individualism, and sexual and chemical experimentation. The music provided the foundation for a counterculture, the members of which shared an array of distinguishing markers and practices. The typical "looks" of rock musicians and fans since the 1950s generally involved some type of threat, flouting traditional gender and racial identities and conventions of bourgeois decorum. Pre-rhinestone Elvis Presley copped his style from African American Beale Street dandies; he "knocked the shit out of the color line" (Guralnick 1994:134) with his clothes long before the racially ambiguous voice singing "That's Alright Mama" hit the airwaves.

Later, in the 1960s, rock style privileged androgyny and exoticism as aesthetic protest to postwar middle-class normalcy. However transgressive of mainstream values these countercultural markers were, they were nonetheless encouraged by entertainment corporations and myriad other producers of "lifestyle products," as they served to isolate a consumer demographic and thus enabled these industries to rationalize production and marketing techniques.

Yet by the 1960s, rock music had arrogated to itself "a 'missionary purpose': its task was to carry hippie values into the heart of the commercial beast" (Frith 1981:221). The rock artist was typically styled a "negative dialectician" in the Adornian sense, using art to indict and to locate a way out of the rationalized system of domination effected by modern capitalism. The more profound and fertile the opposition, the greater the value of the art. For political progressives, rock held promise as a formidable coalition-building force for the social movements of the New Left.

The mass consumption of rock, supposedly a folk form with radical, "alternative" values, was seen as evidence of political change among American youth. Ideologues such as Tom Hayden and Eldridge Cleaver agreed that the "liberation" of white youth could be rooted in rock: this was only a short step away from the idea that "cultural revolution" of "freeing one's mind" (through psychedelic means or otherwise) was an alternative to, or the very manifestation of, political revolution (Buxton 1990:428).

Though the rock culture of the 1960s certainly suggested that "the normal culture of teenagers was becoming infiltrated by grander ideals" (Gitlin 1987:205), retrospective claims about the singular nature of 1960s rock culture have often been excessive: "Rock culture became a collective voice that made sense of revolution. . . . By articulating, reflecting, and reinforcing the social flux of the period, the rock culture became a human force pushing for a better world" (Plasketes and Plasketes 1987:31). If such a claim is true, it is still only half the story; the rise of rock culture must also be understood as a historical moment in the production of new coalitions of consumers and, consequently, of more supple, sophisticated, and activist strategies of capital.

One of the most powerful and durable symbols of the alliance between rock culture and utopian politics was the Woodstock Music and Art Fair, which took place on Max Yasgur's farm in White Lake, New York, for three days in August 1969. Woodstock was the crowning event in a four-year period of rock festival activity in North America and Britain, in which the grassroots music festival tradition (dating back to the mid-1800s) assumed a more commercial character (see Peterson 1973). This is not to say that music festivals had not been viewed as economic enterprises prior to the 1960s, but in that decade, they became profit-making ventures for promoters, record companies, musicians, and merchandisers. More importantly, they were increasingly identified as microcosmic representations of youth culture. 1967 was the year that festivals "broke." Events such as the Monterey International Pop Festival launched many of the decade's most popular artists, such as Jimi Hendrix and Janis Joplin. The festival garnered media attention as a part of the hippie "Summer of Love" phenomenon centered in Northern California. Where much of the nation saw an assemblage of hedonistic freaks, savvy record company executives saw a critical mass of young record buyers and began to devise ways of selling to it. The Monterey festival (the impact of which, as with Woodstock, was boosted by the subsequent release of a concert film) "helped to formulate and crystallize the image of the 'flower child'" (Peterson 1973:101), the typical member of a new cultural bloc, the market potential of which was as yet untapped.

That the early festivals were largely unmarred by violence made the rock festival all the more appealing to both the hippies and the record companies, as it represented both the affirmation of the countercultural ideal of peaceful political assembly and the enclosure—figuratively and literally—of "a large aesthetically responsive middle-class youth audience that transcended regional tastes" (Buxton 1990:435). Here was the counterculture, which, as the record companies were aware, had "at least as much to do with shopping and consumption as with opposition" (Redhead 1990:17).

Janis Joplin, onstage at the Woodstock festival, announced to the nearly half-million in the audience, "We used to think of ourselves as little clumps of weirdos. But now we're a whole new minority group" (Curry 1989:10). Woodstock, a logistical (and meteorological) fiasco, was nonetheless heralded (both by participants such as Joplin and by media organs such as the *New York Times*) as a defining moment in a generation's self-recognition and, for all its countercultural emphasis, fully in keeping with an American tradition of benign expressive individualism (see Hopkins 1970). The Woodstock Nation was largely a construction of the media, a positive rendering of 1960s youth culture that mythologized the event as utopian, especially after the cataclysm of Altamont in December 1969 (Peterson 1973:110–12), which was plagued by violence and culminated in the murder of a young African American concertgoer by Hell's Angels "security." By 1970 the festival movement was waning, as fears of violence and a more aggressive public reaction to youth culture prevailed, and Woodstock emerged as a nostalgic symbol of hippie idealism, a fleeting moment of countercultural transcendence.

Woodstock's cultural capital aside, economically it was a disaster, at least at first. Woodstock's organizers had declared bankruptcy the morning after the festival, leaving their creditors with some $1.6 million in outstanding debt. Woodstock Ventures eventually made good by signing away the rights to the film to Warner Bros. for $1 million and a small percentage of net box office receipts and eventually broke even through album sales and other licensing revenue (Spitz 1979:487–89). Woodstock's countercultural credibility was perhaps enhanced by the financial debacle, as it could be construed as further evidence of the event's orientation away from commodification. The principal organizers, Robert Pilpel, John Roberts and Joel Rosenman, in their apologia *Young Men with Unlimited Capital* (1974), claimed to share the anticommercial values of the Woodstock Nation over and above their entrepreneurial goals. Whatever the veracity of Roberts's and Rosenman's claims, for contemporary and future concert promoters, Woodstock, which "overran the commercial calculations that spawned it" (Lacayo 1994), was an edifying spectacle of inefficiency and undercommodification.

At the Isle of Wight Festival, held in 1970, many of the 600,000 fans in attendance reacted aggressively to the increased commodification of festivals, one seizing an onstage microphone to complain that "this festival business is becoming a psychedelic concentration camp where people are being exploited" (Strauss 1999b:31). Isle of Wight (at which the performers received considerably larger guarantees) was seen as a betrayal of the benevolent-capitalist ethos of the festival movement. Gate-crashers damaged and breached the wall that had been erected around the concert grounds, and fans taunted performers and organizers for their surrender of the festival movement to Mammon. Such behavior, which would recur in the years to come (as evidenced by the recent consumer riot at Woodstock 1999) was symptomatic of "the great irrationality of the rock festival, the conflict between greedy promoters trying to turn a profit and idealistic rock fans who repeatedly fool themselves into thinking that rock concerts are not, at base, moneymaking propositions, that the music they love is not a commodity" (Strauss 1999b:31).

AFTER "GOODSTOCK": INDUSTRIAL CONSOLIDATION, ADVERTISING, AND CORPORATE SPONSORSHIP

There can be no doubt that the commodification of live music performance has increased dramatically since the late 1960s. The Isle of Wight Festival was perhaps the first to be stigmatized for its promoters' (and artists') explicit desire to profit from ticket sales (admission was three pounds). The fans' uproar strikes one as rather quaint today and finds only a faint echo in criticism of the concert industry in the 1990s. Indeed, one factor in "the selling of rock and roll" to corporate America is the weakening—and in many cases, the severing—of the connection of rock music to utopian politics and to social progressivism more generally. As one commentator in the early 1980s noted, contemporary fans "don't go to concerts to protest something. It's more of, 'Hey, let's go out and party'" (Goldberg 1983).

Today's concert business profits not merely from ticket sales but from industrial consolidation, dual and multiname package tours, merchandising, concessions, corporate on-site advertising and sponsorship, ticket surcharges, and Internet and pay-per-view broadcasts. These new revenue-generating techniques over the past two decades have propelled concert industry earnings to an unprecedented high. The top one hundred concert tours in 1998 grossed $920.5 million, up from the 1997 total of $831.6 million (Sandler 1999). As with other sectors of the culture industry, control of the concert business grows increasingly concentrated. The most striking example of this trend can be seen in the recent purchasing spree of the New York-based SFX Entertainment, which has absorbed competing concert promotion companies across the United States with alarming speed and success. Entertainment industry analysts have spoken of SFX's intention "to create one-stop shopping for performance artists looking to launch a tour across the country . . . to create a vertical enterprise that includes ticket sales, advertising, the bringing in of the talent. Once it's in the venues, it will make money from concessions and advertising" (Bodenchak quoted in McCollum 1998). SFX, which, according to one of its executives, "fundamentally understands the fusion of music and marketing" (Klahs quoted in Kaufman 1997), controlled twenty of the most prominent summer tours of 1999 (Sandler 1999) and thirty-one of the major venues; these numbers are likely to rise as the company becomes, barring the operations of small independent promoters, a de facto monopoly.

SFX claims that it merely seeks to centralize, secure, and "streamline" what has traditionally been an unpredictable and often financially hazardous concert promotion business. Historically, promoters have been in danger of losing money on events, as they have traditionally raised the majority of the capital and assumed the majority of the risk (see Stein 1979). Increasingly, however, SFX will be able to dictate the financial terms of an event to minimize its own exposure and pass on costs to individual consumers through increased ticket prices. Ticket prices for major events, such as SFX's 1999 summer Tom Petty tour, have escalated significantly and rapidly throughout the 1990s, auguring a potential situation in which top artists will "end up only playing for the elite" (Petty quoted in Sandler 1999). The typical industry response to the problem has echoed the standard complaint of the embattled capitalist whose labor force has successfully organized for higher wages. In this case the promoters point to the higher guarantee fees powerful performing artists have been able to negotiate, labor costs that diminish promoters' profits. In turn, promoters increasingly extract their profit from the consumer.

Concertgoers can expect, then, both higher ticket prices generally as well as a stratified ticket pricing and seating system—wider disparity between premium seats and less desirable ones, as in the $125–100–75–45 range for Tom Petty. Also as prices rise, events are likely to become both fewer and more grandiose, as SFX concentrates its resources on lucrative summer tours at massive outdoor venues.

The industry has seen the growth of a de facto ticket monopoly in Ticketmaster, which has centralized and rationalized ticket distribution and sales. Ticketmaster charges ticket buyers and promoters a "convenience charge"—on the average, approximately $5 per ticket—over and above face value, a portion of which goes to the venue. Although Ticketmaster claims it does not force consumers to purchase tickets through its service (or promoters or bands to use its distribution), the availability of tickets through other retail channels, such as venue box offices, is limited and precarious. The company was the subject of a 1994 Justice Department probe, requested by the rock band Pearl Jam, alleging monopolistic business practices. Pearl Jam challenged Ticketmaster's dominance of the industry when it attempted to mount a low-cost, low-ticket-price tour using many of the venues with which Ticketmaster had exclusively contracted. The probe was dropped, and Ticketmaster is currently expanding its operations globally.

Merchandising, too, has radically expanded in product range and price over the past three decades. Merchandising represents another technique of exploiting consumer affect, by offering an item—a T-shirt, poster, button, or program— designed to commemorate the event and testify to the fan's attendance and devotion. Although merchandising has existed since the earliest days of rock and roll—one only has to look at the myriad products to which the Beatles and Elvis Presley attached their names and images—its profitability to artists and promoters was often limited by an inability to enforce exclusive rights to a particular name or image (an inability that persists in the international market, where bootleg recordings and merchandise abound). During the 1970s, artists, promoters, and record companies cracked down on unlicensed merchandise and began to look to T-shirt and other souvenir sales as a fertile source of supplementary income. By the late 1980s, merchandising accounted for a large percentage of overall revenue: fans bought $250 million in T-shirts in 1987, a year in which ticket earnings reached $650 million. Typically, the profits from concert T-shirts are divided between the artist (anywhere from 30 to 45 percent), the company producing and marketing the merchandise (around 12 percent), and the venue (around 40 percent) (Plasketes 1992:155). Of course, concertgoers have seen a sharp rise in the price of merchandise over the past twenty years. A T-shirt from Hall and Oates's 1983 tour sold for $8; today, the Backstreet Boys, a group popular with teenagers and preteens, charge $26.

Although many promoters acknowledge that "high prices are eliminating a significant segment of the concertgoing population" (Scher quoted in Sandler 1999), recent trends indicate an aggressive "upscaling" of the concert experience and a neglect of rock's traditionally young and lower-middle-class constituency. The new ideal concert consumer tends to be older and more financially solvent, yet the logic of concert marketing remains much the same as it was in the Woodstock era, with the relatively expensive ticket not merely entitling the consumer to enjoy "the incomparable live sensation" (Scher 1997) but also symbolizing membership in an "affective alliance." "The thinking has always been," one promoter explains, "if it's a band they feel they must see, the fans will find a way to pay for it" (Vallon quoted in Sandler 1999). Nostalgic for the affective musical experiences of their past, baby boomers are desirous and able to relive (and repurchase) them, usually at premium prices. Hence the continuing concert successes of the Grateful Dead (until their disbanding in 1996), the Rolling Stones, the Eagles, Paul Simon, and Bob Dylan, who recently performed for a large sum at a corporate banquet before an audience that, to say the least, "hadn't booked him to shake up their world-view" (J. Miller quoted in Woodworth and Boyers 1999:212). Of the top five grossing tours in 1996, four (Eagles, Kiss, Bob Seger, and Neil Diamond) were "reunion tours" of older artists, most of whom were trading on older fans' nostalgia (Kiss, for example, recreated its 1970s theatrical show and played its old songs to sold-out crowds). These four tours grossed a combined $171 million. In 1991, only two of the top five tours (the venerable Grateful Dead and Paul Simon) specifically targeted an older cohort of fans (Scher 1997).

Related to the reunion tour phenomenon, an entire subculture of latter-day hippies has cohered around the Woodstock myth and the attempt to reconstruct the affective alliance of the 1960s counterculture. Insisting on the primacy of the concert experience over professionally recorded and industrially distributed popular music, these zealous fans made the Grateful Dead one of the top-grossing acts in the concert industry. "The death of (guitarist) Jerry Garcia" in 1996, one promoter lamented, "pulled millions out of this industry" (Scher 1997). The vacuum, however, was soon filled by several younger neohippie "jam bands" patterned on the Grateful Dead's musical aesthetic and concert ritual. Of the top ten grossing concerts in July 1999, two were dates by Phish, which has capitalized on the success of the Grateful Dead and inherited much of its younger audience. Each concert grossed well over $1 million (*Billboard* 1999:13), though Phish (like the Grateful Dead before it) has never had a hit single nor a particularly high-selling full-length recording. These audiences for these lucrative tours are generally white and middle-class, and despite some illicit drug use, they tend to be reliable and tractable consumers who regard the event as an affirmation of their way of life for which they are willing and able to pay. Concert promoters are eager for these types of audiences, whereas other types, such as fans of hip-hop artists, are regarded with caution or are ignored.

Describing the "hip-hop nation" as "another problem that affects the concert biz's bottom line," one trade publication has noted the inability for the industry to reproduce massive hip-hop record sales at the concert box office (Sandler 1999). The publication did not inquire too deeply into this dilemma, chalking it up to the logic of the market, but there is little doubt that racism continues to dictate many of African Americans' leisure consumption options to a degree that whites would find intolerably narrow. As with the Woodstock Nation, the menacing hip-hop nation is largely a construction of the media, emerging out of one particular incident, a rap concert at the Nassau Coliseum in Long Island in September 1988, in which a nineteen-year-old man was stabbed to death. After this, concert venues across the country began to cancel or restrict hip-hop shows, citing threat to life and property; the media demonization of rap audiences after the Nassau Coliseum event and affirmation of the venues' decisions had a chilling effect on the promotion of hip-hop tours. "Because black youths are constructed as a permanent threat to the social order, large public gatherings will always be viewed as dangerous events" (Rose 1994:134). The developments that have enriched and expanded the concert industry more generally, such as corporate sponsorship and advertising, seem unlikely to reach the hip-hop nation, as those consumers with relatively little purchasing power are increasingly ignored in favor of those with deeper or deepening pockets, such as neohippie audiences. In 1991, the top ten grossing tours included one African American act, Bell Biv Devoe; in 1996, the list of headliners was exclusively white.

Perhaps the most significant development in the concert industry (indeed, in the sports and entertainment industry more generally) over the past two decades has been the increasing corporate presence at live events, both in terms of advertising and tour sponsorship. It is likely that the presence of video commercials at concert venues will grow as a result of industrial consolidation, having originated in 1984 as an ostensible means for offsetting the costs of giant video display units by promoters and venue operators. The ads continue to be valued by advertisers who seek "the opportunity to get to such a 'difficult to reach audience in a dynamic environment'" (DiMauro 1984:82). As with the increase in ticket price, corporate involvement with rock is directly related to the rise of the baby boom generation to social and economic dominance. "It's these people," notes one promoter, "the kids from the '60s, who first realized that rock audiences were an advertiser's dream" (Specter 1983).

In addition to advertising, direct corporate sponsorship of tours and events has increased steadily since the early 1980s. Although corporate sponsorship of musical performance was certainly nothing new—Royal Crown Cola and other companies had bankrolled *The Grand Ole Opry*—it was not until 1981, when the beauty-products company Jovan sponsored the Rolling Stones tour, that corporations began to view big-name rock concerts as legitimate ways to reach an important consumer demographic. Pioneering the contemporary sponsorship relationship, the Rolling Stones gave Jovan and, later in the 1980s, Budweiser, advertising space on tour merchandise and concert tickets and stages and even bore corporate logos on their musical instruments (Matzer 1996). Jovan also obtained use of the Stones' name and imagery for broadcast ads, promotional giveaways, and products.

Often corporate sponsors will also demand logo presence on the concert merchandise, as in the presence of Camel cigarettes and Tecate beer logos and advertising copy on T-shirts, hats, and other items from the 1983 Eric Clapton and Tom Petty tours, respectively. During the 1980s, several bands and corporations entered into similar deals, including Schlitz with ZZ Top and The Who, U.S. Tobacco with the Charlie Daniels Band, Jordache with Air Supply, and Canada Dry with Hall and Oates (Specter 1983). From 1987 to 1997, overall corporate sponsorship spending in the United States and Canada rose 337 percent, to $5.9 billion (Button 1997).

Of course, corporate sponsorship is intended to generate an affinity between a particular product and the lifestyle a particular musical artist represents. Researchers studying the market effects of sponsorship found that 56 percent of those questioned indicated that the tie-in between Pepsi and Michael Jackson "made them feel more positive about the brand" (Gross 1989). Strikingly, it has often been the bands that have approached the sponsors in search of lucrative partnerships, as with Journey's full-page solicitation in *Advertising Age* (a trade journal that had championed Jovan's move into concert sponsorship) for potential sponsors of its 1983 tour of the United States and Japan (Specter 1983). In addition to the obvious appeal of the extra revenues generated by corporate sponsorships, bands stand to profit from the greater exposure corporate advertising budgets can provide (see Matzer 1996). The slump in record sales during the early 1980s led to diminished tour and promotional support from record companies, a trend which, despite an upturn in the industry's sales, continues to this day. Recently many artists, facing more competition for radio/video exposure, have welcomed opportunities to participate in corporate advertising campaigns. One record company executive has asserted that "artists understand a commercial will lead to more familiarity for them and their music and can translate into increased record sales" (Olson 1999).

From the vantage of promoters, corporate advertisers, record companies, and most large acts, sponsorship deals have enabled more bands to mount more elaborate and sustained tours efficiently and in the black; many fans have greeted the arrangements with less enthusiasm, as the sponsorship clearly fails to benefit them in any substantial way. Indeed, many fans have protested the joining of two large business entities (the bands and the corporations) for the extraction of greater profit from the consumer. An editor of a popular magazine noted that, for all the infusion of Schlitz's capital into The Who's 1983 tour, ticket prices continued to rise: "The groups get the money, the companies get the advertising exposure, and fans are left with things that I don't think they want very much, like free posters" (Specter 1983).

For those rock fans unable or unwilling to brave the high cost, crowds, and traffic associated with live concerts, the industry has recently begun marketing pay-per-view and Internet broadcasts of live events, a practice pioneered by the sports industry. Concerts are regularly available on cable and satellite television all over the world. Several industry giants (including SFX) have begun purchasing and investing in Internet businesses to facilitate "cybercast" performances. Such a development creates opportunities for the industry to further profit from live performances, as the broadcasts can be archived and viewed repeatedly. The industry is hopeful that music consumers will "ante up for live broadcasts, download archived concerts or relive a show they recently saw in person" (Strauss 1999a). The incomparable—because it cannot be replicated—live experience becomes here a recorded commodity much like the music industry's traditional products, capable of generating profit again and again.

In August 1994, a week before the twentieth-fifth-anniversary reproduction of the Woodstock festival was to be held in Saugerties, New York, a cover story for *Time* leveled a question at its readers: "Is Anyone Hip?" The article charted the rise of "hip" from the 1950s to its eventual demise as a marker of rebel distinction in the present day. Of course, no discussion of hipness would be complete without invoking the halcyon days at Max Yasgur's farm:

> For those who attended the original Woodstock, it was possible to imagine that they were present at history's largest convergence of the privileged few, the hip minority. Of course, they saw it as the birth of the Woodstock Nation, a giant step toward the hipping of the world at large. It's going to be harder to think of next week's festival that way. Though the crowds will come determined to break whatever mold they are poured into, it won't be easy to escape the feeling that this time Woodstock will be history's largest convergence of the mass market. (Lacayo 1994)

The *Time* article presented an update on the Woodstock myth first articulated two decades earlier under the same masthead: Woodstock was the anticommercial Eden from which we fell, and there is no getting back. In the tradition of countercultural nostalgia, *Time* presented a critique (the tone of which was rather hip and ironic itself) of the commodification of previously marginal and resistant subcultures of which Woodstock was singularly representative.

Meanwhile, in another sector of the Time-Warner empire, subsidiary Atlantic Records was set to release a four-CD boxed set of previously unreleased live tracks from the watershed event as well as a "Best of Woodstock" compilation. In addition, a "director's cut" of the original *Woodstock* film, the rights to which Warner Bros. Pictures had acquired in Roberts and Rosenman's bankruptcy fire sale, had opened in theaters across the nation in June, with a new home video version to follow. *Time* would later condemn the 1994 event as "a corporatized simulacrum" (Farley 1994) of the original: sponsored by Pepsi, Apple Computer, and Häagen-Dazs, Woodstock '94 would cost promoters, who would pocket $135 apiece from 225,000 latter-day Aquarian ticket holders, $30 million, and it would generate pay-per-view television earnings between $5 million and $8 million (Farley 1994). The director of the original film, Michael Wadleigh, seemed particularly outraged at the repackaging of the Woodstock myth. He was, however, preparing an antidote:

> Woodstock is the only event that got a generation named after it, and it didn't happen by putting up a lot of Coca-Cola signs. . . . If you look at the film footage, I defy you to find a single corporate logo. That wasn't what the festival was about. I think with all these other events coming down, they're changing the Woodstock Generation into the Pepsi Generation, turning Peace and Love into Peace and Love Inc., trying to rip it off and make a buck from it. So I said, "Let's do a director's cut and these new albums to show the kids what the real event was about." If you want the real stuff, the anti-corporate stuff, this is it. (Rosenblum 1994)

Evidently Time-Warner's marketing blitzkrieg of "original Woodstock" products failed to strike Wadleigh as ironic. Even assuming that the original event had constituted "the anti-corporate stuff," how could a corporation be expected or trusted to deliver it? As Wadleigh's words indicate, rock culture continues to be powered and informed by articulations of resistance, anticommercialism, and authenticity, however cognitively dissonant they may be. Five years later, at Woodstock '99, held at the former Griffiths Air Force Base in Rome, New York, promoter John Scher forsook both nostalgia and duplicity, affirming that "we've never denied we're going to make a profit on this one" (Czelusniak 1999:14). When asked what could have been done better at the festival, at which infrastructural failure, violence, looting, and rape occurred, Scher answered (perhaps unaware of the extent of the trouble), "Commercial opportunities were not exploited as fully as they might have been" (Samuels 1999:81). Yet Woodstock '99, the grounds of which were festooned with corporate logos, made only desultory reference to the peace-and-love spirit of the 1969 event. Rather, the more recent festival was an example of the "commodification of dissent," in which a later movement of rock-culture disaffiliation was mined, processed, and repackaged to spur consumption by young people and those who styled themselves young. This other movement was punk rock.

"THE ANTI-CORPORATE STUFF": PUNK, ALTERNATIVE, AND THE COMMODIFICATION OF RESISTANCE

By the mid-1970s, what rock had gained in economic vitality it had proportionally lost in its ability to articulate authenticity and opposition. One writer noted that "rock has effectively eased to a halt, even if economically you wouldn't have noticed" (Morley 1992:202). Punk arose as a scathing critique of the alliance of rock and capital and of the estrangement of rock artists and the means of musical production from rock fans; it attacked rock for the sins of bombast, pretension, and artifice. The antidote was a return to rock's anarchic roots, a purging of the will-to-art and the commercial gigantism the form had developed. The excesses of 1970s "arena rock"—giant concert venues and inflated ticket prices, impeccably and exorbitantly produced recordings, virtuoso performances, mythologized star personalities, and an expansion in merchandising—provoked a backlash that splintered rock culture. This splintering came on the heels of massive consolidation within the music industry in the late 1960s, part of a more widespread merger phenomenon that narrowed industrial and media control into concentrations without precedent (see Bagdikian 1997). By 1973, ten corporations accounted for 82.9 percent of the U.S. domestic market, the record sales of which amounted to well over $2 billion—worldwide, nearly $5 billion (Chapple and Garofalo 1977:82–87, 186–90).

The aesthetic sensibilities of punk diverged radically from the high-art aspirations and explicit politicization of 1960s rock. In 1976, a writer in *Melody Maker* diagnosed "a growing, almost desperate, feeling that rock and roll should be stripped down to its bare bones again" (Coon 1992:195). Punk song titles ("No Future," "Pretty Vacant," "I Wanna Be Sedated," "Gimme Gimme Shock Treatment") and the unwillingness of punk musicians to play mellifluous, radio-friendly, salable pop and rock songs—often coinciding with the inability to "play" one's instrument in a traditional sense—embodied the sonic aspect of punk's "Refusal" (see Hebdige 1990). Consonant with an abrasive musical program, visually punks "consciously sought cultural forms offensive to mainstream sensibilities and incorporated them into the ensemble of punk subcultural appearance" (Gottdiener 1995:182). Its style—taken here to mean "a collection of signs bound together in 'homologous' relationship" (Willis 1993:379)—involved the appropriation and reinterpretation of signs and commodities as a sort of semiotic guerrilla warfare, in which deliberately transgressive marking of bodies with leather and spikes, swastikas, mohawked and spiked hair, garish makeup and clothing marked one as a member of the insurgency. Being a punk meant being, in the midst of a chaotic and contradictory barrage of visual and sonic codes, "hip to the show" (Shank 1994:107), an adept in a communal performative practice of resistance beyond the reach of hegemony. It is crucial to note that punks' affective alliances were generated through live performances, usually in small clubs, in which the audience played a pivotal and active role (Shank 1994:91–161), in contrast to the stoned-out passivity and pathos of distance that characterized the listening habits of most (recorded) rock fans, as well as most arena rock shows.

Rock culture and the strategies of those who would sell to it had always cohered around those images and models of disaffiliation and rebellion, whose threat had been neutralized or subsumed—one thinks of Chevrolet's use of Elvis's vanilla doppelganger Pat Boone. Yet one of the most effective strategies adopted by the postwar culture industry (and indeed by most marketers of consumer products) consisted in a new strain of advertising rhetoric, which both mimicked and nurtured the counterculture's sense of itself as oppositional (see Frank 1997). Characterizing a product or service as "hip," nonconformist, or even radical became a common technique; ads would often speak in the voices of the ostensible enemies of mainstream consumption—Marxist radicals, racial Others, hippies, and other rebellious outsiders. As a strategy, it was brilliant, because it recast consumption as the crucial site of self-making and authentic interaction with the world. Yet as the advertisers and corporations soon found, images and rhetorics of rebellion were as subject to obsolescence as the products themselves. Over time, once-dependable figures of disaffiliation (for example, hippies) no longer generated the responses advertisers desired. Rock's animating spirit of resistance, however moribund, had to be reinvigorated for its products (and the products with which it was allied) to generate affect and continue to sell. By the late 1970s, new marginalities had to be identified, cultivated, and pressed into the service of capital.

Once disdainful of punk, the mainstream culture industry soon got hip to the show. After its "brief, formative moment of opportunity and danger" (Langford 1999:52), punk "was quickly recuperated into a new kind of pop music that accurately reproduced the latest conditions of consumer capitalism" (Savage 1989:166). Hence punk—a name denoting insignificance and criminality—became "new wave; a marketing statement utilizing the powerful stimulus 'new' to indicate a change in product" (Gottdiener 1995:173). "Brace yourself for the New Wave explosion," *New York* magazine wryly warned its readers in 1980, "the renegade subculture that began on the Lower East Side is going big time" (Post 1980:53). The next year, a young man with spiked hair and wraparound "new wave" shades could be seen hawking Fig Newtons on a new network called MTV.

Beginning in the 1970s, the expansion of independent ("indie") record labels, which produced and distributed recordings on both a local and national scale, provided a means of resisting the increasing concentration of industry capital and the product standardization on FM radio play lists and record store shelves (both radio and music retailing underwent tremendous consolidation during the 1980s). Although small-scale production had existed since the advent of the commercial recording market, the indie-label-as-opposition trend blossomed in the wake of punk. Opposition to increasing concentration of capital was not an explicit goal for most indie label owners; they simply wanted to put out "good stuff" for themselves and those with similar tastes. Some were simply entrepreneurs, colonizing "the seams and spaces of the modern culture industry that are vacated or ignored by conglomerates" (H. Gray cited in S. Lee 1995:21).

Many indie labels nevertheless saw themselves as "cultural articulations," defenders of musical art against its old enemy, commerce (or at the very least, untrammeled commerce). They sought industrial autonomy, the ability to produce and distribute their product in as self-contained and self-determined a manner as possible, isolated from the interference of the crass economism of the major labels and also from the leveling influence of pandering to "the popular taste." Although undoubtedly business entities, these labels struggled to temper the economic rationality of running a business with the desire to establish and curate a subcultural sanctuary for both producer and consumer. Indie labels enjoyed a great deal of "symbolic capital" (Bourdieu 1993) despite the regularity of bankruptcies (with a few notable exceptions) among them.

The redoubtable symbolic capital (the "street creed") of the indie labels' stance was evident in the musical press. Of course, given the right process of exchange, symbolic capital can be transformed into economic capital. The mainstream culture industry, recently embarked on a rapid diversification of product—amid, ironically, another wave of consolidation (see Frith 1988; Sanjek and Sanjek 1996)—increasingly turned its attention to the formerly dark warrens of the musical underground and the audiences (however numerically meager) the indie labels had assembled. Indies "enabled the inquisitive consumer to sample forms of music the majors avoided or denigrated" (Sanjek and Sanjek 1996:657); however few the number of this type of consumer, it was a type the major labels required, if only for market research into the potential Next Big Thing. By the late 1980s, indie labels began to be regarded as a sort of "minor league," heavily invested with symbolic capital, from which the major labels—who by 1995 controlled 85–90 percent of the industry market share (Sanjek and Sanjek 1996:672–73)—culled their hit-making talent.

The mainstream recording industry in the 1990s (dominated by six corporations) thus found its salvation in formerly marginalized and transgressive musics—urban hip-hop and suburban hard rock, or "grunge." Advertisers set their sights on the personae—artists and fans—informing and informed by the critiques these forms articulated. The major labels' foray into indie rock territory—locating and signing rock bands from vital local indie scenes such as Seattle—inaugurated a new genre, *alternative*. The name denoted the strategy with which the industry positioned these bands' recordings as new and exciting alternative products to those already on the shelf.

The loud, aggressive music of artists such as Nirvana and Pearl Jam (both drawn from independent labels), the looks and poses of the band members themselves, and the politics they, to a greater or lesser degree, espoused, became potentially powerful marketing tropes that, like their 1960s counterparts, could link a seemingly disparate group of lifestyle products. Though the abrasive alternative bands were aesthetically of a type formerly viewed by corporations as poor sponsorship risks, those that "wear chains and sing lyrics that are difficult for the corporate image" (Gross 1989), these bands nonetheless had the power to "loosen the wallets" of a crucial age demographic, "the next wave of consumers waiting in the wings: media-savvy high-school and college students whose combined purchasing power approaches $1 billion each year" (Boehlert 1995a). Yet there were impediments to the wholesale appropriation of "alternative" by corporate interests.

Rock music has always, to some degree, articulated the *"reconciliation* of rebelliousness and capital" (Frith 1981:2); at the same time, that reconciliation must be negotiated carefully lest either element grow too dominant and dissolve the crucial tension on which rock's appeal is founded. For rock's older, deeper-pocketed, and more nostalgic audiences, an artist's positive stance toward self-commodification and fan exploitation may constitute no serious threat to that artist's popularity and affective power. Alternative artists, by contrast, risked considerable diminution of their appeal by partaking in such industrial devices as corporate sponsorship and product promotion. Indeed, to be marketable, alternative rock artists must shun or, at the very least, *appear* to shun corporate affiliation; they must, to paraphrase the boast of *Woodstock* film director Michael Wadleigh, give the kids the *real* stuff, the anticorporate stuff. The music industry recognized that the lucrative arrangements in which alternative artists shill for corporations simultaneously mar those artists' ability to project a salable image of integrity and authenticity. Hence the industry, concerned about the appeal of its product, claimed to be "sensitive to overcommercializing the music of Generation X," fearful that alternative acts' "disaffiliated stance might be undercut among listeners by any blatant commercial tie-ins (Matzer 1996). "Rarely," one commentator observed of the alternative paradox, "has corporate America had so much trouble having its checks cashed" (Boehlert 1995a).

Alternative rock as a profitable genre continues to depend on the constant affirmation of the artists' disaffiliation, which can come through music and lyrics, subcultural style, or in rare cases, political views or activism. However, even the most "radical" alternative artists find themselves in the quandary of their own incorporation and their inefficacy at registering any significant transgression. One such band, Rage Against the Machine, claims to "galvanize and inspire its fans to fight back against abuse and injustice wherever they rear their ugly heads." After the violence at Woodstock '99, the band's guitarist was invited by the *New York Times* to write his reaction. Morello inveighed against Woodstock '99's "crass commericialism" and "concert organizers who gouged the kids with grossly overpriced water, beer, and food," and suggested an affinity between the looters and rapists at the event and the corporate entities that sponsored it. The historical meaning of Woodstock '99 would have to be deferred, Morello wrote, "until these vandals and pyromaniacs grow up to become the C.E.O.'s of media conglomerates, like their predecessors at the original Woodstock" (quoted in Strauss 1999b).

Morello's critique seems heartfelt. His words avow a political stance of social justice and egalitarianism; but his anticorporate diatribe fails to mention the fact that his band nonetheless willingly booked and played the event, or that Rage Against the Machine's recordings are produced and distributed by Epic, a subsidiary of the media conglomerate Sony. For its part, Epic most likely welcomed Morello's critique; Rage Against the Machine's ability to affect fans with their denunciations of U.S. foreign policy, racism, and corporate greed was the reason Epic signed them in the first place, as such sensibilities are regarded by corporations less as threats to the consuming order than as niche-market tastes. Similarly, Pearl Jam was lauded for its quixotic legal battle with Ticketmaster, in which it took a stand against a corporate entity whose practices it felt were limiting the band's autonomy and fleecing its fans. Months after band members testified before Congress, Reebok issued a press release that declared "concert ticket prices are so outrageous—and band Pearl Jam is leading the assault," before "announcing a promotion in which customers can win $10 rebates off concert tickets if they try on a pair of Boks shoes" (Boehlert 1995b).

In many ways, Morello's and Pearl Jam's dilemma (being simultaneously anticommercial and commodified) is representative of the more general crisis of oppositional culture at the end of the century: the facility and rapidity with which consumer culture absorbs critique and repackages it for sale.

"There's this notion of capitalism as a kind of Pillsbury doughboy—you can poke it real hard and all it'll do is sort of giggle and pop back out . . . crazy demented punk rock shit came first and Nike, for example, found ways to merchandise and sell it. . . . Capitalism finds its enemies and makes them its best friends" (Johnson quoted in Seiler 1998:59).

However fraught with contradiction, alternative's reconciliation of rebellion and capital has been, on the whole, successful—corporate America's checks were eventually cashed. By the mid-1990s, alternative advertising abounded in print and broadcast media: Henry Rollins, lead singer for the seminal L.A. hardcore band Black Flag signed on to sell khakis for The Gap; a Ford ad equated the excitement of driving a new coupe with hitting an "E" chord onstage at the alternative music festival Lollapalooza; Anheuser-Busch marketed its Bud Dry as "the alternative beer"; and a Nike commercial blared American punks The Stooges' caustic anthem, "Search and Destroy." Ultimately, the alternative culture produced and marketed in the 1990s was the result of "the siege equipment of the consumer age" (Frank 1995:118) laying claim to punk's negativity, having recognized in it a sensibility of immense pecuniary value. It was through alternative advertising that "punk broke"—both in terms of becoming a mass cultural form and in the sense of breaking apart as an antagonistic response to a commodified culture. Alternative rock signifies, then, the industrial takeover of punk and the exhaustion of much of its critical capacity.

CONCLUSION

Rock music surrounds everyday lives; it is enmeshed into advertisements, political campaigns, and the ideology of novelty and youth undergirding contemporary consumer capitalism. Its pervasiveness and affective force make it a cultural practice of tremendous import to the capitalist and the cultural critic alike, as rock has figured both as "a sonic environment for commerce" (Walley 1998:10) and as a soundtrack to progressive social action. Although popular music historically has demonstrated "power to locate people in an affective structure of hope" (Grossberg 1992:396), to inspire and anchor counterhegemonic sensibilities, the alacrity and success with which the culture industry has marketed that affective structure and channeled those sensibilities toward consumption must be soberly acknowledged.

The imagined link between incendiary and anticapitalist (or at least socially therapeutic) politics and rock music grows more and more difficult to reimagine. Rock culture has proven its capacity "to create and construct youth culture as a collective subject" (Redhead 1990:5); but what type of collective subject can be expected to emerge from an increasingly corporate and commodified rock culture? An enormous challenge thus presents itself to cultural criticism invested in rock culture as a political force, namely, to continue believing in it as such, despite evidence of its enervation. The Revolution, to be sure, will not be sponsored.

BIBLIOGRAPHY

Adorno, Theodor (1973). *Negative Dialectics*. Trans. E. B. Ashton. New York: Continuum.

———— (1976). "Popular Music," Trans. E. B. Ashton, in *Introduction to the Sociology of Music*. New York: Seabury.

———— (1990a). "On Popular Music," in *On Record: Rock, Pop, and the Written Word*, eds. Simon Frith and Andrew Goodwin. New York: Pantheon Books.

———— (1990b). "On the Fetish Character in Music and the Regression in Listening,*"* in *The Culture Industry: Selected Essays on Mass Culture*, ed. J. M. Bernstein. New York and London: Routledge: 26–52.

Bagdikian, Ben H. (1997). *The Media Monopoly*. 5th ed. Boston: Beacon.

Baudrillard, Jean (1981). *For a Critique of the Political Economy of the Sign*. St. Louis: Telos.

Bauman, Zygmunt (1988). *Freedom*, ed. Milton Keynes. United Kingdom: Open University Press.

Best, Beverly (1997). "Over-the-Counter Culture: Retheorizing Resistance in Popular Culture," in *The Clubcultures Reader: Readings in Popular Cultural Studies*, ed. Steve Redhead, Derek Wynne, and Justin O'Connor. Oxford: Blackwell: 18–35.

Billboard (1999). "Boxscore Top Ten Concert Grosses," *Billboard* August 14:13.

Boehlert, Eric (1995a). "Madison Avenue Eyes Modern Rock, But Acts Remain Wary," *Billboard* August 5:1(2).

———— (1995b). "Play-by-Play Account of the Pearl Jam Saga," *Billboard* July 8:85(1).

Bourdieu, Pierre (1993). *The Field of Cultural Production: Essays on Art and Literature*. New York: Columbia University Press.

Button, Graham (1997). "And Now, An Event From Our Sponsor," *Working Woman* November:40 (6).

Buxton, David (1990). "Rock Music, the Star System, and the Rise of Consumerism," in *On Record: Rock, Pop, and the Written Word*, ed. Simon Frith and Andrew Goodwin. New York: Pantheon Books.

Certeau, Michel de (1984). *The Practice of Everyday Life*. Berkeley: University of California Press.

Chanan, Michael (1995). *Repeated Takes: A Short History of Recording and its Effects on Music*. London and New York: Verso.

Chapple, Steve, and Reebee Garofalo (1977). *Rock 'n' Roll Is Here To Pay: The History and Politics of the Music Industry*. Chicago: Nelson Hall.

Coon, Caroline (1992). "You Say You Wanna Revolution?" in *The Penguin Book of Rock and Roll Writing*, ed. Clinton Heylin. London: Viking.

Curry, Jack (1989). *Woodstock: The Summer of Our Lives*. New York: Weidenfeld & Nicolson.

Czelusniak, Allen (1999). "Woodstock '99:Three Days of Profit and Music," *PitchWeekly* August 26–September 1:14(6).

DiMauro, Phil (1984). "Commercials Invading Concerts; Rock Fans a Captive Audience," *Variety* July 25:2, 82.

Erenberg, Lewis (1981). *Steppin' Out: New York Nightlife and the Transformation of American Culture, 1890–1930*. Chicago and London: University of Chicago Press.

Farley, Christopher John (1994). "Woodstock Suburb," *Time* August 22:78(3).

Fiske, John (1987). *Television Culture*. London: Methuen.

Frank, Tom (1995). "Alternative to What?" in *Sounding Off! Music as Subversion/ Resistance/Revolution*. ed. Ron Sakolsky and Fred Wei-han Ho. Brooklyn: Autonomedia: 102–19.

——— (1997). *The Conquest of Cool: Business Culture, Counterculture, and the Rise of Hip Consumerism*. Chicago and London: University of Chicago Press.

Frith, Simon (1988). "Picking Up the Pieces," in *Facing the Music*, ed. Simon Frith. New York: Pantheon.

——— (1981). *Sound Effects: Youth, Leisure, and the Politics of Rock 'n' Roll*. New York: Pantheon Books.

George, Nelson (1988). *The Death of Rhythm & Blues*. New York: Pantheon Books.

Gitlin, Todd (1987). *The Sixties: Years of Hope, Days of Rage*. Bantam: New York.

Goldberg, Michael (1983). "Take the Money and Run: Rock & Roll Gets in Bed with Corporate America," *Rolling Stone* July 7:43(4).

Gottdiener, M. (1995). *Postmodern Semiotics: Material Culture and the Forms of Postmodern Life*. Oxford, UK and Cambridge, Mass.: Blackwell.

Gross, Amy E. (1989). "Music Sponsorship: Making a Sound Mix," *Adweek's Marketing Week* January 16:SP9(1).

Grossberg, Lawrence (1992). *We Gotta Get Out of This Place: Popular Conservatism and Postmodern Culture*. New York and London: Routledge: x.

Guralnick, Peter (1994). *Last Train to Memphis: The Rise of Elvis Presley*. Boston: Little, Brown.

Hebdige, Dick (1979). *Subculture: The Meaning of Style*. London: Methuen.

——— (1990). "Style as Homology and Signifying Practice," in *On Record: Rock, Pop, and the Written Word*, ed. Simon Frith and Andrew Goodwin. New York: Pantheon Books: 56–65.

Hopkins, Jerry (1970). *Festival!* New York: Collier-Macmillan.

Kaufman, Gil (1997). "Entertainment Group Buys Large Chunk of Concert Business," *Addicted to Noise, the Online Rock & Roll Magazine* <http://www.addicted.com.au/> December 18 [accessed August 1999].

Kleinhans, Chuck (1994). "Cultural Appropriation and Subcultural Expression: The Dialectics of Cooperation and Resistance." A Paper for Presentation to the Northwestern Center for the Humanities. Evanston, Ill.

Lacayo, Richard (1994). "Is Anyone Hip?" *Time* August 8.

Langford, Jon (1999). "Concealing the Hunger," in *Stars Don't Stand Still in the Sky: Music and Myth*. ed. Karen Kelly and Evelyn McDonnell. New York: New York University Press: 51–55.

Lee, Martyn J. (1993). *Consumer Culture Reborn: The Cultural Politics of Consumption.* London and New York: Routledge.

Lee, Stephen (1995). "Re-examining the Concept of the 'Independent' Record Company: The Case of Wax Trax! Records," *Popular Music* 14.1:13–31.

Lipsitz, George (1990). *Time Passages: Collective Memory and American Popular Culture*. Minneapolis: University of Minnesota Press.

——— (1994). *Dangerous Crossroads: Popular Music, Postmodernism, and the Poetics of Place.* London: Verso.

Marcus, Greil (1990). *Mystery Train: Images of America in Rock 'n' Roll Music.* New York: Obelisk/Dutton,.

Matzer, Marla (1996). "Superwellknown Sponsors," *Brandweek* October 7:28(6).

McCollum, Brian (1998). "SFX Buys Oakland County Show Promoter Cellar Door," *The Detroit Free Press* August 15.

Miller, Daniel (1987). "Material Culture and Mass Consumption," in *Social Archeology*. ed. Ian Hodder. Oxford, UK and Cambridge, Mass.: Blackwell.

——— (1995). "Consumption as the Vanguard of History: A Polemic By Way of an Introduction" in *Acknowledging Consumption: A Review of New Studies*. ed. Daniel Miller. London and New York: Routledge.1987

Miller, James (1999). *Flowers in the Dustbin: The Rise of Rock and Roll, 1947–1977.* New York: Simon & Schuster.

Morley, Paul (1992). "New Pop UK, " in *The Penguin Book of Rock and Roll Writing.* ed. Clinton Heylin. London: Viking,.

Olson, Catherine Applefield (1999). "Artists Now Proud to Pitch," *Billboard* May 8:S-13(1).

Peterson, Richard A. (1973). "The Unnatural History of Rock Festivals: An Instance of Media Facilitation," *Popular Music and Society* 2.2 :97–123.

Pilpel, Robert, John Roberts, and Joel Rosenman (1974). *Young Men with Unlimited Capital*. New York: Harcourt Brace Jovanovich.

Plasketes, George M. (1992). "Taking Care of Business: The Commercialization of Rock Music," in *America's Musical Pulse: Popular Music in Twentieth-Century Society*. ed. Kenneth J. Bindas. Contributions to the Study of Popular Culture. Westport, Conn. and London: Greenwood Press: 149–66.

Plasketes, George M., and Julie Grace Plasketes (1987). "From Woodstock Nation to Pepsi Generation: Reflections on Rock Culture and the State of Music, 1969–Present," *Popular Music and Society* 11.2 :2–52.

Post, Henry (1980). "Business the New Wave Way," *New York* November 3:53–64.

Pratt, Ray (1990). "Rhythm and Resistance: Explorations in the Political Uses of Popular Music," in *Media and Society*. ed. J. Fred MacDonald. New York: Praeger.

Redhead, Steve (1990). *The End-of-the-Century Party: Youth and Pop Towards 2000*. Manchester and New York: Manchester University Press.

Rose, Tricia (1994). "Black Noise: Rap Music and Black Culture in Contemporary America," in *Music/Culture*. ed. George Lipsitz, Susan McClary, and Robert Walser. Hanover and London: Wesleyan University Press.

Rosenblum, Trudi Miller (1994). "Time Warner Plans Woodstock Redux," *Billboard* June 18:1(2).

Ross, Andrew (1989). *No Respect: Intellectuals and the Popular Culture*. New York and London: Routledge.

Samuels, David (1999). "Rock Is Dead: Sex, Drugs, and Raw Sewage at Woodstock 99," *Harper's* November: 69(13).

Sandler, Adam (1999). "Summer Rockers are Road-Wary (1999 Summer Concert Season)," *Variety* May 31.

Sanjek, Russell, and David Sanjek (1996). *Pennies From Heaven: The American Popular Music Business in the Twentieth Century*. New York: Da Capo Press.

Savage, John (1989). "Tainted Love: The Influence of Male Homosexuality and Sexual Divergence on Pop Music and Culture Since the War," in *Consumption, Identity, and Style*, ed. Alan Tomlinson. New York and London: Routledge/Comedia: 153–171.

Scher, John (1997). "Let's Take It Outside, Shall We," *Brandweek* February 24:22–25.

Seiler, Cotten (1998). "Something in the Water: Independent Rock Music in Louisville, Kentucky." Master of Arts thesis. University of Kansas.

Shank, Barry (1994). "Dissonant Identities: The Rock'n'Roll Scene in Austin, Texas," in *Music/Culture*. ed. George Lipsitz, Susan McClary, and Robert Walser. Hanover and London: Wesleyan University Press.

Southern, Eileen (1971). *The Music of Black Americans: A History*. New York: W. W. Norton.

Specter, Michael J. (1983). "Rock Puts on a Three-Piece Suit," *New York Times* October 2.

Spitz, Robert Stephen (1979). *Barefoot in Babylon: The Creation of the Woodstock Music Festival, 1969*. New York: Viking Press.

Stein, Howard, and Ronald Zalkind (1979). *Promoting Rock Concerts*. New York: Schirmer Books.

Strauss, Neil (1999a). "'69 or '99, a Rock Festival Is a Combustible Mix," *New York Times* August 8:1, 31.

——— (1999b). "Raging at the Media," *New York Times* August 5:B3.

Volpacchio, Florindo (1991). "The Mother of All Interviews: Frank Zappa on Music and Society," *Telos* 24.1:124–136.

Walley, David (1998). *Teenage Nervous Breakdown: Music and Politics in the Post–Elvis Age*. New York and London: Plenum Press.

Weinstein, Deena (1999). "Art Versus Commerce: Deconstructing a (Useful) Romantic Illusion," in *Stars Don't Stand Still in the Sky: Music and Myth*. ed. Karen Kelly and Evelyn McDonnell. New York: New York University Press.

Willis, Susan (1993). "Hardcore: Subculture American Style," *Critical Inquiry* 19:365–83.

Woodworth, Marc, and Robert Boyers (1999). "Rock Music and The Culture of Rock: An Interview with James Miller," *Salmagundi* 118–19, 206–23.

11

Fantasy Tours: Exploring the Global Consumption of Caribbean Sex Tourisms

Beverley Mullings

In the past ten years, increasing attention has been paid to the existence of a global sex tourism industry. Newspapers and magazines are replete with stories documenting the growing visibility of this industry in Asia, Africa, Latin America, and the Caribbean. Although the most popular destinations associated with these services traditionally have been in Europe and Southeast Asia, increasing attention is being paid to places once considered "off the map." This chapter examines the factors behind the growing visibility and expansion of sex tourism services in off-the-map locales. Focusing on the Caribbean, the relationship between the growth of this niche tourism service and current transformations in the production and consumption of contemporary tourism is explored. By examining the development of sex tourisms in the Caribbean, it is possible to see how the spatial boundaries that once ordered sex tourism production and consumption are being transformed. Although commodification of the bodies of Caribbean men and women has become a standard feature of sex tourism in the region, how these services are understood, practiced, and consumed within each island differs widely. In other words, the uniqueness of place has stimulated different types of sex tourism consumption.

TRANSFORMATIONS IN TOURISM PRODUCTION AND CONSUMPTION

Two main accounts have emerged from the literature examining the changes in the production and consumption of tourism in the late twentieth century. In the first account, which has been explored largely by sociologists and anthropologists, the changing nature of tourism is viewed as part of a more general transformation in the practice of consumption (Urry 1990; Featherstone 1991; Warde 1992; du Gay 1996; Lury 1996; Baudrillard 1998). Drawing upon the earlier work of Pierre Bordieu (1984), they argue that the social significatory function of consumption has been greatly heightened in the 1990s and has become increasingly nonmaterial in form. Introducing the notion of habitus, Bordieu argued that individuals and social classes utilize unconscious dispositions and classificatory systems to differentiate themselves from others. Habitus therefore acts as a cognitive structure that gives people a sense of their place in the world.

Not all forms of consumption, however, are determined by the desire among social classes to differentiate themselves. Michel de Certeau (1984) suggests that practices of consumption, apart from being the process through which individuals situate themselves within a social hierarchy, may also be a way of creating group identities through the assemblage of distinctive combinations of style. Although consumption has always played a significatory role, Scott Lash and John Urry (1994) state that in recent times, consumers have become more conscious of the symbolic value of certain types of commodities. There is much debate over the existence of symbolic properties in all forms of consumption (Warde 1992; Abercrombie 1994), but it is generally agreed that cultural commodities such as art, literature, and music have become major symbolic indicators of identity. Colin Campbell (1989) also notes another characteristic of contemporary consumption, that is, its insatiability. He argues that modern consumption is driven by the desire to experience in reality the pleasures that are created or enjoyed in the imagination. He states:

> The individual is much more an artist of the imagination, someone who takes images from memory or the existing environment, and rearranges or otherwise improves them in his mind in such a way that they become distinctly pleasing. No longer are they taken as "given" from past experience, but crafted into unique products, pleasure being the guiding principle. (Campbell 1989:78)

This form of consumption that he describes as imaginary hedonism, however, is ultimately disillusioning because real consumption can never be as good as its fantasized version. The persisting cycle of imagined pleasures and disappointments then becomes the driving force behind the insatiable character of modern consumption.

Tourism is one of the industries most transformed by the changing nature of consumption (Urry 1990, 1995; Rojek and Urry 1997) because it is an activity that revolves around the collection of cultural signs—objects and experiences that contrast with the everyday life of organized and regulated work. The collection and consumption of cultures also has the ability to act as a marker of identity.

Tourists can be differentiated by the modes of travel they choose, the places they visit, and the times they travel. Fantasy is also a crucial feature of tourism, because it is through the imagined pleasure of new places that travel actually occurs.

Central to the tourism experience is the visual consumption of landscapes and people in places that promise to provide the traveler with intense pleasures that are different from the everyday. Urry (1995) describes this visual form of consumption as the "tourist gaze" and argues that it gives a particular heightening to other elements of the tourist experience, particularly to the sensual aspects (1995:132). Thus the activities undertaken by tourists tend to be distinctive from everyday "at home" life, and the landscapes and places subject to the tourist gaze often tend to be extraordinary and unconnected with usual activities such as work and domestic and personal life. These factors shape interactions of tourists in places and with the people they meet.

Several writers have attracted attention to the fact that since the 1980s, a new breed of traveler has emerged. Described as the "new middle classes" (Gershuny and Miles 1983; Featherstone 1991), these groups became the new cultural intermediaries initiating and transmitting new consumption patterns, including the search for "authentic" holidays in developing countries. Mowforth and Munt (1997) argue that the third world is deeply implicated in the current pursuit by the new middle classes for new forms of identity differentiating consumption. They posit that increasingly certain forms of travel have become symbols that differentiate the "middle classes" from "the rest." Many third world destinations play an important role in the consumption of modern or "new" tourism, because they continue to be viewed as untouched, authentic and appreciated by a few. As such, travel to many places in the third world confers upon the modern middle-class traveler a certain sense of distinction, of social position by virtue of the symbolic meanings attached to the certain types of activities in particular third-world places. And the symbolic meanings need not always be directly connected to the act of travel itself, for as Allen and Hamnett (1995) argue in the case of trekkers to Nepal, it is not travel to a far-off destination that confers kudos on the modern travelers but rather their ability to appreciate ecology.

In the second account of the changing nature of tourism, writers have tended to view the changes as largely production driven, reflecting an ongoing crisis of capital accumulation and the need to speed and stretch circuits of capital to maintain profit levels (Harvey 1989; Ioannides and Dabbage 1998). Indeed, David Harvey (1989) argues that contemporary consumer desires are created by producers through advertising, much of which manipulates desires and tastes through images that have nothing to do with the product. Drawing upon the work of industrial theorists, these authors claim that since the 1980s, firms within the tourism industry have become more responsive to individual tastes to remain profitable (Poon 1989, 1990: 84; Britton 1991; Urry 1995; Mowforth and Munt 1997).

From travel agents and airlines to hotels, tourism producers have begun to introduce differentiated tourism products and segment markets and use information
technologies such as computer reservation systems (CRSs) to create strategic
market networks. Shaw and Williams (1994) argue that the profit motive is also
an important factor behind the increasing commodification of tourism. In creating more customized products for consumption, tourism has had the effect of
turning places and people into commodities. Mowforth and Munt (1997), for
example, argue that tourists now consume people, landscapes, and places in the
third world in much the same way they do other objects and commodities.
Mowforth and Munt argue that despite the seemingly softer nature of new ecologically aware forms of tourism, individual representatives of the new middle
classes (travelers, backpackers, and so on) are just as culpable in the process of
commodification.

The commodification of places and the people that live in them has become
particularly prevalent since the late 1970s as more and more governments have
come to view tourism as an important source of capital. Increasingly public and
private agencies are beginning to cooperate in the creation of infrastructure and
promotional mechanisms to facilitate tourism development. The impact of these
alliances, argues Urry, has been the increased commodification of places, as:

> An array of tourist professionals develops who attempt to reproduce ever-new ob-
> jects for the tourist gaze. These objects are located in a complex and changing hi-
> erarchy. This depends upon the interplay between, on the one hand, competition
> between different capitalist and state interests involved in the provision of such
> objects and on the other hand changing class, gender, and generational distinctions
> of taste within the potential population of visitors. (Urry 1995:133)

Focusing on place brings both these perspectives on consumption and production together, because as Urry argues, practices of consumption have no proper
place of their own; rather they operate within a space delineated by, but not
equivalent to, systems of production (1995:89). He also claims that there is an
interdependence between how goods and services are consumed and how places
are consumed. This interdependence can be seen in the way that images of places
are used to market products, in the fact that certain goods and services can be
consumed only in certain places, and in the way that images of place are constructed out of local products and services associated with those places. The nature
of the spaces, and consequently, the places, created by the changing consumption and production of tourism, however, must also be considered in the context
of the wider forces of change at the global scale. It is through the changes in the
organization of global capitalism that many of the changes in consumption and
production in particular places have their genesis. Using the Caribbean as an example, this chapter will show how contemporary processes of tourism production
and consumption have created the region as a place for sex tourism consumption.

THE GLOBAL CONSUMPTION OF SEX TOURISMS

Although several writers have begun to document the spread of sex tourism to areas once considered off the map (Kempadoo and Doezema 1998; Lim 1998; Oppermann 1998), few have examined the particularities of place that have facilitated this spread. The factors that have led to the Caribbean becoming a place for the consumption of sex tourism are closely connected to the way that tourism in the region is being produced and consumed and the global and local factors that are currently shaping both processes.

The trade in sexual services has always constituted an element within the tourism and travel culture. Indeed, much of the adventure associated with travel in the nineteenth century was bound up with the anticipation of coming into contact with the dangerous, sexual "other." Describing the pleasure derived from the visual consumption of sights during the nineteenth-century travel experience, Chris Rojek and John Urry (1997) point to the inevitable objectification of people and landscapes that occurred as the upper classes became the voyeuristic consumers of lower-class urban dwellers. The promiscuity associated with public life in these areas also contributed to the commodification of women who sold their sexual labor, as these women became culturally fixed as tourist sights. Consumption in this instance, however, was not always confined to the visual, as Rojek and Urry noted: "But some [men] of course sought out the touch and feel of the other through crossing to the dark side of the city and engaging with the diverse charms of prostitutes, opium dens, bars and taverns. This was known as 'slumming.' Underprivileged areas and criminogenic zones came to be redefined as tourist sights" (1997:7).

The fear and desire associated with women "sex traders" in public space in the nineteenth-century city was mirrored in early travel encounters in the third world. Constructed as sexually aberrant and particularly lascivious, women of color embodied all the mysteries and dangers associated with travel adventure (McClintock 1995). Fantasies associated with travel to the unknown, combined with common-sense theories regarding the naturally libidinous appetites of "native" women, served to justify sexual practices by European males that would have otherwise been considered morally transgressive in Europe. Bishop and Robinson (1997) note the contradictory and self-serving nature of the discourse that surrounded the sexual knowledges created about third-world people. Drawing heavily on Denis Diderot's critique of French morality, they argue that although Europeans believed the sexuality of people of color to be more natural and pure, their closeness to nature simultaneously served to reinforce their inferiority and distance from modern civilization. The eroticization of people of color as reflected in eighteenth- and nineteenth-century travel texts served to create fantasies of the Other that in many places became self-fulfilling realities. As writers such as Truong (1990) and Jones and colleagues (1998) have demonstrated, prostitution in Southeast Asia increased dramatically only after traditional patriarchal systems of slavery and concubinage were adapted to meet the desires of European male travelers and soldiers, traders, and emissaries in their adventures into the infinitely mysterious and dangerous spaces of the Other. In the Caribbean, women's sexual labor was also appropriated to satisfy the fantasies and desires of European males. The system of slavery and indentureship in this instance provided the local conditions that justified such sexual conduct, for as chattel, women were considered actual commodities at the disposal of their owners.

Commercial and more formalized forms of sex tourism developed in the 1940s and 1950s, as women's sexual labor came to be viewed as an economic asset to the tourism industry. During this period in several third-world countries, sex workers were incorporated into the tourism industry to satisfy the rest and recreational needs of military personnel. This form of work played an important role in the growth of tourism in places such as Thailand and the Philippines because it contributed significantly to national foreign exchange earnings. Truong states, for example, that in Japan during the period of post–World War II reconstruction, the government officially praised the geishas who served U.S. servicemen as patriotic for bringing in the foreign exchange needed to rebuild the country.

In the Caribbean, a small but significant sex tourism industry catering to military personnel also developed during this period. Kamala Kempadoo (1996–97), for example, documents the opening of the largest single brothel in the Americas in 1949 by the Dutch colonial government on the island of Curaçao. The brothel, nicknamed "Campo Alegre" (the Happy Camp), was set up to cater to the sexual needs of single men on the island, many of whom were employees of the Dutch Marines and the U.S. Navy. Sex tourism also blossomed in Cuba during the 1950s as tourism surpassed sugar as the main foreign-exchange earner. Dubbed by *Time* magazine as a "fleshpot city" Cuba, like Curaçao, developed into a well-known center for the sale of sexual services (quoted in Schwartz 1997:162).

Given the existence of an organized sex tourism industry in the Caribbean as early as 1949, what distinguishes today's sex tourism from that of the 1950s? The distinction lies in the ways in which certain types of producers and consumers in both the real and virtual segments of the sex tourism industry have commodified Caribbean men and women for consumption, the meanings attached to the consumption of Caribbean sex services, and the characteristics of the consumers of these services. In addition, contemporary sex tourism differs from that which existed in the 1950s because this activity is now part of a global and interconnected industry. No longer is sex tourism limited to a few elite consumers in one or two particular regions or places. Today exotic sensual encounters with the Other can be consumed both at "home" in exotic dance bars staffed by women from developing countries or away in destinations once considered off the map. Consumption today need not even require physical movement. Through the Internet, consumers can now travel to locales where virtual erotic encounters with exotic women can be consumed for the price of a small membership fee. Although the global interconnectedness of contemporary sex tourism distinguishes it from its predecessor, the process itself is paradoxical because it is only through the provision of the unique and the particular that localities are drawn into the global.

CONTEMPORARY SEX TOURISM

To map the contours and structure of global sex tourism, it is necessary to define sex tourism. Sex tourism is often defined as a form of prostitution that is closely linked and dependent upon the patronage of tourists within a country. Such a definition is particularly narrow, however, because sex tourism today includes both real and virtual exchanges of sexual services for monetary reward. No longer is it necessarily the case, either, that the purchaser of sexual services travels to the place of supply, because increasingly many sex workers are in destinations, often in large first-world cities, to provide services for "locally situated" tourists. Even where it is established that sex tourism involves the physical exchange of sex services for financial reward, it is often difficult to establish whether all such transactions should be counted as part of the industry. For example, it is not clear whether repeat tourists who develop long-term relationships of trust and obligation with particular sex workers should be considered in the same way as the tourists who purchase services from an unfamiliar person they will never meet again. It also is not clear whether a sex tourist is a person who travels with the explicit intention of purchasing sex or whether tourists who purchase sex services during the process of holiday travel should be so defined. It is likely that the more formalized "sex tours" as exist in the Philippines, Cambodia, Thailand, Brazil, and the Dominican Republic represent only a small segment of the sex tourism market and that, in fact, the nature of exchanges between tourist and sex workers varies significantly with the popularity of particular sex tourism localities. Similar blurred distinctions exist in the definition of a sex worker. Is a local person who develops an intimate relationship with a foreign visitor who provides financial support always a sex worker? If the nature of the services exchanged involve companionship and comfort rather than sexual intercourse, does this also change how the service provider is defined?

CARIBBEAN SEX TOURISMS

Although still small and for the most part informally organized, the Caribbean is increasingly recognized as a region with a vibrant sex tourism industry (Kempadoo 1999). Unlike Thailand, where sex tourism is primarily associated with female sex workers, the Caribbean islands today are sites for a range of different types of sex tourisms, with each island catering to particular niche markets. Thus not only has a globally integrated sex tourism industry spread to the Caribbean but these activities have become market segmented between Caribbean islands. Islands with predominantly "black" populations of African descent, such as Jamaica and Barbados, for example, increasingly cater to the consumption demands of white heterosexual women primarily from Europe, whereas islands with predominantly Latino populations such as Cuba and the Dominican Republic cater to the consumption demands of white heterosexual men from Europe and North America. With each market segment developing its own product name, sex tourism in the Caribbean appears to have mirrored the growing variety of consumption lifestyles catered to in other differentiated commodities. Thus as figure 11.1 shows among the Caribbean islands, Jamaica has become a specialized place for the consumers who seek the services of *Rent a Dreads*: black men with Rastafarian dreadlocks; Barbados and Trinidad for *Beach Boys*: black men with well-developed bodies; Cuba for *Jineteras*: young Latinas; the Dominican Republic for *Sanky Pankies*: Latin men offering hetero- and bisexual services; and Curaçao for *Sandoms*: fair-skinned women. It is clear from the nature of the market segmentation that race and gender ideologies play an important role in the creation of the Caribbean sex industry. Indeed, the current market segmentation and niching suggest that these services are not simply locally derived but rather are actively created by the same global processes of consumption and production that have expanded and formalized the industry in Southeast Asia. Exploring the mechanisms through which tourist fantasies and dreams are transformed into commodities for consumption provides some indication of the roles of producers and consumers in creating what Henri Lefebvre (1991) describes as the "space of the dream."

PRODUCING CARIBBEAN SEX TOURISM

Although potential consumers may dream of erotic encounters with exotic humans in far-off lands, these fantasies are dependent upon a whole battery of producers to become reality. As Truong demonstrates in her examination of the political economy of sex tourism in Thailand, this activity is an enormously lucrative one that contributes to the wealth of businesses, public agents, and ultimately the state. Today those who benefit from the consumption of sex tourism often extend beyond the boundaries of most island states to include a range of other actors that include advertisers, travel agents, airlines, and Internet providers. As a recent survey article in the *Economist* (1998) estimated, the turnover of the sex industry as a whole is now at least $20 billion a year, with a growing proportion of the trade being organized via the Internet.

In the case of the Caribbean, as island governments have come to rely heavily

Figure 11.1   The Caribbean Sex Trade

upon tourism as major sources of gross domestic product (GDP), so too has their reliance on fantasy images of the Caribbean to market their product (see table 11.1). Tourism in the Caribbean in 1999 accounted for 20.6 percent of GDP, 16 percent of jobs, and 25.7 percent of all capital investment to the region (WTTC 1999). Compared with other regions such as Latin America, North America, and Southeast Asia, Caribbean economies are the most dependent on the tourism sector for their economic prosperity. As other export sectors such as garment assembly and bananas have declined, Caribbean governments have needed to develop new market niches to maintain their share of the global tourism market. In Jamaica, for example, the government has vigorously supported private-sector innovations such as the all-inclusive holiday, heritage tourism, and ecotourism.[1] Although all of these innovations have been successful in generating greater foreign exchange earnings, they have also contributed to the growing alienation of local communities, few of whom formally participate in the tourism industries (Mullings 1999). The restructuring of the tourism industry in other islands has had similar consequences (Pattullo 1996; Cabezas 1999). Cabezas (1999), for example argues that as competition throughout the region has increased, most of the economic resources of the Dominican Republic have been geared toward building infrastructure for the country's guests rather than its citizens. This bias

Table 11.1   Ranking of Tourism's Contribution to Selected Regional Economies

1999 Gross Domestic Product	Employment (% of Total)	1999 Capital Investment (% of Total)
1. Caribbean 20.6	Oceania 16.0	Caribbean 25.7
2. Other Western European Countries 15.4	Caribbean 15.8	Other Western European Countries 16.1
3. Oceania 14.7	Other Western European Countries 15.6	European Union 15.8
4. European Union 14.1	European Union 14.5	Oceania 13.9
5. North America 11.8	North America 11.9	Sub-Saharan Africa 11.7

Source: WTTC 1999

in the direction of investment has only served to further exacerbate the existing disparity in wealth between tourists and locals and has forced many locals into the gray and black markets of the industry in search of work. Thus as formal state-supported tourism niche products have grown, so too have informal niche ones, such as sex tourism.

Although the formal and informal tourism services that have grown in the Caribbean in the past ten years appear to be independently operating entities, in reality they are part of a single, unified economic operation. In the case of sex tourism, not only do some workers in the formal tourism sector provide infor-mal sex services but sex tourism also directly attracts tourists, providing benefits to the formal sector institutions such as airlines and hotels.

Given the benefits that the trade in sex services confers to the overall tourism industries, many Caribbean governments have been inclined to turn a blind eye to the local suppliers in this burgeoning niche market. In Cuba, for example, al-though the government has recognized the rapid growth of sex tourism on that island, it has chosen to view the resurgence of this service as the product of moral degeneration rather than economic desperation. Indeed, in an effort to deflect responsibility for the growth of Cuban sex tourism from the state, Fidel Castro stated in 1993 that thanks to socialism, Cuban girls must make the cleanest and best-educated prostitutes in the world (Gordon 1997).

Few governments directly support the sex tourism industry, but they cannot be excluded from the range of institutions that have indirectly fostered its devel-opment. Through the discourse of advertising, state and private sector institutions routinely provide a range of texts through which fantasy, identity, and meaning are constructed. These texts are essential and effective tools for influencing travel destination decisions. As Truong points out:

> Without advertising, the tourism product means little else than household-related services (food, accommodation, rest) provided to the traveler away from home, or landscape and cultural traits, products of nature and human history. With advertis-

ing, all these aspects become incorporated into the "tourist market basket of goods and services." In this connection, the significance of the ideological constructs of the advertising industry cannot be separated from tourism itself. (Truong 1996:374)

As competition for travelers has increased in the Caribbean so too have the capital outlays that the state and private sectors have been willing to spend on advertising to attract new consumers. Most recently in Jamaica, for example, the government committed J$1.24 billion (US$33 million) to a promotional campaign to market the country's tourism product (Mullings 1999). Although most of the images that have been used to market the Caribbean have relied upon the traditional elements of sun, sea, and sand to create fantasies about the nature of the available consumption experiences, others have traded heavily upon images of sex and servility to market tourism. In Jamaica, alongside the traditional images of beautiful natural landscapes and friendly locals have sprung promises of wild and wanton sexual encounters. One resort, Hedonism II, for example, draws heavily upon these sexual images to market itself as an adult resort. As one of its advertisements claims:

> Hedonism II is an active vacation for the mind, body, spirit and soul. Very simply put, if it feels good, do it. . . . Eat and drink what you want, when you want, as much as you want. It's all included. Meet a friend, find a romantic, secluded spot and contemplate one of life's eternal questions such as "is a piña colada better with light or dark rum?" . . . Ask a total stranger to rub oil on your back. This is Hedonism II and there is no place quite like it anywhere. . . . For paradise found, come to Hedonism II. This spectacular resort is set in 23 acres of jungle garden. It is a celebration of nature in its most magnificent form. . . . The grounds abound with lush palms and fruit trees, splashed with the bright colors of tropical flowers and perfumed with island fragrances of romance and adventure. There are two separate white sand beaches. One nude, one not. (<http://www.honeymoontravel.com/hedonism.html>)

The marketing of Caribbean destinations as places of sexual adventure is not a harmless exercise. It is through the production of knowledge about the Caribbean that travelers are provided with places to act upon their fantasies. Such knowledge as produced through advertising media therefore represents a form of power in which the ability to put into circulation certain understandings of place and the people therein occurs with little or no definitional input by those who form part of these wisdoms. The unequal power relations inherent in these forms of place marketing have been exacerbated by the growth of Internet-based sex travel companies. Here firms, many of which are foreign based, provide information about the places, people, and requirements for a sex tourism adventure. Information is almost never supplied by local service providers themselves, who are usually portrayed instead as objects for consumption. Playing upon the new culture of travel, with its need to distinguish the individual traveler from other mass tourists, many of these sex travel sites offer consumers new landscapes and people for consumption by portraying what ultimately is the purchase of sexual services into the opportunity for romantic adventure. Thus as one site, Fantasy Tours, claims:

> This tour is designed for the sensual traveler. For persons looking for a travel package that incorporates both mind and body. It is for the fun-loving, pleasure-seeking adventurer. Let your dreams and passions come to life. Visit, see, and experience places and things normally not seen by the average traveler. Tropical landscapes, exotic flora and fauna, and beautiful people. Feast on delicious island dishes; quench your thirst with exotic refreshing tropical drinks, party into the wee hours of the morning and awake to make passionate love under a seductive sunrise. . . . The possibilities are endless. Age, color, or race is not an issue. Love, romance and affection are openly excepted [*sic*] in the Islands. Love and romance are definitely not taboo topics as many of us are used to at home. (<http://www.fantasytours.com/erotic.html>)

The effect of Internet-based sex tourism production should not be underestimated. To offer the individual traveler the opportunity to fulfill preexisting sexual fantasies about the Other, these firms must create knowledges about Caribbean men and women that conform to the fantasy. In so doing, local men and women become mere commodities for consumption devoid of individual identities. The inevitable commodification of *all* Caribbean men and women that occurs when producers seek to create people as sexual commodities can be seen in the following quote taken from an Internet sex tourism site that markets Cuba as a destination:

> The girls that are easiest to find are usually black and from the Orient. I think the girls in the Dominican Republic, which are all mixed race, are more beautiful than these Cuban girls. But the black Cubans do not have the same dark complexion as the Haitians. . . . Actually just about any unmarried Cuban girls is available, many of them just don't know about it, until they make friends with a tourist. (Desiree's guide to Cuba, <http://www.sexyguide.com/cuba>)

Although state and private institutions have been important participants in the creation of the necessary conditions for the consumption of sex tourism to occur, their roles have been often viewed as indirect or secondary. Much attention instead has been paid to sex workers, who are often portrayed as aberrant misfits who prey upon unsuspecting tourists (Cohen 1986; Strout 1996; Government of Jamaica 1998). Yet sex workers are just as influenced by the changes occurring in the culture of consumption as sex tourists, and although economic need is usually the primary reason for supplying these services, fantasies about the Other also play an important role. Many writers have examined the economic conditions that have forced women and men in the Caribbean to become sex providers to tourists (Pattullo 1996; Kempadoo 1996–97; Kempadoo and Doezema 1998; Cabezas 1999; Campbell et al. 1999; Mullings 1999), so this chapter does not reexamine these issues. Instead, it focuses on the ways in which the changing culture of consumption has also influenced the meanings attached to sex tourism among sex workers.

To successfully sell one's sexual labor to tourists, a person must engage in a particular type of performance, one that conforms as closely as possible to preexisting stereotypes. Across the Caribbean, these performances vary with the predominant market niche that exists. Thus men and women in the Caribbean must understand and embrace what it means to be a *Beach Boy, Jinetera, Rent a Dread,* or *Dominicana* to perform the role successfully. Unlike in Southeast Asia, most sex workers in the Caribbean tend to be own-account workers, with few intermediaries such as pimps involved (Kempadoo 1999). Although this organization of work allows sex workers greater control over their earnings, many must find the money to pay for the clothing, makeup, and nightclub fees that function as the venture capital of this trade. Such performances can therefore be expensive and onerous, particularly when the consumer is neither physically nor emotionally attractive. The extent to which sex workers engage in product-marketing performances is clearly documented by Phillips (1999) in her description of Beach Boys in Barbados:

> The beachboy's attire is usually that of beach shorts of some brand name variety worn in a manner to show off his well-endowed proportions. His appearance, an obvious marketing strategy, is based on the Western female's notion of the quintessential hypersexual black male—skin darkened almost blue-black to acclaim his pride in his afro-ancestry and to suggest an untamed, primitive nature and an exotic appeal . . . when he goes to a club, immediately he will begin showing his "natural rhythm" gyrating to the latest calypso and reggae tunes, sometimes showing his "natural athletic ability" with a few seemingly improbable flips and splits.

Although most sex workers engage in these performances for their remunerative potential, many are also spurred on by fantasies that are constructed about sex tourists and their ability to satisfy the economic and emotional needs of workers. Like sex tourists, therefore, sex workers also engage in the objectification and aestheticisation of the Other, but unlike sex tourists, they do not have the power to commodify. To have a white holiday-friend who is an economic provider, who offers the opportunity for travel and emigration, represents for many sex workers the ultimate symbol of economic and occupational mobility. The acquisition and consumption of such a symbol often lies at the heart of many encounters between tourists and sex workers and encourages people to conform as best as possible to the sexual ideal fantasized about by the sex tourist. The symbolic status that a potential white partner represents to many sex workers has also been observed in Cuba by Coco Fusco (1998), who states, "The fact that black and mulata jineteras are succeeding in marrying Europeans at an unusually high rate also makes these women objects of envy in a country where many people are using every means possible to migrate" (160).

In fact, many sex workers do not view their activities as prostitution but rather a way to meet people who might help to change their immediate personal circumstances (Pruitt and LaFont 1995; Phillips 1999). Thus although sex workers may be considered direct producers of the tourism experiences that many sex tourists desire, these performances are as much acts of consumption as they are acts of production.

THE CONSUMERS OF CARIBBEAN SEX TOURISM

Much of literature on sex tourism has focused on providers and the conditions under which they work (Truong 1990; Kempadoo and Doezema 1998; Lim 1998); however, more recently, several writers have begun to examine the characteristics, practices, and motivations of sex consumers (Cohen 1986; Meisch 1995; Pruitt and LaFont 1995; O'Connell Davidson 1996). As Oppermann (1998) points out, the invariable image of the sex tourist as an older white man in less-than-perfect shape traveling to the third world for sexual pleasures ordinarily not available at home masks a range of other consumers and motivations in the industry. Consumers of contemporary Caribbean sex tourism are both male and female, young and old, and in search of a variety of comforts, many of which extend beyond simple sexual gratification. Examining the characteristics and consumption habits of a range of persons who might be considered sex tourists in the Caribbean provides some insights into the range of needs that this form of consumption fills.

In a study of sex tourism and sex tourists in Cuba, J. O'Connell Davidson (1996) found that there were two main groups of male sex tourists: those who acknowledged the nature of their relationships with Cuban women and those who tended to deny them or at least view these encounters as situationally determined. She argues that among the self-professed sex tourists, there was much hostility toward the women they sought. This hostility was manifest in the popular adage used by many in this group: "Find them, feed them, fuck them, and forget them" (1996:43). In a more recent study O'Connell Davidson and Sanchez Taylor (1998) explored in more detail the underlying motives behind the consumption practices of self-professed sex tourists. They argue that although price was a considerable demand-inducing factor, Caribbean sex workers also provided their clients with the opportunity to engage in gender performances believed to be unattainable at home. For male sex tourists, many of whom come from Canada, Italy, and Germany, women in the Caribbean are viewed as the opposite or Other of wives or girlfriends back home. Unlike white Western women who were often portrayed as cold, domineering, and unwilling to perform traditional patriarchal domestic gender roles, Caribbean women were imagined to be warm, willing to please, and not tainted by the ideologies of gender equality. For many male sex tourists to the Caribbean, local women were also viewed as the ultimate embodiment of the natural, mysterious island available for exploration and conquest. For the sex tourist to the Caribbean, local women therefore satisfy all of the criteria necessary for the fulfillment of a holiday; they represent an alternative to the everyday world of work and the everyday social relations encountered at home, and they create the space for dreaming and fantasy that forms such an integral part of the travel experience.

With the rise of Internet-based sex travel companies, other motivations for the consumption of sex tourism have appeared. A dominant desire that is expressed in many of the tourism and travel Web-based sites that cater to single males is the need to find women who are untainted by the commercialism of places where sex tourism has become a service for mass consumption. Thus as one sex travel site boasts:

> We not only look at well-known centers of the sex industry but also inform you about those undiscovered by mass tourism. Places where girls are young, and inexpensive and the competition for them is low. Read about exotic countries like GHANA which has excellent beaches, relatively little AIDS, and beautiful girls for as little as $10 a night! ("World Nightlife Guide for Women" 1998)

This advertisement suggests that there is some dissatisfaction on the part of some sex tourists with the level of competition and mass nature of the sex industry in some places and therefore offers new sites for consumption, where the "natural purity" can be ensured by the youth of the girls who sell their sexual labor. In other travelogue sites in which sex tourists share tales of their travel adventures, similar themes reflecting the search for places "undiscovered by mass tourism" also emerge. At one site, *Travel and the Single Male*, sex travelers describing the merits of Cuba as a sex tourism destination stress the importance of meeting women who are not professionals. As one writer reminisces of his Cuban sex excursion:

> I loved the variety. I loved the fact that one could pick up non-pros. In fact, in one local Miramar fast food place that my guide and I visited several times . . . there was lots of flirting with a counter girl and the time she wasn't there . . . the waiter along with our pizza, brought napkins . . . except on one of them, was a note and a number from a girl sitting at a different table!! She wasn't a stunner or anything . . . but still, consider the goddamn environment. It simply cannot get any better. (<http://www.singletravel.com/cuba_faq/Bogey_LaHabana.html>)

The desire to consume an authentic and exotic commodity untouched and untainted by other travelers mirrors the transformations occurring in other forms of tourism consumption. The insatiable desire for a new sex tourism encounter, a new body for consumption, is currently the driving force behind the spread of the industry both regionally and internationally. Although the traditional sex tourist might have visited Thailand to consume the mysteries embodied in the "oriental" body, the contemporary self-professed sex tourist now visits not only Thailand but also Cuba and Kenya to consume the delights of the "third world" body. The ability to sample and compare the sexual labor of women from around the world distinguishes the contemporary self-professed sex tourist from those who they view to be mass sex tourists. Mass sex tourists are those who consume in places that are already well known, where there is already some level of formalization of the sex trade, and where the women encountered are all "professionals." The distinction that is attained by the global sex tourist then comes from the knowledge that is attained not just about the sexuality of the Other but from acquiring intimate sexual knowledge of *all* Others. This is the social distinction that only a few sex tourists can attain, given the high cost of airfare and accommodation required for such global expeditions. The importance of acquiring knowledge about the sexuality of all third-world women can be seen in the way that Internet sex tourism sites market their services. As one Internet site promises:

> TET is the world's premier foreign sex intelligence source. Each uncensored issue brings you essential first-hand information impossible to find anywhere else. In the sterile late 20th century world of 1-900 number rip offs, followed by plastic virtual reality sex—TET revives the unabashed 70's ideals of sex, liberty and the pursuit of bodily pleasure (<http://www.erotictravel.com/about.htm>)

Although there is power to be derived from the sexual consumption of a wide range of "authentic" and pure third-world women, this power can only be realized if that knowledge is made public. As Urry (1995) points out, an important part of the social experience involved in many tourist contexts is the ability to consume particular commodities in the company of others. It is here that the Internet has played a crucial role in the creation of a global sex tourism industry because it has provided an important aspect of what people buy when they act as tourists, that is, a particular composition of other consumers. So as Urry argues, "Satisfaction is derived not from the individual act of consumption but from the fact that all sorts of other people are also consumers of the service and these people are deemed appropriate to the particular consumption in question" (Urry 1995:131).

Internet sites such as *The Erotic Traveler* or *Travel and the Single Male* (TSM), which currently boasts six thousand members and seventy-five postings per day, create a community of other consumers who heighten the pleasure of the sex tourism adventure. Through this medium, travelers not only share tales of sexual adventure but also arrange and coordinate trips and give advice on the best places to go and prices to pay. Whether a real or virtual traveler, the Internet assures each sex travel writer that his conquests will be observed and possibly envied by other members of the community.

Essential to the authentication of the adventure claims of sex travel writers is the acquisition and display of objects from each trip. Many sex tourists who contribute stories to Internet sites authenticate their experiences with photographs of the women they have sexual encounters with. These photos often appear to be personalized objects of some sentimental value; nevertheless, they become public commodities for anonymous audiences to view. As Celia Lury argues, "While the object may have 'personal,' 'sentimental' meaning in its final resting place, this is a meaning which is not deemed intrinsic to the object and, thus, is not publicly valued" (1997:79).

Photography plays an important role in the visual appropriation of place that has become a part of the tourist gaze. Cranshaw and Urry (1997) argue that it is a powerful signifying practice that produces a dominant set of images while simultaneously hiding the constructed nature of that image. In doing so, photographs contribute to dominant ideologies in a society by enhancing and reproducing selected images and presenting them as accurate representations. The photographs that are shared by many sex tourists with other fellow travelers are equally powerful because they construct all Caribbean men and women as commodified bodies or objects for consumption. The reduction of Caribbean sex workers to their bodies open to the gaze of other sex travelers in cyberspace is evident in the lack of effort made to maintain the anonymity of sex workers. The faces of sex travelers (who are always clothed) are often carefully computer modified to make identification impossible, but sex workers are always displayed without any modifications.

Although the self-professed sex travelers conform to many of the stereotypes of the sex tourist currently in vogue, they only represent a proportion of sex tourism consumers. Oppermann (1998) drawing on a series of studies conducted in 1995 by Kleiber and Wilke (1995) with German tourists, demonstrates the ambiguities that surround the identifying of a sex tourist. Kleiber and Wilke asked more than six hundred male tourists on holiday in five third-world destinations whether they intended to engage in sex with local women before departing their destination and whether they considered themselves to be sex tourists. They found that although approximately 70 percent intended to engage in sex with local women, only 20 percent considered themselves to be sex tourists. Their findings suggest that there may be other meanings attached to the consumption of sexual services that form part of a travel experience and that sex tourists may not conform to the standard stereotype. Indeed there is much evidence that many tourists who consume sex with locals as part of their travel experience may be motivated by the desire to experience a particular type of romantic experience unlikely to be attained easily at home.

In her exploration of the relationship between love and late capitalism, Illouz argues that commodities have penetrated the romantic bond so deeply that they have become "an unacknowledged spirit reigning over romantic encounters" (1997:11). She argues that in Western culture, romantic love has become the expression of a utopian model that celebrates the sovereignty of the individual above and often against the rule of the group. Through romantic love, individuals are able to transgress group-maintained divisions based on gender, class, and national loyalties. In effect, the pursuit of romantic love creates the conditions for social orders to be transgressed. Illouz argues that in contemporary Western culture, romantic love has become incorporated into the sphere of leisure, and all forms of transgression are now mediated through the consumption of market-based commodities. Market consumption now infuses all romantic rituals and indeed now forms the structural base of most romantic moments. Even moments that are domestic and intimate, she argues, often involve the presence of communications technologies such as the TV or the indirect presence of another commodity such as a gift of some kind or both.

The commodification of romance observed by Illouz is evident in the consumption practices of some sex tourists. The desire by some tourists to achieve the romantic ideal in their relationships with sex workers epitomizes the modern commodification of love. The search for the romantic utopia in these relationships is usually impossible to achieve because they tend to mask the irrevocable unequal relations of power that lie at the heart of all tourist–sex worker liaisons. Many tourists are seduced by the fantasy that is constructed of the Other and seek to create a more romantic and committed link. It is quite common for relationships of trust and obligation to develop, where sex workers promise fidelity for the duration of a tourist's holiday and see that person exclusively during subsequent visits. Although there is an underlying expectation of financial reward in all of the relationships that develop between sex workers and the tourists they service, this expectation is overshadowed by the discourse of romance.

Examining the relationships and motivations behind the sexual relationships that develop between foreign men and Thai girls, Cohen (1986) argues that many middle-aged married or divorced men become infatuated and strongly attached to women that they pick up from a bar or coffee shop. These romantic attachments, however, are problematic because these foreign men, or *farangs,* are often unable to safeguard these relationships or ensure the fidelity of their holiday girlfriends once they return home. Similar types of relationships have been documented by Andre Codrescu (1998) in his description of the romantic relationship between Jack, a fifty-two-year-old American, and Yasmina, a fifteen-year-old Cuban whom he picked up a year earlier at a salsa bar:

> It was unbelievable. At this fiesta in Santiago, I had one girl waiting outside by the rum truck and I was by the wall with this other girl I had just met. But when Yasmina showed up with some high school friends, I told them all, "No more, I met the one."
> . . . Yasmina wanted to stay the night with Jack, but Cuban girls aren't allowed in tourist hotels. Instead they went to the all-night Club 300, where they swayed the

night away and saw the pink dawn rise over the cathedral in Parque Cespedes. By dawn Jack had found love. . . . Jack was determined to make Yasmina his and to prevent her from becoming a Jinetera or a prostitute. To that end, he began sending her $100 a month through a Canadian bank. They speak on the telephone every week, which isn't easy because Yasmina's family doesn't have a telephone. (1998:32–33)

From these accounts it is clear that although the romances that develop between tourists and sex workers are committed ones often sustained over long periods of time, these liaisons are borne out of a specific type of relationship that can only be maintained by the continued commodification of emotions and financial exchange. Most men who develop romantic relationships with sex workers are deeply aware of the poverty that has driven many young girls out onto the streets. The men are also aware of the responsibilities many sex workers often bear for maintaining the welfare of their families. Financial contributions therefore become not only a way of ensuring continued romance but also an important expression of concern for welfare that goes beyond that expressed by the self-professed sex tourist. By making financial contributions to sex workers and their families, the relationship between romance and commodified love becomes inextricable.

The commodified search for romantic love is not confined to the relationships that develop between sex workers and male tourists. Pruitt and LaFont (1995) have also documented the nature of the relationships that develop between white female tourists and male sex workers in Jamaica, who are popularly described as "rent a dreads." Describing these relationships as romance tourism, they argue that female tourists are motivated to enter such relations of financial and sexual exchange by a desire for romantic love. Pruitt and LaFont acknowledge that the pursuit of romance with local Jamaican men is a transgressive act but view such behaviors as part of the general challenge to gender-based constraints that has occurred as greater numbers of women have begun to travel alone. "As Western women construct new identities, their spirit of adventure is often expressed by more than just a new outdoor style. Continually expanding the boundaries of the feminine requires perpetually new experiences, including a new kind of romance" (Pruitt and LaFont 1995:425).

Based on ethnographic interviews, they argue that the women who engage local men in romantic relationships span all nationalities, ages, and socioeconomic relationships. Most of the relationships are cross-racial and last in duration from a few weeks to a few months. During this time, relationships are strengthened by the financial support offered by the women, who will pay for meals and entertainment during the holiday and continue to send money and gifts upon their return home. In some cases, gifts may include airplane tickets for their holiday boyfriends to visit them at home or even more expensive outlays such as motor vehicles. Like their male counterparts, many women also construct fantasies about the Other that serve to differentiate the men from those encountered back home. For many female tourists to Jamaica, the spirituality of Rastafarian men, their reputed closeness to nature, combined with the mystique of the reggae counter-culture, represents an attractive opposite to white males. Although the relations of power that govern these relationships contradict conventional notions of male/female hegemony, they reinforce notions of racial hegemony. Women who engage in these forms of romance tourism with male sex workers wield considerable economic power over the men they become involved with and are able to determine the pace and continuity of such relationships. The men, although publicly performing traditional masculine gender identities, must ensure that the romantic fantasy is maintained to assure the continued emotional and financial support and possibility for eventual emigration. But the pursuit of the romantic ideal, when mediated through remunerated sexual relations, is often doomed to failure. For those who develop long-term committed relationships, the realities of the economic inequalities that created the liaison in the first place ultimately becomes a terminal source of instability:

> Cast in the role of financial provider, the women may become enmeshed in an exchange relationship that did not define their initial impulses. . . . Furthermore if the woman decides to remain in Jamaica, unless she is independently wealthy, she may lose the financial advantages she brought to the relationship or grow weary of the economic demands placed on her. . . . The challenges become even greater if the relationship moves to the tourist's country of origin where the man has little of the cultural capital needed to achieve the success he desires in Western society. . . . With the man's role as culture broker and tour guide no longer necessary, educational, age, and racial differences which seemed inconsequential in the host country are magnified. (Pruitt and LaFont 1995:434)

The motivations behind the consumption practices of tourists who enter into financially remunerated sexual relations with local men and women vary tremendously; however, one cannot discount the unequal relations of power that undergird all such relations. For as long as the inequalities between the first and third worlds, men and women, and production and reproduction remain as skewed as they currently are, new opportunities for profit from the commodification of these differences will continue to emerge.

THE FUTURE OF THE CARIBBEAN AS A SEX TOURISM DESTINATION

The historical relationship between the sex trade and tourism in the Caribbean suggests that this is not a new phenomenon that will go away in the future. Indeed, given the downward economic spiral that has engulfed many of the islands in the region, it is likely that the production of sex tourism will continue and even expand in the future. But what of consumption? The drive to consume symbols that distinguish the individual traveler from the mass tourist is a phenomenon that is also likely to continue unabated. This form of consumption, however, will probably spread geographically as markets in popular sites become unfashionably saturated by hordes of mass tourists, forcing new "virgin" sites to be found. Given the inevitable insatiability of contemporary consumption, it is therefore likely that sex tourism will eventually shift to new and yet unexplored islands, bodies, and places outside the Caribbean. Though it is thereby unlikely that the production of sex tourism will end in the near future, the intensity of demand for existing sexual services will. The insatiable nature of contemporary sex tourism consumption poses a dangerous threat to places such as the Caribbean that are heavily dependent upon the tourism for the majority of their foreign exchange earnings. For as existing sex tourism sites lose their power as symbolic indicators of particular consumer identities, such places will need to create new and more sensuous commodities for consumption. In the case of the Caribbean, where sex workers tend to be older than in Asia and are more likely to be self-employed (Kempadoo 1999), there will be greater pressure for younger workers to enter the market and more incentives for more organized forms of service provision (possibly though pimps) to develop. The outlook for the region is therefore not encouraging. As younger sex workers enter the industry and as service provision is taken over by the more organized criminal sector, the propensity for human rights abuses and public health risks is likely to increase considerably.

Focusing from a global perspective on the consumption of sex tourism services, this industry is likely to expand steadily in the future. As romance and leisure become interconnected experiences that can be commodified into objects for market exchange, so too will the conditions for continued fantasy and desire. For the possibilities and pleasure of romance and sexual intrigue will continue to act as the stimulus behind the search for new spaces where erotic encounters can be purchased. As communication media such as the Internet become more sophisticated in their ability to create cyberdestinations to satisfy these fantasies, they may ultimately become the strongest competitors to real sex tourism destinations. Yet ironically it is only through the disappointment of real consumption that opportunities for new pleasures will continue to emerge.

NOTES

1. The "all-inclusive" concept pioneered by the Superclub group has created a truly "cashless" vacation. Each resort caters to a particular segment of the tourism market (families, hedonists, and heterosexual couples) and for a prepaid price, vacationers are entitled to the unlimited consumption of the hotel's goods and services.

BIBLIOGRAPHY

Abercrombie, N. (1994). "Authority and Consumer Society," in *The Authority of the Consumer*, ed. R. Keat, N. Whiteley, and N. Abercrombie. New York: Routledge:43–57.

Allen, J., and C. Hamnett, ed. (1995). *A Shrinking World? Global Unevenness and Inequality*. New York: Oxford University Press.

Baudrillard, J. (1998). *The Consumer Society: Myths and Structures*. Thousand Oaks, Calif.: Sage.

Bishop, R., and L. Robinson (1997). *Night Market: Sexual Cultures and the Thai Economic Miracle*. New York: Routledge.

Bourdieu, P. (1984). *Distinction: A Social Critique of the Judgment of Taste*. London: Routledge and Kegan Paul.

Britton, S. G. (1991). "Tourism, Capital and Place: Towards a Critical Geography of Tourism," *Environment and Planning D. Society and Space* 9(4):451–78.

Cabezas, A. (1999). "Women's Work Is Never Done: Sex Tourism In Sosúa, the Dominican Republic," in *Sun, Sex and Gold: Tourism and Sex Work in the Caribbean*, ed. K. Kempadoo. Boulder, Colo.: Rowman & Littlefield.

Campbell, C. (1989). *The Romantic Ethic and the Spirit of Modern Consumerism*. Oxford: Blackwell.

Campbell, S., et al. (1999). "Come to Jamaica and Feel All Right: Tourism and the Sex Trade," *Sun, Sex and Gold: Tourism and Sex Work in the Caribbean*, ed. K. Kempadoo Boulder, Colo.: Rowman & Littlefield.

Codrescu, A. (1998). "Picking the Flowers of the Revolution," *New York Times Magazine* February 1:32–35.

Cohen, E. (1986). "Lovelorn Farangs: The Correspondence between Foreign Men and Thai Girls," *Anthropological Quarterly* 59(3):115–27.

Cranshaw, C. and J. Urry (1997). "Tourism and the Photographic Eye," in *Touring Cultures: Transformations of Travel and Theory*, ed. C. Rojek and J. Urry. New York: Routledge:176–95.

de Certeau, M. (1984). *The Practice of Everyday Life*. Berkeley: University of California Press.

du Gay, P. (1996). *Consumption and Identity at Work*. Thousand Oaks, Calif.: Sage.

The Economist (1998). "The Sex Industry: Giving the Customer What He Wants." February 14:21–23.

Featherstone, M., ed. (1991). *Consumer Culture and Postmodernism*. London: Sage.

Fusco, C. (1998). "Hustling for Dollars: Jineterismo in Cuba," in *Global Sex Workers: Rights, Resistance and Redefinition*, ed. K. Kempadoo and J. Doezema. New York: Routledge:151–66.

Gershuny, J. and I. Miles (1983). *The New Service Economy*. London: Macmillan.

Gordon, J. (1997). "Cuba's Entrepreneurial Socialism," *Atlantic Monthly* 279(1):18.

Government of Jamaica (1998). Honourable Francis Tulloch's Contribution to the Budget Debate. May 5, 1998. "The Way Forward," Unpublished Document.

Harvey, D. (1989). *The Condition of Post Modernity*. Oxford: Basil Blackwell.

Illouz, E. (1997). *Consuming the Romantic Utopia: Love and the Cultural Contradictions of Capitalism*. Berkeley: University of California Press.

Ioannides, D., and K. Dabbage (1998). *The Economic Geography of the Tourist Industry.* New York: Routledge.

Jones, G., (1998). "Prostitution in Indonesia," in *The Sex Sector: The Economic and Social Bases of Prostitution in South East Asia*, ed. L. L. Lim. Geneva: International Labour Office:29–66.

Kempadoo, K. (1996–97). "'Sandoms' and other Exotic Women: Prostitution and Race in the Caribbean," *Race and Reason* 1(3):48–53.

———, ed. (1999). *Sun, Sex, and Gold: Tourism and Sex Work in the Caribbean.* Boulder, Colo.: Rowman & Littlefield.

Kempadoo, K., and J. Doezema, eds. (1998). *Global Sex Workers: Rights, Resistance and Redefinition.* New York: Routledge.

Kleiber, D., and M. Wilke (1995). *Asia, Sex und Tourismus: Ergebnisse einer Befragung deutscher Urlauber und Sextouristen.* Baden-Baden: Nomos-Verlagsgesellschaft.

Lash, S., and J. Urry (1994). *Economies of Signs and Spaces.* London: Sage.

Lefebvre, H. (1991). *The Production of Space.* Oxford: Blackwell.

Lim, L. L., ed. (1998). *The Sex Sector: The Economic and Social Bases of Prostitution in South East Asia.* Geneva: International Labour Office.

Lury, C. (1996). *Consumer Culture.* New Brunswick, N.J.: Rutgers University Press.

———. (1997). "The Objects of Travel," in *Touring Cultures: Transformations of Travel and Theory*, ed. C. Rojek and J. Urry. New York: Routledge:75–95.

McClintock, A. (1995). *Imperial Leather: Race Gender and Sexuality in the Colonial Contest.* New York: Routledge.

Meisch, L. A. (1995). "Gringas and Otavalenos: Changing Tourist Relations," *Annals of Tourism Research* 22:441–62.

Mowforth, M., and I. Munt (1997). *Tourism and Sustainability.* New York: Routledge.

Mullings, B. (1999). "Globalization, Tourism, and the International Sex Trade," in *Sun, Sex, and Gold: Tourism and Sex Work in the Caribbean*, ed. K. Kempadoo. Boulder, Colo.: Rowman & Littlefield.

O'Connell Davidson, J. (1996). "Sex Tourism in Cuba," *Race & Class* 38(1):39–48.

O'Connell Davidson, J., and J. Sanchez Taylor (1998). "Fantasy Islands: Exploring the Demand for Sex Tourism." Paper presented at the conference "The Working Sex," Kingston, Jamaica, July.

Oppermann, M., ed. (1998). *Sex Tourism and Prostitution: Aspects of Leisure, Recreation and Work.* New York: Cognizant Communications.

Pattullo, P. (1996). *Last Resorts: The Cost of Tourism in the Caribbean.* London: Cassell.

Phillips, J. (1999). "Tourist-Oriented Prostitution in Barbados: The Case of the Beach Boy and the White Female Tourist," in *Sun, Sex, and Gold: Tourism and Sex Work in the Caribbean*, ed. K. Kempadoo. Boulder, Colo.:, Rowman & Littlefield.

Poon, A. (1989). "Competitive Strategies for a 'New Tourism,'" in *Progress in Tourism, Recreation and Hospitality Management*, ed. C. Cooper. London: Belhaven Press:1:91–102.

——— (1990). "Flexible Specialization and Small Size: The Case of Caribbean Tourism," *World Development* 18(1):109–23.

Pruitt, D., and S. LaFont (1995). "For Love and Money: Romance Tourism in Jamaica," *Annals of Tourism Research* 22(2):422–440.

Rojek, C., and J. Urry (1997). *Touring Cultures: Transformations of Travel and Theory.* New York: Routledge.

Schwartz, R. (1997). *Pleasure Island: Tourism and Temptation in Cuba*. Lincoln: University of Nebraska Press.

Shaw, G., and A. Williams (1994). *Critical Issues in Tourism: A Geographical Perspective*. Cambridge: Blackwell.

Strout, J. (1996). "Women, the Politics of Sexuality, and Cuba's Economic Crisis," *Socialist Review* 25:5–15.

Truong, T. D. (1990). *Sex, Money and Morality: Prostitution and Tourism in Southeast Asia*. London: Zed Books.

———— (1996). "Serving the Tourist Market: Female Labour in International Tourism," in *Feminism and Sexuality: A Reader,* ed. S. Jackson and S. Scott. New York: Colombia University Press: 373–78.

Urry, J. (1990). *The Tourist Gaze*. London: Sage.

————(1995). *Consuming Places*. New York: Routledge.

Warde, A. (1992). "Notes on the Relationship Between Production and Consumption," in *Consumption and Class: Divisions and Change*, ed. R. Burrows and C. Marsh. London: Macmillan:15–31.

Williamson, J. (1986). "Woman Is An Island: Femininity and Colonization," in *Studies in Entertainment: Critical Approaches to Mass Culture*, ed. T. Modeleski. Bloomington: Indiana University Press.

"World Nightlife Guide for Women" (1998). *Sex Travel Information Service: A Travel Guide for Men,* <http://www.sex-adventures.com/world.htm> [accessed June 1999].

WTTC (1999). *WTTC Travel and Tourism: Creating Jobs*. London, <http://www.wttc.org/WTTCGATE.NSF>[accessed June 1999].

12

Commodification and Theming of the Sacred: Changing Patterns of Tourist Consumption in the "Holy Land"

Noam Shoval

Because of the religious importance of the Land of Israel, or the "Holy Land," to the monotheistic religions, for hundreds of years, tours to the area assumed the nature of a pilgrimage and fulfilled a moral and spiritual role for the traveler. A visit to the Holy Land was not, however, a matter of intellectual contemplation or aesthetic observation alone. Rather, it involved fantasy, prayers, and dreams (Rinschede 1992). In this respect, the issue of the authenticity of the historical sites was only of minor significance to the pilgrims as long as they believed and accepted the common knowledge of their own particular creed about the historical and religious geography of the Holy Land. In fact, the personal, spiritual experience of the individual pilgrim-visitor was molded by the socially constructed spatial pattern of specific sites that became "holy places" according to the particular mythological and historical narrative of each religion and denomination (Shachar and Shoval 1999).

From the middle of the nineteenth century onward, however, the authenticity of this socially constructed geography of holy places was frequently questioned, especially by members of Protestant denominations. For example, Mark Twain wrote a sarcastic critique of the Catholic and Orthodox geography of the holy places after a visit to the Holy Land in 1867 (Twain 1869). As a result, the Protestants created their own geography of holy places during the second half of the nineteenth century, emphasizing locations and desirable elements (whether more authentic or not) that were more suitable for this particular denomination, such as open spaces, proximity to nature, and interpretations closer to the written scriptures. For example, the Protestants changed the location of the Garden Tomb (or

"Gordon's Calvary") from the traditional Catholic/Orthodox-sanctioned place of the Holy Sepulcher in Jerusalem to a site that was established outside the present city walls (Kochav 1995).

The modern archaeological research that began in the Land of Israel toward the end of the nineteenth century—which was also the time when the Jewish people were resettling there, a process that led eventually to the establishment of the State of Israel—created many new tourist sites. In general, the Jewish pilgrims and some of the Christian pilgrims, especially from Protestant denominations, saw the resettlement of the people of Israel as an essential stage for the beginning of the fulfillment of their prophecies. Consequently, they added these new locations to their tour itineraries in the Land of Israel along with an entirely different narrative for the geography of the Holy Places. In contrast, the various Catholic and Orthodox denominations and Muslim pilgrims kept their traditional itineraries after the creation of the State of Israel and merely added new archaeological sites relevant to their religious narratives. In fact, even today, when constructing the itineraries of these Catholic, Orthodox Christian, and Muslim pilgrimages, the territory is still referred to as the "Holy Land" and not the State of Israel.

Western society has undergone major changes in the second half of the twentieth century. One of many aspects involves the issue of consumption and its increasing role in both society as a whole and social interaction in particular. Several theoretical approaches have conceptualized these social changes at the macro level. George Ritzer (1996) developed a theoretical approach he called "the McDonaldization of society." This perspective on modern society was strongly influenced by Max Weber's theory of rationalization and is a grand narrative viewing the world as growing increasingly efficient, calculable, predictable, and dominated by rational nonhuman technologies. According to Ritzer, these principles were applied to the delivery of fast-food franchising. The worldwide success of McDonald's stimulated entrepreneurs to apply the same techniques to the delivery of an increasing number of other services.

Whereas George Ritzer's approach is concerned with the mechanisms of production for franchised consumer services, a different perspective on consumption spaces emphasizing marketing and environmental design and using semiotic theory was presented by Mark Gottdiener (1997), who focused on the increasing use of themed environments in society to entice consumers. "The themed environment with its pervasive use of media culture motifs that define an entire built space and are clearly tied to commercial enterprises characterizes more and more daily life in westernized countries" (Gottdiener 1997:4). According to Gottdiener, while the rationalization of service provision, or McDonaldization, certainly explains a part of the new consumer environment, attention must also be paid to the increasingly significant role of signs and the manipulation of symbolic themes in the construction of consumer spaces. In the development of so-called sacred or holy places in Israel for religious tourism, both the McDonaldization of franchising and the semiotic processes of thematic representation define the new, commodified tourist environments.

The aim of this chapter is to present how the process of commodified representations is leading to the creation of tourist services and attractions in the Holy Land that use themed environments to attract visitors to sites where they consume material or spiritual merchandise. The phenomena of franchised commodification and theming are relatively new when compared with the millenniums-old traditions of the different monotheistic religions in the Holy Land. Therefore the pace of "infiltration" by these processes into the staging of religious services and attractions in Israel has been relatively slow until recently. Now holy sights are increasingly themed in Israel.

One possible explanation for the success of themed environments could be related to the geographic origins of the tourists. More than 80 percent of the inbound visitors to Israel originate from North America and Europe (Central Bureau of Statistics 1998:table 4), where the theming of new spaces has already become central to everyday life. Therefore these tourists feel more comfortable in environments shaped by the new logic of franchising and theming. Now entrepreneurs and even religious leaders are aware of this strong demand for themed environments and are trying to take advantage of this concept to promote their businesses or ideologies.

PILGRIMAGE, RELIGIOUS TOURISM, AND TOURISM

The sociological analysis of the relationship between tourism and religion has focused primarily on the question of the similarities and differences between the tourist and the pilgrim (MacCannell 1990; Cohen 1992; Smith 1992). Tourism and religion are both closely related and diametrically opposed modalities of social conduct. They are historically related through the institution of the pilgrimage from which modern tourism developed (Cohen 1998:1). Some sociologists of tourism went beyond this historical relationship and claimed that there exists a structural affinity between tourism and the pilgrimage. Dean MacCannell (1990) in particular argued that the modern tourist is a "secular" pilgrim, paying respect to the diverse symbols of modernity embodied in tourist "attractions." However, religion and tourism are also mutually opposed because tourism is often an inversion of ordinary life, giving vent to the satisfaction of hedonistic drives contrary to religious precepts (Turner 1969). A foreign tour is a vacation from everyday life as it is lived in the home country, including the norms and customs of that life. Cohen (1998) argued that both pilgrims and tourists may visit the same sites but for very different reasons: the former to worship, the latter merely to observe and participate in the pilgrim's experience but without the pilgrims' belief in the location's spirituality. For these reasons, some authors such as Adler (1989) sought to conceptualize a category of travelers that is between pilgrims and tourists, called "religious tourists," that both tour and worship on their journey.

Empirical evidence (see Shachar and Shoval 1999) on the subject of segmented patterns of consumption and activity among inbound tourism to Israel suggests that when patterns of consumption are analyzed, most tourists who define their main purpose of visit as a "pilgrimage" could be better characterized as "religious tourists." The same observation was found regarding those defining their main purpose of their visit as "touring." Differentiating between "pilgrims" and "religious tourists" has its methodological difficulties, but one way to distinguish between the two groups is by analyzing the sites they visit. If "secular" sites or sites that belong to other religions have also been included in the tour, the visitor may be considered a "religious tourist." Contrary to the past, it would appear that during the last several decades in Israel, there has been a shift from organized "pilgrimage" toward the more eclectic experience of "religious tourism."

PILGRIMAGE AND TOURISM TO THE HOLY LAND

David's transfer of the Ark of the Covenant to Jerusalem and the building of the Temple by his son, Solomon, transformed Jerusalem during the period of the First Temple, mid-tenth century B.C.E., into a religious center and a focus of Jewish pilgrimage. This trend continued and even strengthened during the period of the Second Temple, reaching a peak in the first century of the Common Era. Within the same broad context, Jesus and his disciples came as pilgrims to Jerusalem during one of the Passover festivals. As a result of this famous journey, Jerusalem became one of the most holy sites for Christianity, if not the holiest, as well as a focal point for Christian pilgrims. Approximately six hundred years later, Islam adopted Jerusalem as one of its holiest places too, distinguishing the city by several religious traditions, such as the Night Journey of Mohammed and the location of his ascension to heaven. Along with the increasing holiness of the city for the three monotheistic religions, came the notable component of pilgrimage.

Modern secular tourism, which took shape in Europe in the form of the "grand tour," began in the sixteenth century (Towner 1985). It was not until the nineteenth century that secular tourists began arriving in the Holy Land at an evergrowing pace (Ben-Arieh 1979). The obstacles to the increase of such tourism were the relatively great distances from the countries of origin, coupled with problems of security and the lack of a suitable infrastructure for tourism when visitors arrived (Brendon 1991:120–23). The improvement of the physical infrastructure, including touristic infrastructure, during the twentieth century and the consistent increase in international tourism throughout the world resulted in the growth of tourist arrivals to the Holy Land.

By the 1990s, more than two million tourists arrived in Israel annually (Central Bureau of Statistics 1998:table 1). Almost 60 percent of this number were Christians (26 percent Catholics, 24 percent Protestants, 8 percent Orthodox), 25 percent were Jewish, 4 percent belonged to other religions, and 13 percent claimed to have no affiliation (Midgam 1998:table 3). In addition, more than 70 percent of the tourists to Israel came from Europe (49.1 percent) and North America (23.6 percent) (Central Bureau of Statistics 1998:table 4). Of the tourists who defined their main purpose of visit as "pilgrimage" in 1997, more than 80 percent arrived in organized groups, compared with a rate of 46.4 percent of the total number of tourists arriving in organized tours (Midgam 1998:table 9). The high proportion of religiously motivated tourists that come in organized groups could be explained by the fact that an important aspect of the religious pilgrimage is being part of a group. This holds true, at the very least, for the three monotheistic religions (Turner and Turner 1978). Another interesting fact is that most of the religiously motivated groups (Christians and Jews) were led by their religious leaders during their journey to the Holy Land and the members of the group were also usually members of the same congregation.

COMMODIFICATION, THEMING, AND SIMULATION OF RELIGIOUS SITES

Recent research in cultural studies pays special attention to the phenomena of commodification and commercial theming in everyday life (see Gottdiener 1997 for further bibliographical notes). In the past, there has been an interest in the use of images and symbols in different religions (Eliade 1969), but until recently, there has not been enough research on the new forces that shape consumption in contemporary society such as McDonaldization, theming, and the process of commodification with specific regard to religious sites that are objects of pilgrimages. It is important to note that theming and commodification are not new phenomena when discussing organized religion per se. For example, both the Orthodox and Catholic churches were undoubtedly designed as themed environments with the intention of influencing the believers for religious reasons (not primarily for commercial reasons as in the use of theming today). Commodification did *not* play a part in any early theological teachings in any of the monotheistic religions, but it seems that not long after the crystallizing of the different religions, the religious establishments formed enormous economic institutions that began to commodify many aspects of the religion. One example is the selling of indulgences by the medieval Catholic church, not to mention the money paid to functionaries for performing ritual tasks in all the organized religions.

Model of Jerusalem in the St. Louis World's Fair of 1904

At the turn of the century and the first two decades of the twentieth century, world's fairs and other types of exhibitions had exhibits devoted to science, technology, and so on, but they also included distant cultures and exotic entertainment, with representations of cities and foreign settlements. At the St. Louis Word's Fair of 1904, there was a Filipino village and an Indian reservation. But there was also a huge model of Jerusalem, on a 1:1 scale, erected by private entrepreneurs (Vogel 1993:213–15). The centrality of this exhibit to the layout of the fair and the extraordinary effort required to construct it indicates the strong significance Jerusalem played in the imagination of the American people.

Presenting models of Jerusalem for educational purposes as a substitute for an actual visit to the city was not a unique practice in the second half of the nineteenth century (see Rubin 1999 for a detailed discussion of this issue). The St. Louis Fair model was significant because it was the first time (and the last time, at least until somebody in Las Vegas builds a hotel with a Jerusalem or Holy Land theme) that such a large representation was built. It was constructed on thirteen acres and included the most important landmarks and sites of the city—the Dome of the Rock, the Holy Sepulcher, the Western Wall, the Markets of the Old City, Jaffa Gate, the Citadel, the Way of the Cross, and three hundred buildings and alleys imitating the street pattern of the Old City. The model was surrounded by a wall representing the walls of the Old City (Rubin 1999). An account from the fair claims that hundreds of Jerusalem's inhabitants were brought along to live their "everyday" life within the exhibit (Rubin 1999; *The Piker*, June 1904:29). This observation is not out of context, as there are other accounts of "live actors" in such ethnographic representations. For example, the Filipino village mentioned above, which was erected by the federal government to commemorate the American conquest of the Philippines, included a working exhibit population of 1,200 men and women (Rydell 1993:18–23). Many of the visitors to the Jerusalem model participated in Christian religious services that were conducted in the several churches, including weddings performed inside the "Holy Sepulcher," which were historically prohibited in the "real" church in Jerusalem (Rubin 1999:7).

These types of exhibitions devoted to travel and the exotic were in response to the growing interest in faraway places and exotic cultures, on the one hand, coupled with the high costs and dangers associated with such travels, on the other hand. Later, these "travel substitutions" were replaced by travelogues shown at the movies and on television and videos, and in more recent years, by cable television programs on travel and by "virtual reality" technologies for home use (Rubin 1999).

Even as early as 1904, the benefits of visiting a modeled environment as a substitute for exotic travel were touted, in postmodern fashion, as more educational than the real thing. Consider this excerpt from the World's Fair bulletin:

Many visitors to Jerusalem—in fact . . . the preponderating majority . . . get only a superficial acquaintance with the city, and fail to have impressed upon their minds the significance of the many things they see. . . . The visitor will not only be an onlooker . . . but it will be thoroughly explained to him, enabling him to grasp its full significance in every respect. (*World's Fair Bulletin* 1903:35)

The Time Elevator—Jerusalem

Today more and more of the tourist's limited time is spent at historical/religious sites in different kinds of audio-visual experiences, models, and so on, and less and less is spent at the authentic archeological sites or even museums. Because the duration of the average visit to Israel is declining (ten nights at present, down from fourteen a decade ago) a progressively greater emphasis is now placed on educational media displays and staged "experiences" that help the tourist better understand the complicated history of the land. In this process, the emphasis is on constructed effects and virtual experiences instead of on active touring of the area, which, for example, is the way native Israelis enjoy their country. The newest representation attraction of this kind is the "Time Elevator—Jerusalem," which opened in 1999 in the center of Jerusalem and is located only three hundred yards from the walls of the Old City.

As described by an Israeli journalist:

Time Elevator—Jerusalem offers a lively zip through thirty centuries of local history in just as many minutes. A movie theater on the ground floor of Jerusalem's press center (three hundred yards from the Old City's walls) has been converted to house this big-screen multi-sensory "experience." Moving simulator-type seats and zooming effects on the screens have you hurtling down time tunnels into the past; personal audio-headsets provide narration in different languages. Starting out at Mount Moria with a dramatized version of Abraham almost slaying Isaac, you then whiz through selected episodes of the city's history. . . .Glide over the computer-reconstructed grandeur of Roman Jerusalem. . . .Your guide and narrator through all of this is the timeless Chaim Topol, aptly cast in the role of the "Biblical" Shalem, the child of two mothers granted the gift of eternal life by King Solomon. (Kershner, *The Jerusalem Report*, February 5, 1999)

Nazareth Village

Baudrillard-type simulations are not confined to Jewish areas in Israel. They have recently been used by Israeli Arabs to promote their own religious tourism industry. Today the modern city of Nazareth is a bustling regional center for a quarter of a million Arabs in the northern part of Israel. Many Christian tourists that visit the city expect to find the calm and peaceful village where Jesus was brought up, but after experiencing the town's conflictual environment, principally a result of tensions between Muslim and Christian Arabs, they are frequently disappointed. In addition, a huge Catholic cathedral overshadows the historic core and actually serves to "drive out" believers, mainly from the various Protestant denominations who were hoping to experience natural or "authentic-looking" sites.

An initiative by Protestant groups both locally and from abroad sought to solve this situation by reconstructing an "authentic" first-century-C.E. village simulating the time when Jesus lived that would be close to the historical core of the city. To date, US$2 million out of the planned sum of US$30 million have been invested in this project (Kesselman Business Plan 1997:7). The following excerpt was taken from the leaflet sent to potential donors:

> This authentic site is the only land left that would have been farmed by Nazareth villagers at the time of Jesus. . . . When complete, a working village surrounded by vineyards, olive groves and terraced crops with villagers dressed in first-century costumes will vividly illuminate the social patterns and farm practices that inspired many of Jesus' parables. (Kesselman Business Plan 1997:2)

In "Nazareth Village," actors with written texts will play specific roles, like the characters of Mickey and Donald at the Disney parks. The cafeteria will serve both Western food and "dishes characteristic of the first century" (Kesselman Business Plan 1997:2). It may not be surprising that the initiative for such an attraction came from Protestant denominations in the United States because there, people have been heavily exposed to themed environments in their everyday lives. As with the Jewish tourists visiting the Jerusalem elevator, Christian visitors to Nazareth find it more attractive to remake a representation of their holy site that better fits the image they have in mind, and in this case, one that will avoid the overshadowing presence of the Catholic Basilica of the Annunciation planted in the center of town. In fact, different market surveys carried out for this project among tourist guides, congregational leaders, and tour operators showed that all North American Christians (i.e., both Protestants and Catholics) were very enthusiastic about the idea, whereas the Europeans in general feared that Nazareth Village would be an "American Production," that is, a site that would sacrifice authenticity on the altar of technological simulation (Kesselman Market Study 1997:46).

Interestingly enough, the proposed Nazareth Village simulation represents a case of an imitation of something that never existed in the past, in a location that is without any doubt *not* in historical Nazareth. So much for historical authenticity. No matter how many resources have been invested in scientific research ($2 million out of a total of $30 million planned for the entire project), it could never be as exact as the original. As Jean Baudrillard (1989) notes about such simulacra, they are imitations of things that never actually existed, copies without originals. Similarly, "Main Street USA" in Disneyland is meant to evoke a typical main street anywhere in the United States but it is not actually from anywhere. It mobilizes images that people have already formed about what a typical American small town should be like. Indeed the effect of a visit to Disney World may be to render the experience of actual main streets in small towns quite disappointing, if not lacking (Bryman 1996:126). This reliance on simulation at the present time can also be seen at large shopping malls with displays that create a sense of "hyper-reality" in which the fake seems more real than the original (Eco 1987).

The Nazareth Village will not be a typical theme park for entertainment and leisure because of its function as a site for religious tourism, but it does represent the creation of a new type of theme park—one that combines evocative religious symbolism with commercial outlets selling merchandise. The hyperreal dimension of such an experience lies in the intended result of the simulation as providing people with a more satisfying visit than that available in the actually existing city of Nazareth.

COMMODIFICATION AND THEMING OF THE RELIGIOUS TOURISM INFRASTRUCTURE

From Christian Hospices to Themed Hotels

As mentioned before, there is an ongoing theoretical debate among sociologists about the relationship between tourism and pilgrimage. In reality, there is no actual difference in terms of how a pilgrim, a religious tourist, a secular tourist, or a businessman uses the touristic infrastructure when visiting Israel. Pilgrims, in particular, use the same accommodations as other visitors. The use of Christian hospices, which once comprised the majority of the traveler accommodations in the Holy Land prior to this century, has declined a good deal, compared with stays at modern hotels, especially for organized groups that get special rates. Hospices still exist today, but they comprise no more than a fraction of the total accommodation stock in the nation. This means that religious tourists or pilgrims are not disconnected from the everyday life they left at home because, as tourists, they sleep in a chain hotel (and earn a little extra mileage on their frequent-traveler program), watch CNN in the room, and eat in international franchised restaurants. Because of global franchising, in fact, pilgrims or religious tourists from North America or Western Europe do not really leave their "home" or environment when traveling. In this sense, the organized pilgrimage groups (or the organized groups of religious tourists) could be seen as fitting Cohen's (1972:164–182) typology of tourists. They qualify as participating in organized, mass tourism "in search of the familiar, [and] travel[ing] in the security of their own environmental bubble" (1972:180) on the guided tour.

Recently, in response to the high volume of tourism, hotels have turned to the use of themes to enhance their attractiveness in competition with other accommodations. The first of these (not surprisingly) appeared in the resort town of Eilat, a hot desert location at the very tip of Israel, where typically the hotel itself is the main attraction. Sandwiched in between Egypt and Jordan, Eilat is located on the Red Sea. The major hotels, some of which are now themed, have waterfront access, and all have pools, so they serve as the place where tourists spend most of the day. Lately the use of theming has migrated north to Jerusalem. Local newspapers announced the construction of a new Holiday Inn Royal Plaza in Jerusalem under the franchise of Holiday Inn, which will be a themed hotel using aspects of both the Old and the New Testaments. There is little doubt that the phenomenon of theming, so powerful in the United States (Gottdiener 1997), will increasingly characterize tourist projects in Israel.

Fast-Food Franchised Restaurants

In addition to the increased use of theming, the constructed tourist environment in Israel makes liberal use of international franchise operations in a process of McDonaldization. Brand names such as McDonald's, Burger King, Pizza Hut, Subway, Dunkin' Donuts, Nathan's, and others have appeared in Israel over the last decade as a result of the increase in GNP per capita that has allowed the local population to spend part of its income on this kind of consumption. Another reason for the switch to international franchising was the end of the Arab boycott on Israel as a result of the ongoing peace process. Those commercial firms that knuckled under to the boycott in the past are now free to begin their commercial penetration of Israel.

The franchised brand names are always popular with large segments of the "tourist population," mainly Americans and Canadians, because they are fixtures from back home. A good example of the centrality of franchised fast food to the religious tourist experience is in this account from a member of an evangelical group from California that visited Israel during 1997:

> The bus then proceeded to the town of Meggido. We stopped at a modern shopping center that had a number of restaurants. When the double golden arches [McDonald's] were spotted, a cheer went up from the group; not just from the children. Most of the group ignored the Arab restaurants; heading straight for McDonald's! Of course, for the sake of my grandkids, I had to maintain my personal tradition of eating in McDonald's in each country that I visit. (Arnett 1997:17)

Franchised fast food in Israel does not just appeal to Christians from the United States. Orthodox Jews visiting Israel who are prohibited by dietary laws from eating at such places back home find that once in Israel, many of the familiar chains operate kosher kitchens. In the United States they can only gaze at the "promised land" of McDonald's but cannot enter because these restaurants are not kosher. Upon arriving at the "promised land" of Israel, however, the religious dietary laws of Kashrut observed in most of the international chains permit them to participate in the "American Dream" at last. It is interesting that these very places that represent an international food business that is opposed to the Orthodox religious way of life of these people are nevertheless visited en masse without Rabbinical hindrance in Israel even though the companies still represent the same way of life and are only forced by the Israeli state to comply with dietary laws. And as described in one of the Jerusalem newspapers concerning this phenomenon: "Once Jerusalem attracted tens of thousands of Jewish American tourists because of the Western Wall, the Old City and the significance of the city to the Jewish people. Today they are coming here because the Kosher fast-food restaurants are flourishing downtown."

Another interesting example of a themed restaurant (that is, not a fast-food restaurant) is the Cardo Culinaria, located in the middle of the Jewish quarter of Jerusalem's Old City. Drawing on design techniques of simulation, it is advertised as a "reconstruction" of an "authentic" Roman gastronomic experience. The Cardo Culinaria markets itself to tourists, especially Jews, who would prefer to have a reconstructed historical dining experience than to eat at Arab restaurants, even if that "history" is simulated. As its ads attest:

> Step back in time to an era of lavish banquets, accented by Roman frescoes, marble tables and terra cotta oil lamps. The Culinaria Experience takes you back to Jerusalem of 2,000 years ago when you are greeted with trumpet blasts by an envoy of the famed Roman legion. The Legionnaire will escort you to a marble table authentically set with oven-glazed pottery plates and cups overflowing with unending, delicious delicacies and plenty of wine and drink. . . . Return to a livelier era of dining experience where digestion is soothed by a subtle lulling of the harp and flute while fire jugglers and jesters thrill and amuse you and your guests at events like Bar Mitzvahs, Sheva Brachot, Britot and even Weddings.

The narrative of this advertisement is ironic because it is targeted at Jews, many of whom are religious, to come and celebrate their religious family festivities in a restaurant with a theme dedicated to Roman culture. This is the very same Roman Empire that systematically opposed Jewish religious rites when Rome ruled the area, and the same Roman legion that ultimately and brutally destroyed Jerusalem and carried off the Jews into the Diaspora. As Baudrillard might remark, these "trifling" details of the real do not inhibit the free use of simulacra for commercial purposes because the commodified images and signs are not based on any reality at all.

CONCLUSION

This chapter analyzed the infiltration of themed environments such as those in contemporary American/Westernized consumer culture into the realm of religious consumption in the Holy Land. There exists clear evidence for the increasing use of this pattern of consumption, especially among Protestant denominations. However, it seems that in the case of pilgrims and religious tourists to the Holy Land, there is still a significant percentage who are motivated by a genuine "search for authenticity," according to MacCannell (1990), though Chris Rojek claims that the "quest for authenticity is a declining force" (1997:71). Yet there remains a paradox, because the current quest for authenticity is experienced through the newer forms of theming and McDonaldization. In recent years, in both the Jewish and Christian sections of Israel, the purveyors of religious tourism have increasingly turned to commodified and manufactured experiences, to multimedia extravaganzas and simulation.

This process, if it continues to characterize historical and religious tourism, brings into question the entire issue of a pilgrimage to the Holy Land (as it also indirectly questions the act of traveling to other places.) If a tourist flies in a commercial jetliner, rides around in a Volvo bus or rented car from one of the big auto makers, sleeps at a franchised Holiday Inn or Howard Johnson hotel, eats at McDonald's or a Movenpick restaurant, and visits audio-visual displays and themed, artificially simulated environments, what is left of the "authentic" aspect of the religiously inspired journey? In other words, if travel is dominated by simulation, why bother to travel? Once experiences are commodified and packaged, they can also be shipped globally to any location, as the 1904 model of Jerusalem in St. Louis suggests. Significant sites that have been the subject of simulation lose their locational specificity, as has been the case with Disneyland, which manifests itself in Japan and France as well as two locations in the United States. In sum, the contemporary development of sites relevant to religious tourism in Israel may seriously undercut the significance of the authentic historical locations and trivialize their meaning.

BIBLIOGRAPHY

Adler, J. (1989). "Youth on the Road: Reflections on the History of Tramping," *Annals of Tourism Research* 12:335–54.

Baudrillard, J. (1989). *America*. London: Verso.

Ben-Arieh, Y. (1979). *The Rediscovery of the Holy Land in the Nineteenth Century*. Jerusalem: Magnes Press.

Brendon, P. (1991). *Thomas Cook: 150 Years of Popular Tourism*. London: Secker & Warburg.

Bryman, A. (1996). *Disney and His Worlds*. London: Routledge.

Central Bureau of Statistics (1998). *Tourism 1997*. Jerusalem.

Cohen, E. (1972). "Toward a Sociology of International Tourism," *Social Research* 39(1):164–82.

——— (1992). "Pilgrimage and Tourism: Convergence and Divergence," in *Sacred Journeys: The Anthropology of Pilgrimage*, ed. S. A. Morinis. Westport, Conn.: Greenwood Press.

——— (1998). "Tourism and Religion: A Comparative Perspective," *Pacific Tourism Review* 2(1):1–10.

Eco, U. (1987). *Travels in Hyper-Reality*. London: Picador.

Eliade, M. (1969). *Images and Symbols*. New York: Sheed and Ward.

Gottdiener, M. (1997). *The Theming of America: Dreams, Visions and Commercial Spaces*. Boulder, Colo.: Westview Press.

Kesselman Consulting and Coopers and Lybrand (1997). Nazareth Village Business Plan. Tel Aviv.

Kesselman Consulting and Coopers and Lybrand (1997). Nazareth Village Market Study: Final Report. Tel Aviv.

Kochav, S. (1995). "The Search for Protestant Holy Sepulcher: The Garden Tomb in Nineteenth-Century Jerusalem," *Journal of Ecclesiastical History* 46(2):278–301.

MacCannell, D. (1990). *The Tourist: A New Theory of the Leisure Class*. 2nd ed. New York: Shocken Books.

Midgam—Consulting and Research Ltd. (1998). Tourists Survey: January–December 1997. Jerusalem: Ministry of Tourism.

Rinschede, G. (1992). "Forms of Religious Tourism," *Annals of Tourism Research* 19(1):51–67.

Ritzer, G. (1996). *The McDonaldization of Society*. Thousands Oaks, Calif.: Pine Forge Press.

Rubin, R. (1999). "When Jerusalem Was Built in St. Louis: A Large-Scale Model of the Jerusalem in the Louisiana Purchase Exhibition, 1904," *Palestine Exploration Quarterly: Holy City in a World Fair (1904), Jerusalem and the Land of Israel,* 132:59–70.

Rydell, R. W. (1993). *World of Fairs: The Century of Progress Expositions*. Chicago: University of Chicago Press.

Shachar, A., and N. Shoval (1999), "Tourism in Jerusalem: A Place to Pray," in *The Tourist City*, ed. D. R. Judd and S. S. Fainstein. New Haven: Yale University Press.

Smith, V. L. (1992). "The Quest in Guest," *Annals of Tourism Research* 19(1):1–17.

The Piker, St. Louis, Mo., June, 1904.

Towner, J. (1985). "The Grand Tour: A Key Phase in the History of Tourism," *Annals of Tourism Research* (12)3:297–333.

Turner, V. (1969). *The Ritual Process*. Chicago: Aldine.

Turner, V., and E. Turner (1978). *Image and Pilgrimage in Christian Culture: Anthropological Perspectives*. Oxford: Basil Blackwell.

Twain, M. (1869). *The Innocents Abroad*. London: Collins-Clear Type Press.

Vogel, L. I. (1993). *To See a Promised Land: Americans and the Holy Land in the Nineteenth Century*. University Park: Pennsylvania State University Press.

World's Fair Bulletin (1903). St. Louis, Mo. August.

13

The Consumption of Space
and the Spaces of Consumption

M. Gottdiener

There is no consumption of space without a corresponding and prior production of space. Recently much attention has been paid to the latter, and this chapter will summarize this discussion only briefly (Lefebvre 1994; Gottdiener 1994). However, our understanding of the production of space possesses an interesting conceptual core.

THE PRODUCTION OF SPACE

Traditional societies thousands of years ago found themselves suspended in a vast uncharted domain, the natural environment. They produced a modest space for themselves of vernacular housing, constructed from materials at hand that tailored the concept of shelter to the needs of the environment: shelter from rain, cold, sun, enemies, and/or animals, as the case may be. Because the particular environmental factors differed, the architecture of settlement spaces among traditional societies across the globe displayed great variation.

Beyond the boundaries of any particular village, settlement, or primitive town, however, nature lay waiting in a great, uncharted domain. Mental maps marked off the tiny known world from this enormous, unknown natural realm. Best exemplified by the concept of "Terra Incognita," the separation of the primal domain was often signified on medieval maps by pictures of dragons or sea monsters on the sea or on the land by the phrase "here there be tygers." Alongside *topia*, to use Michel Foucault's phrase, there existed the undomesticated and often frightening places of the imagination, or *heterotopias*, of the unknown natural realm.

Now things have changed in two broadly conceived ways. First, the production of space is directly and intimately part of the capital accumulation process that is increasingly tied to global linkages in the investment, disinvestment, construction, reconstruction, renovation, and redesign of real estate. In short, settlement space today is a resource turned into a commodity by the political economy of contemporary capitalism that can be bought, sold, rented, constructed, torn down, used, and reused in much the same way as any other kind of investment. The production of space now follows its own subset of the laws of capital accumulation (Lefebvre 1991; Gottdiener [1985] 1994; Harvey 1973; Feagin 1988).

Second, the vast uncharted domain of the natural world has disappeared. Satellite technology that maps the entire globe into discrete parcels is but the end result of the great age of exploration that began for Europeans during the Middle Ages but earlier for Asian and Polynesian peoples. Every region of the earth is photographed, mapped, fragmented into parcels, homogenized, labeled, and either commodified for present capital investment or claimed by the state and expropriated by political interests, such as in "national parks" or "game preserves." Now commodification, surveillance, and regulation of land are all pervasive and globally ubiquitous as practices of capital and/or the state. The so-called natural realm of the imagination has disappeared as a place on earth, and imaging activity has been transferred today to visions of outer space and planetary exploration.

By "production of space" is meant the process of capital accumulation as it transpires in the real estate sector or the "second circuit of capital" (Lefebvre 1994; Gottdiener 1994), a process that involves investment, circulation, and profit realization through the commodification of land. The history of industrial societies in the West can be broken down into phases corresponding to ways the built environment was transformed by the second circuit of capital (Gottdiener 1994). The mercantilist phase of the global system produced the great port cities of the world during the 1600s and 1700s. Industrial capitalism produced the industrial city, such as the "great towns" of England (Engels 1973). There the separation of society into the two main classes of capitalists and workers was reflected in the separation of housing for the wealthy from the mass of residential dwellings for laborers and their families. A "consumption of space" is mentioned during this period, but only in a limited sense. Use values for workers were confined to the requirements of housing, because neither capital nor the state provided segments of land for free recreational use in the early industrial city. Use values for capital consisted of prime locations for businesses and factories, with the consumption of space confined to the ownership and use of landscaped land exclusively for the privileged, such as country clubs, yacht and harbor facilities, and resort places in the country.

Later in the 1800s, reformers concerned about the social evils of industrial capitalism surfaced to reclaim a part of accumulated wealth for public purposes. In the United States, for example, the City Beautiful Movement, inspired by the Garden Cities of England, pressured the state to create parks, recreational facilities, and green spaces for free public use, such as the great urban park landscaping schemes of Frederick Law Olmstead in the United States. Central Park in Manhattan, Prospect Park in Brooklyn, Golden Gate Park in San Francisco, Delaware Park in Buffalo, and Fairmont Park in Riverside, California, are some examples of Olmstead's work. At the same time, world's fairs, such as the Pan-Am Exposition of Buffalo in 1901, and commercial but inexpensive amusement spaces, such as Coney Island in New York City or Brighton in England, provided alternatives spaces for the masses to the dreary, boxed-in areas of housing within the inner industrial city. These regions were limited extensions of spatial production for the general purpose of enjoying space, of consuming space, made available to the public, sometimes for a modest fee, as in the case of the amusement park or public zoo.

In the early nineteenth century, as societies struggled to break free of the one-dimensional land-use schemes produced by capitalist industrialization through green-space-planning schemes, tourism was developed systematically as a commercial enterprise, enabling people to consume specially prepared spaces. This "consumption of space" through tourism was initially out of reach for the working class. Wealthy and middle-class patrons, however, enjoyed an increasing variety of tourist experiences ranging from the development of Niagara Falls, New York, as the de rigueur "honeymoon" spot for newlyweds in the United States to organized African safaris for wealthy Americans and Europeans. State regulation of public lands developed national parks that were also included in the organized travel vacation known as "tourism" (Rojek 1985; MacCannell 1989). Tourist destinations were produced by capital investment in hotels, resorts, and road and airport infrastructure; public services such as electricity and police protection; and particular normative offerings for guests, such as sumptuous meals, golf and/or tennis, and nighttime lounge entertainment. They also precluded the existence of a "safe" environment, that is, nature tamed for human use. This process of pacification has expanded to more elaborate levels in conjunction with the development of modern-day tourism and includes global support for dictators that pacify "unruly" populations (see below).

By the 1950s, in the United States the preponderance of capital investment was still cycled into the production of housing and the built environment of industry. The process referred to as "the consumption of space" remained a limited affair. But settlement space configuration began to change in a most fundamental way. Developers, banks, government agencies, and individual as well as corporate investors belonging to the second circuit of capital began the mass development of suburbia. The burgeoning middle-class population along with well-paid segments of the working class took up residence on an unprecedented scale in areas outside the central city that were developed for housing by agents of the second circuit of capital. Single-family home construction and real estate investment became a multibillion dollar industry during the 1950s in the United States. By the 1970s, the plurality of the American population was residing in the suburbs, not the central cities, of the nation. Thus, the urban configuration was radically altered to a *new form of settlement space*, the *multicentered metropolitan region* (Gottdiener 1994). Everyday life became based on a regional routine of commuting, including the separation across the metropolitan landscape of places of work from housing and shopping. It was only at this point, after 1950 in the United States, that a critical mass of locations and activities involving a large enough population could be called "the consumption of space."

THE CONSUMPTION OF SPACE

Organized family outings on Sundays to urban "pleasure zones" such as public green spaces or amusement parks are aspects of the consumption of space. So too are trips to the country club for a round of golf or the weekend cottage at the seashore, although they are considerably more expensive and carry the affluent class's imprimatur. Activities involving the consumption of space have in common the use of a thoroughly commodified and/or regulated environment, commodified by capital and/or regulated by the state. Thus, once advanced industrial societies progressed after the 1930s to the extended commodification of everyday life, most activities involved some form of spatial consumption as the built environment itself assumed the backdrop of an increasingly ubiquitous consumer culture.

In the 1930s, for example, the ersatz decoration of individual housing became thoroughly commodified by the design ethos of modernism propagated by design ideologies, such as the Bauhaus (Baudrillard 1968). Idiosyncratic furnishings were replaced in the home by the norms of modernist interior design with its systematic consuming of modules—kitchen sets, dining room sets, living room sets—that synchronically reinforced compatible ambiance (Gottdiener 1995). Under pressure of modernist interior design, as well as the extension of home ownership to the majority of the population through government programs and the advances of the real estate industry, shelter was converted into the consumption of space.

As tourism became an activity of the middle class as a result of the development of the tourist industry as a mass, commodified sector of the economy, it too became exemplary of the consumption of space. As Henri Lefebvre (1991) observes, instead of the circulation of commodities among people, as in the stage of industrial capitalism, tourism involves the circulation of people to specific locations that are consumed as spaces—spaces of leisure, sport, recreation, "nature," amusement, "history," or simply "otherness." As the latter suggests, the phenomenon of cultural *difference* is as important to tourism as any spectacular site. One visits New York City from a base in London not to experience a city per se but a *difference*. Familiarity with urban culture from years of living in London enables the tourist to negotiate the strange environment of New York because of common urban features. The tourist consumes the differences that the foreign space offers. Sunday motor trips into the country from the city pursue the same tourist quest for difference if only for a shorter time and at less expense.

The consumption of space is clearest in the stereotypical tourist activity of picture taking. Photography has been transformed over the years by industrial processes of the most advanced kind and the artistic activity has been commodified and mechanically retooled for easy access by the most unaccomplished amateurs in everyday life. An amazing variety of formats, films, and cameras are now available to tourists seeking to capture images for show, storage, and documentation of trips. Intrinsically a part of the consumer "vacation" is the consumption of places themselves that are documented with the help of the photography industry that is now extended to videotape technology. In short, the production and consumption of films, video tapes, still cameras, video cameras, accessories, and processing labs articulates together with the production and consumption of tourist spaces—the molding of beaches, "natural" scenic wonders, and "pleasure environments"; the construction of hotels; the building of infrastructure; the acquisition, training, and support of staff; and the pacification of foreign places with unstable political climates through state and corporate means. These components, in turn, articulate with the vast tourism industry consisting of advertising; travel agents; service personnel in hotels; the car, rail and air transportation industries; rental activities; and the pictorial modeling of *astral* visions of desirable destinations by media-driven culture, including novels, magazines, TV, and the cinema.

Any discussion of the consumption of space through tourism would not be complete without mention of the production of places to shop that are always a part of any destination. Indeed, many travel "vacations" are, in reality, shopping trips. The intent is the same whether discussing the activity of suburban housewives who journey by plane to places with famous megamalls, such as the giant Mall of America in Minnesota, or the organized bus trips of northern Greeks to Istanbul, Turkey.

Of particular interest are the trinket shops that can always be found adjacent to tourist sites. In some cases, they contain products once produced by local craft skills that have been appropriated, reimaged, and retooled for mass production. In others, souvenirs manufactured in low-wage, third-world countries are mass marketed in advanced societies, such as little statues of the Eiffel Tower, coffee mugs imprinted with scenic images, or sealed snowy paperweights with tiny images of natural wonders. Third-world labor is also employed in the production of T-shirts, hats, jackets, and the like that are equally available in tourist shops for consumption. This trinket industry is also part of the global circuit facilitating the accumulation of capital through the stimulated circulation of people to sites around the world for the consumption of tourist spaces.

THE SPACES OF CONSUMPTION

In 1996 almost one million people took a tour through a modest, former physician's home that became Graceland, the estate of Elvis Presley, in Memphis, Tennessee. The tour begins on the other side of the busy highway in a cleverly constructed visitors center in which the tickets, costing more than $20 a person, are hyped to expectant crowds. Elvis memorabilia is everywhere in this building. Minibuses take ticket purchasers, each supplied with a portable audio cassette guide, across the street to view Presley's home and estate. Inside the house itself, there is no Elvis memorabilia, only the *momento mori* of the physical surroundings that were once the site of his everyday life, including the second floor bathroom where he died (the entire upstairs is closed to the public).

Graceland works as a space of consumption for the consumption of Elvis's former space. The tour is engineered to move people from the ticket counter to the exit in the most efficient manner and hopefully within a reasonable time to make room for other gawkers circulating through the same space. Disneyland (another "land") located in Anaheim, California, perfected this kind of circulation as a space of consumption back in the 1950s. Now that site and its larger twin, Disney World, in Orlando, Florida, are the most visited places on the globe. For the consumption of space to work as an extension of the realization and subsequent accumulation of capital, space not only had to be commodified, as has been seen, but also engineered appropriately as a space of consumption. During the last two decades, there has been a veritable explosion of such spaces in the United States and possibly elsewhere. Many of these sites explicitly use themes to organize the decor that purposely articulate with the larger consumer/media culture of society.

Themed environments seem to be everywhere, and most of them are successful as commercial enterprises. There are themed restaurants, malls, airports, hotels, gambling casinos, fast-food courts, sports stadiums, and lately, even themed museums or monuments, such as the Holocaust memorial in Washington, D.C. Personal celebrations, such as weddings, anniversaries, and vacations, increasingly rely on themes. Symbolic motifs vary across a full spectrum drawing from popular culture in a variety of ways. Sometimes pure themes such as the "Wild West" or "tropical paradise" define commercial spaces. At other times, motifs are mixed together in a postmodern pastiche of new combinations, such as the decor of the Luxor Hotel and Casino in Las Vegas, Nevada, which features an elaborately themed rendition of an Egyptian pyramid as its exterior shape and inside had a huge restaurant called the "Manhattan Buffet," signified by the logo of New York's skyline (in 1998, this place was renamed "Pharoah's Pheast," but other juxtapositions like it can still be found in Vegas).

The growing reliance on themes for commercial spaces is relatively recent. Until the 1970s, shopping places were recognized by their names or the labels of famous clothing manufacturers and designers. People shopped at Gimbals', in downtown New York City, because it was a well-known, full-service department store. Today, Manhattan's Gimbals' is gone and relatively few people shop in any city's downtown. The major portion of retailing sales takes place in suburban shopping malls, many of which are fully themed environments. People are drawn to the motif of the mall and/or its reputation as a space of consumption and then find places to shop within it, rather than being attracted to a particular store because of some unique marketing ploy. In fact, the hundreds of small boutique mall stores rely on the impulse buying of consumers as they walk within the mall environment, thereby consuming its space—itself an important activity of suburban shoppers. Below is a look at some examples of spaces of consumption recently appearing as articulations between commercial places and media-driven culture.

The Themed Restaurant

Until quite recently, Americans rarely ate in restaurants. The norm was to cook meals at home. Dining out was reserved for a special occasion. Eating at the local community diner was an exception to this practice, because it offered a substantial breakfast or meat-and-potatoes lunch at reasonable prices. Frequenters of diners were mainly people on the move, such as truck drivers, traveling salespeople and delivery men, or single adults, again especially males or "bachelors" who did not have families. The roadside diner was an important place during the 1930s and 1940s, at the first blossoming of today's now mature automobile culture. Many of these structures were simple affairs that restricted their advertising to the daily specials. They counted on traffic and the sparsity of competition to bring customers their way. Nevertheless, a few of these establishments exploited advertising in competition for business and some managed to develop thematic devices. One classic case was the original McDonald brothers' roadside hamburger stand on Route 66 just west of San Bernardino, California. The brothers embellished their simple diner with a golden logo in the shape of a large "M." Over the years, as the original stand grew into the multinational, multibillion dollar corporation under new, franchise-thinking owners, this arched logo would undergo many stylistic transformations as it melded with the *theme* of the "McDonald's" experience.

As Robert Venturi, Denise S. Brown, and Steven Izenour (1972), observed, the diner is essentially a simple shed adorned with symbols. The decorated shed became the forerunner for the themed restaurants of today. Now competition among fast-food franchises or restaurants, coupled with increasing affluence and the new consumer norms that support frequent meals outside the home, have pushed eating establishments into the use of thematic devices. Some restaurant chains exemplify total themed environments. Typical of the new trend are the dining places constructed by the Specialty Restaurant Corporation (Wright 1989). It often renovates failed factories, as in the case of the Cannery Restaurant of Newport Beach, California, which operated from 1921 to 1966 processing seafood until pollution from suburbanization forced its closure. The interior of the factory was gutted and converted into a restaurant. Instead of throwing out the original machinery, however, the designers recycled it as sculpture. Artifacts from the manufacturing process became part of the decor. Thematic elements unified around the motif of the local fishing industry, such as photographs, ships' compasses, and navigational equipment, are pinned to the walls. Employees dress in uniforms that recall a version of the 1920s. Aspects of the cannery motif, therefore, pervade the entire space as a totally themed environment. Of course, the current cannery is only a simulation—not a real fish-processing plant but a fish restaurant *disguised* as a factory. Such simulations are increasingly more characteristic of society, prompting one culture critic to argue that reality itself has disappeared (Baudrillard 1983).

Perhaps the best-known fully themed franchise is the Hard Rock Café concept that started in England. Catering to young adults and serving comparatively simple meals centering on the staple of hamburgers and french fries, this restaurant chain has become so successful that it can be found in the capital cities of several countries, and recently, a Hard Rock Casino has opened in Las Vegas. The thematic motif of this franchise derives from the rock music industry, including nostalgic elements from its origins in the 1950s. The distinctive theme, fed constantly by the connection to popular music, is developed further by ambitious merchandising made available at all restaurant locations, including sales of Hard Rock Café T-shirts with the location on the logo, jackets, and tote bags.

Because the totally themed environment proved successful for the Hard Rock Café franchise, its form has been copied more recently by other operations. Perhaps the most spectacular example is the recently launched chain called Planet Hollywood, started by several movie superstars—Arnold Schwarzenegger, Sylvester Stallone, Bruce Willis, Demi Moore, and others—which is now having financial difficulties. As with the Hard Rock Café, Planet Hollywood commodifies its connection to a popular culture industry—this time, it is the movies. Restaurant walls are decorated with Hollywood memorabilia. Once inside a typical franchise, the customer finds virtually the same type of fare as at the Hard Rock Café, that is, basic American diner food. In fact, other than the themed environments of these two examples, there is little to differentiate them from any other local

American diner existing in virtually every town in the United States. The *themed* environment makes the difference. Difference is produced not through products but contrasts in the themed environment alone.

Now there is an explosion of themed restaurants both in central cities and suburbs. Some recent examples that have all been franchised across the country are: the Fashion Café (started by several supermodels), the Harley-Davidson Café (after the famous motorcycle), and the Rain Forest Café (using an "environmentally conscious" theme). According to a *Time* article,

> In the past couple of years, a business exceeding more than half a billion dollars has emerged that the trade calls "eatertainment." Theme restaurants, a combination plate of amusement park, diner, souvenir stand and museum, have become the fastest-growing segment of the restaurant industry, turning up the heat on fast feeders such as McDonald's and the segment known as casual dining. . . . This heady expansion leads to projections that eatertainment will be a $5 billion baby by the turn of the century—assuming the theme dreamers continue to titillate a fickle been-there, done-that public. (Angelo 1996:56–57)

In the last few years, renovations of existing restaurants by spectacular interior designers have spawned a new type of theming called "imagist architecture" (*Designweek* 1994). One of its exponents, Chicago designer Jordan Mozer, is known for his widely fantastic, kinetic interiors that turn restaurants into representations. His *Vivere* restaurant in Chicago has been described as "a dizzying baroque symphony of dancing mosaics, huge sculpted copper spirals, custom-blown glass lamps, and a squid-shaped iron gazebo that houses the host station" (Allen 1994:93). For all its tour de force, Gaudi-influenced shapes, Mozer's design logic for *Vivere* was based on a single theme, the rise to prominence of the restaurant's owners as represented by a spiral motif that is repeated throughout the interior. "It's the basis for columns, chandeliers and other light-fittings, for an entry gazebo and as inlays in the granite bartop" (*Designweek* 1994:18). Similarly, Mozer's *Iridium* restaurant in the Lincoln Center area of Manhattan was inspired by the theme of music as represented sineasthesially in forms deriving from kinetically portrayed musical notes, instruments, and the ballet.

Other restaurant franchises that have not been as successful commercially but that also use fully themed environments feature French village motifs, Southwestern decor, and New York City deli style. There is also a diverse deployment of nostalgia themes, such as 1950s "oldies," country farmhouses, and ethnic symbols that are mechanically replicated, as in the quasi-Italian "Olive Garden" restaurants (more successful than most). A typical nostalgia-themed restaurant is the "Ruby Tuesday" chain—the name comes from an old Rolling Stones song. This restaurant is particularly interesting for its postmodern *implosion* of times and places that stretch over almost an entire century while the decor manages to integrate the varied referents in the exploitation of popular nostalgia. Its walls are lined with reproductions of ads and public signs from the 1920s, 1930s, and 1940s. The decor of the booths, however, reaches farther back, to the last century. The booths are illuminated by a remarkable display of imitation Tiffany lamps (originally dating to the 1890s) and stained-glass windows. The nineteenth- and early twentieth-century implosion is complemented by "old tyme" ceiling fans and Victorian era–style hanging plants. Lastly, no Ruby Tuesday's restaurant would be complete without its authentic-looking, but simulated, plastic tin roof.

The marketing of a restaurant as a thematic environment also deploys aspects of merchandising to attract customers. Fast-food places often run promotions by providing special gifts that reflect corporate motifs or representative characters. Even when not engaging in special promotions, themed restaurants carry through their coordinated designs down to their napkins, plates, cups, and table decor. As seen with the Hard Rock Café, Planet Hollywood, and others, commercialism can extend to the aggressive merchandising of clothing such as T-shirts and jackets with signature logos.

The use of themes for restaurants seems to coincide with the post–World War II boom in franchise merchandising. Because each restaurant belongs to a web of eateries marketed through association with a national or global company, it must convey that link through the use of signs. Franchising pays for national advertising, so individually owned places can use the chain decor through interior design, employee uniforms, and cups, plates, bags, and napkins with the corporate logo. But themes are important in ways other than franchising. Their increasing use also coincides with the growth in popularity of fully enclosed shopping malls. In this later case, other uses for motifs are realized in the creation of a consumer space on a large scale.

The Themed Mall

Malls, just like the restaurants previously discussed, vary regarding the extent to which they carry through thematic designs. Yet they also increasingly use overarching motifs and coordinated design schemes in total environments that link the place of consumption with the larger context of media-driven culture. As described above, restaurants compete with each other for cash customers. Malls began, however, not in competition with other malls, because only recently have they proliferated, but in competition with the downtowns of cities. Their direct rivals were for many years the large department stores located in the center of the metropolis. Consequently, malls had to advertise themselves as a *place* to go, and they still do. This kind of advertising for a particular site of consumption or location within an urban region is, besides the ads placed by individual department stores, aimed at attracting customers to a specific space. As a special destination, malls require some overarching means of identification. Consequently, they often adopt an image meant to be attractive to potential consumers who always have the choice of where to do their shopping. In this way, they are different than the city downtown, which is not a unified commercial space and does not advertise itself as a location.

There is another reason why malls adopt a unified image. Whereas the central city remains a public space that allows free interaction among a variety of people for any number of purposes, the mall is a highly regulated, *private* commercial space that is expressly designed to make money as a place for consumption. This instrumental function of the mall, for realizing capital, must be disguised because it would not be attractive to consumers. As a result, almost every mall has an overarching motif that attempts to convey it as a unique and desirable location *for its own sake.* As with restaurants, the mall theme is a simulation, a facade, but as a motif for the entire space, it sets the symbolic tone for the interior.

Malls have been very effective as commercial spaces. They account for more than half of all retailing sales in the United States. In many metropolitan areas, malls have been so severely competitive that they have forced downtown shopping districts out of existence. Buffalo, New York, for example, has several large, successful suburban malls ringing the central city, but the last big department store located downtown closed in 1995. During the 1960s, suburbanization and mall development were so devastating to central cities that the cities required large infusions of cash from federal government renewal programs to float schemes that would bring customers back to the downtown. Few of these efforts were successful.

Suburban malls have changed the nature of retailing competition by introducing the dimension of space. In the past, when central city department stores dominated all commerce, only individual stores themselves had to advertise. Once suburbanization reached a mass level after World War II and malls were introduced as retailing outlets dispersed within the larger metropolitan region, the downtown of the city became only one location among several alternate destinations for shoppers. Each retailing center, suburban or urban, had to compete with every other center as a specific destination, as a desirable space of consumption for commuters. Besides advertising that expresses competition among stores, therefore, mall advertising is also a response to competition among the alternate locations of retailing centers. The latter kind of promotion takes the form of thematic appeals, especially for malls that project a special image of their own. Lately, even central cities have begun to advertise themselves to shoppers. Thus, retailing competition over the years has taken on a dimension of spatial competition, and it leads to a greater use of themes. In addition, because of place competition, there is a tendency over time for malls to be bigger and bigger so that more store possibilities are offered to potential visitors.

The largest mall in the United States is the Mall of America, in Bloomington, Minnesota, outside of Minneapolis, that opened for business on August 21, 1992. In many ways, this "megamall" is, in fact, a separate small city itself. Developers pushed the total environment form a step further by constructing a closed and immense interior space (sometimes called a "hyperspace" because of its size and disorienting qualities; see Jameson 1984). The Mall of America covers 78 acres, with more than 4 million square feet of floor area that includes 2.5 million feet of actual retailing space, has more than four hundred specialty shops and four large department stores, and contains a fourteen-screen movie theater, nightclubs, bars, nine areas of family entertainment, more than twenty-two restaurants, and twenty-three more fast-food outlets. But that is not all. At the center of this three-story complex, beneath an immense hyperspace of skylights, mall developers located a seven-acre theme park run by Knott's Berry Farm of southern California. The park has trees and bushes, a controlled climate, twenty-three amusement rides including a roller coaster, fourteen places to eat, and high-tech virtual-reality simulations. Promotional literature for the megamall claims that it is as big as eighty-eight football fields, can contain twenty of Rome's St. Peter's Basilicas, and is five times as large as the famous Red Square in Moscow. According to its Canadian developers, the megamall site in Minnesota was chosen among alternatives in several states because of key factors including the presence of 27 million people in the surrounding region and their household income that is above the national average. In addition, local governments put up more than $100 million in transportation upgrades for the surrounding area, including the construction of large multistoried parking ramps.

The Mall of America cleverly ties its overarching theme to the grand symbol "America." Developers decorated the exterior facade in stars and stripes and red, white, and blue. Its patriotic decor can mean so many things to so many different people that it serves as a consummate mass-marketing device. Ironically, the original developers of the mall were Middle Eastern immigrants to Canada, but that did not prevent them from feeding an "all-American" simulation to the hungry consumers of the Minneapolis–St. Paul region. The interior of the megamall articulates the polysemic patriotic theme, with others shaping the major shopping sections. Restaurants are often like the ones analyzed in the last section, with individual themes of their own. Most of them are chain franchises such as Hooters (featuring skimpily clad waitresses), Tony Roma's (a chain of rib restaurants), Ruby Tuesday's, Fat Tuesday, the Alamo Grill (southwest food), the California Café (a simulation of southern California style), and Gators (another diner food chain), among others. Each of these themes relates to each other only in the loosest possible sense as belonging to the tapestry of American folklore simulations.

Retailing activities within the mall subdivide space into four main areas. Each, however, relies on the same type of simulation—recapturing urban ambiance in a varied version of the city street scene. It seems that malls cannot escape from their main competitor—the downtown, public space of the classic central city. The four shopping areas of the Mall of America are: North Garden, Main Street USA; West Market; South Avenue; and East Broadway.

Despite its sometimes overreaching metaphors that try to connect with urban spaces in real cities, this mall's decor is only a thinly veiled disguise for what is essentially an immense indoor commercial shopping area. This is true of other malls too. The grand themed environment of the mall functions as a sign-vehicle that aids its role as a container of many commercial enterprises because it is also attractive as a desirable destination itself. What makes the Mall of America different is its large scale and overabundance of family entertainment opportunities, including the seven-acre theme park. It represents a consummate linkage between retailing and the effort to attract families in competition with the downtown of the city that has little family entertainment of its own. This mall is a totally themed environment, but its motifs, like the case for other malls as well, are subservient to the principal need of conformity with the decors of its tenant shops. Commercialism—and not the overarching themes of the classical city, that is, religion, cosmology, or politics—dominates the *contemporary* mall form.

The Las Vegas Casino

In their spectacularly prescient book *Learning from Las Vegas* (1972), the architects Venturi, Brown, and Izenour identified the phenomenon of Las Vegas architecture as a new and foundational departure from modernism. According to the authors, modernist architecture attenuated the symbolic dimension of buildings to the benefit of the austere functionalist "program" of the International School. In modernism, meaning was to be communicated through the characteristics of form rather than through symbol and allusion. "The creation of architectural form was to be a logical process, free from images of past experience, determined solely by program and structure" (1972:7). Las Vegas architecture represents the rejection of modernism. It is, in fact, constructed as if modernist doctrines never existed. Instead of the austerity and functionalism of the International School's program, Las Vegas architecture is the apotheosis of signs and symbols. The guiding logic of this architecture is and has always been unadulterated commercialism.

As Venturi and associates point out, the Las Vegas environment is a victory of symbols-in-space over the modernist project of forms-in-space. The symbolic environment fits the needs of an automobile-dominated landscape with immense distances and high-speed travel, "where the subtleties of pure architectural space can no longer be savored" (1972:153). The vast spaces of the desert-dominated Southwest, with its fast-paced interstate highways, requires a commercial environment with "explicit and heightened symbolism" composed of "watts, animation, and iconology" (1972:19).

The function of architecture within a commercial environment designed for the auto is the seduction of the consumer. Las Vegas is a multidimensional experience of seducing pleasures—money, sex, food, gambling, and nightlife. Las Vegas constitutes a specialized space; it is one of several global "pleasure zones," such as Monte Carlo (now the name of a new casino) and the French Riviera (the Riviera is also the name of a Las Vegas casino), the Greek islands, Rio (also another Las Vegas casino), Disney World, Marienbad, or the Taj Mahal. According to Venturi and associates, "Essential to the imagery of pleasure-zone architecture are lightness, the quality of being an oasis in a hostile context, heightened symbolism, and the ability to engulf the visitor in a new role: vacation from everyday reality" (1972:53).

Las Vegas casinos, which are themed consumption spaces designed principally for gambling, epitomize this type of pleasure zone architecture. In recent years, casinos have extended their use of symbols from the heavily denotative electric signs that signify place through names, such as the Desert Inn, to iconic representations comprising the entire casino building itself, such as the Luxor Hotel and Casino, which was constructed as a large, Egyptian-style pyramid.

It is, in fact, at this level of the literal signs, the advertisements of Las Vegas attractions and the iconic building of casino forms, that the fantasy themes and appeals of the casino/resorts are best articulated. With this practice, some overarching thematic device is introduced, such as the risqué, continental decor of the Riviera, or the pirate theme of Treasure Island. The particular fantasy theme is then developed through facades, the language of signs and pictures that *connote* a specific ideology or set of cultural meanings that relate to the announced theme. The metaphorical relation is declared first as a unifying idea, often through iconic representation of the casino exterior, and then developed as a particular set of connotations within the same sign. This complexity, this rapid-fire transmission of distinct messages that simultaneously denote specific forms of information, such as the contents of a meal and its price, and connote thematic associations, such as the invitation to participate in a fantasy environment, is communicated to both pedestrians and drivers of automobiles alike.

The Las Vegas gambling economy is situated within structures that are combinations of casinos, hotels, and often, resorts. Most of the spectacular resort/ casinos are located on the Strip because of the need for sprawling space. The downtown area, or "Glitter Gulch," is dominated by casinos specialized for gambling or hotel/casinos, such as the Golden Nugget, which are also nice places to stay.

According to Venturi and associates, most of these structures are examples of the "decorated shed." They are rather similar buildings that are designed for gambling or hotel occupancy. However, they are overlaid by elaborate signs. The Las Vegas casino functions, in fact, as one big sign. Each casino possesses a separate theme that is some overarching code or ideology. "It is hard to think of each flamboyant casino as anything but unique, and this is as it should be, because good advertising technique requires the differentiation of the product" (Venturi et al. 1972:34). The varied thematic devices, with the casino functioning as one large sign of itself, creates an emergent system of signification through difference. Each differentiated casino, as a separate theme, standing juxtaposed against other casinos, produces an overarching intertextuality that is the grand text of

Las Vegas, a system of difference at the level of the Strip or downtown environ-ment itself. This grand text does not intend to convey any particular message but instead becomes the profusion of signs that is the overarching environmental ex-perience of Las Vegas. As individual casino themes are altered, or as new casi-nos are built, the system of difference also changes and the Las Vegas experi-ence becomes more varied and deeply modulated.

Starting from the southern tip of Las Vegas Boulevard (also known as the Strip) and working northward, for example, the following casinos and their overarching themes are juxtaposed. The Mandalay Bay is furthest south and displays a tropi-cal paradise fantasy theme. Going north on that side of the street are the spec-tacular hotels—the Luxor, an Egyptian pyramid fantasy, and the Excalibur, a medieval castle and King Arthur fantasy. Across the street is the Tropicana ca-sino with its highly articulated tropical/Brazilian/Polynesian fantasy.

On the east side of the Strip and continuing north—crossing north from the Tropicana—is the largest casino/hotel in the world, the MGM Grand, with an illuminated lion at the entrance. This complex elaborates the theme of Hollywood glamour and MGM memorabilia. On that same side of the street and continuing north are the Aladdin, with its Arabian nights theme, and Bally's, which exploits the ambiance of continental luxury and a "Monte Carlo" setting. Right next to Bally's is the new casino/resort Paris, which recreates the Eiffel tower at two-thirds scale and, inside, contains a simulated version of the great city. Across the street from the Aladdin was the Dunes Hotel/Casino, which also exploited an Arabian theme but which was replaced by the Bellagio, another continental luxury themed resort. It shares the block with several small motel/inns, including the Broadway and the La Quinta, which themselves exploit specific thematic devices in their motel chain logos, although they lack the elaboration and development of the casinos. Two casino/resorts are located on this western side of the Strip, the giant New York–New York Casino and Hotel, with its incredible replication in miniature of the entire New York City skyline, and the Monte Carlo, a literal reference to the famous gambling mecca of Europe.

Continuing north and crossing Flamingo Road on the western side is the Caesars Palace complex, which has undergone several expansions. The Palace modulates the overarching themes of Caesar's Rome and classical Italian archi-tecture. Across the street heading east are the Barbary Coast, with its theme of old-time, nineteenth-century San Francisco, and the Flamingo (Bugsy Siegel's hotel), which retains its twin themes of continental luxury and Hollywood glam-our. Above the Flamingo is the Imperial Palace, which has limited thematic ele-ments deriving from Japanese architecture, and the Holiday Inn Motel. Across the Strip on the west, however, is the giant Mirage complex, which exploits both Hollywood glamour and tropical paradise themes. The Mirage has a nightly dis-play of an erupting volcano for the benefit of passersby on the Strip. North of it is the casino/hotel Treasure Island, with its Caribbean pirates theme. It too offers a repeating show of a battle between two ships within an artificial Caribbean lagoon. Across the street from the Mirage is the giant, multibillion dollar hotel/resort casino, the Venetian, which reproduces St. Mark's Square and the canals of Venice on the casino's second floor. In short, within less than a mile, it is possible to see simulations of Paris, New York, Monte Carlo, Egypt, Camelot, Bellagio, Ancient Rome, Venice, and Tahiti.

Further up the Strip to the borders of downtown and Glitter Gulch are the Sands Hotel/Resort/Casino and the Desert Inn—both with an Arabian Nights theme, and across the Strip, the Frontier Hotel, which introduces a Wild West, cowboy theme for the first time and allows a thematic segue into the downtown, with its overly endowed Wild West–themed casinos such as the Golden Nugget, Binion's Horseshoe, and the Four Queens.

Before entering the downtown area, several other large casinos are encountered. On the west side of the Strip, next to the Frontier, is the Stardust, an immense hotel/motel complex that expresses a limited association with Hollywood glamour. Heading north is the Westward Ho casino, which exploits the downtown cowboy theme, and the gigantic Circus Circus complex, with an obvious circus theme that includes the performance of live circus acts and a recently completed theme park. On the east side of the street are several small hotel/casinos and then the Riviera casino/hotel, which displays a continental, Monaco/French Riviera theme. North of it is the Wet and Wild water theme park, and on the city-limits dividing line, Sahara Avenue, is the Sahara Hotel, another Arabian fantasy thematic attraction.

Semiotically speaking, difference is not created in the system of signification by all thematic casinos. The downtown is uniformly structured by an Old West theme with little variation from casino to casino. Three Strip casinos (before the demolition of the Dunes and Sands, it used to be five) share an Arabian Nights theme and three of them—the Alladin, Desert Inn, and Sahara—are close to each other. The continental theme is also shared by several casinos that are in close proximity, including the Flamingo, the Monte Carlo, the Paris, the Bellagio, and Bally's, and further north the Riviera. Thematic similarity, rather than semiotic difference, characterizes these casinos.

In the most recently developed section of the Strip, however, overarching casino themes are produced through difference, thereby creating a multithemed and multileveled symbolic environment. That is, meaning is produced through difference, by contrasts between one casino theme and another. For example, the casinos Mandalay Bay, Luxor, Tropicana, Excalibur, and MGM Grand are all within a short walking distance of each other. The Aladdin, Bally's, Caesars Palace, and the Barbary Coast, situated at the cross section of the Strip and Flamingo Road, also constitute a highly differentiated thematic contrast. Crossing Dauphine Way there is a third complex consisting of the Mirage, Treasure Island, and the Imperial Palace, which though not as graphic in its thematic contrasts, is nevertheless spectacular because of the elaborate outdoor shows in front of the Mirage and Treasure Island. Pedestrians can effortlessly walk from the fiery conflagration of the volcano eruption at the Mirage to the warring conflagration of pirates versus the British in front of Treasure Island.

Metonymy and the juxtaposition of themes produce a spectacular system of signification that defines the Las Vegas environment as a profusion of signs. The entire outside area becomes one immense and multithemed consumption space designed principally for the purposes of casino gambling but stimulating through the use of fantasy images from Hollywood movies, travelogues, and television. Venturi and associates were the first to remark about the graphic contrasts that they attributed to Las Vegas as an "architecture of inclusion" (1972:53). Since they wrote, these metonymical differences have increased. Standing at the entrance of the Tropicana one can see in a single, scopic gaze an immense three-story lion (MGM Grand entrance, now being altered to placate the superstitions of Asian visitors), the medieval edifice of the Excalibur castle, and the giant sandstone sphinx and glass pyramid of the Luxor. Within the field of view one can also see tall gas station signs with their corporate logos, gigantic casino signs advertising food and showcase entertainment, bus stops, parking lot signs, and advertising for various products on walls and fences.

In sum, the entire external environment of the Strip creates its own system of signification through metonymical contrasts and has become an immense, themed consumer space. The pastiche of inclusive architecture is quite remarkable and ranges from the symbols of ancient Egypt, through tropical fantasies, medieval apparitions, neoclassical, Roman, rococo, baroque, mock Tudor, Taj Mahal, Arabian Nights fantasies, and the fantasized Wild West or Barbary Coast of San Francisco.

THE ROLE OF SYMBOLS OR THEMES IN THE CIRCUIT OF CAPITAL

A nation of consumers must be fed by appeals to consume even when the goods they are presented with have dubious use-values. Basic human needs are relatively simple and consist, as every third-grade school child can attest, mainly of food, clothing, and shelter, not to mention a job that can provide for these necessities. The needs pumping up a consumer society, however, extend much beyond these basics, and furthermore, even the basics are elaborated by the practice of consumption almost beyond recognition from the picture painted for schoolchildren. Shelter for most people, for example, means a basic three- or four-bedroom suburban house complete with a fully equipped kitchen and recreational room. Consumers also view the commodities that stock such a "basic" home as "necessities." They desire dishwashers, refrigerators, microwave ovens, conventional ovens, stoves, and assorted electric gadgets in the kitchen; also television

sets, videotape players, stereo equipment, CD players, portable phones, and leisure furniture and bedroom sets in the family room and bedrooms. Many of these
commodities are either manufactured abroad or contain components manufactured
abroad. The principal task in this country, as it has shifted away from industrial
production, has become that of desiring these goods as necessities that cannot
be done without in daily life. Thus, as the shift has been made to a nation of service and information-processing industries, the function of consumption has per-
sisted and grown in importance.

For the most part, the production of desire for such commodities at the intense
level that it exists in today's society depends directly on symbolic mechanisms.
Signs and themes play a central role in the proper priming of the consumer society. Society has matured into possessing a fully themed mass culture. Mass advertising fuels the spending activities of society through the production of desire. Marketing procedures encompass today not only the appeals made by
advertising, such as those found on TV or in magazines, but also appeals within
the built environment itself, that is, in the suburban and city consumerscapes, or
the stores and malls that remain responsible for the realization of capital. The
key economic relation of the consumer society is not the exchange of money for
goods, as it was in the nineteenth century, but the link between the promotion of
desire in the mass media and advertising and the commercial venues where goods
and services can be purchased. Store environments are but an extension of TV,
magazine, and newspaper advertising. They provide material spaces for the realization of consumer fantasies primed by movies; rock videos; the record
industry; commercial advertising; lifestyle orientations from religious, ethnic,
racial or class origins; and even political ideologies that are propagated in community discourse or at the place of work.

This chapter puts forth the argument that, ever since the 1970s, themed consumer spaces are more and more important to commercial capital. Their increasing use is a result of competition among retailing and service providers, many
of which are now franchised. As consumer spending became the engine of growth
in the economy after the Great Depression of the 1930s, even as manufacturing
was deindustrialized in the 1970s, the abundance of companies producing similar items created a need for competitive marketing practices that helped develop
an image-driven culture, along with the mass media. These efforts now occur on
a grand scale and include the deployment of architectural design, environmental
engineering, advertising, mass-media technology, and recreational science in the
service of selling an experience along with commodities.

The new economic realities of a consumer-oriented economy derive from the
crisis base of capitalism that is, above all, a crisis in the realization of capital
among highly competitive global producers. Although most of the countries in
the world possess immense productive capacity, their development depends on
the ability of corporations to sell goods and services after they are produced.

Increasingly, the problem of capital realization is solved through the creation of image-driven, themed environments that are attractions themselves but also contain outlets for the sale of commodities. People today consume symbols *and* environments along with goods and services.

If the increasing use of themed environments can be explained as a response to the realization problem of capital, its implementation has occurred through changes in marketing since the 1970s. This chapter has argued that retailing was once dominated by prestige department stores centrally located in the downtown sections of cities. As cities themselves have declined as places to live for the affluent middle class, the commercial functions of their downtowns have also deteriorated. Suburban malls, in contrast, have enjoyed remarkable success during this same period—since the 1950s. Malls are themed consumer environments that attract people to their location in competition with other locations and not necessarily to specific stores. They provide a certain experience that derives from today's highly developed, image-driven, commodity-driven, popular culture. The environment of the mall is an engineered extension of mass advertising and mass media.

Presently, the range of themed environments varies according to the particular goods or services sold. In the case of theme parks, motifs are closely connected to proven mass-media commodities, such as Disneyland or the "Camp Snoopy" theme of Knott's Berry Farm. Some themed restaurants also derive directly from the mass media, such as Planet Hollywood or the Hard Rock Café. Other cases are examples of postmodern pastiche because they mix and match images as their thematic elements form a large variety of sources and times, such as the decor of the Ruby Tuesday's chain. Because malls are in competition with city centers or other large agglomerations of stores, they seek to capture an urban ambiance as their milieu. The mall environment depends on pedestrian traffic and numerous retailing outlets, including both department and specialty stores. A common motif of mall decor is the urban or European "village" that is often constructed as a microenvironment or series of environments within the mall space itself.

All of this variety cannot compare with the explosion of fantasy motifs characteristic of Las Vegas. That city is a veritable laboratory of environmental themes. Casinos and their function of gambling are disguised as entertaining spaces. Proliferating themes nevertheless articulate with well-known, often hackneyed and clichéd motifs of Hollywood films and television. Casino images range from environments that invoke the "Wild West" to ancient Egypt to the European Middle Ages to an invocation of "tropical paradise." New casinos are being built each year, and because of increasing competition, they innovate new thematic environments. Yet there remain close connections between this activity and the popular themes of movies, music, television programming, and other forms of mass culture. In fact, the themes of Las Vegas casinos are the clearest examples of the way the new spaces of consumption are consciously designed as extensions of the commodity/culture milieu comprising magazines, advertising, television, music, movies, and increasingly, computer cyberspace. As such, their decors and motifs will be modulated in the future by shifts in popularity of significant signs and desirable images or commodities.

Themed environments work not only because they are connected to the universe of commodities and are spaces of consumption but also because they offer consumers a spatial experience that is an attraction by itself, that is, they promote the consumption of space. People may come to the mall, for example, to shop, but they also come there to see and be seen, much like people have done for centuries through daily visits to the town square or central city downtown. For this reason, future changes will not only involve fashionable shifts in the content of desirable images but also changes in the types of environments offered to consumers in conjunction with retailing.

NOTE

1. This chapter contains revised material from an article of the same title first appearing in *Architectural Digest* 131: April 1998. Reprinted by permission of the publishers, John Wiley and Sons, U.K.

BIBLIOGRAPHY

Allen, T. (1994). "The Shapes of Things to Come," *Chicago*, December:93–95.

Angelo, B. (1996). "Hungry for Theme Dining." *Time*, July 22:56–57.

———— (1968). *Le Système des objets*. Paris: Denoil–Gonthier.

Baudrillard, J. (1983). *Simulations*. New York: Semiotext(e).

Designweek (1994). "Feast Your Eyes." April, 1:18–19. London, U.K.

Engels, F. (1973). *The Condition of the Working Class in England*. Moscow: Progress Publishers.

Feagin, Joe (1988). *The Real Estate Game*. Upper Saddle River, N.J.: Prentice-Hall.

Gottdiener, M. (1994). *The Social Production of Urban Space*. 2d ed. Austin: University of Texas Press.

———— (1995). *Postmodern Semiotics: Material Culture and Signs of Postmodern Life*. Oxford: Blackwell.

———— (1997). *The Theming of America: Dreams, Visions, and Commercial Spaces*. Boulder, Colo.: Westview Press.

Harvey, David (1973). *Social Justice and the City*. Baltimore: Johns Hopkins University Press.

Jameson, F. (1984). "Postmodernism, or the Cultural Logic of Late Capitalism." *New Left Review*, 146:53–92.

Lefebvre, H. (1991). *The Production of Space*. Oxford: Blackwell.

MacCannell, D. (1989). *The Tourist*. New York: Schoken Books.

Mall of America (1992). *Guide*. Minneapolis, Minn.

Rojek, C. (1985). *Capitalism and Leisure Theory*. London: Tavistock.

Venturi, R., D. S. Brown, and S. Izenour (1972). *Learning from Las Vegas*. Cambridge, Mass.: MIT Press.

Wright, T. (1989). "Marketing Culture, Simulation, and the Aesthetization of Work and War." *Social Text*, Spring.

Index

abundance, Baudrillard on, 79
activists, consumers as, 41, 44
Adams, Henry, 101
Adorno, Theodor, 203–4
advertising, 15–16, 282; in music industry, 209–16
African Americans, music industry and, 212–13
alternative music, 216–21
ambiguous violence, 160
anti-supper, 12
architecture, of Las Vegas, 277–81
Arditi, Jorge, 71–89
artists, consumers as, 41, 43
ATM fees, 186
auction sites, 84
authenticity, tourism and, 229–30, 262

Baade, Robert, 189
Baltimore Ravens, 187, 189–93
banking: fees in, 186; McDonaldization of, benefits of, 36
Barbados, sex tourism in, 234–35
baseball: professionalization in, 180–82; strikes in, 182

The Basketball Diaries, 162
Baudrillard, Jean, ix, 18–19, 58, 259; on gift giving, 6; and Internet, 83; and popular music, 204; on shopping, 79–81; on sign value, 20
Bauhaus, 268
Beach Boys, 234–35, 239
belonging, 23–24
birds, as replacement providers, 149–50
Black Flag, 221
Black Sox scandal, 179–80
Blade Runner, 99–100, 106
Blake, William, 102
body: consumption and, 131–52; end of, 131; in sex tourism, 242; in tourism, 61–64
Bogdan, R., 66
Boone, Pat, 217
Bourdieu, Pierre, 39–40, 45–46
brain-suck, 93–109; definition of, 94
Braudel, Fernand, 11
Brazil, sex tourism in, 233
breastfeeding, 136–37, 142–47; support networks and, 146–47
Brown, Denise S., 272, 277

287

bureaucracy, 5

calculability, 5, 33–34
calculus of objects, Baudrillard on, 79–80, 85
Calvert, Karin, 120
Cambodia, sex tourism in, 233
Campbell, Colin, 14, 228
Camus, Albert, 98–99
Capek, Karel, 99
capital: Bourdieu on, 45–46; circuit of, themes and symbols and, 281–84
capitalism: changes in, x; consumer, 203–26; consumption and, 12–17; culture of, 111; and love, 243–44
Capra, Frank, 96–97
Cardo Culinaria, 261
care work, 76
Caribbean, economy of, 235–36
Caribbean sex tourism, 227–50; consumers of, 240–46; contemporary, 232–33; future of, 246–47; production of, 234–40
Carneal, Michael, 170–71, 173n23
Carolina Panthers, 186–87
Carroll, Jim, 162
cars, and brain-suck, 94–95
casinos, 277–81
Castro, Fidel, 236
Certeau, Michel de, 228
Cerulo, Karen A., 153–76
Chapman, Rex, 197–98
Charter Ownership Agreements, 196
children: as consumers, 115, 119; fashion for, 111–29; merchandising for, 148; prostitution of, 63–64
choice, illusion of, 79–80
choosers, consumers as, 41–42
Christian hospices, 259–60
Cincinnati Bengals, 196
citizens, consumers as, 41, 44
class perspective: critique of, 58; on tourism, 56–57
Cleaver, Eldridge, 207
Clement, Priscilla, 146
clothing, 27; children's, 111–29; meaning of, 112

Codrescu, Andre, 244–45
colonialism: and sex tourism, 57, 232; in *Star Trek*, 97–98; and tourism, 60, 64
commercial personae, 112–13, 183
commodification: of childhood, 111–29; disadvantages of, 183–84; of milk, 131–52; of religious sites, 255–62; of sacred, 251–64; in sex tourism, 227–50; of sports, 177–201; of violence, 153–76
commodities: Baudrillard on, 79; Marx on, 3–4; PSLs as, 193; recontextualizing, 86–87
communicators, consumers as, 41–42
competition, and McDonaldization, 38
computer culture, 93–96
concert industry, 206–16
conspicuous consumption, x–xi, 7–9; origins of, 12
conspicuous leisure, 7–9
conspicuousness, 7; and social positioning, 7–8
consumer capitalism, 203–26
consumer cultures, 21–25
consumerism, x; rise of, 10–12
consumers: of Caribbean sex tourism, 240–46; children as, 115, 119; and McDonaldization, 45–47; and milk reform, 137–42; types of, 40–44
consumer society: credit and, 15; and Cunanan, 104–5; and normality, 100
consumption, ix, 3–31; and capitalism, 12–17; changes in, ix; classical approaches to, 3–10; contemporary, 228; contemporary approaches to, 10–17; creativity of, 204; and identity, 21–25; new forms of, 20–21; and postmodernism, 51; shopping and, 71–89; of space, 265–85; as task, 282; of tourism, changes in, 227–30; visual, 229, 243
consumption emphasis, critique of, x, 17
consumption ethic, 112
consumption spaces, 28–29, 93, 265–85; proliferation of, 24; and re-enchantment, 20–21; variety of, and McDonaldization, 39–40

contextual sequences, 156, 158–59
control, 5; with nonhuman technologies, 33, 35; over products and processes, 35–36
Cook, Daniel Thomas, 111–29
Cooke, Jack Kent, 195
Cooke, John Kent, 197
Coppola, Francis Ford, 161
corporate sponsorship, in music industry, 209–16
cosmopolitanism, 51–52; critique of, 63–64
country, consumption and, 131–52
credit, 15
Cuba, sex tourism in, 232, 234–36, 238, 241, 244–45
culture(s): Baudrillard on, 18–19; of capitalism, 111; of consumption, 16–17, 21–25; deterritorialization of, 66; Durkheim on, 5; image-driven, 20–21; of rock music, 203–26; of tourism, 59
Cunanan, Andrew, 104–6
Curacao, sex tourism in, 232, 234–35

dairy industry, 147–50
Dark City, 98–100
Darlington, Thomas, 141
Dead Man Walking, 163
decorated shed, 272, 278
democratization, and consumption, 13
denim jeans, 27–28
DePalma, Brian, 162
desire, production of, 282
DeVault, Marjorie, 76–77
deviant violence, 159
Diallo, Amadou, 170
Diana, Princess of Wales, 103–6
Diderot, Denis, 231
difference, and tourism, 269
DiMaggio, Joe, 180
Disneyland, 259, 270
Disney World, 55, 270
dissimulation, 19
diversity, and McDonaldization, 39
domestic life, in Victorian era, 143–46

Dominican Republic: economy of, 235–36; sex tourism in, 233–35
Do the Right Thing, 163
doublecasting sequences, 156, 159
Douglas, Mary, 75–76
Drysdale, Don, 180–81
DuGay, Pau, ix, x
DuPuis, E. Melanie, 131–52
Durkheim, Emile, 3, 5–6

Earnshaw, George, 115–17
e-commerce, 81–86
ecotourism, 54
Eco, Umberto, 58–59
efficiency, 5, 33–34
Elizabeth I, queen of England, 12
Elway, John, 198
emotion: and normality, 101; substitute, 103–4
Epic, 220–21
Ewen, Stuart, 16
exchange value, 25–29
explorers, consumers as, 41–42

family life, in Victorian era, 143–46
FANS, Inc., 189
fantasy: and sex tourism, 234–35, 237–40, 245–46. *See also* re-enchantment
fashion, 12–13; in children's clothes, 111–29; and culture, 27; Douglas on, 75; and identity, 16
Fashion Café, 273
fast-food franchised restaurants, 260–61
Fayed, Dodi, 105
Featherstone, Michael, 20, 22
feminism, 63
fetishization: of commodities, 4, 9; of resistance, 18
field, 39–40, 45–46
Firat, Fuat, 17–18
Fiske, John, 18
Flood, Curt, 181
food: consumption of, 131–52; themed environments and, 271–74
football, commodification in, 177–201
Foucault, Michel, 74–75, 266
framing practices, in shopping, 86–87

Frankfurt School, 17, 203
free agency, 181, 183
friendship, in Victorian era, 145

Gabriel, Yiannis, 40
Galbraith, Kenneth, 14
Gallaro, Georgio, 154
games, 178; versus sports, 179
Gap, 221
Garcia, Jerry, 212
gender, and milk merchandising, 147–49
gender perspective: critique of, 58; on
    shopping, 72–77; on tourism, 57–58
Giddens, Anthony, 22
gift giving, 6; Baudrillard on, 79
Giordano, Jeremy, 154
globalization, tourism and, 65
The Godfather, 161
Goffman, Erving, 125
Goldman, Robert, 16
Goodman, David, 135
Gottdiener, Mark, ix–xvii, 3–31, 58, 66,
    252, 265–85
Graceland, 270
Grateful Dead, 212
grunge, 219

habitus, 45–46, 228
Halton, Eugene, 93–109
Hard Rock Café, 272
Harley-Davidson Café, 273
Hartley, Robert, 134, 137–38, 140–41
Havel, Vaclav, 97
Hayden, Tom, 207
Head, Edith, 123
health care industry, McDonaldization of,
    37–38
hedonists, consumers as, 41–43
Heininger, Mary Lynn Stevens, 143–44
Hendrix, Jimi, 208
heterotopias, 266
high consensus acts, 168
Hightower, Jim, 135
hip-hop, 212–13, 219
Holy Land. *See* Israel
Horkheimer, Max, 203

hotels, themed, 259–60
Hourney, 214
housework, and shopping, 76
human labor, substitution of nonhuman
    technology for, 33, 35

identity: in children, 125; as commodity,
    111; consumption and, 16, 21–25;
    shopping and, 86
identity seekers, consumers as, 41–42
illusion of abundance: Baudrillard on,
    79; and Internet, 83
image-driven culture, 20–21
independent record labels, 218
Internet: and children, 114; music
    industry and, 215; and self-identity,
    25; and sex tourism, 234, 237–38,
    241–43; and shopping, 81–86
Invasion of the Body Snatchers, 97
Iridium, 273
Isle of Wight Festival, 209
Israel, 56, 68n2; tourism in, 251–64
It's a Wonderful Life, 96–97
Izenour, Steven, 272, 277

Jackson, Michael, 214
Jacksonville Jaguars, 196
Jamaica: economy of, 235; sex tourism in,
    234–35, 237, 245
Jerusalem, 254; model of, 256–57
Jesus Christ, 102, 106
Jews, and McDonald's, 261
Jineteras, 234–35
Joplin, Janis, 208
Jordan, Michael, 183

kali yuga, 100–101
Kalvert, Scott, 162
Kasson, J. E., 66
Kellner, Douglas, 18
Kempadoo, Kamala, 232
kinship networks, in Victorian era, 145
Kiss, 212
kitsch, 59
Koskovich, Thomas, 153–54
Koufax, Sandy, 180–81

Krippendorf, Joost, 53

Lang, Fritz, 99–100
Lang, Tim, 40
Lasch, Christopher, 97
Lash, Scott, 228
Las Vegas casinos, 277–81
Lauer, Edgar L., 126n9
Lears, Jackson, 14, 124
Lee, Spike, 163
Leetch, Brian, 183
Lefebvre, Henri, 3–4, 234, 268
leisure: conspicuous, 7–9; and romance, 244; technology and, 96
lifestyles, types of, 75
Lingis, A., 58, 62
love: capitalism and, 243–44; shopping and, 77–78, 81
low consensus acts, 168
Lury, Celia, 22, 243
luxury, 11

MacCannell, Dean, 53
magazines, for children, 114
Mall of America, 275–77
malls, 24–25; themed, 274–77. *See also* megamalls
Marcuse, Herbert, 203
Marcus, Greil, 204
Martin, Emily, 131
Marxism, and PSLs, 193–95
Marx, Karl, 3–4; critique of, 10–11, 177
Mason, Christopher, 104
materialism, and normality, 102–3
Mauss, Marcel, 6
McCracken, Grant, 11–12
McDonaldization, x, 33–49, 252; benefits of, 36; consumers and, 45–47; critique of, 56; definition of, 33; degrees of, 38; misrepresentation of, 36–37; principles of, 33; variations in process of, 37–39
McDonald's, 260–61, 271
McTourism, 52, 55–56; body and space in, 62; critique of, 56
Mead, Margaret, 121

meaning: of clothing, 112; of shopping, 86–87
media: and mourning, 103–4; and violence, 153–76
mediation, of personal relationships, shopping and, 77–78
megamalls, 269, 275–77
Meloy, Reid, 105
merchandising: in music industry, 211; and Shirley Temple, 122–23; of toddlers, 111–29
Merchant, Carolyn, 131
Metropolis, 99–100
metropolitan region, multicentered, 268
Microsoft Man, 97
middle classes: new, 22, 229; in Victorian era, 146
militarization, and sex tourism, 57, 232
milk: versus breastfeeding, 142–47; consumption of, 131–52; industry of, 147–50
Miller, Daniel, 77–78
Mills, C. Wright, 7
Mintz, Sidney, 135
Modell, Art, 189–90
modernism, 107; critique of, 14; design ethos of, 268; Las Vegas architecture and, 277
modernity: conceptualization of, 67n1; principles of, 51; study of, 66–67
money, Marx on, 3–4
Monterey International Pop Festival, 208
mother: as consumer, 116, marketing to, 112; new parenting and, 121–24
mourning, media and, 103–4
Mozer, Jordan, 273
Muhleman, Max, 186
Mukerji, Chandra, 11
Mullaly, John, 139–41
Mullings, Beverley, 227–50
multicentered metropolitan region, 268
Murray, Ken, 192–93
music, commodification of, 203–26
music industry: and alternative music, 216–21; and concerts, 206–9; consolidation of, 209–16

National Football League, commodification in, 177–201
nation-state, and modernity, 51
nature: end of, 131; industrialization and, 148
Nava, Mica, 72–75
Nazareth Village, 257–59
neotribalism, 22–23
network society, 64
new parenting, 121–25
New Wave, 218
Niagara Falls, 267
Nietzsche, Friedrich, 99
Nike, 221
Nirvana, 219
normality: in consumption society, 100; materialism and, 102–3; versus wisdom, 105
normal violence, 159–60

Oakland Raiders, 187
O'Connell Davidson, J., 240
Oh, Minjoo, 71–89
Olive Garden, 273
Olmstead, Frederick Law, 267
organizational size, and McDonaldization, 38–39
Ovadia, Seth, 33–49
owners, and PSLs, 193

Packard, Vance, 15
Paley, William, 139
Pan-Am Exposition, 267
Papson, Stephen, 16
parenting, new, 121–25
Parker, Ida, 134
pay-per-view, music industry and, 215
Pearl Jam, 211, 219, 221
pecuniary emulation, 7–8
Pepsi, 214
performance, in sex tourism, 239
performer sequences, 156–58
personalization, 84
personal relationships, mediation of, shopping and, 77–78
personal seat licenses (PSLs), 186–93; future of, 195–98; Marxism and, 193–95; mechanism of, 186

Philippines, sex tourism in, 232–33
Phish, 212
photography, 243, 269; and sex tourism, 243
pilgrimage, 52, 253–54; to Israel, 254–55
Pillsbury, Richard, 135–36
Pilpel, Robert, 209
place, commodification of, 230
Planet Hollywood, 272–73
players, 178; commodification of, 185; contracts of, 180–81
pleasure, in consumption, 18
pluralism, 53
political ecology, of consumption, 131–52
polysemy, and shopping, 75–76
popular music, sociology on, 203–6
postcolonialism, 60
postdemocratic system, 97
postmodernism, 51, 93, 107; and consumption, 17–21; counterargument to, 52; debate on, 63; and shopping, 79–81; and tourism, 53, 58–60, 62–63
posttotalitarian system, 97
Potterville, 96–98
predictability, 5, 33–35
Presley, Elvis, 207, 270
product endorsements, 183
production: of Caribbean sex tourism, 234–40; changes in, ix; and childhood, 113–14; of desire, 282; Marx on, 3; and modernity, 51; of space, 265–68; of tourism, changes in, 227–30
productionist emphasis, critique of, 10–11
Protestant ethic, and capitalism, 14
Prout, William, 139–40
provisioning, 76–77
PSLs. *See* personal seat licenses
punk, 216–21

race: music industry and, 212–13; and sex tourism, 57–58, 239–40, 246
Rage Against the Machine, 220

Rain Forest Café, 273
rap music, 212–13
rationalization: of art, 107; negative
 aspects of, 55; seeing through, 56;
 Weber on, 33, 36
rebellion, commodification of, in rock
 music, 203–26
rebels, consumers as, 41, 43–44
Redclift, Michael, 135
reductionism: avoidance of, 26, 28;
 critique of, 18–23
Reebok, 221
re-enchantment, 20–21; Internet and, 83;
 tourism and, 51–70
reflexivity, 63
Reisman, David, 125
religion: Durkheim on, 5; and milk
 reform, 138
religious tourism, 253–54; infrastructure
 of, 259–62
Rent a Dreads, 234–35, 245
representational positioning, 19–20
reserve clause, 180–81
Reservoir Dogs, 165
resistance: commodification of, 216–21;
 in consumption, 18; music
 consumption as, 204; to PSL plans,
 189
restaurants, themed, 271–74
Richardson, Jerry, 186
Ritzer, George, 5, 14–15, 20–21, 33–49,
 52, 252
Robbins, Tim, 163
Roberts, John, 209
rock culture, 203–9
rock festivals, 208–9
Rojek, Chris, 51–70, 231, 262
Rolfe, Dock, 154–55
Rollins, Henry, 221
romance tourism, 244–45
romanticism, and capitalism, 14
Rorty, Richard, 59
Roseneau, Sidney, 126n9
Rosenman, Joel, 209
Ruby Tuesday, 273–74
Ruppert, J., 180
R.U.R., 99

sacred, commodification of, 251–64
sacred and profane: in childhood, 113–
 15, 124–25; Durkheim on, 6
St. Louis Rams, 186–87, 189, 191
St. Louis World's Fair, 256–57
Sandoms, 234–35
Sanky Pankies, 234–35
Scarface, 162
Scher, John, 216
Schuldson, Michael, 16
science: modernism and, 51; postmodernism
 and, 101; in Victorian era, 148
Scorsese, Martin, 161–62
Seiler, Cotten, 203–26
Seiter, Ellen, 121
self: performative versus natural, 125;
 virtual, 25
self-identity: as commodity, 111;
 consumption and, 16, 24; Internet
 and, 25
sex tourism, 57–58, 227–50; and child
 prostitution, 63–64; definition of,
 233; global consumption of, 231–33;
 stages of, 57
SFX Entertainment, 210, 215
shopping, 12–13, 71–89; for children's
 clothes, 115–17; importance of, 78;
 Internet and, 81–86; as irrational, 71,
 75; meanings of, 86–87
Shoval, Noam, 251–64
signs, 17–21
sign value, 9, 20, 25–29, 204
sign wars, 20
simulation, 19, and consumption spaces,
 28–29; of religious sites, 255–59
slumming, 231
Snyder, Daniel, 196–97
social action, formula for, 45
social positioning, conspicuousness and,
 7–8
society: changes in, 21–22, 136; Durkheim
 on, 5; network, 64. *See also* consumer
 society
sociology: crisis in, 62–65; on popular
 music, 203–6; on shopping, 72–78;
 of tourism, 53–60
solidarity, 5

Sommerhof, Roy, 192–93
Sony, 221
souvenirs, 269–70
space: consumption of, 265–85; production of, 265–68; in tourism, 61–62, 64–65. *See also* consumption spaces
spectators, 179
Spencer, Leland, 134
sports, 179; commodification of, 177–201; professionalization of, 179–81; success in, spending and, 183–85; trends in, 197
Star Trek, 97–98
status, 5; in Victorian era, 146
Steadman, John, 193
Stephens, Sharon, 124
The Stooges, 221
story sequencing, 156–59; and assessment of violence, 165–68; consciousness of selection of, 163–65; definition of, 153; and de-normalization of violence, 169–71; importance of, 155–56; selection of, 159–63
The Stranger (Camus), 98–99
Strickland, Rod, 183
strikes, in sports, 181–82
structuralism, and tourism, 53–58
style, Douglas on, 75
Super Bowl, ticket licensing for, 196
support networks, and breastfeeding, 146–47
surplus-profit, 194
Susman, Warren, 124
swill milk, 136–38
swing theory, 75
symbolic exchange, 9–10
symbols, and circuit of capital, 281–84

Tarantino, Quentin, 165
Taxi Driver, 161–62
techno-colonization, 94–96
technology: and brain-suck, 108; human versus nonhuman, 33, 35; and leisure time, 96

teleology, 107
television, and brain-suck, 108
temperance, and milk reform, 140–41
Temple, Shirley, 121–24
terrorism, and tourism, 64
Thailand, sex tourism in, 232–34
themed environments, 66, 252, 270–81; hotels, 259–60; malls, 274–77; restaurants, 271–74; and tourism, 58
theming: and circuit of capital, 281–84; and consumption spaces, 28–29; of religious sites, 255–59; of religious tourism infrastructure, 259–62
Ticketmaster, 211, 221
Time Elevator, 257
Tocqueville, Alexis de, 145
toddler, 111–29; use of term, 117
topia, 265–66
totemism, 6
tourism, 51–70; changes in, 227–30; and consumption of space, 267; and crisis in sociology, 62–65; increase in, 52–53, 64–65, 255; in Israel, 251–64; postmodernism and, 51; religious, 253–54; sex, 227–50; sociological studies of, 53–60
tourist gaze, 229, 243
transportation, and milk consumption, 141
Trinidad, sex tourism in, 234–35
Twain, Mark, 251

uncharted territory, 265–66
upright child, 120–21
Urry, John, 56, 228, 231
use value, 25–29

Veblen, Thorstein, x–xi, 6–10
velocity, 62
Venkatesh, Alladi, 17–18
Venturi, Robert, 272, 277
Versace, Gianni: death of, 104–6; funeral of, 103–4
victims, consumers as, 41, 43
victim sequences, 156–57

violence, 153–55; assessment of, story sequencing and, 165–68; de-normalization of, 169–71; factors affecting, 154; media and, 153–76; prevalence of, 154; sequences of, 156–59
violence types, 159–60; and story sequencing, 160–61
Virilio, P., 62
virtual self, 25
visual consumption, 229, 243
Vivere, 273
voluntarism, and tourism, 53–54
Vreeland, Jason, 154

Wadleigh, Michael, 216, 220
Washington Redskins, 195–97
wealth, 5
Weber, Max, 3–5, 14, 33
Wells, H. G., 101

West, Vera, 123
Wolfenstein, Martha, 121
women: employment of, 136–37; and milk consumption, 132; sex tourism and, 231–32, 240–41, 244–45; in Victorian era, 143–46. *See also* gender perspectives
Woodstock, 207–9
Woodstock '94, 215–16
Woodstock '99, 220
work: changes in, ix, 26; and modernity, 51; women and, 136–37
World Congress Against Commercial Sexual Exploitation of Children, 63

Yankees, 183

Zappa, Frank, 203
Zelizer, Viviana, 113

About the Contributors

Jorge Arditi is associate professor at the State University of New York at Buffalo. His book, *A Genealogy of Manners: Transformations of Social Relations in France and England from the Fourteenth to the Eighteenth Century*, was recently published by the University of Chicago Press. He has published articles on the sociology of knowledge, on agency and identity, on the transformations of manners and changing infrastructures of social relations, and on poststructuralism, among other themes. He is now engaged in a study of the ethical implications of poststructuralism.

Matthew D. Bramlett is a faculty research assistant in the Department of Marketing at the Robert H. Smith School of Business at the University of Maryland, College Park. He recently finished his dissertation, earning his Ph.D. in sociology at the University of Maryland, College Park. His dissertation is an event history analysis of the effects of children on the stability of marriages and cohabitations. His current research focuses on high-technology services sold to business-to-business customers. His other research interests include the commodification of sports and the exploitation of the consumer in professional sports, and the fertility effects of family planning programs in developing countries over time. He is a member of the Population Association of America and a member of the Family, Sociology of Population, and Race, Gender and Class sections of the American Sociological Association. His forthcoming publications include an analysis of business customers' repatronage behavior based on services experience, and an analysis of the cross-cultural determinants of customer value in interorganizational relationships with a high-technology service provider.

297

Karen A. Cerulo (Ph.D. Princeton University) is associate professor of sociology at Rutgers University. Her research interests include media and technology, symbol systems, and culture and cognition. Professor Cerulo's articles appear in a wide variety of journals and annuals, including *American Sociological Review*, *Annual Review of Sociology*, *Social Forces*, *Sociological Forum*, *Sociological Inquiry*, and *Communication Research*. She also is the author of *Deciphering Violence: The Cognitive Order of Right and Wrong* (Routledge, 1998) and *Identity Designs: The Sights and Sounds of a Nation*—winner of the Culture Section's "Best Book Award, 1996" (The Rose Book series of the ASA, Rutgers University Press, 1995). *Second Thoughts: Seeing Conventional Wisdom through the Sociological Eye* (co-authored with Janet M. Ruane) was just released in its second edition (Pine Forge/Sage, 2000). Currently, she is at work on a new book entitled *Individualism . . . Pro-tem: The Scripting of American Social Relations.*

Daniel Thomas Cook received his Ph.D. in sociology from the University of Chicago and now teaches at the University of Illinois. The author of several articles on the commodification of childhood, Cook is currently working on a manuscript that historicizes the connection between the rise of "the child" as consumer and children's emergent status as persons in twentieth-century American culture, to be published by Duke University Press.

E. Melanie DuPuis is assistant professor of sociology at University of California, Santa Cruz. Her major research interests are Sociology of Agriculture and Food, Industrial Organization, Sociology of the Environment, Culture and Consumption, Policy. She is the co-editor of *Creating the Coutryside: The Politics of Rural and Environmental Discourse* from Temple University Press

M. Gottdiener is professor and chair of the Department of Sociology at the University at Buffalo. He has also held the position of full professor at the University of California and at the City University of New York. His research interests include urban sociology, contemporary theory, cultural studies, and semiotics. Gottdiener is the author/editor of twelve books, including *The Social Production of Urban Space*, *Postmodern Semiotics*, *The Theming of America*, and *The New Urban Sociology* with Ray Hutchison, and co-author of *Las Vegas: The Social Production of an All-American City.* He is the managing editor for North America of *Urban Studies* and is on the executive editorial board of *City* and the editorial board of the *Journal of Consumer Culture.* His forthcoming book is *Life in the Air: The New Culture of Air Travel*, to be published by Rowman & Littlefield.

Eugene Halton is co-author of *The Meaning of Things* (Cambridge University Press) and author of *Meaning and Modernity* and most recently *Bereft of Reason* (both with University of Chicago Press). He teaches sociology and humanities at the University of Notre Dame. He has written recently on the fifties, living rooms, dreaming, the obesity epidemic, megatechnic America, and the displacement of organic and inward nature by the modern mechanized outlook.

Beverley Mullings is assistant professor in the Department of Geography at Syracuse University. Her research interests are focused on the institutional prerequisites for the creation of sustainable industry. She has published several articles on the gender impacts of industrial restructuring in the Caribbean.

Minjoo Oh is a doctoral candidate in the Department of Sociology at the State University of New York at Buffalo. Her research examines the relations of food and identity from a post-Colonial perspective, in particular, as they are affected by the global spread of consumerism. She has also written a Foucauldian reading of the Confucian self, in which she develops the notion of a particular microphysics connected to subjectivity in Korea.

Seth Ovadia is a Ph.D. candidate in the sociology department at the University of Maryland, College Park, where his areas of concentration are theory and stratification. In addition to his work on McDonaldization, he is currently working on studies of the varying patterns of segregation in American cities and how to use intersection theory in empirical research.

George Ritzer is professor of sociology at the University of Maryland where he has been a Distinguished Scholar-Teacher and won a teaching excellence award. He has served as chair of two sections of the American Sociological Association— Organizations and Occupations and Theoretical Sociology. In addition to *The McDonaldization of Society* (1993, 1996, 2000; translated into a dozen languages), his other efforts to apply social theory to the everyday realms of the economy and consumption include *Expressing America: A Critique of the Global Credit Card Society* (1995), *The McDonaldization Thesis: Explorations and Extensions* (1998), and *Enchanting a Disenchanted World: Revolutionizing the Means of Consumption* (1999). At the other end of the spectrum, his contributions to metatheorizing include *Sociology: A Multiple Paradigm Science* (1975), *Toward an Integrated Sociological Paradigm* (1981), and *Metatheorizing in Sociology* (1991). He has recently edited *The Blackwell Companion to Major Social Theorists* (2000), is currently co-editing (with Barry Smart) *The Handbook of Social Theory*, and is co-founding editor of the *Journal of Consumer Culture*. In 2001, Sage of England will publish two volumes of his collected works.

Chris Rojek is professor of sociology and culture at Nottingham Trent University. He is the author of many books, most recently *Leisure & Culture* (St Martin's Press, 2000). He is currently working on a *Handbook of World Sociology*, celebrity and culture and the sociology and cultural studies of Stuart Hall.

Cotten Seiler is a Ph.D. candidate in American studies at the University of Kansas, currently working on a dissertation on the ideological origins of the Interstate Highway System. He is also an expert on rock music as an American cultural form.

Noam Shoval completed his doctorate in the Department of Geography at the Hebrew University of Jerusalem, Israel. He has studied with professor Arie Schachar and together they have published several articles on Religious- based Tourism. Currently he holds a post-doctorate at the University of London.

Mark D. Sloan is the academic coordinator of the University of Maryland Gemstone Honors program. He is finishing his doctoral degree in sociology at the University of Maryland, College Park. His dissertation is entitled "The Effects of Technology Shifts on Unemployment and Social Structure in the United States." His current research focuses on the environmental factors influencing educational attainment among elite honors students in higher education. Other research interests include professional and amateur sports culture, the socio-economics of race, and the shaping of contemporary society by technology. He is a member of the Society for the Advancement of Socio-Economics, the American Sociological Association, and the American College Personnel Association.